D0214949

"POINT FROM WHICH CREATION BEGINS"

BAG

"Point from which creation begins":
The Black Artists' Group of St. Louis

Benjamin Looker

Missouri Historical Society Press
St. Louis
distributed by University of Missouri Press

07 06 05 04   1 2 3 4

Library of Congress Cataloging-in-Publication Data

Looker, Ben, 1978-

    Point from which creation begins :

    the Black Artists' Group of St. Louis /

    by Benjamin Looker.

        p.   cm.

    Includes bibliographical references, discography, and index.

    ISBN 1-883982-51-0 (hardcover : alk. paper)

  1. Black Artists' Group. 2. Jazz--Missouri — St. Louis--History and

criticism. 3. African American musicians — Missouri — St. Louis. I. Title.

    ML3508.8.S7L66 2004

    781.65'09778'66 — dc22

      2004016406

Distributed by University of Missouri Press

Cover images: top: Oliver Jackson, *Untitled, 1968*, mixed media on canvas,
    66" x 66". Reproduction courtesy of the author and Anne Kohs &
    Associates. bottom left: BAG actors and dancers in *Poem for a*
    Revolutionary Night at Christ Church Cathedral in St. Louis, November
    1969. Photograph courtesy Michael E. Emrick. bottom right: Oliver
    Lake (left) and Baikida Carroll in a duo concert, c. 1973. Photograph
    courtesy Baikida Carroll.

Design: Creativille, Inc.

Printed and Bound by Friesens, Canada

TABLE OF CONTENTS

FOREWORD

In the late 1960s and early1970s, I was immersed in the academic world, first as an undergraduate and then as a master's candidate in my home state of Michigan, later acquiring my Ph.D. in the strange and magnificent land of New Mexico. I knew little of St. Louis, and the African American experience was only a peripheral and primarily philosophical concern to me. I appreciated music of all kinds and tried to keep up with news from the art and theater worlds. But that wasn't my "scene." It is not surprising that I was familiar with neither the Black Arts Movement nor, specifically, the Black Artists' Group in St. Louis.

As I perused Benjamin Looker's manuscript on the St. Louis Black Artists' Group, I realized that this tiny but influential piece of American and cultural history could so easily have been lost, sunk with only the faintest ripple into the whirlpool of the past. These African American artists in St. Louis who gathered together for mutual support as well as larger concerns were an extraordinary group of talented, dedicated, and socially aware people. Collectively or individually, they became an impressive force in the transformation of the artistic landscape of America and ultimately the world. Equally effective were their commitments to heightened black identity and, at the same time, multicultural appreciation. BAG members and other African American artists in similar movements didn't stop there; their philosophies encompassed concerns for civil rights, economics, education, and politics.

Julius Hemphill, a BAG member and talented musician, called the experience a "springboard to innovation." In a mere four years, BAG members would begin to scatter beyond the confines of St. Louis, dispersed by a host of different circumstances. Yet subtly—and until now nearly anonymously—their influence washed over, around, and through St. Louis and beyond, as surely as the Mississippi rolls steadily by our city. Here these artists created a place for common aspirations and shared memories, a successful building of community in a too-often unwelcoming city. It was in no way a secret or subversive movement; in the artistic community, particularly among African American artists who know our region, BAG and the nationwide Black Arts Movement are remembered. But I believe that the larger population will enjoy a measure of surprise and enlightenment in discovering the "point from which creation begins" in our very own place. It is fortunate for all of us that the BAG story has been retrieved and told for the widest possible audience. Sharing our stories is an essential ingredient in the process of developing an inclusive and cohesive community, and those who share their stories attain a common ground that merits sustaining for future generations.

I will never know what it was like to be a 1960s African American musician or artist struggling for his or her place or opportunity, but I can share the story by listening to the tale and finding common ground in the hopes and dreams that all humans have in some respect. I can always learn more about my city and the people of diverse and multiple perspectives whose stories built this place and this community. Benjamin Looker has contributed to the all-inclusive narrative of St. Louis; without his superlative research and detailed narrative, this story might have been lost to many of us, and a piece of our past would thus have been absent from the story we seek to promulgate in all its parts.

—Robert R. Archibald, Ph.D.
President, Missouri Historical Society

PREFACE

Thanks to Benjamin Looker's careful and empathetic study, the geographical, political, cultural, racial, and artistic territory in which St. Louis's Black Artists' Group came into self-awareness and formation will be re-etched (like familiar scarifications) into the memory of those who were there in the fire and ferment of the 1960s and '70s. The fabled, multi-tiered, and therapeutic stresses of those spatial and temporal terrains—exploding and imploding in regional, national, and worldwide bellies—also resulted in permanent acoustical and optical scarifications. Their legacies, which now reside in the purview of both "orature" and formal pedagogy, have become a natural part of the artistic, investigative, pioneering, and activist spirit that was passed like a baton among descendants, heirs, and beneficiaries of BAG and the Black Arts/Black Power Movements. BAG's trailblazing achievements include being centrally responsible for the creation of a regional Black Arts Movement (BAM); making what Miles Davis called "that St. Louis [art] thing" accessible to the world in both traditional and radicalized forms; establishing beachheads in Europe (including Sweden and France) and Africa; making influential sound waves among musical innovators and audiences in New York's "loft movement"; and extending the St. Louis "thing" across the globe by founding the World Saxophone Quartet.

St. Louis's and East St. Louis's historic role in developing and fostering the twin roots of African American racial-social consciousness and musical-literary arts is cogently framed by the strategic geographical-industrial position of these two cities. Both served as winnowing and threshing floors for strategists aiming to advance the cause of black freedom and equality and to eliminate the viruses of racism (recall the Dred Scott decision in St. Louis and the 1917 race riots in East St. Louis).

Both cities also acted as conduits (via railways, packinghouses, and water-ways) for the upriver migration of blues, jazz, and gospel from New Orleans, various points of departure in Mississippi, and Memphis. Each was a nurturing and processing ground for musical culture, feeding it to other midwestern locations such as Kansas City and Chicago, as well as East Coast cities such as Philadelphia and New York. Looker richly sums up this influential metroplex by referring to St. Louis as a "hinge" city, "fixed geographically and musically midway between Chicago and New Orleans."

Under Looker's "def licks," BAG's portraiture emerges as a multi-arts and activist confluence grooving on vibrant tributaries of events, individuals, and organizations, including the densely layered socialization rituals that BAG members experienced while growing up in the Ville or attending St. Louis's segregated public schools (Sumner High in particular) and the historically black Lincoln University in Jefferson City, Missouri. Other tributaries ranged from musicians and mentors such as Clark Terry, Elwood Buchanan, Miles Davis, George Hudson, Eddie Randall, Chuck Berry, Ken Billups, Ike Turner, and Freddie Washington to Pulitzer Prize–winning poet Gwendolyn Brooks and French playwright Jean Genet (whose work *The Blacks* served as BAG's inaugural arts event). Nor does Looker overlook BAG's enormous debt to dancer-choreographer Katherine Dunham's Performing Arts Training Center (PATC) or to John Coltrane, Ornette Coleman, Albert Ayler, Archie Shepp, and Chicago's Association for the Advancement of Creative Musicians (AACM). Aware that they were part of a larger national and global cultural ambience, BAG participants pioneered the ideal—a "holistic" (if that's the right word) multi-arts commune often touted but never fully realized by other BAM collectives.

In particular, BAG's holism was aided in its conceptualization, implementation, and empowerment by Dunham's PATC and Southern Illinois University's Experiment in Higher Education (EHE). Located in East St. Louis, the EHE, which also housed PATC, was a veritable fulcrum of art, radical curriculum development (especially emerging black studies programs), pan-Africanism (and other cutting-edge ideologies), activism, and leadership training for the movement. The mere presence of the legendary Katherine Dunham—not to mention the radicalized and unorthodox faculties and student bodies of EHE and PATC—augured well for the various social, political, and aesthetic thrusts in St. Louis and urban America at large. Complementing Dunham's presence and importance was that of St. Louis painter-thinker Oliver Jackson, whose portrait is also deftly etched by Looker. Jackson, an unheralded but brilliant architect of pan-African concepts, aesthetics, and curricula, was also chief theoretician at the EHE-PATC complex and helped usher in black studies programs at Southern Illinois University–Edwardsville, Oberlin College, Ohio University, and California State University–Sacramento, where he laid the theoretical groundwork for a pan-African studies department that still thrives.

Jackson conceived and put into place the sets and images for Images: Sons/Ancestors, an ambitious and hugely successful mixed-media performance of the African Continuum (Jackson's favorite phrase) at St. Louis's Powell Symphony Hall in February 1971. (Jackson also took the continuum concept to CSU–Sacramento where, working with dramaturge Paul Carter Harrison, he gave the name Sons/Ancestors to CSU's award-winning African American theater program.) The African Continuum program showcased BAG members (and associates such as pianist John Hicks and Senegalese master drummer Mor Thiam) at the peak of their powers—and in one of the city's literal and symbolic citadels of European-Anglo-American art and culture. Images, a variant of which BAG would produce repeatedly throughout the bistate region, meshed "high" black art with symbols and repositories of "high" white art and told volumes about the backgrounds of BAG members and allies, including their intensive cross-cultural and cross-fertilized aesthetics and training. Such "crosses" included the aforementioned upbringing and chops-cutting, explorations of African art and thought (thanks to Jackson's prodding), and the impact of and/or collaborations with European classical-modernist-radical composers such as John Cage, Arthur Custer, and Karlheinz Stockhausen. Underlying all of these confluent energies were the magnetic, diverse, and painful origins of St. Louis, from the ever-green burial sites of the Osage and Underground Railroad hideaways to Pierre Laclède's dominions and Scott Joplin's "rags" to W. C. Handy's blues and the East St. Louis race riots (which inspired the formation of the St. Louis Urban League).

BAG was not, by any stretch of the imagination, the best-known BAM collective—that distinction, as Looker duly notes, belonged to such groups as LeRoi Jones's (Amiri Baraka's) New York Black Arts Repertory Theatre and School (and Spirit House in Newark), Oakland's Black House, Chicago's Organization of Black American Culture (OBAC), and Los Angeles's Watts Writers Workshop. However, St. Louis had ties to more popular and influential BAM units: BAG poet Bruce (Ajulé) Rutlin attended workshops at Gwen Brooks's home in Chicago, for example, and St. Louis native Quincy Troupe, a member of the Watts Workshop, maintained ties with BAG members, some of whom he had known since high school. Troupe helped link BAG and East and West Coast BAM artists and activists through associations with Baraka, Sun Ra, Ornette Coleman, Larry Neal, Jayne Cortez, K. Curtis Lyle, Stanley Crouch, and others.

Under the leadership of Julius Hemphill, the brilliant jazz-voiced Rutlin, poet-composer Oliver Lake, baritonist Hamiet Bluiett, and the restlessly inventive Lester Bowie, BAG stretched out, simultaneously embracing and developing what East St. Louis jazz deejay Leo Chears called "different bags." BAG's "bags" included poetry (a.k.a. the spoken arts) with Robert Malinké Elliott, Shirley Bradley LeFlore (then wife of BAG trumpeter Floyd LeFlore), and, later, highly original Watts Workshop transplant K. Curtis Lyle. The dance and theater components flourished under the leadership of Georgia Collins (borrowed from Dunham's PATC), Portia Hunt, Muthal Naidoo, and the idiosyncratic and brilliant Vincent Terrell. Visual artists Emilio Cruz and Oliver Jackson vigorously engaged their respective interests as BAG launched mixed forms that encompassed everything from "guerilla" theater to all-night sidewalk jam sessions.

Looker's examination of the impact of racial dynamics on BAG and black music and musicians nationwide is particularly telling as he surveys the demographics and economics of race, black migration, and audiences. Social and economic gains and setbacks created by the northern migration of blacks were mirrored by the successes and plummeting fortunes of the musicians. The burgeoning new black middle class initially aided in the flourishing of jazz clubs and a buying market for recorded jazz, but new patterns of segregation—supported by entrenched St. Louis racism—kept black musicians from playing in white venues even as the black sources of support for jazz dried up. The downturn in support came courtesy of the open (and ambivalent) arms of suburbia. Looker spends well-directed energy on this phenomenon, including the role of big, small, and self-operated recording companies. For example, we are told that in 1972 no less a genius than Julius Hemphill sat in his LaClede Town home, hand-labeling copies of his inaugural and seminal recording, *Dogon A.D.*, for distribution to radio stations, jazz magazines, and music critics.

Looker's rich reportage and evaluative writing highlights the sticky issue of black artist-audience interactions and protocol—a particularly complex and often avoided subject but one that is always circulating on the grapevine. With BAG, artist-audience communication (or lack thereof) was paramount because of the collective's new and radically out-there "bag," in the face of an already diminishing audience in an already conservative "belt" (and already in a former slave state). Alternately heartbroken from playing to near-empty houses and exhilarated by standing-room-only audiences, BAG also underwent merciless and unabashedly negative criticism from elder statesmen and peers married to conventional and "acceptable" ways of performing music, poetry, theater, and dance. In one of the most judicious and courageous discussions in print, Looker examines all sides of this issue—economic, social, racial, geographical, class, gender, and taste. Noting that perceptions are central to the issue of artist-audience relationships, he discusses stereotypes that each side holds of the other. Should an audience have to snap fingers, shake booties, and/or pat feet? Can they just sit and listen?

Down on the threshing floor of aesthetics, ideologies, perceptions, issues, and managing and playing a day-to-day schedule, BAG continued its dynamic program of "musical institution-building," employing three primary initiatives:

> First, and most crucially, BAG's artists resituated . . . and redefined the traditional spaces for jazz performance. In discarding the customary club gigs . . . they eluded aesthetic restrictions and cultivated an inner-city listenership whose ears would otherwise have remained deaf to their brand of music. Second, by initiating reciprocal activities with other like-minded collective[s] . . . they helped to create a broad, supportive network of experimental musicians through the Midwest. And, finally, by starting their own record labels [Mbari, Universal Justice] . . . several of BAG's musicians tried to create an alternative cultural space for their music, one in which they could at least partly escape the commercial pressures threatening to squeeze the life out of the music.

Among the aforementioned experimental Midwest collectives with which BAG interacted were Katherine Dunham's Performing Arts Training Center (where Hemphill taught) and Black River Writers Press in East St. Louis; Mor Thiam's Senegalese-spiced drum and dance ensemble; AACM of Chicago; St. Louis/East St. Louis institutions and venues such as Gateway Theatre, Circle Coffee Shop and Bookstore, Berea Presbyterian Church, IMPACT House, Webster College, Sheldon Memorial Hall, City Art Museum in Forest Park; and Detroit's Creative Musicians Association, John Sinclair's Artists Workshop, and Phil Ranelin and Wendell Harrison's Tribe. However, these connections, vibrant as they were, could not compete with the changes and challenges generally experienced by jazz musicians and BAG's free-avant-experimental grooves in particular.

Reasons for BAG's breakup and death—in its St. Louis matrix—have been attributed to numerous differences and tensions, from economic and administrative to artistic and ideological to personal and aesthetic. According to Hemphill, BAG, which hadn't "cultivated" younger cadres of artists, lacked the material and emotional support to stay alive. The drying-up of audience support was also a factor, as noted by BAG members and friends. BAG remained in the African American "grain," however; according to Looker, when five of its members headed to Paris in 1972, they "replicated the transatlantic journey of half a century's worth of African American musicians, visual artists, and writers." However, in Paris, Sweden, and elsewhere in Europe, the economic and attitudinal ups and downturns took heavy tolls on the artists as they had in St. Louis, and BAG members headed for New York and the "loft scene," where colleague Hamiet Bluiett (who had earlier opted not to go to Paris) had established a foothold.

In New York, BAG again "grooved" on the winnowing and threshing floor of aesthetics and entrepreneurship and returned to the gig life in 1976, riffing out of its reincarnated "bag" as the World Saxophone Quartet. The rest, as they croon, rests with "bags" of stories about BAG's grooves.

Yes, BAG folded—but its folding, as that of other Black Arts Movement collectives across the country, did not signal the collapse of the numerous spin-off "BAGs." Just check out a sample listing of the contemporary bistate heirs to BAG's legacy: writers Arthur Brown, Chris Mullen, Jabari Asim, Andrea Wren, Sylvester Brown, Ruth Miriam Garnett, Chris Hayden, Sherman L. Fowler, and Darlene Roy (and members of the eighteen-year-old Eugene B. Redmond Writers Club in East St. Louis); participants in the highly visible and audible spoken arts movement; musicians Glenn Papa Wright, Reginald Thomas, Montez Coleman, Russell Gunn, Delano Redmond, and Keyon Harold; dance/drum ensembles such as the Bakari Institute, Sylvester "Sunshine" Lee's Community Performance Ensemble, Deborah Ahmed and Black Dance St. Louis, and the East St. Louis Center for the Performing Arts; and acting ensembles such as St. Louis Black Repertory, Unity Theater, and Pamoja Theater. Even more popular and commercially successful artists and entertainers like Cedric, Nelly, Chingy, and the Hudlin Brothers' filmmaking team can trace their origins back to BAG—not to mention TV producer and St. Louis fiction sensation Lyah LeFlore, daughter of BAG artists Floyd LeFlore and Shirley Bradley LeFlore.

Benjamin Looker has set a pace and a standard for "bagging" the grooves of modern and contemporary Black Arts Movements in a cultural, racial, artistic, and economic context. Now the work of biographers, autobiographers, ethnologists, musicologists, sociologists, cultural workers, and philosophers—coming out of the new, newer, and newest "BAGs"—must begin.

—Eugene B. Redmond
Poet laureate of East St. Louis, Illinois,
and founding editor of Drumvoices Revue

INTRODUCTION

One by one, a crowd of nearly two thousand spectators filed into the grand rococo foyer of St. Louis's Powell Symphony Hall, escaping from a chilly February wind. The event that drew them on that evening in 1971 was a multimedia performance extravaganza, a concert dubbed Images: Sons/Ancestors. The organizers envisioned their program as a sweeping ceremony, a "concert–ritual prayer" that would outline the African provenance of the most contemporary black American artistic work. The trio of artists coordinating the show—saxophonist and composer Julius Hemphill, visual artist Oliver Jackson, and poet Michael Harper—took the African Continuum as their name, and that unit was itself a progeny of the local arts cooperative the Black Artists' Group (BAG). Over the past three years, the latter group had established itself as a powerful center of gravity for a constellation of young black artists working in St. Louis, and Hemphill and Jackson, both members of BAG, planned the Images concert as an elaborately orchestrated focal point for the fresh creative energies that their collective had released onto the local arts scene.[1]

Here on the stage of Powell Hall, they had assembled some of the area's most dynamic black performers: fellow members of BAG, musicians from Chicago's Association for the Advancement of Creative Musicians, and Senegalese percussionists drawn from the East St. Louis arts center founded by the celebrated dancer Katherine Dunham. With the passage between the program's two sections, "Sons" and "Ancestors," the artists signaled an intention to delineate the connections between expressions of music and language from the African American present and from a distant African past. As the somewhat enigmatic program notes explained, the performance was to be a "calling forth of the spiritually dynamic forces and powers of the cosmos" to revitalize "that harmonious existence which perpetuates itself as the African Continuum."[2]

The midtown area in which the concert took place, once a vibrant district for theater- and moviegoers, had dwindled to a collection of abandoned auditoriums and vacant plots, with the few remaining movie marquees blinking garishly over deserted streets. But Powell Hall, an ornate 1920s movie palace just renovated as home for the local symphony orchestra, stood proxy for the city's efforts to resurrect the moribund neighborhood. With African American performers generally excluded from the city's finest temples of elite art, the symbolism of the Powell venue must have resonated with the audience almost as much as the presentation of music, visual art, and poetry. The sumptuous surroundings were an anomaly in some ways, a startling contrast to the usual BAG events staged at makeshift locations scattered around the inner city, or at the revamped industrial building that served as the organization's headquarters. And yet, as Oliver Jackson explains, the Images event was "more than a symbolic gesture; it was a thrust to be able to use these great halls to put forward very serious work," presentations at which "having an African American audience was fundamental to the performance." The concert exemplified a number of the issues coming together in the life of BAG, in particular its members' assertive drive to expand and redefine the context for their art.[3]

The ten musicians tuned up their instruments amidst African artwork donated by local collectors and Jackson's own multileveled backdrop. But somewhere in the city, an unknown person, perhaps irritated by the bold artistic assertions that BAG had made over the previous three years, or enraged that a site dedicated to elite Anglo-European art would be used as the venue for such an event, picked up the telephone and called in a bomb threat. Minutes after the concert had begun, a tuxedoed theater official rushed onto the stage and ordered the auditorium cleared. The crowd poured onto the damp pavement of North Grand Boulevard as a police bomb squad roared up, and only after half an hour of milling around outside was the audience finally allowed back inside. Michael Harper's verse once again called the musicians to the stage, and a single stark drumbeat on the jembe pulsated through the hall, polyrhythmic layers building before making way for an eruption of hard swing from the entire ensemble, which then proceeded to sweep through a plethora of jazz styles. Julius Hemphill's lush, luminous score moved under the poet's fractured mosaic of images—visions of jazz legends come and gone, of a sinister St. Louis combining "music, death and minstrelsy," until the poem "High Modes" announced the ritual's climax, a "union of sons/ancestors" finally leading the audience "back to the well: Africa, / the first mode . . ."[4]

Staging an intricately choreographed production for such a large audience rounded off Hemphill's efforts with BAG over the past three years and validated what he would attempt to reproduce soon thereafter on his heralded debut album, *Dogon A.D.* And, though not exclusively a BAG performance, the Images concert incorporated a number of sources grounded in the collective's life and mission. The collision of aesthetics with social conflict was always an integral part of BAG, and nowhere more so than in the music that was so central to the movement. But the most explosive convergence at work that February night lay not offstage but onstage, not in the attempted intimidation but in the visual mix of contemporary American and traditional African art, and in the ensemble's sonic orientation, a sometimes uneasy union of traditional and contemporary that engrafted the scion of free jazz onto the venerable but still vital St. Louis musical trunk. Across four years of multimedia performance work similar in spirit, if not in location, to the Images event, the collective's members responded boldly to the social conditions then shaping the contemporary arts scene.

—»—≡—◉—BAG—◉—≡—«—

St. Louis has always been careful to cover its tracks, razing its history so it can start over again with a clean slate. But beneath every city lies a ghost town of spectral buildings and streets, and Mound City is no exception. Cars zip along the expressway over the burial ground of the Osage, over the orchards of the explorer Pierre Laclède, over the caverns where the beer baron William Lemp stored his brew and built a ballroom and put a revolver to his head, and right past Tom Turpin's Rosebud Café, where an echo of Scott Joplin sitting at the keyboard might still reverberate in the summer air. Other echoes of the past, too, occasionally manage to cut through the insistent drumbeat of the now, and one of these whose voice has been muffled but not quite silenced is the Black Artists' Group. During the turbulent years of the late 1960s and early 1970s, this seminal arts cooperative formed and flourished in St. Louis, bringing together and nurturing young African American experimentalists involved with theater, dance, poetry, and jazz in order to present a socially engaged and politically charged brand of performance art to the city's African American and progressive white communities.

While the collective's story may be largely unrecalled, its members are not, and many alumni have gone on to garner national and international renown. The organization formed a seedbed for a generation of innovative artists: musicians such as Oliver Lake, Julius Hemphill, Baikida Carroll, and Hamiet Bluiett; writers and directors such as Malinké Elliott, Ajulé Rutlin, Shirley LeFlore, and Vincent Terrell; dancers Georgia Collins and Luisah Teish; and visual artists Emilio Cruz and Oliver Jackson. All of these, and a host of lesser-known but still vibrant performers, honed their craft together in a retrofitted industrial building on St. Louis's near north side, surrounded by the physical evisceration of a deindustrialized city core. Members also formed alliances with other significant African American artists of the area, most notably Katherine Dunham, long a luminary of the international dance world; the poet and activist Eugene Redmond; and transplanted former members of the Watts Writers Workshop in Los Angeles. Though the city could never provide adequate opportunities for avant-garde artists to build long-term careers, the musicians, actors, dancers, poets, and painters of BAG struggled to heighten black consciousness and explore the far reaches of interdisciplinary performance—all while carving out a place for themselves within the context of local spaces, institutions, and politics.

Over the course of the decade, African American artistic collectives had sprung up around the country as part of a diffuse social and aesthetic outgrowth known as the Black Arts Movement. Emphasizing self-reliance and self-representation, these organizations derived much of their aesthetic direction from a reinvigorated attention to African ancestry and a newly nationalistic black consciousness in the United States. And if, as some movement essayists charged, the Harlem Renaissance of the 1920s had been compromised by its orientation toward white audiences and patrons, they would attempt to sidestep this error, presenting a self-consciously racialized version of identity to the very communities from which the artists emerged. In keeping with doctrines of cultural autonomy, cadres of young musicians, dancers, poets, and actors took their performances out of the white-controlled sites where they had traditionally been exploited to forge new artistic venues in storefronts, community centers, churches, coffeehouses, converted industrial buildings—in short, wherever they could get a hearing and address the nation's working-class black neighborhoods. Often evanescent, these manifestations of contemporary black culture shot briefly across the American sky, leaving in their wake questions about race, community, and nation.[5]

Although the critics' gaze has focused mostly on the coasts, a richer, more complex, and more problematic vision of the Black Arts Movement emerges when regional cooperatives such as BAG are brought back into the light. By the late 1960s, the tenets of the movement had penetrated the nation's cities from Detroit to Denver, Minneapolis to Memphis, and these impulses resonated with BAG's founders. Inspired by similar arts cooperatives around the country—particularly Chicago's Association for the Advancement of Creative Musicians—the group's members fused modernist technique with local experience, and they combined traditional forms of blues, jazz, and narrative expression with a communal focus and ideas of cultural autonomy. Unlike many other artistic collectives of the period, BAG was fundamentally committed to a collaborative interweaving of its members' diverse artistic mediums. Most significant, perhaps, were BAG's music and theater components. The musicians built on the free-jazz vocabulary developed through the decade by such pioneers as Ornette Coleman, John Coltrane, and Albert Ayler, and their innovations later energized the vital mid-1970s avant-garde jazz community in New York. Meanwhile, BAG's actors and directors served up an engaging synthesis of the avant-garde European techniques of Bertold Brecht and Jean Genet with plays by a new generation of black writers and materials improvised from contemporary African American culture, developing a dramatic approach that nonetheless remained grounded in local, working-class issues such as education, jobs, housing, and police brutality. While often pushing the limits of their mediums, these artists also created new models for interdisciplinary cooperation and arts-driven social activism.

Debates over civil rights, black nationalism, and the role of the arts in political struggle all found form in BAG. But in contemporary collectives around the country, these general trends expressed themselves in local and usually very different contexts. BAG came to maturity in the environment of the distinctive issues, institutions, and concerns with which the collective was enmeshed on a day-to-day basis, and also in the milieu of the broader intellectual and political tides running high in African American communities through the country. The group's experience in St. Louis worked as interface between the global and the local, the general and the particular. Though inspired by general ideologies gaining currency in the nation's radical intellectual circles, the group's leaders were driven, as well, by specific and particular needs within the local setting. The organizations emerging from the Black Arts Movement, while bound together by intellectual and ideological ties, were essentially grassroots in nature, and thus connected in specific urban locales and around particular spaces and issues. Like many similar arts cooperatives, BAG recast city spaces and institutions to fit its own agenda, creating new centers, nodes, and landmarks for the African American populace of St. Louis's north side.

Many of the collective's founders, as former BAG saxophonist J. D. Parran asserts, "were entering new territory culturally and politically as well as artistically." Indeed, the decade's busy intersection of politics and the arts, dramatized by groups such as BAG, blurred the lines between social commitments and aesthetic production. Accordingly, within the St. Louis milieu the organization's members cultivated three overlapping roles: as artists, as activists, and as community members. In their roles as artists, participants sought to inject messages of cultural liberation into their work. The dramatists took on controversial new plays by writers such as Sonia Sanchez and Amiri Baraka; the musicians incorporated the Afrocentric impulses of much of the period's free jazz into their sounds; and the creative writers attempted to wrest poetry from the academy and return it to the city's streets and neighborhoods.[6]

A few of the group's artists crossed those boundaries not just in their aesthetic work, but also in their fluid movement between the realms of artistic creation and on-the-ground organizing. As activists, several members engaged in some of the high-profile social causes in St. Louis— supporting the nation's first rent strike in federal public housing, as just one example—and affiliated themselves with local civil rights and nationalist political organizations. And finally, stressing their roles as engaged community members, BAG's artists turned toward the city's black citizenry, frequently mounting productions in low-income areas of St. Louis's north side and establishing a free arts academy for local African American youths. In addressing themselves to the city's black community, the artists followed one of the central tenets of the Black Arts and Black Power Movements. Yet in allying with such multiracial progressive groups as the Human Arts Association, they acted out a more integrationist ideology than that of many radical arts groups elsewhere, thereby insisting upon the universality of their aesthetic vision.

What enabling conditions made an organization such as BAG likely, or even possible? What resources fueled its trajectory across the local and ultimately the national arts landscape? The group's emergence depended on a number of factors, including the contemporary urban condition in St. Louis, the intellectual currents of the Black Arts and Black Power Movements, a tightly knit local network of artists and institutions that had developed through the mid- and late 1960s, and funding responses from liberal reformist foundations. First came the rapidly changing situation in American urban areas, in terms of population, economic viability, cultural stature, and even physical fabric. Hammered by deindustrialization, suburban flight, destructive urban renewal clearances, and a full ration of other urban troubles, St. Louis, along with its industrial neighbors throughout the Midwest, was fast becoming a harbinger of what American cities everywhere could expect. Only a few short blocks separated Eero Saarinen's sleek, stainless-steel Gateway Arch from the bedraggled near north side, but like the zebra stripes of a crosswalk, the metropolitan area remained segregated into tightly contained neighborhoods where black and white, rich and poor, were fenced off by physical and social barriers embedded deep in the city's history. The Black Artists' Group to a large degree responded to the contemporary urban condition—the disenfranchisement of the city's black communities as well as their rich substance and lively tenacity.

Alongside this crisis in northern industrial cities came a newly assertive nationalist sentiment, the civil rights movement transposed to a different key. Despite the far-reaching goals of the Johnson administration's civil rights legislation, by the mid-1960s the political mood in much of black America was one of exasperation. The nonviolent protest movement may have garnered sizable improvements in the field of public access, but progress had seemingly stalled in the arenas of jobs, education, and housing. With an anti–civil rights backlash building in the North, a new set of leaders came to reject the pacifist tactics and integrationist goals of the older civil rights groups. Less conciliatory, less willing to wait on gradual change, and less inclined to seek white approval, they called for African Americans to demand economic autonomy and the right to cultural self-determination. Many of them lent to the movement a revived focus on African heritage, one that had gained further inspiration as liberation movements in Africa gradually pried loose the grip of European colonial control. The Black Power slogan, inaugurated by Stokely Carmichael in 1966, resonated with increasing numbers of African Americans as the image of white and black hands clasped came to seem naïve or even maudlin.

In St. Louis itself, these trends had given rise to a densely interwoven network of local arts institutions, existing almost entirely outside the traditional realm of the academy. A younger and more radical generation of local writers and performers emerged, a fresh cohort that self-confidently cast the arts as a potent tool in the struggle for social and political liberation. While BAG achieved the highest degree of recognition, that organization was only one among many such efforts percolating through the metropolitan area. In 1967, Katherine Dunham had founded a dynamic performing arts center just across the Mississippi River in East St. Louis, Illinois. At the same time, a bevy of cultural nationalist organizations—among them Black Culture, Inc.; the Zulu 1200s; and the Black River Writers—sprang into being as fast as participants could think of names for them, while influential arts programs arose at community centers funded through the federal government's War on Poverty. In the close quarters of urban St. Louis, geographically the smallest of major American cities, young black musicians, painters, dancers, and poets rubbed shoulders in a way almost bound to ignite artistic sparks.

And finally, for a brief time, some real money was available to support the organization. As BAG's founders busily assembled their group in summer 1968, local arts executives and philanthropic foundations were developing plans for an inner-city arts initiative in St. Louis. Although these executives shared BAG's view of the arts as a powerful social instrument, the program they envisioned embodied many condescending notions about the proper role of the artist in black communities. Nonetheless, the collective was able to take advantage of these funding resources. And while outside grants did not create BAG, the money did allow it to develop as a full-fledged institution, with a school, its own building, staff, and nonstop arts programming until the group's dissolution four years later.

⟶⟩══◉BAG◎══⟨⟵

The Black Artists' Group coalesced out of a long tradition of black music in St. Louis and was fostered by a number of institutions—high schools, churches, neighborhoods—where the artists came of age, and the first chapter narrates the upbringing of its members and the 1968 formation of the group against this backdrop. The context in which the newly formed collective found itself was one of both turmoil and opportunity, as local Black Power adherents mustered their strength and issued insistent challenges to the city's establishment. Responding to polarization and unrest, liberal reformists from local arts bodies and philanthropic foundations developed new programs that worked in symbiosis, but also in conflict, with BAG's artistic thrust, as the second chapter explains. As the organization struggled to its feet, members developed local networks within the black community, opened a school, and interacted with multiracial organizations emerging from the countercultural and campus protest movements. The third chapter describes how arts and community played off one another as both stimulant and irritant in BAG's first several years. The fourth chapter narrates the cooperative's deliberate effort to erase disciplinary boundaries, incorporating music, poetry, theater, dance, and visual art, often in large-scale multimedia productions.

The collective remains most widely known, however, for the fleet of jazz improvisers and composers that it spawned, its musicians not only expanding aesthetic boundaries themselves, but also serving as inspiration for many of the artists working in other media. The fifth chapter explores in greater depth the manner in which BAG's musicians added a unique voice to the changing local and national jazz scenes, both by crafting new sounds and by pioneering new approaches to the economic obstacles facing jazz musicians of the period. But when their Missouri locale finally threatened to throttle artistic creativity, key members took their passions and skills farther afield. In 1972, as internal divisions and a lack of funding put pressure on the organization, five of the leading musicians relocated to Paris, where they joined a burgeoning free-jazz scene and made the connections that would allow them to move to New York. The sixth chapter follows the group's unraveling in St. Louis and several members' migration to Europe. By the mid-1970s, many of BAG's musicians had arrived in New York amid a flowering of experimental music in the partially abandoned loft buildings of Lower Manhattan. There, three of them cofounded the World Saxophone Quartet, one of the most influential avant-garde jazz ensembles of the 1970s and 1980s. The seventh and final chapter sketches the development of this loft performance scene and BAG's place in it.

In 1971, several months after the Powell Hall concert, BAG saxophonist Oliver Lake recorded his first album as a leader—*NTU: Point from Which Creation Begins*. In retrospect, his title seems to encapsulate not only the fresh and challenging music on that record, but also the legacy of BAG, whose aesthetic and social commitments sometimes coalesced and sometimes diverged. But art is a place where contradictions do not destroy one another, to paraphrase St. Louis poet Howard Nemerov, and the productive tension that led to BAG's formation prepared the ground—the "point from which creation begins"—for a reshaping of the St. Louis and, by extension, the American arts landscape.[7]

Chapter 1

A City Built to Music: St. Louis foundations

Roots and branches, cultivation and growth, current and flow—such metaphors often stand proxy for the continuity of development through American musical history. This is especially true with regard to the movement of jazz from its putative origins in New Orleans, up the Mississippi River to St. Louis, and outward to Chicago, Kansas City, New York, and beyond. And, admittedly, there *is* a satisfying organic sense to those metaphors, as exemplified by the 1999 Smithsonian documentary *The Mississippi: River of Song*, which traces musical traditions in the towns that border the great river. The title of the series evokes a kind of uninterrupted movement, even if the current somehow moves in the wrong historical direction, from Minnesota down to Louisiana.[1]

The confluence of elements that was the St. Louis Black Artists' Group drew from a variety of sources and locales, but always centered in the fabric of the city itself—its neighborhoods, its schools and churches, its clubs. The historical and cultural antecedents of BAG help fix its place in American musical history, but to get closer to the truth we must set alongside the placid certainties of terms such as roots, current, flow, and the like, a set of less comfortable terms—discontinuity and reconnection, atrophy and regeneration. The development of an artistic life in St. Louis, especially for African Americans, was not one of steady progress, no "crystal stair," to quote another Missouri native, Langston Hughes. And yet the story of BAG in its earliest incarnation is a story attached to a particular place in time, shaped by the history of that place, its past and present; a story that reaches back to an older St. Louis and forward to the first formal recognition, with BAG's inaugural multidisciplinary performance of Jean Genet's play *The Blacks* in 1968, that something new had come into being.

⊹⊱◈BAG◈⊰⊹

BAG's St. Louis connection flows through all sorts of channels from the city's musical past, sometimes hidden, sometimes surfacing in unexpected places. Markets, ports, and railway junctions where people from many regions and walks of life congregate often become centers for artistic innovation, nodes along a sometimes coursing, sometimes interrupted current. Through the nineteenth and early twentieth centuries, St. Louis along with Chicago functioned as just such a portal, linking the vast regions and natural resources of the Great West with the industry and trade networks of the East. Although the railroads eventually redirected the region's trade to Chicago, St. Louis's remaining trade links with the South made the city a natural destination for the immigration of musical talent, especially from the southern states, a movement that continuously infused nutrients into the creative system. But here, again, metaphor describes and dramatizes, but sometimes oversimplifies. True, St. Louis and its sister cities of East St. Louis and Brooklyn, both across the Mississippi River in Illinois, remained central to a network of musicians held together by railroads, rivers, and highways that converged on the area. But this was a process—or maybe a condition—that included blockages, stops, and starts.[2]

Though St. Louis has long been a vibrant center for African American music, through the nineteenth and much of the twentieth century, opportunities for formal training were severely curbed by the harsh segregation policies of the city's schools and musical institutions. With limited success, African American musicians responded to these economic and social challenges, just as BAG would do in the 1960s. Due in part to their exclusion from the city's white musical institutions, nineteenth-century black musicians had formed a number of organizations to provide training and at least rudimentary economic protections, ranging from the nation's first black musicians' union to the Luca Conservatory of Music for black students. The city's African American musical life was fostered in a variety of settings—a tradition that would stretch from church choirs, fraternal organizations, and drum-and-bugle corps to hard-bop combos playing the club circuit in the 1950s and 1960s.[3]

Already by the 1860s the region was a major hub for black music. Ragtime pianist and composer Scott Joplin arrived in the city in 1885, and during the next several decades, ragtime music wafted continuously through the saloons lining Chestnut and Market Streets. Early in the century, a visitor could hear blues as well, in working-class clubs on the riverfront, in East St. Louis's Valley district, and at informal rent parties. Roughing it through St. Louis in 1892, the bluesman W. C. Handy slept on the cobblestoned Mississippi levee, sheltered only by the arches of Eads Bridge. There he caught the distant strains of blues fragments that years later filtered into the song that would make him (and the city) famous: "The St. Louis Blues." By the 1920s, blues had almost completely supplanted ragtime as the staple of the city's nightlife. Like the blues players, most local jazz musicians found their employment on the Missouri side of the river in the 1910s and 1920s. But the jazz scene became more active on the river's Illinois side during the 1930s and 1940s, with a host of clubs sprouting up in East St. Louis and Brooklyn. By the 1950s, the region had produced a number of nationally recognized jazz musicians, including guitarist Grant Green and saxophonist Jimmy Forrest, and touring bands such as Eddie Randle and his Blue Devils, and George Hudson and his Orchestra. The area became known especially for its trumpeters—Harold "Shorty" Baker, Dewey Jackson, Clark Terry, George Hudson, and Miles Davis—playing what Davis later called "that St. Louis thing."[4]

But just as economic security and vulnerability walked hand in hand through the streets of black St. Louis, so did cultural opportunity and indifference. Many of the most prominent musicians had left during the early 1950s to build careers elsewhere. The city lacked the recording opportunities and radio airplay to give a boost to aspiring musicians or to retain rising stars, a problem especially acute for African Americans. The 1950s saw a flurry of independent record labels spring into existence in St. Louis, but none managed to last for long. At the same time, the area's radio stations remained dominated by white disc jockeys and white pop music, making it difficult for local African American artists to make headway. And though as a teenager growing up in St. Louis in the late 1930s and early 1940s, rock-and-roll pioneer Chuck Berry remembers listening to blues, boogie-woogie, and swing on a black radio station from Illinois, it was the only station in the metropolitan area that would play artists such as Muddy Waters, Tampa Red, and Rosetta Thorp. By the early 1950s, St. Louis radio had only two black disc jockeys, and the city's beleaguered record companies had difficulties getting airplay for their black artists.[5]

Birth, growth, decline, and death. The organic metaphor suggests that the cycle should have come to an end. But the current of song, seemingly having dried up to a trickle, surged once again in the 1950s with the reemergence of urban blues dance styles and an influx of talent from the South, galvanizing St. Louis's popular music scene. From Mississippi came Ike Turner and his Kings of Rhythm; from Mississippi via Memphis, Oliver Sain and Little Milton Campbell; and from Arkansas, the guitarist Albert King. Clubs on both sides of the river flourished once again, their audiences moving to the new rhythms at nightspots with memorable names like Helen's Moonlight Lounge, Sadie's Personality Bar, the Dynaflow, and the Shadow Box. When Missouri's early bar closing hours shut them down, the bands packed up for the river's Illinois side and played until daybreak, at venues ranging from opulent nightclubs to dilapidated roadhouses where East St. Louis trailed off into the dirt roads of rural Illinois. And throughout the decade, much of the city's entertainment was controlled by the black social clubs that hired bands to play weekend dances for crowds of hundreds. Meanwhile, on the jazz scene, such musicians as Oliver Nelson, Jimmy Forrest, and Grant Green were busy charging up their audiences. As Miles Davis recalled, "After St. Louis closed down at night, everybody over there came to Brooklyn [Illinois] to listen to the music and party all night long. People in East St. Louis and St. Louis worked their asses off in them packing and slaughtering houses. So you know they was mad when they took off work. They didn't want to hear no dumb shit off nobody." The scene was jerrybuilt, vulnerable to the slightest economic tremor, but founded in a bedrock of musicality on which BAG would build in the decade that followed.[6]

⇔▬◉ʙᴀɢ◉▬⇔

This was the groundwork that gave footing to a cadre of young musicians—Oliver Lake, Lester Bowie, Floyd LeFlore, and Hamiet Bluiett, among others—who would provide the early impetus for BAG's 1968 genesis. Born within a few years of each other around 1940, all of these musicians grew up in black neighborhoods on the city's north side, or just across the river in East St. Louis and its environs. Living in the small and relatively concentrated black community of the north side, many of them knew one another from elementary school on up. They came of age amidst a lively amateur and semiprofessional local music scene, with members of the black community actively participating in drum-and-bugle corps, school music programs, church choirs, and dance and jazz ensembles. Oliver Lake, whose family had moved to St. Louis from the small Arkansas town of Marianna shortly after his birth, formed close friendships in his early years with Lester Bowie, born in Maryland and raised in Arkansas and St. Louis, and Floyd LeFlore, born in Mississippi and raised in St. Louis. Meanwhile, just across the river, Hamiet Bluiett grew up in the Illinois town of Brooklyn, a former Underground Railroad stop founded by free blacks in 1837. His aunt and uncle ran a Brooklyn nightclub, and Bluiett remembers the local musical traditions as "a different way of thinking. It was the drum-and-bugle corps all mixed up with hoot'n'holler gospel. We got barbecued up in that church. Slow-cooking."[7]

Jazz scholar Paul Berliner notes that "exposure to their own community's music as well as that of the mainstream is one advantage commonly afforded minority children in America." An advantage *taken*, perhaps, rather than "afforded"—but whether it was Lake listening raptly to the jukebox at his mother's restaurant in the Ville neighborhood; LeFlore soaking up tales from his uncle, the guitarist Bucky Jarman; or Bowie sitting at the feet of a musician father and older brother, all of them absorbed something of the sonic traditions that marked out St. Louis as a musical compendium. Baikida Carroll, a younger member of the group, later commented that "being in a black community, there is music around all the time. You never assume that you're going to play it, but at the same time, it is so around you in almost every aspect of day-to-day living." Even as the city's black population was squeezed in an economic vise, the young musicians grew up in neighborhoods teeming with a rich musical life that was central to the African American community.[8]

Not surprisingly, racial segregation typified the neighborhoods in which these musicians were raised, a product of actions by the government, real estate industry, and white homeowners' associations. As the city's black population had spread westward from early neighborhoods near the Mississippi River's downtown shores, clusters of African Americans were increasingly encircled by restrictive covenants forbidding deed owners from selling or renting to nonwhites—leading to the development of black enclaves dotted through the city's northern half. Between the early 1940s and the late 1960s, over 5 million African Americans left the South for northern cities—many of them settling in St. Louis. But even after the Supreme Court ruled restrictive covenants unconstitutional in 1948, white St. Louisans developed sophisticated systems for maintaining de facto residential segregation, using zoning laws, redlining, and racial steering to confine blacks to restricted neighborhoods.[9]

Due to rigid limitations on residence elsewhere in the city, for much of the twentieth century African Americans had clustered in a northwestern St. Louis district known as the Ville. Though in 1920 only 8 percent of that neighborhood's residents were black, by 1950 the Ville was 95 percent African American and firmly established as the heart of the city's black middle class, with professionals accounting for one in seven of its residents. Nevertheless, the diverse neighborhood hosted a wide variety of residents, with businesspeople, lawyers, and doctors living side by side with manual laborers. The Ville contained a dense cluster of the city's major black institutions, including several schools, a hospital, churches, and commercial districts. While much of black St. Louis lived in tenuous economic circumstances, the Ville provided educational and professional opportunities to many of its residents.[10]

The Ville's Sumner High School became fertile ground for the cultivation of African American musicians in St. Louis. The first black high school west of the Mississippi, Sumner had opened in 1875 after black parents sued the district for refusing to educate their children, and in 1911 it relocated to a distinguished Georgian building in the Ville. Sumner enjoyed a national reputation for its excellent faculty, and in 1931 boasted the first African American instrumental music instructor to be employed by the St. Louis School Board. The school's musician-graduates included Jimmy Forrest in the late 1930s, Chuck Berry in the late 1940s, and Tina Turner and opera star Grace Bumbry in the 1950s. The respect given especially to jazz by Sumner's music teachers offered encouragement to budding students.[11]

In the mid- and late 1950s, a new cadre of musicians matriculated there, one that would include core members of the Black Artists' Group and its sister organization in Chicago, the Association for the Advancement of Creative Musicians (AACM). Oliver Lake, Lester Bowie, and Floyd LeFlore found themselves at Sumner with a group of students that included drummers Philip Wilson and Jerome "Scrooge" Harris, trumpeter David Hines, and pianist John Hicks. Of his Sumner High days, Bowie remembers, "We had some really hip musicians. Hicks was cool even then—he had a hip little trio, he had a suit and tie, he had that look. Philip was cool, too. Philip was like an organ trio-type dude." LeFlore played in the band and began to hang out with his more musically oriented classmates, discovering records by musicians such as the hard-bop icon Horace Silver. And although Lake only started playing the saxophone seriously the year following his 1961 graduation, he too was involved in the music scene during his Sumner High days, playing percussion in a drum-and-bugle corps.[12]

Trumpeter Lester Bowie was the most active on the local scene as a high schooler. Coming from a long line of musicians—his father was a trumpeter and school band director, his grandfather a trombonist, and his great-grandfather an organist—Bowie gravitated naturally to a musical career. But because of his father's experiences with segregation as an orchestral musician, Bowie dismissed the idea of a career in classical music. "When he came up," Bowie explained, "there was no hope of a black man getting with a symphony orchestra in the States, so I didn't even consider that." As a youngster, the story goes, Bowie practiced by his open bedroom window in hopes that the legendary Louis Armstrong might stroll through the area and hear him. Trumpeter Bobbie Danzie, one of Miles Davis's closest childhood friends, took Bowie under his wing. At age fifteen, Bowie was a member of the black musicians' union, playing in clubs, school bands, and church recitals and sitting in with older musicians. Through his teens and early twenties, Bowie played professionally in St. Louis, toured the South with doo-wop backup bands, rhythm-&-blues acts, and even carnival tent shows, and barnstormed the central Missouri blues circuit with groups such as Jack Harris and the Invaders.[13]

By the early 1960s, the Sumner High youngsters were hanging out with a number of other improvisers, saxophonists James Jabbo Ware and J. D. Parran and trumpeter Baikida Carroll among them. Ware was raised in Tennessee by his grandmother and spent summers in St. Louis with his parents, eventually moving there permanently in 1960, while Parran had grown up in St. Louis, gaining his early musical exposure in public school bands and the Baptist Church. Baikida Carroll, born in 1947, absorbed his musical interests from his parents: as a teenager, his mother used to cut school to catch Miles Davis matinees at a small club called Rhumboogie's, and his father was an amateur saxophonist and pianist. During Carroll's sophomore year at Soldan High School, he joined the school band, and by that summer he was gigging with the rhythm-&-blues groups of Albert King and Ike Turner, where he eventually met Lester Bowie.[14]

Jazz educator David Baker has emphasized the significance of the "enlightened high school band leaders" who have historically nurtured young talents in African American communities around the country, and the St. Louis area's schools had a number of these figures: Ken Billups and Clarence Wilson at Sumner High, Vernon Nashville at Soldan High, Elwood Buchanan at East St. Louis's Lincoln High, and George Hudson at Elijah Lovejoy High. Nashville, in particular, took a leading role in these musicians' educations, starting a rehearsal band that met on Saturdays at the black musicians' union hall. The hall, sitting half a block from the celebrated Riviera nightclub, hosted a nonstop bustle of local musicians who dropped in for shoptalk and jam sessions after wrapping up late-night gigs. Bowie, Ware, Parran, and Carroll regularly gathered there to play in Nashville's rehearsal band. Older musicians stopped by to offer them encouragement and advice, while saxophonist Oliver Nelson and drummer Chick Booth contributed charts. At the same time, the dynamic rhythm-&-blues scene that animated the city's clubs and halls provided early employment opportunities for the young musicians. They honed their skills on weekends backing Ike Turner, Albert King, Little Milton, and Oliver Sain, as a more soulful style of blues gained popularity in the nation and in St. Louis.[15]

⊸━❖ BAG ❖━⊷

St. Louis's role as a musical watershed was confirmed again by the arrival of the saxophonist Julius Hemphill, who stepped onto the local scene in the mid-1960s and would become one of the most influential BAG members. Born in 1938 in Fort Worth, Texas, Hemphill was an only child, raised by his mother after his father's early death. He spent his formative years in a Fort Worth district called the Hot End, where, as he remembered, "the back door was in the country and the front door was semi in the city." Growing up in the Hot End, Hemphill was steeped in the sounds of rhythm and blues, rural blues, and swing, and surrounded by the cadences of the church, where his mother Edna played piano. "Oh, it was rich musically," Hemphill remembered, recalling the snatches of blues and country music that churned out of the Hot End's countless jukeboxes and through his bedroom window; "without moving an inch, I was exposed to all of this. I can't remember when I didn't know about Louis Jordan. . . . In my neighborhood, Louis Jordan was the *man*." Sprawled on the carpet listening to his aunt's extensive record collection, the young Hemphill also came across the sounds of Johnny Hodges, Duke Ellington, Sarah Vaughan, and Lester Young.

Bused miles to a black high school even though there were several white schools within walking distance of his home, Hemphill played clarinet and, later, saxophone in the school band, studying with the reedman John Carter while growing up a few blocks from the home of

Ornette Coleman, a distant cousin. Even so, as a teenager his interests gravitated more to sports than to music.[16]

But what Hemphill did have in common with a number of the St. Louis contingent was another important institution, the historically black Lincoln University in Missouri's state capital, Jefferson City. Though the call of sports remained strong—Hemphill tried out for football at the University of California, Berkeley—he deepened his musical interests after transferring to Oakland Junior College and finally to Lincoln, a two-hour drive from St. Louis. There, Hemphill met members of the Sumner High cadre of musicians, among them Lester Bowie, Oliver Lake, and John Hicks. The drummer Ronald Shannon Jackson, another Fort Worth native at Lincoln University, recalled that the new friends "spent as much time performing together as studying." However, the school's conservative music department frowned upon jazz, and Hemphill and his friends had to pursue their jazz studies outside the school environment. Hemphill and Bowie later had some negative recollections of Lincoln. "It was *verboten* to be playing what they called street music in there, jazz kind of thing," said Hemphill, recalling that students who gathered in practice rooms for jam sessions ran the risk of suspension.[17]

Even so, it was at Lincoln University that Hemphill made a fundamental commitment to music. "I lost all my money gambling when I got up there, so all I could do was practice," he later laughed; "I practiced through many a meal time." David Baker, after finishing a stint as a sideman with the Stan Kenton band, taught brass at Lincoln and instructed Hemphill in music theory. Shuttling between school in Missouri and his family's Fort Worth home, Hemphill continued to be exposed to the blues and jazz traditions of the South, sitting in at Dallas clubs and touring the tiny juke joints scattered through the backwoods of West Texas. Like Oliver Lake, who once commented that he "studied first in the university of the streets," Hemphill, too, noted that "I learned what I learned in school. The rest of it I learned in West Texas and on the south side in Dallas, jumping up and down on the blues boys' bandstands and bebop bandstands."[18]

Passion for their art turned almost any situation to advantage for the future BAG members, and whether in college or in the armed

Saxophonist and composer Julius Hemphill, BAG's first chairman.

⋗═◉BAG◉═⋖

Photograph courtesy Portia Hunt.

forces, they remained attentive to the muse. Most of them were in and out of town during the early or mid-1960s, but whatever the circumstance, they all managed to focus on their music. Floyd LeFlore, Baikida Carroll, Lester Bowie, and Julius Hemphill were musicians in the service, and Bowie also gigged with blues bands on the side. Meanwhile, Hamiet Bluiett became a member of the navy band, where he developed his expertise in the high registers by playing alto saxophone parts on the baritone.[19]

When he had almost finished his degree in music education, Hemphill was suspended from Lincoln (legend has it that he skipped final exams to hear John Coltrane in St. Louis) and lost his service deferment, joining the army when it became clear that he would be drafted. Stationed at Fort Hood, Texas, and Fort Leonard Wood, Missouri, his military specialty was saxophone, though he learned flute and soon switched over to that. Hemphill ended up as leader of the 399th Army Dance Band. But Hemphill strongly disliked the rigid rules and make-work tasks that were a part of army life, and he frequently took unauthorized leaves. He also resented the discriminatory practices of the armed forces. After reading *The Autobiography of Malcolm X* while in the service, Hemphill later remembered thinking, "Right, give me a rifle and send me down to Mississippi or something and let's fight a battle that I think needs fighting." At one point, Hemphill tried to be declared unfit for service by hanging Nation of Islam materials in his locker before an inspection. At the end of his initial sign-up period, Hemphill refused to re-enlist.[20]

After high school, Baikida Carroll, too, reluctantly entered the army. Several of his neighborhood friends had been drafted and killed in Vietnam, and Carroll considered seeking refuge in Canada or Holland from the bloodbath that the war was swiftly becoming. Convinced instead by his high school band director, Vernon Nashville, to use his musical talents to avoid combat, Carroll attended the Armed Forces Music School in Virginia before being stationed in Germany for three years. While studying composition at the conservatory in Würzburg, Carroll was inspired to start an after-hours big band as an outlet for his compositions.

BAIKIDA CARROLL IN FRANCE, 1973.

Photograph courtesy Baikida Carroll.

At the same time, he listened with growing enthusiasm to the free jazz of the 1960s, especially the music of Ornette Coleman, Don Cherry, Archie Shepp, and Albert Ayler. The charts he wrote for his nighttime ensemble reflected the avant-garde impulses of these contemporary trailblazers.[21]

Back in St. Louis sporadically through the mid-1960s, whether from Lincoln University or the armed forces, the musicians renewed their connections through the local R&B scene. Oliver Lake, one of the few who had not spent time in the armed forces, returned to the city from Lincoln University in 1965. Now a serious student of the saxophone, Lake sought out the tutelage of more established local musicians such as saxophonists John Norment and Freddie Washington, pianist John Chapman, and bassist John Mixon. At that time, LeFlore had recently returned from the service and lived around the corner from David Hines and Lester Bowie, who shared an apartment on Washington Boulevard. Seeing the dedication of his former schoolmates, LeFlore ratcheted up his practicing and would "go to places and jam all night long." Meanwhile, Hemphill moved to St. Louis after leaving the army. He worked a string of blue-collar jobs—as a furniture salesman, shipping clerk, milk truck driver, and bread salesman—before finding employment as a substitute music teacher with the St. Louis Public Schools, where his wife Lynell also taught. After turning to rhythm-&-blues gigs to supplement his income, Hemphill began to explore avant-garde music in his spare time. J. D. Parran writes, "I vividly remember the excitement generated by Julius's presence on the scene. Oliver Lake raved about Julius, placing his prowess above all other saxophonists in town." The voluble, six-foot-four saxophonist quickly developed a local reputation as an astonishingly creative improviser, becoming known in musical circles as "The Professor."[22]

But whether it was accompanying Ike and Tina Turner on their frantic cross-country tours or backing Oliver Sain and Little Milton on local funk and rhythm-&-blues gigs, by the late 1960s the young jazzers were finding little sustenance on the commercial scene. Carroll found it "cool for finances, but creatively I wasn't being inspired." Hemphill, meanwhile, grew particularly disenchanted with commercial work after his unique solo style got him fired from a spring 1968 midwestern tour with Ike Turner. Neither could St. Louis's mainstream jazz scene satisfy their desire to stretch further. "I really wasn't content playing the material from the '40s, '50s and '60s and so forth," Hemphill later recalled; "at this time everyone was pretty much concerned with a particular region of music, people were mainstream, which was alright, but it didn't satisfy me." Instead, the musicians were inspired by the free and avant-garde music coming from the East Coast: the late-period work of John Coltrane and the sounds of Ornette Coleman, Archie Shepp, and Albert Ayler. Lake, Hemphill, and their comrades delved into these fresh styles rather than continuing in the R&B and mainstream jazz traditions that held St. Louis's music scene in their sway.[23]

This small but healthy cadre of free jazz musicians developed their new sounds almost unnoticed by the wider music-listening public. Floyd LeFlore remembers that "there was a great deal of frustration going on, 'cause there wasn't an opportunity to perform, really. Some of the older guys, the traditionalists around here, wouldn't even let us sit in. You know, they used to talk about us bad. 'They can't play,' and that kind of shit." More by necessity than by choice, their combos almost never included a complete rhythm section, foreshadowing their future nonstandard groupings. Just as "nonstandard" were their rehearsal spaces: Carroll and Hemphill, for example, met not in the proverbial smoky jazz club, but at the Forest Park golf course where Carroll often practiced his trumpet. Shut out of club venues, experimentally minded musicians met to rehearse at other unlikely locations, forging their styles at each other's apartments and at an old garage in North St. Louis nicknamed the Hairy Hut, where dozens of musicians would gather to jam through the night.[24]

-->≡◉BAG◉≡<--

Meanwhile, an important catalyst for the St. Louis musicians was revving into life three hundred miles to the north in the form of Chicago's Association for the Advancement of Creative Musicians (AACM), whose voltage generated a musical current far beyond its immediate locale. Lester Bowie established the first connection with his move to Chicago. Bowie had met the gospel-turned-soul singer Fontella Bass while gigging with Little Milton in St. Louis, and they soon were married. By the mid-1960s, Bass's popularity was on the rise, and when she inked a deal with Chicago's top blues label, Chess Records, Bowie became her musical director. Late in 1965, the couple decided that musical opportunities were better in the Windy City and relocated to Chicago. Soon thereafter, Bass burst into the national limelight with her rollicking soul hit "Rescue Me."[25]

Bowie supported himself in Chicago by playing studio sessions and advertising jingles, but soon after arriving in the city, he encountered the AACM. The free and avant-garde jazz scene that he found in Chicago eventually became the model for the musicians remaining in St. Louis. In the early 1960s, a cadre of young black Chicago musicians had clustered around the composer and pianist Muhal Richard Abrams— a mentor and father figure—joining his Experimental Band, a group exploring free jazz and collective improvisation, as well as modernist compositional techniques such as polytonality, chromaticism, and serialism. In a city whose musical life had been in decline since the end of World War II, the mavericks who gathered around Abrams had little outlet for their experimentation. But Abrams seemed to be opening a new channel. In May 1965, he and his colleagues formalized their efforts and founded the AACM, an organization composed primarily of members of the South Side black community. Through their collective, these musicians aimed to take control of their own artistic destinies.[26]

Years later, Bowie remembered his delight when he first sat in with the AACM, explaining that "it was shocking, because I hadn't seen that many weird cats in one room before." Enthralled by their musical departures, he soon joined the collective, as well as an AACM subunit, the Roscoe Mitchell Art Quartet (later the Art Ensemble of Chicago), which included Mitchell and Joseph Jarman on reeds along with the bassist Malachi Favors. When Bowie first encountered the Art Ensemble, the only member making a living entirely from music was Favors, who had a regular gig at a Holiday Inn. Bowie's marriage to the new soul star

Fontella Bass, and his connections through her to studio work, made him one of the few AACM musicians who could make a decent living from music. But it was his musicianship and organizational skills that won him the presidency of the collective in 1968.[27]

Bowie's involvement with the AACM accelerated the idea of forming a black musicians' collective in St. Louis. Several of the Missourians piled into Oliver Lake's old Nash to visit Bowie in Chicago, and LeFlore later noted the impact: "We drove up there and heard this free, this avant-garde music. . . . And it was just so overwhelming for me, I didn't know what to play, you know." Lake, too, was struck by the "strength that had come about from their unity." And when Hemphill traveled to Chicago, he even considered joining the AACM, only to be deterred by the organization's regimented code of conduct. "I just got out of the army," he remembered later with a laugh; "I don't ever follow nobody's rules!" Still, the power and depth of the AACM's musical program created mounting excitement among the St. Louis group. Lester Bowie, with his frequent trips between Chicago and his hometown, fueled the development of both the AACM and BAG, and later formed the most tangible link between the two organizations.[28]

While the AACM had evolved from Muhal Richard Abrams's Experimental Band, the progenitors of BAG swung on the axis of the Oliver Lake Art Quartet. After checking out the scene in Chicago, Lake formed a combo in 1967 that gave St. Louis its first taste of the new sounds on offer in Chicago and New York. Rounding up his old schoolmates Floyd LeFlore and Jerome "Scrooge" Harris, and adding local bassist Carl (later Arzinia) Richardson, Lake introduced his Art Quartet in 1967 at the Circle Coffee Shop in LaClede Town and followed up that concert with a more elaborate presentation at Sheldon Memorial Hall in the city's midtown district. By early 1968, the Lake Art Quartet had embarked on several new projects, including a soundtrack for the short experimental film JAZZOO. Lake crafted an impressionistic, free-floating, yet funk-based soundtrack that pulsated under images of Saint Louis Zoo animals stirring in the early morning hours, and the project eventually took first prize for experimental film at the Atlanta Film Festival.[29]

⊶⊷⊷⊛BAG⊛⊶⊷⊷

Although BAG is often depicted as purely a musical group, it actually was the result of parallel movements toward consolidation in both the jazz community and the black theater community in St. Louis. Music, as always with BAG, was the catalyst. But from their high school days, the musicians were friends with budding poets, painters, and actors. For one, they associated with the poet Shirley Bradley LeFlore, who had attended Sumner High School and Lincoln University with many of the musicians, and had recently married Floyd LeFlore. The poet Ajulé (originally Bruce) Rutlin, a Soldan High School graduate, also became a friend. Rutlin recalls that "most of those guys had been hanging out for years and talking about doing things, so I was always part of that, and my house was one of the places where they would meet to hang out and talk." The young musicians gathered at Rutlin's apartment on the city's western edge, or came together while checking out the local music clubs for their old high school friends.[30]

At the same time that future BAG musicians were developing plans for a collective, impetus was also building for a black theater company in St. Louis. Employment opportunities for the young experimental musicians may have been slim, but black actors faced an even more dismal prospect trying to make a living at their craft. In addition to the informal racial restrictions that limited the roles black actors could take on, the St. Louis theater scene was floundering by the late 1960s. While local actors mounted sporadic professional shows, effort after effort to establish a resident professional theater company had failed. But although professional opportunities for African American actors and directors were almost nonexistent, St. Louis's black community hosted a lively amateur theater scene, with plays sponsored by churches and by organizations such as the Urban League. In the 1920s, the Mississippi-born African American theater pioneer Frederick O'Neal had organized the Ira Aldridge Players in St. Louis, before going on to cofound Harlem's seminal American Negro Theatre. Church and civic organizations continued the amateur theater tradition in the 1950s and 1960s, with plays such as James Baldwin's *Amen Corner* as staples. The city did have one regular black theatre troupe, the Persona Players, a company that performed light comedies and operettas at church and civic benefits.[31]

Malinké (originally Robert) Elliott, a young poet, actor, and director, had long mulled establishing a company to lend a sharper focus to the city's developing black theater community. Born in 1942, Elliott attended the integrated Beaumont High School before joining the Air Force and left St. Louis while trying to overcome severe reading difficulties. But during high school, he had spent hours leafing through theater magazines, fascinated by the photographs of New York productions. Despite his reading problems, Elliott resolved that someday he would write for theater. In the Air Force, while stationed at an Alaskan military hospital, Elliott began struggling through novels such as Richard Wright's *Black Boy*, with help and encouragement from an elderly librarian. Surprised and delighted, as he said, to find "books that reflected me," he learned to read proficiently and started devouring all sorts of texts, from French existential philosophy to the landmark works of African American fiction. Shortly later, he was transferred to Topeka, Kansas, where he worked at the Menninger Foundation, a renowned psychiatric clinic, on screening nuclear launch controllers for the Strategic Air Command. The Menninger Foundation sponsored a community theater program, and there Elliott finally waded into dramatic productions.[32]

Returning to St. Louis in 1964, Elliott began to develop a career in drama while delving into the theatrical literature of the Black Arts Movement. At the same time, the momentum for a local black theater company had quickened with the establishment of the Metropolitan Educational Center for the Arts (MECA), a federally funded arts education program in St. Louis, which operated from 1967 to 1970. Under the leadership of the modernist composer Arthur Custer, who had relocated from Philadelphia to head up the project, MECA sponsored five "Saturday Centers" scattered through the metropolitan area, with local artists offering up instruction in visual arts, music, photography, dance, and theater. By 1968, Elliott was teaching drama for MECA's downtown branch, where he worked with Russ Durgin, a white English instructor at an elite prep school. At MECA, Elliott gained experience directing plays in a variety of settings, from churches and warehouses to street corners. The MECA project brought in outside groups such as the Harlequin Players, an award-winning Off-Broadway troupe.[33] But Durgin and Elliott made it their goal to establish a black company using local actors, believing, as Durgin said, that "a corporation of black artists will create art with more integrity at this time in history." While white patrons often couched their support in condescending assumptions that African Americans possessed an innate, instinctual ability for self-expression that negated the need for formal instruction, Durgin and Elliott were convinced that the company they envisioned needed to be grounded in professional training.[34]

The trajectory for a black theater company moved through these official channels, but meanwhile, working-class black actors were assembling a grassroots company. Vincent Terrell spearheaded these efforts. A St. Louis native, Terrell had acquired both an interest in poetry and a strong political consciousness in the army, where he was severely traumatized by the brutal war experience in Vietnam. Returning home, he worked a series of factory jobs while continuing his development as a poet, meeting other aspiring writers at readings in the cafés of Gaslight Square. Terrell developed deep indignation over social conditions in his home city, a sentiment symbolized by the .38 caliber pistol and sawed-off shotgun that, while never used, always sat amidst the jumble of papers in his briefcase. Early in 1968, Terrell, along with the drummer/actor Charles "Bobo" Shaw, started a drama group known as The Society of the Creatively Concerned, or the TSOCC Players, which began performing skits at political rallies that summer. The group infused its early productions with social and political energies. Ultimately the most radically political of BAG's members, Terrell explains that the TSOCC Players "was grassroots, it dealt with issues of the day—police brutality, poverty, just the rigors of living in St. Louis at that time."[35]

LeRoi Shelton, an assembly worker and union shop steward at the city's McDonnell Douglas aircraft plant, quickly joined Terrell's nascent group. Shelton had experience in the theater from his work with the Persona Players, but by 1968, that company's light comedies seemed increasingly out of step with the social imperatives of the time. In the

LeRoi Shelton in a 1969 production of Dorothy Ahmad's play *Papa's Daughter*.

Photograph courtesy Portia Hunt.

Persona Players, Shelton remembers, "We did white shows, and it was very middle-class type stuff. . . . I was tired of the type of stuff I was doing. I wanted to do something where I was making a statement." Spurred by his work with direct-action civil rights groups, and his firsthand experiences of corporate racism at the McDonnell Douglas Corporation, Shelton sought out a venue to address these issues through theater. Charles Shaw's connections with the musicians of BAG later led Terrell and Shelton to the group as an umbrella organization for their own embryonic company.[36]

⟶⟦◉ BAG ◉⟧⟵

Both the fledgling black theater groups and the new music being created by Lake and company needed a physical space and occasions for public performance. Many of these musicians, actors, and writers had been nurtured in long-standing institutions that fostered the arts, and to that they added a newer set of nodes, ones that hosted a small but thriving counterculture more amenable to the formation of a socially committed arts collective. At LaClede Town, the Circle Coffee Shop, and Berea Church, opportunities for artistic experimentation and a young cadre of artists dissatisfied with the city's arts scenes came together in a dynamic mixture.

LaClede Town residents from the nascent BAG included Baikida Carroll, Julius Hemphill, Oliver Lake, Floyd LeFlore and his wife Shirley LeFlore, and the painter Manuel Hughes, in what Hughes remembers as "a natural mingling of artists who happened also to live in the same place." Occupying sixty-five acres near the downtown's edge, LaClede Town was a federally funded, mixed-income housing complex that had opened in 1964. The project was built on part of the Mill Creek Valley site, formerly a 465-acre district of almost twenty thousand residents, 95 percent of them black, that had contained hundreds of viable institutions, from restaurants and beauty parlors to community centers and churches. While many residents saw the Valley as the heart of the black community, urban renewal proponents dubbed the Valley a decaying slum, and in one of the country's largest renewal projects, the city displaced its residents and demolished the district in 1959.[37]

Although LaClede Town came into being by way of the city's now-discredited urban renewal policies, in the late 1960s the four-thousand-resident project enjoyed a national reputation for its successful effort at racial integration. With a population 50 percent white, 40 black, and 10 percent other minorities, the complex was an anomaly in an extremely segregated city like St. Louis. The social mix was unusual as well: residents ranged from truck drivers, bartenders, and journalists to students, political activists, and musicians. Floyd LeFlore fondly remembers the "real cultural experience" that LaClede Town's racial, socioeconomic, and immigrant mix provided. The groceries, bars, cafés, and shops dotted among low-rise townhouses gave the complex a human scale that contrasted with the super-block housing projects typical of the time.[38]

Many St. Louisans viewed LaClede Town as the heart of the city's counterculture, and when the local congressman denounced the complex as "a hotbed of radicalism," the residents wore it as a badge of honor. With its racial and economic diversity and small-scale design, LaClede Town proved an excellent staging ground for artistic endeavor as well as for social activism. The housing project's idiosyncratic and flamboyant director, Jerry Berger, was a former jazz disc jockey in his early forties who swept around town in a chauffeured Rolls Royce. Berger believed the success of the housing community depended on resident participation in its cultural life, and he provided three months of free rent to musicians performing at LaClede Town in order to encourage a creative social environment.[39]

Most of the artists who would later comprise BAG mixed and mingled in 1966 and 1967 at LaClede Town's Circle Coffee Shop and Bookstore, a de facto community center and haven for poets, filmmakers, musicians, and actors. The nearby Berea Presbyterian Church, which administered the Circle for the LaClede Town management, put actor LeRoi Shelton in charge of booking entertainment, and the Circle's tiny stage hosted readings, dance, improvisational theater, and music from the likes of Hamiet Bluiett, Julius Hemphill, and Oliver Lake—all with a strong focus on audience participation. At the Circle, J. D. Parran first

LaClede Town, a low-rise, mixed-income housing project, opened in 1964 and quickly became home to a thriving community of artists and activists.

◆◦━◈◦⊰⊱◦◈━◦◆

St. Louis Post-Dispatch *staff photographer*/ © 1965, St. Louis Post-Dispatch.

took in the instrumental combination of a sax duo sans rhythm section, as Hemphill joined forces with then–St. Louisan David Sanborn. Though originally aimed at LaClede Town residents, the performances soon were attracting overflow audiences from the surrounding neighborhoods, nearby housing projects, and local high schools and universities. At the same time, many of the BAG actors were brought together for the first time in a 1967 Circle performance of *Viet Rock*, an Off-Broadway anti-war pageant that had debuted in New York the previous year.[40]

The Berea connection was not limited to managing the Circle Coffee Shop. In the destruction of Mill Creek Valley, Berea was the only church out of more than forty that managed to fight off demolition. Founded in the late nineteenth century as a black congregation, Berea became racially mixed with the influx of white residents to LaClede Town. A strong anchor in the LaClede Town community, the congregation was also economically mixed, as doctors and lawyers shared pews with housekeepers and factory workers. In the early 1960s the congregation had sent delegations to marches in the South led by Martin Luther King, Jr., and over time it became a meeting place for many of the city's civil rights and antiwar groups. Berea Church moved to the forefront of local social justice campaigns with the arrival in 1962 of Carl Dudley, its first white pastor. Dudley's ceaseless work on housing and welfare rights and the antiwar movement earned him national recognition and plaudits from the local black press.[41]

With so many young black artists living in the nearby LaClede Town, Berea Church became a center for artistic activity in the years preceding BAG's official formation. Artists such as Shirley LeFlore and LeRoi Shelton were active members at Berea, and especially involved in the civil rights activity that came out of the church. Berea, as Shirley LeFlore remembers, "was always open to the arts. We could go there for our civil rights meetings…, and we could have concerts down there." Oliver Lake and Julius Hemphill, though not members, sometimes participated in the performances that frequently formed a part of Berea's worship services. Like many of St. Louis's black congregations, Berea sponsored performances of plays such as James Baldwin's *The Blues for*

Mister Charlie. Several future BAG actors met as part of the church's theater troupe, the Berea Players, even though Dudley recalls that bomb threats occasionally disrupted performances.[42]

The inauguration of the city's Wall of Respect mural (*Up You Mighty Race*) in summer 1968 gave the artistic and political energies coursing through the central city a spatial focus, as well. While modest in scale, the mural became for a short while a central node in the community of black activists, drawing together artists, performers, and political figures in a series of concerts and rallies "to bring on black awareness and black consciousness of black history," as the leader of the Zulu 1200s announced. A number of BAG-related groups participated in the frequent performances at the Wall.[43]

The installation was sparked by the creation of a similar wall in Chicago the previous year. In June 1967, artists from Chicago's Organization for Black American Culture began painting a semi-abandoned building in a South Side neighborhood slated for urban renewal demolition. Collaborating with the surrounding community, artists used portraits of African Americans from politics, sports, and the arts to outline the theme of "Black Heroes," a declaration of black people's right to define their own culture and history. A festival atmosphere quickly prevailed as throngs gathered for jazz concerts, speeches, and poetry readings. With their imaginative addition to the cityscape, artists and residents laid claim to their own neighborhood, temporarily thwarting the city administration's urban renewal schemes for the area. The project touched off a national mural movement, one that came to include over a thousand urban murals by 1975, most of them executed by African American, Asian American, and Chicano artists.[44]

Inspired by the Chicago model, on a blistering Sunday afternoon in June 1968 the local visual artist Leroy White directed activists from the St. Louis civil rights groups CORE, ACTION, and the Zulu 1200s as they began painting the east wall of a ramshackle brick apartment building in the city's central corridor. Curious pedestrians lingered to watch the painters, as speakers from the three organizations exhorted a growing audience. Like similar murals elsewhere, St. Louis's Wall memorialized a pantheon of "black heroes," from recently fallen icons Malcolm X and Martin Luther King, Jr., to contemporary leaders such as H. Rap Brown and the local son Dick Gregory; and from historical figures such as Frederick Douglass and Marcus Garvey to cultural luminaries such as James Baldwin and Amiri Baraka. As the hot summer progressed, artists added portraits to the mural amidst a series of weekly rallies, which included poetry, street theater, jazz concerts, and speeches about African American history and local issues.[45] The Oliver Lake Art Quartet, poets Ajulé Rutlin and Eugene Redmond, and Vincent Terrell's TSOCC Players regularly performed at these gatherings. In a poetry reading at the mural's dedication, Redmond declared the Wall "Built so Blacks can see their (Blackness) tower," and "Towering untouchably / Over timid stares of the 'enemy.'" Though vandals later splattered white paint over the mural, and it eventually disappeared completely before the building on which it resided was razed, for a short time it focused debates about black identity in St. Louis and in the country at large.[46]

⇢⊱⊙≼∴≽⊙⊰⇠

The artistic and political impulses that percolated through LaClede Town, Berea Church, and the Wall of Respect rallies were tangible, but had not taken on formal shape. What was needed to spark the current was a performance that would bring together the theatrical and musical groups, and Malinké Elliott decided that a staging of *The Blacks*, by the French modernist playwright Jean Genet, would ignite both. Genet's 1958 work is a play-within-a-play that, as one critic puts it, "stands as the obituary of [white] mastery." Using a fractured technique emphasizing subversion and struggle, illusion and ritual, the play depicts a white court watching a group of blacks re-enact the fabricated story of a rape in a minstrel-show atmosphere. This act ostensibly reinforces the whites' racist images of the black players, but while the "show" is taking place, other black characters are engaged in revolutionary activities elsewhere.[47]

Elliott and Durgin hunted for black actors interested in taking on the production, finally recruiting from the Persona Players, the

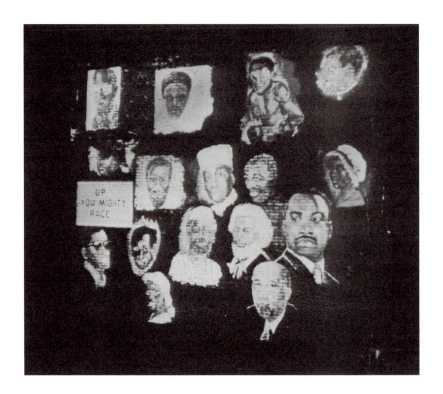

St. Louis's Wall of Respect was painted in summer 1968 on a building at the intersection of Leffingwell and Franklin Avenues. The Wall memorialized prominent African American cultural and political figures, as well as several African and Caribbean anticolonialists. For a short while, the mural site became home to weekly street theater, music, poetry, and political rallies.

—>—◦—<—

Photograph courtesy Fine Arts Department, Saint Louis Public Library.

Harlequin Players, and Vincent Terrell's TSOCC Players. To integrate dance into the performance, they borrowed dancer and choreographer Georgia Collins from Katherine Dunham's arts training center across the river in East St. Louis. During the planning period for the play, Oliver Lake asked Elliott to join forces with the collective that the musicians were planning. The actors and musicians decided that by integrating music into the production, *The Blacks* "would be a perfect vehicle for us all to get together, collaborate, have a common experience, and would be a great foundation to establish a group," as Elliott remembers. The Lake Art Quartet, having notched up over a year's experience, took on the task of providing the music. Lake added three musicians to his group, including Julius Hemphill, and composed a series of chamber pieces as incidental music for the dancers. In both its emphasis on social commentary and its integration of music, drama, and dance, the production presaged many of the multimedia performances BAG would undertake in the ensuing years.[48]

The production was slated for July of 1968, a month when theatergoers in St. Louis were treated to two very different types of all-black drama. In Forest Park, a touring production of *Hello Dolly* with an all-black cast was packing houses at the city's open-air Municipal Opera. At the same time, in suburban Webster Groves, a black court sat in judgment over a traitor who had given up the struggle against the tyranny of whites in *The Blacks*, a performance that marked the beginning of BAG's formal existence. While Genet's play itself revisits some stereotypical attitudes about black rage, *The Blacks* must have been a startling experience for St. Louis audiences. Just at the time that inner-city political groups such as the Black Liberators had begun to unnerve suburban St. Louisans with their radical rhetoric, revolutionary drama shook the stage in the genteel suburb of Webster Groves.[49]

With its aggressive posture toward its audience and its treatment of race and color in the context of a self-consciously modernist theatricality, Genet's play embodied the hybrid nature that would characterize the BAG enterprise. Acutely aware of national and international artistic currents, the group also tuned in to the social and aesthetic

TBAG's inaugural performance of Jean Genet's *The Blacks*, given July 31 and August 1, 1968, at Webster College in St. Louis. Vincent Terrell (right) plays Archibald.

✦⊶⊷❁⊶⊷✦

Photograph courtesy Portia Hunt.

forces at work in the local community. That the performers played to a majority white audience in the suburban enclave of Webster Groves bore out Genet's comment that his play was "intended for a white audience." But Genet had instructed, at the beginning of *The Blacks*, that if it were performed for a black audience, "then a white person must be invited every evening . . . [and] the actors will play for him." If no white person accepted, then "let white masks be distributed to the black spectators as they enter the theater. And if the blacks refuse the masks, then let a dummy be used." Either tactic reverses the usual figure/ground relationship, as the whites who observe become the figure against a ground that is black. The original intention had been to follow up the Webster Groves performance with shows on the north side and in East St. Louis, which would presumably have completed the array of spectators envisioned by Genet, whose opening injunction literalized an ironic reversal of relationships.[50]

This performance of *The Blacks*, with its fully integrated artistic media and uncompromising social stand, promised to spur the challenging organization into life and serve as a model for assimilating a range of black artists. At the rehearsals and performances, Hemphill said, the play's thirteen actors and seven musicians "brought up the idea of forming a collective to influence our own destiny." Though the musicians had originally considered becoming a chapter of Chicago's AACM, they decided instead to create their own organization—one that, unlike the AACM, would include their colleagues from dance, theater, the visual arts, and creative writing.[51]

With Julius Hemphill as chairman, Malinké Elliott as artistic and executive director, and Oliver Lake as treasurer, the group quickly incorporated with the State of Missouri as a not-for-profit organization and settled on the name "The Black Artists' Group, Inc.," with its hip and catchy "BAG" acronym. The following month, the artists consolidated their group by mounting a Sunday afternoon presentation of music, dance, and poetry entitled "The Third World" at the City Art Museum in Forest Park. The first occasion on which the BAG musicians performed as a large ensemble, the concert included many of the major musicians to be associated with the collective—Hamiet Bluiett, Oliver Lake, J. D. Parran, Floyd LeFlore, Charles "Bobo" Shaw, and Jerome "Scrooge" Harris. Players strolled about the stage, drawing bells, police whistles, car horns, and small percussion instruments from a table of sound devices, and spiking traditional horn-driven jazz with a heady dose of free sounds. Ajulé Rutlin added his poetry to the musicians' forays in his extended work "Ballad of the Lonely Blacks," during which Rutlin, in a chant-like mode, outlined his version of the black legacy from slavery to the present.[52]

In the response to this first BAG concert, the musicians got an early taste of how audiences would react to their musical styles, receiving a mixed reaction that would be repeated over and over again through the years of the group's existence. The performance began with an overflow crowd, about two-thirds white. As the music proceeded, a large contingent of the audience walked out, shaking their heads in disgust or incomprehension. But their seats were eagerly filled by the crowds of listeners who had packed into the lobby outside, and who rose in a standing ovation at the concert's end. BAG was now a reality.[53]

→⊢═◎ BAG ◎═⊣←

Born of artistic frustrations and aspirations, the fledgling group had taken flight, and the founders quickly moved to craft an agenda that would fit their own needs as artists as well as the needs of the community at large. The Black Artists' Group had emerged from a long tradition of black artistic life in St. Louis, and though this tradition would form a ground base, the events of the moment proved at least as important, as the city contended with the racial struggles emerging into full view across the nation. Even as its insurgent members posed new and experimental aesthetic challenges, BAG's artists were faced with a daunting set of social and economic challenges. St. Louis replicated the problems of every other large American city, but its unique situation on the hinge of North and South—fixed geographically and musically midway between Chicago and New Orleans—set distinctive possibilities and limits for the newborn organization. Amidst the political maelstrom of the late 1960s, the artists would fashion a program capable of responding to local and national conditions, and they would navigate the corridors of institutional power in order to further this agenda. The collective's aesthetic growth moved to these urban rhythms, spurring its members to create an art that at once acknowledged and challenged, incorporated and transcended local conditions.

CHAPTER 2

Double Vision: Black Arts and urban reform

I f the musical heritage of St. Louis provided essential nour-
ishment to the members of BAG, then the rough hand of
inner-city St. Louis disciplined them into more direct action.
The Black Artists' Group came into being at a time when the fault lines
of black and white society in America gave off tremors that shook the
country's political and social stability. Nowhere was this measured more
seismically than in its cities, where the long-smoldering postindustrial
transformation of urban America flared into national consciousness via
televised images of National Guardsmen reconnoitering the aftermath
of urban rebellions.

In this environment, even nominal allies in the civil rights
struggles contested the role of culture in relation to race and the urban
crisis. Two dominant views of urban culture and the arts had emerged
by the mid-1960s, with a number of way stations in between. On the
one side were leaders and theorists of the Black Arts Movement, who
championed ideas of cultural autonomy and liberation, and urged
African American artists to focus their work on their own communities—which in the North resided overwhelmingly in the inner cities.
On the other side were liberal reformers in government and philanthropic circles, who saw the arts as a tool to promote black social and
political assimilation in the wider culture and, in doing so, inoculate
the nation's cities against civil unrest.

Although the Black Arts Movement's agenda was distinct from
and even in conflict with this liberal Great Society agenda, these two
"arts movements"—both ostensibly grassroots, but the latter planned
from afar—were in many senses symbiotic. The proliferation of community arts organizations in the mid- and late 1960s converged with
money available through the federal government's War on Poverty, city
agencies, or private foundations and corporations. Paradoxically,

funders' reactions to the ideological directions of these groups often ranged from ambivalence to outright hostility. Thus, the patronage they doled out through the byzantine channels of public and private agencies, as BAG would later discover, was often fragile.

BAG came of age as an organization in an environment deeply colored by this dichotomy, which formed just one small part of a larger debate between liberal integrationism and black nationalism, between War on Poverty approaches and radical grassroots organizing, between reform and revolution. To be sure, such approaches often overlapped, as local activists and even revolutionaries watered their organizations with government grants, while that same money potentially subjected them to outside controls. BAG's agility in straddling this uneasy yoking of disparate responses to the urban environment of the 1960s enabled it to develop quickly from a loose amalgam of artists working together on an occasional basis into an organization with a specific purpose, structure, and program.

⤞⊜⊙BAG⊙⊜⤝

The Black Artists' Group originated in a St. Louis which, like most American industrial cities, had been overtaken by new social and economic realities. In the decades following World War II, the city found itself transformed from a sixty-one-square-mile, mostly blue-collar concentration of German Lutherans and Catholics, whites from the Middle South, and black migrants from the Mississippi Delta, into a fragmented hodgepodge of suburbs flung along the lines of superhighways. The population of the central city dropped precipitously, from its high-water mark of 852,000 in 1950 to 622,000 in 1970—losses among the worst in the country. Town fathers could flaunt the city's newly constructed Arch and downtown baseball stadium or its small fleet of middle-income housing developments as signs of renewed vitality. But such projects fell short of early hopes, belying whatever optimism more enthusiastic boosters could muster. "We just can't make it anymore," Mayor Alfonso Cervantes lamented to *U.S. News & World Report* in 1968, pointing to his city's tumbling tax base and the spiraling costs of social services. Like their counterparts throughout the Midwest, civic leaders had to battle the uneasy sense that their city's decline was disastrous and inexorable.[1]

While highway construction, a host of federal housing policies, and other hidden subsidies lubricated white middle-class flight to the suburbs, by the mid-1960s, black migrations from the South to the urban North had produced vast "second ghettos," isolated physically and economically from the city as a whole. St. Louis's north side, the western and southern sections of East St. Louis, and southeastern Alton, Illinois, held most of the metropolitan area's 350,000 African Americans. These areas were saddled with a host of ills—subpar public services, housing, and education, redlining and segregation in real estate and employment, an increasing exodus of the black middle classes, and rising crime rates. Poorly planned urban renewal projects demolished low-income neighborhoods and drove their residents into the overcrowded north side or into the massive postwar housing projects—Pruitt-Igoe, Cochran Gardens, Darst-Webbe, Vaughn—that became tools of policymakers to quarantine the ghetto. In the late 1960s, the St. Louis metropolitan area had the nation's worst case of black unemployment; an average income for black households of only 56 percent that for all households; and 42 percent of the central city's children living in poverty. Inner-city residents grew ever more frustrated by the mounting poverty in the core city and the government's inability or unwillingness to tender an effectual solution. A race and class polarization—pitting the black north side against the mostly white south side, and the city against suburban St. Louis County—became even more firmly entrenched in the region's mental geography.[2]

In the face of what many commentators saw as inevitable and accelerating decline, BAG's leaders envisioned a definite and vital role for the arts in urban St. Louis. To body forth that dream, they reached for the ideas of cultural authenticity and autonomy emerging from the Black Arts Movement. Though rooted in a postwar cultural movement spanning the African diaspora that historian Robin D. G. Kelley dubs Black Bohemia, the movement had begun to take formal shape in early 1960s collectives such as New York's Umbra Workshop, the Harlem

Writers' Guild, and Philadelphia's Muntu Group. These embryonic writers' circles became sites for discussion of philosophical and aesthetic theory, and particularly for explorations of the links among black culture, politics, and the arts. They opened up an intellectual space for writers and theorists such as Larry Neal, Charles Fuller, Ishmael Reed, and Askia Touré to develop new ideas about the proper relationship of the arts to black communities and liberation struggles, as the burgeoning black nationalism of the 1960s reverberated through the arts world. St. Louis registered the vibration as well: Malinké Elliott notes that BAG was "deeply aligned with the Black Arts Movement," focusing on black arts as a means to "the spiritual and cultural liberation of black people from the position we found ourselves in here in the United States, the oppression we were facing."[3]

Nationally, the movement's leaders aimed to create an aesthetic that stressed the unique characteristics of black American culture, that promoted black values, and that encouraged black consciousness, pride, and unity in the face of assaults from white society. Arguing that ethics and aesthetics were artificially separated in Western culture, Black Arts theorists claimed that a legitimate black art should reunite moral and aesthetic sensibilities in order to promote black people's struggles against oppression. Black cultural nationalists turned their backs on assimilation with white society, urging artists to create an autonomous and empowering way of life through what theorist Maluana Ron Karenga called a "functional, collective and committing" art, one that emphasized African and black American modes of expression. Undergirding the Black Arts Movement was the egalitarian notion that ordinary, working-class African Americans—and not just a cultural elite—were capable of producing and appreciating the arts. And the essence of the movement's program was performative. Theater, music, and spoken word would display and transform black culture, becoming a means by which to reclaim a black history that had been distorted or diluted by Western culture, one that could help black people redefine their identities in the present.[4]

In a move often seen as the symbolic inauguration of the Black

Arts Movement, poet and playwright Amiri Baraka (then LeRoi Jones) had left New York's Lower East Side for Harlem following the 1965 assassination of Malcolm X, there setting up his seminal Black Arts Repertory Theatre and School. Baraka wanted to create an institution that would bring radical music, poetry, and drama to the street corners of Harlem. Though his venture was short-lived, dissolving through internal disputes and inadequate funding, the example set in Harlem percolated through the nation's cities, with flagships such as Black House in Oakland and Baraka's own Spirit House in Newark, New Jersey. By the early 1970s, more than 150 Black Arts organizations had sprung into existence across the country, sharing the goal of putting artistic work in service of cultural liberation. And from London's Caribbean Artists Movement to Toronto's Black Theatre Canada, organizations throughout what Paul Gilroy calls the "black Atlantic" marched to a similar rhythm.[5]

Movement leaders, however, sometimes underestimated the amount of Black Arts activity in the country's interior. "Our 'nationalism' only extends to Harlem, Philly, or Detroit," the poet Askia Touré complained, declaring that leading cultural nationalists clustered in those cities to be "black" and "hip" rather than spreading the new consciousness through the nation. Nevertheless, scores of groups had flickered into life across the Midwest, South, and Pacific coast. Home to important black publishing outlets, Chicago and Detroit were in the vanguard. Over the course of the decade, those cities developed vibrant institutions such as the Organization of Black American Culture, Kuumba Workshop, and Afro-Arts Theater in Chicago; and Broadside Press, Concept East Theater, and Boone House in Detroit. Following in their wake, other midwestern cities were soon afloat with Black Arts Movement activity. Artists emerged from organizations like Cleveland's Afro-Set Black Arts Project and East St. Louis's Black River Writers, and major writers associated with the movement taught at midwestern educational institutions such as Oberlin College and Ohio University.[6]

→≫◉◎◉◎◉≪←

By the late 1960s, St. Louis and East St. Louis were also home to a growing number of groups that fostered both black nationalist political activity and the Black Arts aesthetic. In the political world, a cascading series of organizations moved steadily to the left, as young activists dismissively turned their backs on the insular worlds of local ward politics. Disenchanted by sluggish progress in employment, housing, and municipal politics, direct action groups jostled the traditional black leadership rooted in the church, the NAACP, and the Urban League, and leaders such as poet Eugene Redmond lobbed verbal fusillades at the older, integrationist civil rights groups in the local press. While militant activists plunged into campaigns ranging from housing reform to economic development to police brutality, young black artists were busy crafting institutions that promoted a strong and assertive black aesthetic in the face of cultural and economic pressures. Though they lacked extensive contacts on the coasts, Black Arts Movement devotees in St. Louis developed networks of mutual support and cooperation with writers, musicians, and publishers scattered through the cities of the midwestern manufacturing belt.[7]

The Black Power and Black Arts Movements materialized in the region most visibly, at first, in East St. Louis, Illinois. And if St. Louis mirrored the ills attendant on a postindustrial and racially troubled society, its sister city across the Mississippi River seemed to magnify every urban problem of the late twentieth century. By the late 1960s, the formerly flourishing railway hub had lost most of its large employers and a sizable percentage of its population. East St. Louisans looked across the Mississippi to see the glistening $37 million Gateway Arch and adjacent development, while their own riverfront became home to a tangled web of expressways that displaced hundreds of families. The black community of East St. Louis, 44 percent of which lived below the federal poverty line, was devastated by deindustrialization, endemic unemployment, and the almost complete exclusion of blacks from municipal government in the face of an entrenched white political machine. Local newspapers exposed blatant political corruption, triggering both a federal investigation of organized crime's influence in local elections and an increasingly militant reaction from young black citizens. Activists responded both to the national currents of the Black Power Movement and to the local conditions created by the gutting of resources in their own communities.[8]

East St. Louis's black nationalists challenged the white political machine for a voice in running schools, local government, and War on Poverty agencies and attempted to wrest control of the city's neighborhoods from absentee investors and landlords. At the same time, angry white leaders increasingly relied on repression by the police to keep radicals at bay. The city's main black nationalist groups—the Warlords, the Black Egyptians, and Black Culture, Inc.—melded a philosophy of armed self-defense with community development and cultural programs. The Warlords had begun as a teen gang, but in 1968 their new leader, Charles "Sweed" Jeffries, introduced a different orientation centered on community progress and eventually established the Olatunji Center, a short-lived academy for high-school dropouts. The Black Egyptians, formed in the aftermath of the Martin Luther King, Jr., assassination, initially stressed their paramilitary orientation. But realizing, as one leader said, that local African Americans "didn't view us as their protector," the group added job training and community business efforts to its agenda. Meanwhile, Black Culture, Inc. mapped the dissemination of black artistic and intellectual development as the avenue toward political solidarity and revolution. These East St. Louis activists stoked the paranoia of police agencies, including the FBI, which sternly rebuked local agents for not properly infiltrating the groups.[9]

These impulses toward cultural and economic autonomy rippled through East St. Louis's arts world, as well. Many of the local writers and artists in the thick of inner-city life were closely linked with political organizations nourished by Black Power principles. The primary leader was the poet and activist Eugene Redmond, who crafted a series of writing workshops that promoted the Black Arts aesthetic. Born in 1937, Redmond had grown up in East St. Louis's Rush City and South End neighborhoods and attended Lincoln High School—an artistic seedbed from which Miles Davis, actress and director Barbara Ann Teer, and jazz singer Leon Thomas had emerged. Redmond began publishing his verse in literary magazines in the mid-1960s, developing a poetry whose images and energy were fueled by a passionate attention to African American identity in community and nation. His early works skirmished with contemporary events, ranging from the FBI and H. Rap Brown to the "hollow hungry eyes" of his own city, and were quickened by musical subjects, invoking a pantheon of jazz masters as "Sturdy invisibly hooded holymen." In association with such poets as Sherman Fowler and Henry Dumas, Redmond organized several important writing workshops, including the Rap-Write Now Creative Workshop and an overlapping group, the Black River Writers, a performance and publishing collective that issued poetry chapbooks, fiction collections, and spoken-word recordings by area writers.[10]

Redmond's early career illustrates the manner in which adherents of Black Arts Movement principles could draft in liberal reformist agencies to support their own agendas, a tactic that BAG would use in the years following. For his arts projects Redmond often drew on existing political structures for financial support, mixing an alphabet soup of agencies as stock for the Black River Writers collective—the Experiment in Higher Education (EHE), IMPACT House, and the Grace Hill Settlement House, where he directed a Head Start program. The EHE was a government-funded education project in East St. Louis that provided the first two years of college to high school dropouts, while IMPACT House was nominally the headquarters for a job training and recreation program. At the EHE, Redmond taught alongside artists and academics such as Dumas, sociologist Joyce Ladner, and painter and BAG member Oliver Jackson. The academy quickly became an "intellectual repository," as Redmond says, for the "systematic study of revolution and movements in the world." Students and teachers immersed themselves in black history, radical philosophy, and theoretical texts on social change, and much of the area's radical leadership emerged from the EHE. They brought their knowledge and texts to IMPACT House, a youth hangout and cultural center that stirred the EHE's cadre of nationalist intellectuals with disaffected local youths into a heady brew of radical politics. Musicians used the center for a series of Sunday concerts and "Summer Black Festivals" featuring political oratory, blues and jazz, African percussion, and art exhibits, a program that culminated with the formation of Black Culture, Inc.[11]

⋅⊶⊕※⊙⊶⋅

Eugene Redmond forged his arts projects, he remembers, in a set of overlapping spaces and institutions that formed "a volatile vortex of culture and activism." And as the 1960s wore on, this vortex pulled in participants on the Missouri side of the Mississippi River. There, a number of nationalist groups, ranging from artistic to cultural to paramilitary, formed as well. In St. Louis, the Zulu 1200s and the Black Liberators surfaced in mid-1968, followed by over half a dozen others in 1969 and 1970. The Zulu 1200s emerged from the Mid-City Community Congress, an umbrella organization consisting of block groups, churches, and small businesses in the heart of the city. With leftist activist Ocie Pastard at the helm, the congress became headquarters for much of the area's civil rights organizing, and the base for the Zulu 1200s. More concerned with fostering black culture than political revolution, the Zulu 1200s sponsored educational programs and campaigned for affordable inner-city housing. Nevertheless, after City Hall rejected their bid to use a vacant firehouse as a cultural center, many of the Zulu 1200s soured on working through traditional channels and became more radically politicized.[12]

Meanwhile, the Black Liberators sprang into existence under the leadership of twenty-three-year-old activist Charles Koen. Koen had cut his teeth in the civil rights movement at an early age, spending his seventeenth birthday in jail after demonstrating for integrated facilities in his native Cairo, Illinois, and joining the Student Non-Violent Coordinating Committee (SNCC) while studying ministry in college. Soon, he was shuttling among various civil rights organizations dotted through the small towns of southern Illinois. Koen spent a good deal of time in East St. Louis, but with all the leadership slots filled in that city's radical organizations, he turned his energies to St. Louis in mid-1968.

Koen adopted a colonial analysis of black urban poverty, arguing that "the ghetto is a black nation. We're all colonized people." Though briefly a member of the Zulu 1200s, Koen felt that their cultural program neglected revolutionary imperatives, and left the group to form the Black Liberators in July 1968.[13]

Operating out of an Easton Avenue office in the city's heart, the Liberators adopted a set of tenets based on those of the Black Panther Party of Oakland, California, the nation's most high-profile revolutionary nationalist group. Soon, they attracted several hundred members, mostly working-class African Americans in their late teens and early twenties. The Liberators first demanded that white policemen be withdrawn from the area, and planned to establish a "black patrol" to protect the community from police brutality. They campaigned for political candidates, printed a short-lived newspaper, provided draft counseling for African Americans seeking to avoid conscription, and put on a symposium series featuring national figures such as Stokely Carmichael, Julius Lester, and James Foreman. Eventually, Koen was named SNCC's Midwest deputy chairman and tried, with mixed success, to form alliances with East St. Louis's Warlords and Black Egyptians.[14]

Combined pressure from local police and the FBI, however, quickly dampened the Liberators' fire. They were drawn into a series of exchanges with the authorities that included spurious arrests for "unlawful assembly," the destruction of their office and firebombing of their car, and the severe beating of Koen and his deputy, Leon Dent, in the basement of a local police station—actions that the *Sentinel*, a black weekly, blasted for pushing the city "to the brink of civil disaster."[15] Meanwhile the internal dissent that wracked the Liberators and similar organizations was heightened by the FBI's covert counterintelligence program (dubbed COINTELPRO), designed to "expose, disrupt, misdirect, discredit, or otherwise neutralize" suspected communists, New Left activists, civil rights leaders, and black nationalists. In St. Louis, the FBI fostered divisions with an anonymous flyer praising the Zulu 1200s as "black, strong and proud" and denigrating the Liberators as run by "white honkie ministers." Agents also sent anonymous letters alleging that members of the Liberators were government informers, and one to Koen's wife accusing him of infidelity.[16]

Though the Liberators soon disappeared from the headlines, other St. Louis organizations sprang up for similar purposes, including the Black Defenders, the Black Patriot Party, and the Black Nationalists. Many of these groups paired a paramilitary orientation and revolutionary rhetoric with community development efforts—running free children's breakfast programs, promoting black-owned businesses, crafting plans for low-income housing, and operating recreation and education centers.[17] Nevertheless, a drumbeat of negative coverage from St. Louis's two daily newspapers—the right-wing, red-baiting *Globe-Democrat* and the centrist *Post-Dispatch*—convinced many readers that their only purpose was to battle the police. And, with the refrain that predictably followed any demonstration or uprising of the 1960s, St. Louis media and politicians regularly blamed local militancy on "outside agitators," as if conditions were so good that only rabble-rousing visitors could stir the city's African Americans to protest.[18]

Much of this activity was occurring in tandem with broader civil rights initiatives in St. Louis, which followed a similar pattern of radicalization. St. Louis had one of the country's earliest and most important chapters of the Congress of Racial Equality (CORE), which embraced nonviolent resistance and direct action, in contrast to the NAACP's legal gradualism or the Urban League's moral suasion. In the decade following its 1947 birth, the group used sit-ins and pickets to force the integration of public accommodations. By the late 1950s, CORE had shifted its attention to employment issues, allying with the NAACP's youth wing to press local businesses on hiring discrimination. Tactics such as these triggered harsh condemnations in the city's two major newspapers, the *Globe-Democrat*, for example, asserting in a front-page spread that CORE's leadership was heavily infiltrated by communists.[19]

The local civil rights landscape turned like a hinge in the fall of 1963 with CORE's action against discrimination in white-collar banking jobs at the Jefferson Bank and Trust Company, which created a political fallout that galvanized the city's civil rights community through the rest of the decade. CORE had targeted Jefferson Bank for its dismal record and broken promises in hiring African Americans, but when picketers moved into the bank and blocked its doors, they were arrested for violating a court injunction against obstructive demonstrations. Supporters were stunned by midnight arrests of demonstrators, exorbitant bails, abnormally lengthy prison sentences, and the vilification of the protestors by the city's white politicians and media. The Jefferson Bank incident all but wrecked many activists' hopes of change by working "through the system," as activists saw the interlocking nature of the city's white-dominated judiciary, media, corporate, and political spheres. The harsh sentences stemming from the conflict led older CORE members to shy away from confrontational tactics, while younger leaders denounced their alleged middle-class timidity. Feeling that CORE "had battle fatigue," the group's employment committee chairman, Percy Green, led a dissident faction that formed the Action Committee to Increase Opportunities for Negroes (ACTION) in 1965.[20]

Green's focus was squarely on economic issues, rather than the battles over public access that had prompted CORE's early challenges. CORE's mantle as the boldest and most intrepid local civil rights group quickly passed to ACTION. The group electrified the city with its "theater of confrontation" techniques, intended to highlight issues through outrageous and creative protest tactics. Campaigning against corporate discrimination in hiring and promotion, members sprayed insecticide into the Southwestern Bell building lobby, showered paint on Union Electric's headquarters, and chained the doors to the Laclede Gas Company. ACTION also did battle with the city's Veiled Prophet Ball, a segregated debutante event, by deploying pickets and a satiric annual counterfestival known as the Black Veiled Prophet Afro Festival. Viewing white members as beneficial and black leadership as therapeutic for whites, ACTION sidestepped the battles over black separatism that consumed national organizations such as CORE and SNCC.[21]

Meanwhile, by the late 1960s, CORE chapters nationwide had become more militant and less committed to the doctrine of integration. At its 1968 national convention held in St. Louis, CORE changed its constitution to exclude whites altogether, though the St. Louis chapter remained ambivalent about this new nationalist stance, endorsing calls for "Black Power" while maintaining language calling for integration. At the end of the decade, a newly invigorated CORE was undertaking a number of initiatives, including a large-scale boycott of Anheuser-Busch for the brewer's alleged discrimination in hiring.[22]

Just as in East St. Louis, artists on the river's Missouri side were moved by these shifting social currents. The Black Artists' Group situated itself in this increasingly radicalized landscape, even if BAG ultimately chose a response rooted in cultural autonomy and artistic development rather than direct political confrontation. For one thing, many of these artists had participated in the evolving political scene, some through mainline integrationist civil rights groups and others in more radical offshoots. Baikida Carroll, for example, took part in black student union protests at Southern Illinois University's Edwardsville campus, while Shirley LeFlore worked on civil rights and housing issues and helped to assemble a local contingent for the 1968 Poor People's Campaign in Washington, D.C. And Ajulé Rutlin, as a longtime member and former chairman of the local CORE chapter, brought a history of social activism with him to BAG. LeRoi Shelton was a member of ACTION, charged with recruiting sympathetic suburban housewives to the group's direct-action protests as observers, to monitor the behavior of the police. Meanwhile, Jerome "Scrooge" Harris and Vincent Terrell were active participants in the Zulu 1200s, while Bill Archibald, an actor in Terrell's TSOCC Players, was the Zulu 1200s' head commander. Referring to groups like the Black Liberators, Rutlin says, "We were all suffering under the same oppression, so it was natural for us to feel a commonality."[23]

But regardless of whether or not artists participated directly, this new social and intellectual turbulence contributed to a volatile and creative milieu for the arts. To some, the city seemed poised in a state of uneasy tension between conservative forces and a radical set of challengers, and, says Malinké Elliott, "that was the air we breathed every day." For many of the artists, this ideological and political turmoil acted as a kind of brownfield for the imagination, radiating fresh challenges and possibilities in radically unstable combinations. The Black Power Movement, Oliver Lake later remarked, had created an "energy towards having groups in the community" in St. Louis, one adopted by performers as well. New impulses on the social front encouraged local African American artists to band together, to assert direct control over their own creative activities.[24]

⊷⟌◉ BAG ◉⟍⊶

Whatever their connections with political organizing, young black artists in the metropolitan area gained a center of gravity with the opening of East St. Louis's Performing Arts Training Center (PATC) in 1967. One of the most important centers for black arts in the Midwest, the PATC was the source from which BAG eventually drew many of its dance and theater artists. The institution was founded by the world-renowned dancer, choreographer, and anthropologist Katherine Dunham, who brought to East St. Louis decades of experience studying art's social functions. As a social anthropology student at the University of Chicago in the 1930s, Dunham had focused her fieldwork on black dance traditions of the Caribbean. She later codified her research into a dance system known as the Dunham Technique by reassembling elements of Haitian dance into movements that could be integrated with Western dance idioms. By the late 1950s, Dunham had established an international reputation, built on her own Broadway and Hollywood performances as well as educational experiments such as the Katherine Dunham School of Cultural Arts in New York City—an attempt, she explained, "to take *our* dance out of the burlesque [and] to make it a more dignified art." Though her technique and her education projects, Dunham tried to counter racialist notions about the "innate" performing talents of blacks.[25]

Dunham also infused her productions with advocacy for social justice, ranging from her choreographic work on the New York Labor Stage's *Pins and Needles* in 1939 to her ballet *Southland*, a 1951 production that depicted a lynching for international audiences despite interference from the U.S. State Department. She spent the 1950s and early 1960s touring and working as a choreographer for opera, theater, and film in over fifty countries, and served as a cultural adviser to Senegalese president Léopold Senghor. At the First World Festival of Negro Arts, held in Dakar, Senegal, in 1966, Dunham declared that "dance is not a technique but a social act," one that emerges from "man's social living." Over the ensuing decades, she would attempt to make this connection between dance and "man's social living" with her move to East St. Louis, where she employed her developing ideas about the role that the arts should play in America's most economically devastated black communities.[26]

Dunham opened her cultural arts center in East St. Louis under the auspices of Southern Illinois University and soon allied with Eugene Redmond and his cadre of writers and activists. The soft-spoken dancer arrived at a time of civil unrest and found the city to be "a reservation at the end of the world." Dunham later explained, "[L]ike so many people my age, I thought the civil rights movement was going to change everything . . . , and to return to find that the situation was worse than it had ever been, that the violence was so heightened, was shocking." Despite a smattering of underfunded neighborhood centers established through the War on Poverty, there were few formal artistic opportunities in East St. Louis, a city without a theater or even a single cinema. Dunham and her husband rented a small house amidst derelict buildings and vacant lots and opened it as a meeting place to those interested in the arts. Determined to cultivate an artistic garden in the city, she invested an immense amount of energy in launching the PATC, which initially taught Dunham Technique dance to the city's working-class youths.[27]

Making use of her connections with the international arts world, Dunham recruited former members of her touring dance company as teachers. Operating on a shoestring budget, Dunham initially hired seven staff members, who taught dance to a class of local teacher-trainees. As with her New York schools during the 1940s, students at the PATC did not simply study dance. Rather, they took an array of courses in the social sciences, philosophy, history, and humanities, while Julius Hemphill of BAG headed up a small music program. The PATC also developed a semiprofessional dance company composed of staff and students, ran community service programs, and operated the Dynamic Museum, a collection of artifacts from Dunham's three decades of world travels. Dissatisfied with the strictures of the American education system, Dunham held up the PATC's "new horizons of thinking" as a counterweight to the "ivory towers of the apartheid colleges and universities."[28]

Moved by her developing pan-Africanist commitments, Dunham tried to establish some sort of exchange among her three homes of Senegal, Haiti, and East St. Louis. And at the PATC, she drew on her vast experience studying black religious ceremonies in the Caribbean and West Africa, envisioning ritual as a source of stability and social bonding while also an impetus toward political solidarity and action. Her interest in Haitian cultural lore led her to incorporate similar "folk traditions"—pillars of leadership, local heroes, and ritual events—into performances that dramatized neighborhood characters and experiences. For example, when the local CORE activist Taylor Jones was killed in a car accident in 1967, his death left a tremendous void in the community. Honoring Jones's request for celebrations rather than mourning upon his death, Dunham recalled, "[O]n the day of his death about a thousand young people did sing and dance in the streets on their way to City Hall carrying torches and, of course, this terrified the Establishment. . . . I took the initiative and wrote the verse, and then we had this in song and dance." Dunham, along with Eugene Redmond, crafted the multidisciplinary tribute *Ode to Taylor Jones*. Incorporating dance, musical, and theatrical elements from several pan-African contexts, the *Ode* instantly became a local favorite, and its cast of students, activists, and professionals toured the production through the Midwest.[29]

A moderate, older leader, Dunham attempted a difficult balancing act, trying simultaneously to challenge the city establishment and mobilize the community while tamping down potential violence from the city's youthful militants. And her local involvement went far beyond the teaching of dance. "There is no such thing as being there as an artist, being there on a cultural mission without being there on a total mission," she explained. Commanding respect from disparate factions, including the paramilitaries of the Warlords and Black Egyptians, she tried to restore hope to the city and to reshape its social and cultural life. Skeptical activists warmed to Dunham when she defended a young dance student whom she felt was unjustly arrested, a move that briefly landed her in jail for disorderly conduct. Dunham also claimed responsibility for breaking up a drug district known as "The Corner" by encouraging dealers to write theatrical pieces based on their own experiences. The arts activity she fostered in East St. Louis, Dunham felt, helped avert major unrest during the city's tense summers.[30]

Though Dunham insisted that African Americans were not "culturally deprived," but rather were "culturally rich and opportunity poor," she also saw the arts as a means to overcome alienation, promote social participation, and avert violence.[31] But even as liberal leaders sought to bolster Dunham's programs, seeing her as a bulwark against civil disorder, the FBI exploited endemic tensions between the fifty-seven-year-old dancer and the brash young revolutionaries of East St. Louis. In the spring of 1969, the Bureau's local office distributed a bogus underground newspaper purportedly produced by radical black students. The FBI-authored publication ridiculed several black leaders, Dunham among them, in an attempt to divide and discredit activists. One article derided her for "40 years of trying to make it the honkie way," and claimed that her interest in the local community was disingenuous and self-serving.[32]

In the end, this type of covert meddling proved to be more an annoyance than a roadblock. But for all Dunham's success, her vision was sometimes rejected by younger, more radical activists. And navigating the choppy waters of local politics proved tricky as Dunham tried to head off what she saw as "an impending crisis." On the one hand, Dunham worried about the influence of visiting militants from Detroit and Chicago (particularly the Blackstone Rangers), who urged young East St. Louisans to launch a muscular offensive against the city establishment. On the other hand, she was appalled by the city police department's intensified campaign against local black nationalists. Privately, she feared that municipal leaders were eager for the city to erupt into riots, as a cynical excuse to crack down on dissidents and replace black riverfront neighborhoods with pricey high-rise apartments.[33]

⋅⇥⊜BAG⊜⇤⋅

Although they sometimes disagreed, people like Katherine Dunham, Eugene Redmond, and BAG's leaders were deeply engaged in thinking about the sociological functions of the arts, about the degree to which art should focus on specific political issues, and about the possibility of a definable black aesthetic. But while artists in BAG and groups like the Black River Writers drew much of their intellectual capital from the philosophies of the Black Arts Movement, government agencies and private foundations also cast the arts as a sociological tool, though in a very different sense. Alarmed by the uprisings that swept America's cities, many white liberals gravitated to the notion that arts programming might foster black political and social participation, channel frustrations, and thus mitigate the anger that led to violent urban rebellions.

The idea emerged in part from the "culture of poverty" theories constructed by social scientists in the early 1960s, which swiftly became the orthodoxy within publicly and privately funded anti-poverty projects. Though eventually adopted by conservatives, the culture-of-poverty analysis was originally championed by liberals who promoted increased social spending. These theories explained poverty by pointing to the culture and lifestyles of the poor, presenting poor people as passive, locked in a self-perpetuating world of dependency, and lacking the motivation to change their degraded condition. Viewing the poor, and especially the black poor, as culturally deprived and socially disorganized, liberal bureaucrats developed therapeutic programs that aimed to "socialize" the poor, to change their character rather than to alter the distribution of political and economic resources.[34]

The War on Poverty, seen through this lens, needed a cultural front. Through the intervention of sympathetic white elites, black culture could supposedly be used as a tool to overcome "alienation," promote black social participation, and revitalize depressed neighborhoods. Spurred by fears that urban disorders would continue and even intensify, city governments, federal agencies, and private foundations ear-marked dollars for inner-city cultural programming. Through the 1960s, as many as a thousand settlement houses and storefront community centers, funded through the Johnson administration's Great Society programs, sprang up in the nation's cities, many of them with arts components. Scores of cities launched hastily assembled arts programs that typically were curtailed at the end of each summer, known derisively as "riot insurance." Despite the often-cynical motives of government planners, participants on the ground charged energetically into the establishment of storefront arts academies, writing workshops, dance seminars, and filmmaking courses, emphasizing the teaching of cultural history and pride to African American children.[35]

These two contradictory views of the arts converged in St. Louis. While artists such as Malinké Elliott and Eugene Redmond explored and enunciated the ideas of the Black Arts Movement, liberals in the city's arts and political worlds were developing what became known as the Inner City Arts Project, a scheme to dispatch artists into the area's most devastated neighborhoods. This project would eventually provide BAG with its early funding.

The planners focused on St. Louis's Model Cities target area. The Johnson administration, hoping to pacify disgruntled big-city mayors who accused previous War on Poverty initiatives of usurping their authority, had launched the Model Cities Program in 1966. The idea was that small, sharply defined "target areas" would receive concentrated local, federal, and private resources as demonstrations of how impoverished neighborhoods could be rebuilt within five years. In St. Louis, a north-central area centered on the Yeatman district emerged from internecine struggles as the chosen target area. The seventy-thousand-resident district was over 85 percent African American, contained much of the city's public housing, and was marked by high unemployment and poor social services. Although several of the small-scale Model Cities initiatives proved beneficial, the program was marred by acrimonious disputes and leadership changes. Embattled almost from the start, St. Louis's Model Cities Agency made increasingly unrealistic promises to community groups in its target area in order to sustain political support while waiting and hoping for federal funds that always seemed to be less than expected.[36]

For some, though, the program mapped the right path. The chief of St. Louis's Arts & Education Council, Michael Newton, enthusiastically championed the idea of serving up arts to the Model Cities target area. From studies that he had commissioned, Newton learned with dismay that the district contained no professional artists. His consultants advised the Arts & Education Council to develop an inner-city arts program that would foster communication between white and black, rich and poor citizens, and that would stress the participation of poverty-zone residents. Based on these studies, Newton inserted into St. Louis's Model Cities application a proposal for a cultural enrichment program that would make artists-in-residence available to inner-city residents.[37] Newton then pitched his scheme to administrators at major philanthropic foundations. Norman Lloyd, a composer-turned-administrator who was director for arts at the New York based Rockefeller Foundation, expressed keen interest in Newton's plan. And closer to home, the St. Louis–based Danforth Foundation had recently started an urban affairs program, despite one trustee's qualms over the semblance of "political involvement" and the possible "displeasure of city fathers." Somewhat more reluctantly, that foundation also agreed to consider Newton's ideas.[38]

While the officials who crafted the project acted out of a sincere concern over the economic conditions of the inner city, they also leaned heavily on paternalist notions of the causes of and cures for black poverty. The project's administrators saw the root causes of poverty as psychological rather than structural and stressed the idea of the arts as a potent means to socialize and assimilate the poor. Newton believed that an attack on poverty that "overlooks its psychological manifestations" would be ineffective. And while the annual uprisings that reverberated around the nation had left St. Louis largely untouched, the possibility of civil unrest always loomed. The arts, he felt, could function as a form of therapy, thus allowing "the inner feelings of the residents of those areas [to] find an authentic voice." Similarly, the Rockefeller Foundation diagnosed the "underlying ills" of the inner city as "voicelessness, isolation, [and] depersonalization"—problems for which the arts could "offer a direct remedy." Somewhat more condescendingly, local Model Cities director Donald Bourgeois chimed in to urge the necessity of an arts program in an area with "so much potential for destructive use of time." An idle mind, it seems, was the revolutionary's workshop.[39]

Proponents of the arts as urban palliative had a model ready, one that was heavily funded by the Rockefeller Foundation. The Watts Writers Workshop, the most prominent among scores of such efforts, had been formed by the renowned screenwriter Budd Schulberg in the wake of the devastating August 1965 uprising in South Central Los Angeles. Schulberg hoped that literary training could mitigate the anger that led to urban rebellions, and he developed the workshop as a training and performance space for aspiring writers from the black neighborhoods of Watts. With Schulberg's Hollywood connections as resources, the workshop almost instantly became a national media darling, attracting television and magazine features, invitations to testify before Congress on urban reform, and visits from novelist Claude Brown and Senator Robert F. Kennedy. But the media hoopla and political applause masked underlying tensions. Irritated by white paternalism and rejecting the concept of the arts as vaccine for urban uprisings, thirteen of the younger writers split off in fall 1968 to form an independent and more radical group, the Watts 13. Still, liberal reformers, groping for a panacea for the nation's urban crisis, saw in the Watts Writers Workshop a creative solution available for export to other cities. Through an investment in arts in the inner city, the expressive energies of urban minority populations could supposedly be fostered at the same time as radical challenges to the status quo were blunted.[40]

The example set in Los Angeles energized the administrators crafting plans for a similar project in St. Louis. Newton lavishly praised Schulberg's intervention, claiming that the Watts project showed how the arts "gave a form of power to the residents" and allowed the disenfranchised black poor to communicate with the more privileged sections of society. Dunham invited workshop members to visit her center in East St. Louis, while Norman Lloyd at the Rockefeller Foundation saw Dunham's PATC and the Watts group in tandem, speculating that both areas could become "new centers of sophistication in the arts, as young Negroes flock to these centers." While critics found approaches like Schulberg's to be tinged with paternalism, such efforts differed markedly from an arts strategy that saw most federal arts grants earmarked for urban schools used for ticket purchases or onetime imported performances, with black children bused to white symphonies and museums while the African American artistic heritage was ignored.[41]

In March 1968, Newton sat down with Katherine Dunham, MECA director Arthur Custer, and Kenneth Thompson, a Rockefeller Foundation vice president, to hammer out the details for their own program. Those gathered all brought widely differing viewpoints to the conference table, as they mulled the advantages and complications of placing artists-in-residence in the inner city as resource persons for the training of "talented ghetto children." The St. Louis contingent argued that the "vacuum in the arts" in the inner cities meant that "resistance is less strong against white collaboration," though only, as Dunham suggested, if the artists took care not to appear to be members of the establishment and avoided reinforcing the stereotype of the black artist as "song and dance man." Despite Thompson's brusquely condescending concerns over whether artists would "lounge in the ghetto or do basic teaching of real quality," the group was enthusiastic about the possibilities for the program's success.[42]

In its final version, the plan for the Inner City Arts Project had two prongs. It called for a cultural enrichment center based in East St. Louis, and an artists-in-residence program (AIR Program) in St. Louis's Model Cities target area. The East St. Louis center would, for all purposes, be an expansion of Katherine Dunham's PATC. Reassured by Dunham's participation and stature, the Rockefeller and Danforth Foundations put up matching grants of $100,000 each, with the money to be evenly divided between the PATC and the St. Louis AIR Program. Local arts leaders eagerly speculated that the initiative might become a "national demonstration," while Mayor Cervantes lauded the plan's relevance to the Model Cities agenda of providing "a voice for the poor and voiceless." Their enthusiasm was shared by outside observers: the St. Louis project, opined the *Wall Street Journal*, "involves nothing less than enlisting the arts in today's efforts to preserve the city from social disintegration."[43]

⟶⟫⟦◉ BAG ◉⟧⟪⟵

While these administrators developed their inner-city arts initiative, BAG's leaders watched with keen interest. From his teaching position with the MECA arts education project, Malinké Elliott had a front-row seat for the planning of the program. Meanwhile, Julius Hemphill was acquainted with the local Model Cities Agency through his work as editor for the *Model City Voice*, a newspaper for the target neighborhoods. Although deep and fundamental differences between BAG's agenda and that of the project's funders would eventually surface, the group quickly took advantage of the available funding to support its own programs. Once the grants were approved, Elliott advised his colleagues in BAG to apply for the new artists-in-residence positions. The Arts & Education Council hired Hemphill, who was already chairman of BAG, as the director for the AIR Program, while Elliott took a seat on the project's advisory council. While the $100,000 grant was only a small fraction of what Michael Newton had originally wanted, to Hemphill and Elliott—who were then making ends meet as a substitute schoolteacher and a janitor—the amount seemed enormous.[44]

With Hemphill at the helm of both projects, BAG now had a means to expand its own activities and personnel. By September 1968, two months after BAG's inaugural performance of *The Blacks*, Elliott and Hemphill had the grant money at their disposal. They quickly looked to fill the five artist-in-residence slots for the AIR Program. They first hired their BAG colleagues Oliver Lake and Ajulé Rutlin as directors of the music and creative writing components, and Georgia Collins from the PATC to head the dance component. Collins had wide experience as a professional dancer, having trained at the American School of Ballet and the Talley Beatty School and performed professionally with Dunham and with the Alvin Ailey Dance Theater. Elliott and Hemphill then headed off for New York to recruit artists to supervise the visual arts and film departments.[45]

For the visual arts position, they had their eyes on Emilio Cruz, an African American painter of Cuban descent. The thirty-year-old artist was already developing a strong national reputation, having participated in prominent group exhibitions and winning several prestigious fellowships. Cruz at first was reluctant. But, strongly affected by the deaths of Malcolm X, Martin Luther King, Jr., and other leaders, Cruz felt called upon to join the St. Louisans as "my chosen way and my personal struggle." Eventually Hemphill persuaded Cruz to move to St. Louis with his wife, Pat, a civil rights organizer and worker with a War on Poverty project in Queens. As the resident film director, the BAG leaders chose Thurman Faulk, a producer who had worked on various feature films and at New York's Circle in the Square Theater, as well as with HARYOU ACT, a Johnson administration anti-poverty program in Harlem. Because of their overlap in personnel, the Black Artists' Group and the foundation-funded AIR Program soon became almost indistinguishable, operating for a time under the joint moniker "AIR-BAG."[46]

For many of the cultural nationalist organizations of the late 1960s, the idea of corporate or government funding chafed against founding principles. Controversies flared at Baraka's Black Arts Repertory Theatre and the New Lafayette Theatre in New York over whether, and under what conditions, to accept such support. The AACM in Chicago, meanwhile, refused to seek outside backing, feeling that grants from external institutions carried the danger of introducing controls on their aesthetic and social mission and would reinforce the paternalism they sought to eradicate. Likewise, some BAG members were dubious about the impulses behind the Inner City Arts Project, seeing it as striking an easy pose. Shortly after his arrival from New York, Emilio Cruz came to the conclusion that "all they wanted was a symbolic cleanup." Baikida Carroll explains that the consensus within BAG was that the funders "had no idea what we were doing aesthetically. Their agenda was to pay

GEORGIA COLLINS, BAG's FIRST DANCE DIRECTOR.

Photograph, 1969, courtesy Portia Hunt.

Senegalese percussionist Mor Thiam, shown here at St. Louis's Forest Park, migrated to the area in 1969 and served as an artist-in-residence for Katherine Dunham's PATC.

us to blindly represent their interpretation of the role of the arts in the inner city, which had more to do with political posturing than art." But despite such concerns about the funders' motivations, BAG's leaders felt that they could pursue their own agenda more fully with the $100,000 grant.[47]

Meanwhile, the injection of foundation dollars allowed Dunham to expand her East St. Louis operations at a rapid pace. She developed all sorts of initiatives: in one instance flying local activists to New York to discuss social issues with noted psychoanalyst and social theorist Erich Fromm, with whom Dunham had developed a close friendship in the late 1940s. The PATC hired instructors who offered courses ranging from dance and theater to martial arts to French, Japanese, and Yoruba conversation. In addition to talent drawn from New York and Europe, Dunham recruited master percussionists Mor Thiam of Senegal and René Calvin of Haiti; Zak Diouf, the director of the Senegalese National Dance Company; and Paul Osifo, a renowned wood sculptor from Nigeria. The PATC became an integral part of the community and developed into a crossroads for international artists, drawn particularly from West Africa and the Caribbean. With black artists from around the world congregating there, one poet described the center as a "little African village." Along with their heavy performance schedule at area schools and universities, the PATC's dance-and-drum contingent became a fixture at cultural events and rallies held by the area's black nationalist political organizations.[48]

In its original conception, the entire Inner City Arts Project was to be overseen by Dunham. But, to her chagrin, the BAG artists quickly vetoed that idea. With surprise, Norman Lloyd reported to his superiors at the Rockefeller Foundation that "[t]hese younger artists do not want to accept Katherine Dunham's role as leader." Hemphill remembers that he and Elliott "argued that we didn't need to be under her jurisdiction. . . . We wanted free rein." Rather than following Dunham's lead, the ardently independent young leaders insisted on pursuing their own artistic visions by constructing a program "from the ground up," as Hemphill put it. The Inner City Arts Project thus became two separate entities, operating independently in East St. Louis under Dunham and in St. Louis under Hemphill and his artists-in-residence. But although foundation officials later portrayed the groups at odds, there would always be fruitful commerce between BAG and the PATC. Vincent Terrell was hired as the PATC director of theater, for instance, and over the following years, many performers would migrate to BAG through the doors of the PATC.[49]

⊹⊱∞⊰⊹

The group that had coalesced almost unnoticed at the Circle Coffee Shop and the jam sessions in Forest Park thus entered 1969 with $100,000 of funding and a set of salaried full-time artists hired from St. Louis and New York. Through its incorporation of the AIR Program, BAG found itself precariously balanced between two competing visions of the role that the arts should play in the inner cities: as propagators of cultural autonomy and liberation on the one hand and of social stability and assimilation on the other. The two existed symbiotically for a brief moment, allowing BAG to draw on the ideological strengths of the Black Arts Movement and the funding resources of liberal philanthropists. Although the collective's members rejected the "cultural missionary" aspects inherent to the Inner City Arts Project, they saw the AIR Program funding as a convenient tool to support their own agenda, described by Baikida Carroll as one of "artistic cultural liberation."[50]

BAG's leadership next had to wend its way through these competing agendas while developing the organization as a viable cultural and artistic outlet. To advance its own agenda, the collective would obtain a building, open a school, and take its dynamic performances to a widening circle of locations—from the neogothic halls of Washington University to the slapdash fabric of the city's public housing projects.

Chapter 3

"Poets of Action": The arts and the local village

glance at BAG's idiosyncratic "map" of St. Louis in 1969 reveals much about the group's attempt to position itself in the Gateway City. Rather than drawing the viewer's eye to familiar landmarks—the Arch, say, or Forest Park—BAG orients itself to the city's north side public housing projects. In doing so, the group both comments on the marginalizing of this segment of the black population and signals its intention to center itself in that community. But while an engagement with the surrounding community was central to BAG's mission, members envisioned this community in a variety of ways. Aiming their program primarily at the city's black neighborhoods, they also took their performances to mostly white college campuses, interacted with white countercultural and New Left organizations, and helped to create a multiracial performance group, the Human Arts Ensemble. Through these kinds of alliances, BAG crafted a set of overlapping constituencies, ranging from black separatists to white progressives, while maintaining the group itself as a stronghold for black leadership. Rather than a rigid and confining doctrine, BAG's nationalism was a flexible, experimental concoction, meeting the need for black control over black artistic directions but able to adapt itself to local circumstances.[1]

During the final months of 1968, while Julius Hemphill and Malinké Elliott busily interviewed candidates for the Artists-in-Residence (AIR) Program, BAG's performing units took on a breakneck schedule of presentations. The Oliver Lake Art Quartet, the Julius Hemphill Trio, and Ajulé Rutlin's group, the Poetry/Music Function, popped up at area colleges and universities, appeared at LaClede Town, and gave lecture-demonstrations at public high schools, and Lake took his combo on a concert jaunt to New Haven, Connecticut. At the same time, the AIR-BAG consortium enlisted an advisory Citizens

Committee, composed of prominent members of the black middle class. Alongside this eddy of performance and organizational activity, BAG's artists crafted an increasingly coherent philosophical direction for their organization. In particular, members wanted to explore the role that the arts could play in building and mobilizing the surrounding community. Many of them felt that the poetry, pageants, and musical activities that permeated the city's black community, and especially its congregations, "had a great deal to do with keeping neighborhoods together," as BAG poet Shirley LeFlore says. They were keen to augment this function through their own work, both as artists and as community members. Elliott captured this kinetic sense of purpose in a memorable phrase, urging the artists to become "poets of action."[2]

Seeing their art as a communal creation, national leaders of the Black Arts Movement had rejected Romantic and post-Romantic notions of the individual artist working in isolation or estrangement from his social context. Instead, they stressed art's functional roles, urging that it be created in a communitarian and socially engaged stance. Strongly moved by these credos, BAG's leaders looked to turn away from white consuming audiences and to develop an art firmly planted in the soil of the black community, using black cultural resources as its nutrients. In a series of essays, Elliott elaborated on BAG's philosophical orientation, arguing that "Black arts is family" and that any artistic conception that placed black artists outside of black communities was "a western corruption of that natural unity of aesthetics and ethics."[3]

The Black Artists' Group made this abstract commitment concrete through an energetic engagement with the metropolitan area's African American community—by establishing a physical presence in the black inner city, running an arts training school, taking its teaching and performing programs to public housing projects and neighborhood centers, and, as individuals, participating in various civil rights struggles. Many members saw this agenda as radical and new: Vincent Terrell, for example, maintains that "at the time in St. Louis this was unheard of—going into neighborhoods, churches, community centers, housing projects—and we'd do anything for the people, free." Through a nexus of artistic, political, and cultural practices, they aimed to live within and embody as well as depict and comment on the community. This process began with the group's membership itself. Believing that the creation of a black-controlled artistic forum was essential to the development of a robust black-oriented aesthetic, BAG, like many of its contemporaries, was firm on its restriction to black members only. Many members felt that significant white participation carried the dangers of co-optation or dilution of the group's aesthetic program, a specter that was enhanced by the exclusion or unfair treatment that the city's African American artists so frequently received in white-controlled venues.[4]

The group's philosophical orientation was by no means monolithic. BAG actress Portia Hunt remembers "a whole range of feelings about blackness in the group. Some of our members felt strongly about a very clear black identity, and a lot of individuals were multi-culturalists." Sometimes, though, the imperative to formulate and address a black nation collided with an aim toward universality in the group's artistic vision. In what Elliott describes as "one of the big, central fights throughout BAG," members sharply debated the degree to which white allies should participate in artistic projects. This issue surfaced in running disputes over whether to close the BAG building to whites, whether to hire white instructors to train the group's actors, and whether to solicit white tech support and audiences. For a time, at least, these kinds of disagreements stoked the intellectual energy of the group rather than fueling an explosion.[5]

⇥✦◉ BAG ◉✦⇤

BAG's commitment to its community functioned on a material as well as a psychological and aesthetic level, and a physical presence in the heart of the city seemed necessary to its success. The group's first location signaled this intent, as they began operations in the Gateway Theatre, a small auditorium wedged into St. Louis's Gaslight Square, on the near west side of downtown. A decade earlier, Gaslight Square had been a magnet for painters, musicians, and poets of the Beat generation, with a lively collection of coffeehouses, galleries, and bars catering to this bohemian crowd. After a devastating tornado flattened the neighborhood in 1959, the square rebuilt, based on an influx of insurance money, into a chic entertainment district. Through the early 1960s, crowds of nighttime revelers flocked to the three dozen bars, bistros, and nightspots packed into a block-and-a-half strip on Olive Street and anchored by the swank Crystal Palace.[6]

But by the mid-1960s, Gaslight Square had transformed from its earlier incarnations as casual Beat hangout or stylish nightlife district. Flooded with suburbanites and tourists, the district lost its ethos of nonconformity and diversity. As rock-and-roll clubs and go-go joints opened, old-timers bemoaned the shift from "the grace and intimacy of old" to the "go-go noise and gawking mobs of the recent past." At the same time, the city's newspapers obsessed about crime near the square, frightening off many St. Louisans. In 1966, business was down a fourth over the previous year; in 1968, twenty-two nightclubs sat empty amidst deserted streets. But despite the seeming desolation, creative ventures in Gaslight Square didn't cease. For a brief time, plunging property values again made the district accessible to arts venues and media projects on the fringes of the mainstream, ranging from Boyle Avenue's Exit Coffee Shop to the countercultural radio outlet KDNA.[7]

BAG stepped into this eclectic company when it acquired a Gaslight Square venue as its first home. Buoyed by the infusion of grant money from the Inner City Arts Project, Katherine Dunham had opened an extension of her PATC on the Missouri side of the river in late 1968, leasing Gaslight Square's Gateway Theatre after a local drama troupe that used the space folded. The 270-seat venue was located on the second floor of the turn-of-the-century Musical Arts Building, a fabled site where legendary opera singer Helen Traubel had studied and where Tennessee Williams and William Inge had presented trial runs of their early plays. Because of difficulties in running the center from East St. Louis, the PATC extension quickly fizzled, but Dunham was still saddled with the lease for the Gateway Theatre. She offered the vacant space to Julius Hemphill for the AIR Program that he administered. He installed his office on the second floor, and BAG and the AIR Program made the theater their first home.[8]

On a March evening in 1969, BAG kicked off its weekly concert series at the Gateway Theatre. That night, the imperturbable limestone angels playing their trumpets above the entrance must have been tempted to blow counterpoint with the earthier notes cascading out the door. Musical ensembles led by Oliver Lake and Julius Hemphill joined with poetry from Ajulé Rutlin and a choreographic spectacle from Georgia Collins in a multi-part, multimedia show. And each weekend, the group's various departments would create something new for the Gateway performance series, which ended up running for more than thirty consecutive weeks, meanwhile bringing "a bit of animation back to that neighborhood," as Hemphill later observed.[9]

But while the Gateway Theatre provided a congenial home for large performances, it had no rehearsal space or room for the wider range of activities that BAG's leaders envisioned. Several of the artists-in-residence decided they wanted a building of their own to serve as an administrative center, a performance space, and a classroom building, if not inside the Model Cities target area, then at least within walking distance of it. The first open conflict between BAG and the administrators of the Inner City Arts Project came with the decision on location. The program's administrators had envisioned the AIR Program artists living in vacant apartments at the Pruitt-Igoe housing project, already a national poster child for the worst failures of postwar public housing. Emilio and Pat Cruz, who had recently arrived from New York, were aghast. They felt the plan was "indicative of a separatist and racist notion of how you would treat artists who were African American," as Pat Cruz later remarked. Likewise, Emilio Cruz saw the proposal as merely a cynical attempt to create the impression that Pruitt-Igoe was a viable, active living space, when in fact, "what they were asking for was for people to be destroyed, because the people in Pruitt-Igoe were being destroyed." The funders' dubious logic implied that here was the perfect opportunity for community involvement: the artist as "cultural missionary," bringing light to the dark places of the earth.[10]

The artists swiftly rejected the Pruitt-Igoe scheme. Emilio Cruz quickly pursued a more appropriate and useable headquarters for the

AIR Program, with hopes that BAG could share the same space. Along with Julius Hemphill, Cruz crisscrossed the city's near north side for weeks, hunting for an abandoned building that the artists could afford to rent. Eventually, they chose a two-story, 9,200-square-foot structure, rundown and unoccupied for over a decade, located in a predominantly black district just north of the city's central corridor and two blocks south of the Model Cities target area. With this move, Hemphill recalled, BAG set up its headquarters "right in the midst of the city, in these somewhat devastated neighborhoods." At 2665 Washington Boulevard, the building sat on an industrial strip in the center of thirty-five blocks of decaying commercial and residential structures, sharing the block with a blood bank and scattered light manufacturers. The district's commercial thoroughfares were lined with white-owned grocery stores, pawnshops, and liquor stores, as well as black-owned barbershops, taverns, and storefront churches that served as neighborhood gathering spots. The building was structurally viable and centrally located with respect to the population that BAG envisioned serving.[11]

After days spent scraping out pigeon droppings from the upper floor and weeks of renovations using mostly contributed materials, the artists finally opened the building as headquarters for BAG and for the AIR Program. The group's new home provided ample space for the various divisions—creative writing, music, dance, drama, and visual arts—that comprised the AIR Program, along with a long studio next door for larger theater and music projects. With the surrounding commercial activity dying down at 6 each evening, the musicians' frequent late-night rehearsals disturbed no one. Upstairs, in the spacious, skylighted loft that became his studio, Cruz lived with his wife Pat, ensconced among his many books and paintings. The building boasted a café for a short time, a small library, and a collection of artwork, and members later painted the walls red, black, and green to signal the group's pan-African commitments. In mid-March 1969, a week after inaugurating the Gateway concert series, BAG's artists invited the public into their headquarters for the first time, drawing a diverse and appreciative crowd to hear music and poetry and to view paintings and film by Emilio Cruz and

As headquarters for BAG and the AIR Program, an abandoned warehouse at 2665 Washington Boulevard in St. Louis was renovated by artists.

Photograph by Michael E. Emrick, 1969.

Thurman Faulk, the artists-in-residence from New York. In publicity flyers for the open house, the artists explained that the AIR Program reflected their "conviction that the inner city of St. Louis needs the presence of creative, professional working artists living and working in its midst just as it needs lawyers, doctors, educators, etc."[12]

The building and its location proved fundamental to BAG's mission, giving the area's residents access to the group's programming and its frequently free performances. And location was a political as well as a practical issue. As music clubs were strangled by economic decline, the numbers of arts venues of every kind in the inner city had dwindled, a situation the group tried to address. "Nobody was doing anything for the residents in that area; no one brought them anything," BAG visual artist Oliver Jackson relates, but with the collective's new location, the area's African American populace "could come and hear all this stuff going on, make their *own* decisions about it, and have a place to interact with the artists." While St. Louis institutions of all sorts scrambled to leave the city's boundaries, BAG established itself in the heart of the city.[13]

Despite the occasional debates over whether white supporters should be allowed into the building, Hemphill later emphasized that "anybody want to come in there was welcome; any color of people were welcome." A bustle of volunteers, schoolchildren, and curious visitors from the suburbs filled BAG's new home, and the artists encouraged residents from the nearby Model Cities target area to visit, hang out, and browse through the library. The group's artists were equally enthused. During the daytime, BAG members delivered mail or taught school or worked on assembly lines, but as Jerome Harris, drummer for the Lake Art Quartet, says, "they'd gladly go ahead and get it out of the way so they could get on down to the building." The lights frequently burned through the small hours of the night during marathon discussions addressing aesthetic theory, political philosophy, and black awareness. And soon, the BAG building had joined the PATC, the Experiment in Higher Education, IMPACT House, the Mid-City Community Congress, and LaClede Town as yet another node in an extended network of countercultural arts spaces. Churning steadily through the doors of all these institutions was a diverse crowd, ranging from War on Poverty workers, revolutionary activists, and radical students to philanthropic officials, alternative media mavens, and performance artists of every shape and skill.[14]

-»=◎BAG◎=«-

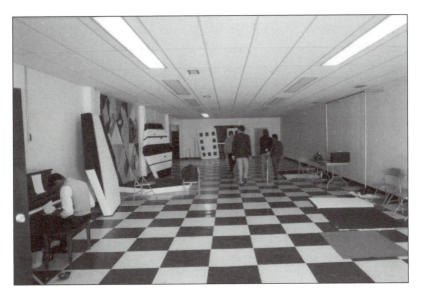

ABOVE: Upstairs interior of BAG's Washington Boulevard headquarters, with paintings by Emilio Cruz in the background.

BELOW: Downstairs in the BAG building.

—⇒╾⊜ᴀɴɢ⊜╼⇐—

Photographs by Michael E. Emrick, 1969.

Education was a key tenet of BAG's Black Arts philosophy, and with the Washington Boulevard building as anchor, BAG quickly opened its arts training school as part of the AIR Program. Many musicians of the 1960s tried, in similar fashion, to intervene in the urban crisis by putting their artistic skills to use. Hemphill, for example, could look to his old teacher from Fort Worth, saxophonist and clarinetist John Carter, who had moved to Los Angeles to teach and perform following the 1965 Watts uprisings, feeling that it was everyone's responsibility "to try to make this place right." The Black Artists' Group based some of its programming on the community-oriented activities of the Black Panther Party, Ajulé Rutlin explains, but the AACM provided the most significant model for the group's educational program. While BAG renovated its Washington Boulevard building, the Chicago collective had been busy setting up its own music school—an effort to emphasize black musical forms in the face of their exclusion from or denigration by the traditional academy. Trombonist George Lewis, a student at the AACM school, remembers that the Chicago musicians had grown troubled by "a wide-ranging denial of African histories [that] could well result in an erasure of cultural memory." To prevent the deleterious musical consequences of this process, the AACM faculty felt that black musicians had to expand their roles vigorously, functioning not only as artists but also as scholars, historians, educators, and cultural critics. At their Chicago school, the teachers presented their own historical and musicological research, focusing primarily on the African American musical heritage, but also examining various world musical traditions. This venture formed a strong blueprint for BAG.[15]

In St. Louis, the artists recruited through the public schools and neighborhood organizations and soon had children lined up outside their doors on summer evenings, eagerly waiting to get into the group's headquarters. By June 1969, enrollment had climbed to over two hundred students, filling the often-free classes in creative writing, music, drama, dance, and the visual arts. Courses in music theory and specific musical instruments were by far the most popular, running every weeknight, and many of BAG's musicians supplemented the work of the salaried artists-in-residence. For example, as a trumpet and theory tutor, Baikida Carroll taught young students such as Bruce Purse, George Sams, and Miles Davis's eldest son, Gregory, who was then leading a local avant-garde trio called the Musical Liberation Front. Meanwhile, Ajulé Rutlin organized writing classes for adults and children, developing a curriculum he called Creative Writing in a Functional Context. He dedicated the first portion of his children's course to challenging the privileging of Standard English over the vernaculars spoken by many inner-city African Americans. To demonstrate that language was an evolving "collection of tools and symbols" rather than a historical given, Rutlin directed the children in an exercise in which they invented their own "language" from scratch. As students gained experience through the arts courses, several were invited to join BAG's music, dance, and drama ensembles.[16]

The popularity and success of this inner-city arts academy encouraged the local school district and the Model Cities Agency to open a handful of community schools based on the same model. But in addition to operating their own school, BAG members also brought their programming to the surrounding area, conducting workshops and classes at YMCAs, public schools, and the neighborhood community centers set up through the War on Poverty. Carroll, for instance, wrote charts for the Young Disciples project in East St. Louis, an effort to provide musical training for economically underprivileged youths. BAG also brought its theater, musical, and dance units to Carr Square, a low-rise public housing complex on the city's north side.[17]

And while Hemphill and Cruz had deemed Pruitt-Igoe an unsuitable accommodation for the artists-in-residence, BAG's members focused a good deal of energy on the shoddily built and poorly managed housing project that sat less than a mile from their headquarters. Warehoused in thirty-three eleven-story buildings towering grimly over a scrub-grass wilderness, the residents were physically and economically isolated from the surrounding city, living in what the local Model Cities chief dubbed "the worst social and physical catastrophe in the country." Though the project was integrated for a short period following its construction, many of the city's African Americans had few housing choices

At a March 1969 open house for BAG's Washington Boulevard building, Emilio Cruz (center) demonstrates drawing techniques to area children as Shirley LeFlore (right) observes.

⇥═◉═BAG═◉═⇤

Photograph by Lloyd Spainhower/ © 1969, St. Louis Post-Dispatch.

after urban renewal demolished thousands of homes in black neighbor-hoods, and Pruitt-Igoe soon became an all-black complex. The artists from BAG were appalled not just by the dire living conditions produced through callous government policies, but also by the lack of more formal artistic opportunities in the area. The housing project included few gath-ering places, and most of the area's black clubs and businesses had been razed. Accordingly, BAG dispatched its theater and music contingents to the project for performances. And though many of the complex's children were enrolled in classes at the BAG building, the group estab-lished a base at Pruitt-Igoe to teach drama, music, and the visual arts. Working with two dozen of the children, for example, Vincent Terrell invented an interactive drama project called Freeze in Motion, which focused on the living conditions at Pruitt-Igoe, and he solicited set designs from Oliver Jackson.[18]

The artists also served as mentors outside the more formal con-text of their school. Nurturing young like-minded musicians was an empowering, assertive move in which the tenets of the Black Arts Movement dovetailed perfectly with the St. Louis musical tradition in which so many of BAG's members had found their voice. Just as older performers such as George Hudson and Vernon Nashville had guided the budding BAG musicians in the early 1960s, BAG members in turn took less experienced artists under their wings, many of whom went on to become recognized performers in their own right. Lester Bowie's brother, trombonist Joseph Bowie, became BAG's youngest member when he joined the group in 1969 at age fifteen. The younger Bowie came in contact with the collective's musicians by playing in an all-city jazz band directed by Hamiet Bluiett, and shortly thereafter he began working with Oliver Lake's combos and with the BAG big band. Joseph Bowie notes that, musically, he was raised in the group: "There was a point where I would just get up and leave my parents' home, and go hang out at BAG all day. It was that kind of vibe for me." Indeed, the building became a magnet for the city's young musicians. Jazz artists often dredge up memories of gathering outside the back doors of clubs as youngsters, straining to hear the sounds emanating from within, and saxophonist Greg Osby tells a similar story about an afternoon spent lingering outside the BAG building: "I was riding my bike and I heard this commotion coming out of this warehouse building . . . I didn't know what was happening, but I was kind of transfixed. My friends just left, and I was down there until nightfall listening to this music. . . . They were getting some otherworldly timbres out of their instruments; there were some other spirits that were being conjured up."[19]

Apprentices sprang into being on a number of fronts, ranging across the arts, even when such relationships did not lead to formal membership in BAG. The saxophonist Luther Thomas, who grew up playing rhythm and blues on the river's Illinois side, began hanging out with older reedmen such as Hemphill, Lake, and Bluiett, and describes these musicians, along with the AACM's Lester Bowie, as "responsible for my musical development." Another of these protégés was Marty Ehrlich, today a prominent New York saxophonist and composer. As a high school student in University City, an integrated suburb on St. Louis City's western border, he met BAG's Malinké Elliott and J. D. Parran while taking a drama class at one of the MECA Saturday Centers. Ehrlich became fast friends with Elliott, who passed along record albums by avant-garde artists such as Ornette Coleman and Albert Ayler. After shifting his interests from drama to poetry and eventually to music, Ehrlich began attending jam sessions with Oliver Lake and Julius Hemphill. This connection would continue years later in New York, when Hemphill became an important mentor for Ehrlich, who played in several of Hemphill's ensembles. BAG's poets, as well, mentored young writers such as Karl Evanzz, a teenage Black Liberators member who later became a *Washington Post* editor and author of books on Malcolm X and Elijah Muhammad.[20]

⇢⟡⟡⟡⟡⟡⟡⟡⟡⟡⟵

BAG developed its precarious success by a complex process of negotiation, sometimes presenting subtly different faces as it restated its goals to various audiences: institutional funders, local activists, the black and white media, and the general metropolitan population. Rather than signaling an inconsistency of purpose, these shifts were strategic movements designed to promote the group's viability within different spheres of the St. Louis community. But there were certain ideas about the organization that members could not accept. The Inner City Arts Project had been established by philanthropic bureaucrats on the assumption that poor, black St. Louisans were "culturally impoverished," and the local press often glibly parroted this idea. The *Globe-Democrat*, for example, claimed that BAG's aim was "to encourage creativity among a people deprived of it." This particular kind of misrepresentation greatly irritated the group's leaders, who frequently emphasized their belief that economic impoverishment did not equal cultural impoverishment.[21]

Elliott heatedly disputed this notion with a local reporter, commenting that the group's goal was "reclaiming and redefining" black culture, while Hemphill nuanced the argument, explaining that BAG intended "to make black people more aware of their creative potential." And that also meant avoiding the impression that BAG knew best what its community needed. "You don't go out in a missionary way and tell people what's good for them and how they will be transformed by art," comments Pat Cruz, who then served as the organization's spokeswoman. Instead, she says, the group aimed to "find out what art forms [people] are engaged in and that they believe in, what ways their lives are enriched by culture. Then you can work together to mutual benefit." Members insisted that they were energizing what was already there, not compensating for alleged cultural deficiencies.[22]

The organization was set up primarily to focus on the arts, and BAG's social thrust was embedded in the content of its artistic presentations, rather than in coordinated political action. But then and now some members maintain the centrality of BAG's political orientation. At the time, Elliott insisted to a skeptical journalist, "In 1969, all black art is political. Don't let anybody tell you anything else." And Floyd LeFlore later commented that BAG "was very political," explaining that urban unrest and social frustrations were "definitely reflected in the artform, and it was also reflected in just our attitude about it." Nourished

BAG MEMBERSHIP MEETING, HELD IN 1969 AT THE COLLECTIVE'S
WASHINGTON BOULEVARD HEADQUARTERS.

-»}=◎BAG◎=}«-

Photograph courtesy Oliver Lake.

by cultural nationalist principles and anchored in a neighborhood that
sat at the center of struggles over housing, police brutality, and economic
empowerment, the group's very reason for being ordained some sort of
social commitment, even though members sometimes disagreed about
the medium and the means for intervention. While BAG's poets and
dramatists often engaged with contemporary social issues in their tren-
chant artistic presentations, several members also participated in local
struggles in more pragmatic and immediate fashion. This political work,
for the most part, was intermittent and individual rather than organiza-
tion-wide. But while not explicitly an activist organization, the collec-

tive did provide an intellectual space where social commitments could concentrate and then shoot off into various trajectories—whether activist or artistic—in the diverse projects of its members.[23]

Such political energies, nonetheless, drove a host of BAG activities. Pat Cruz describes the artists' growing awareness that "to engage people with art, you have to be engaged with what's meaningful to them. And if it's about housing and jobs and civil rights and a sense of equal access—and that's what we believed in anyway—you don't divorce that from your sense of where art fits into that." For example, despite his initial reluctance to come to St. Louis, once there, Emilio Cruz quickly allied with ACTION's leader, Percy Green, and his cohort of civil rights workers. After receiving a primer from Green on the local civil rights situation, Cruz concluded that "there was a very dastardly circumstance going on in that city, . . . one that needed remedy immediately." In conjunction with ACTION, he developed a Wednesday-night series of panel discussions called the People's Forum, held at the BAG building and chaired by his wife Pat. At these forums, area residents and community organizers conferred on civil rights questions and planned coordinated responses. BAG's performers, likewise, maintained contacts with a range of activist groups: playing music at fund-raisers for CORE, ACTION, and the Black Liberators and presenting skits that dramatized issues such as police brutality and fair housing. Suggesting the impossibility of divorcing art from everyday social realities in late-1960s St. Louis, Percy Green explains that BAG became "part of the networking. . . . The artists were able to convey the struggle of the times to another group of people."[24]

BAG's attempts at building counterinstitutions, insulated from the assumptions of the white mainstream, were part of a broader cultural front. The group's agenda, however, was subject to a variety of interpretations by outsiders. Ajulé Rutlin, challenged by a wary journalist on the group's frequent invocation of the word "revolution," explained that for BAG, "revolution" meant "changing our people's frame of reference from white to black." Yet many of the period's cultural nationalists faced charges from revolutionary activists that they were not sufficiently attuned to political realities, and that cultural change was not nearly bold enough a response to the crisis faced by African Americans. While the intense ideological debates between nationalism's cultural and revolutionary wings were not nearly as all-consuming in St. Louis as they were on the coasts, they did surface on occasion. In response, several BAG members tried to make clear the link between artistic endeavor and political needs. For example, in a 1969 *Post-Dispatch* interview, Malinké Elliott adamantly maintained: "Black art is not just a cultural thing. It's also a political thing. I know people need jobs. And they need housing. But this is about black life. It's part of the struggle, too." Looking back years later, Julius Hemphill reflected that while BAG was located in the same neighborhood as groups such as the Black Liberators, its social thrust necessarily took a different form: "We were doing a kind of activism in terms of music and theater and stuff like that, trying to cut across what we perceived as the existing lines."[25]

Occasionally, however, more specific campaigns could galvanize the entire organization. One such event was the citywide rent strike in public housing, which dominated local headlines through most of 1969. Tenants in St. Louis public housing had grown increasingly frustrated by the physical deterioration of their buildings, burdensome rent increases, and callous management. In February 1969, residents in five housing projects began a rent strike that would last for nine months, and they soon had over 35 percent of the city's public housing tenants participating. In addition to withholding their rent payments, tenants picketed and held sit-ins at City Hall, and they devised media-savvy tactics to dramatize their plight, such as sending "welfare menus" and empty food cans to the mayor, the state's governor, and President Richard Nixon. Over the nine months of the strike, tenants pushed the St. Louis Housing Authority toward bankruptcy.[26]

Facing fierce opposition from the Housing Authority, which tried to evict tenants and to seize the rent money they were depositing in escrow accounts, the rent strikers used their strong ties with the African American community to generate support from a range of civil rights groups, including CORE, ACTION, the Black Liberators, the

Zulu 1200s, and the Black Nationalists. They also were supported, to varying degrees, by religious organizations, labor unions, and the local daily newspapers. Fearing that the rent strike might touch off civil disorders—a prospect strategically exaggerated by the tenants' lawyers—nervous federal officials shuttled back and forth between Washington, D.C., and Missouri trying to mediate a solution.[27]

BAG opened its building to public forums and debates about the rent strike, and several members took a more engaged stance. At the weekly People's Forum meetings in the BAG building, participants suggested that the group's artists might support the rent strikers through their performances. Vincent Terrell and his TSOCC Players put on entertainment to raise money for the rent strike effort. And Emilio Cruz and Julius Hemphill rented a flatbed truck as a mobile performance and speechmaking unit to take to the projects, an effort to "reinforce an idea that [the tenants] had external support," as Cruz explains. BAG members such as Terrell, Oliver Lake, and Charles "Bobo" Shaw joined the demonstrations on wheels, and the imaginative scheme garnered participation from the local NAACP chapter and from Percy Green and Sister Cecelia Goldman of ACTION. By bringing their performances to the scene of struggle, the artists hoped to deploy aesthetic and creative means to reach political ends.[28]

BAG's members had lessons to learn themselves on this front, however, and occasionally well-intentioned efforts could be taken differently than they were intended. On one foray into Pruitt-Igoe to support the rent strike, Pat Cruz assumed her designated role as spokeswoman. Between skits and musical interludes from the flatbed truck, she excoriated the local housing authority, claiming that the residents lived under dehumanizing conditions. But the residents, feeling that the artists were condemning them rather than the municipal government, took offense and asked BAG to leave. In retrospect, Cruz ascribes the incident to her being "earnest and naïve," but through both successes and failures in dealing with the surrounding community, members developed an increasingly acute sense of how they could participate in the development of political solidarity.[29]

Whatever minor missteps might have occurred, this early experience in direct political action eventually paid off. In November 1969, under pressure from a variety of community leaders and organizations, city officials finally agreed to rent reductions, tenant representation on the Housing Authority board, programs to put tenants into project management, and improved policing and maintenance. The strike was one factor in pushing the U.S. Congress, two months after the strike settlement, to pass the Brooke Amendment to the 1969 Housing Act, providing federal subsidies to reduce public housing rents and limiting rents to one-quarter of a tenant's income.[30]

⊷┝═◉ ʙᴀɢ ◉═┥⊶

The young black artists housed at BAG, the PATC, the Experiment in Higher Education, and the Black River Writers tapped into a much wider expression of the new consciousness. Nationally, the currents of the Black Power Movement flowed through all types of cultural symbols—slogans, posters, chapbooks, fashions, and songs—all of which helped to mobilize a wider constituency. Like cities around the country, St. Louis and East St. Louis became home to a new crop of black-owned bookstores, black history classes, and black cultural centers, all of which emphasized cultural pride and a consciousness of African roots. Area bookshops such as the House of Negro History, the Black Smith Shop, and the House of Truth sold Afrocentric literature and the latest offerings from movement leaders, while cultural activists organized black history classes outside the confines of the white-dominated universities, at venues such as the local CORE headquarters, the House of Umoja bookshop, and the Black Light Cultural Center.[31]

BAG members and their colleagues in likeminded groups used these cultural outlets to pursue their agenda. At the new bookstores and cultural centers, they sold their poetry chapbooks, gave readings, advertised performances, and networked with fresh bands of supporters. The performers also took to the airwaves with the 1969 inauguration of *Heads Up* on KMOX—the first local television program created by and for the

African American community. Groups such as the Oliver Lake Art Quartet, Ajulé Rutlin's Poetry/Music Function, and actors from BAG appeared periodically on the show alongside political leaders such as Dick Gregory. But the "new black consciousness" espoused by BAG and by figures such as Eugene Redmond was not readily accepted in a conservative city like St. Louis, even within the African American community. The city's oldest black weekly, the stodgy *St. Louis Argus*, editorialized against natural hair and other symbols of cultural liberation, while the city's black-owned bookstores teetered on the edge of closing because of low earnings.[32]

Afrocentric institutions in St. Louis walked a hard road, and alliances with the white New Left sometimes helped to smooth the pavement. So it was not unusual for various BAG members quite deliberately to develop overlapping constituencies that spanned the progressive community, in many cases aligning with strengthening New Left activism at area colleges and universities. Although the protests sweeping the nation's campuses came late to St. Louis, student activism swelled in 1968, catalyzed in part by the Tet Offensive in Vietnam and Senator Eugene McCarthy's antiwar presidential candidacy. The invigorated student protest movement jolted college administrators at campuses throughout the city, led by especially active chapters of the Association of Black Collegians (ABC) at Saint Louis University and Forest Park Community College.[33] But the epicenter for campus protest was Washington University, an elite private institution perched on the city's edge. Campus radicalism quickened public attention in December 1968, when separate contingents from ABC and the radical campus group Students for a Democratic Society (SDS) occupied buildings and issued lists of demands to university administrators. The ABC sit-in ended when the administration agreed to six of ten demands from the group's "Black Manifesto," including the establishment of a black studies program. While the mostly white SDS activists were rebuffed, the twin actions set the tone for a crescendo of protests that would culminate seventeen months later in fierce uprisings against the university's entanglements with the defense industry.[34]

On St. Louis's campuses, radical and avant-garde artists had access to new financial resources, however small, and a politicized audience that was open to their pursuits. Although alliances between black nationalists and collegiate New Leftists were sometimes uneasy, the entrenched conservatism of the surrounding area often led left-wing artistic, countercultural, and activist groups to circle the wagons in the face of opposition. Terry Koch, a local SDS leader, claims in retrospect that "if you were a poet, if you were a black jazz musician, if you believed in abortion rights . . . it was the same as being in the antiwar movement. You were all in it together because you're in St. Louis and you're surrounded by a bunch of rednecks." Although these disparate connections were sometimes transient and fleeting, several BAG members did participate more directly in the mushrooming antiwar movement. Vincent Terrell, for example, denounced the conflict in Southeast Asia in his poem and play "Viet-Bop" and performed the work in Paris on a trip with the American Friends Service Committee, the Quaker antiwar group. Malinké Elliott, meanwhile, shared an apartment with Kendrick Holder, one of the city's most theatrical student peace movement leaders, and together the two organized dozens of audacious demonstrations, sometimes shepherding hundreds of student protesters to the doorsteps of Washington University trustees' homes. On the cultural front, Elliott helped to organize the antiwar Angry Arts Festival on Washington University's campus.[35]

With much of this activity concentrated at Washington University, some of BAG's theater personnel began performing skits at Holmes Lounge, a campus gathering spot frequented by politically active students. Vincent Terrell found going to the campus "solidifying," because with his radical politics, he felt "sort of isolated most of the time." BAG members such as J. D. Parran, who was a graduate student in the university's department of music, performed at campus events such as the Rainbow Festival of Life, a fund-raiser for students arrested in protests against the university's ROTC program. Meanwhile, the university's ABC chapter incorporated members unaffiliated with the school, forming a link between black college students and the surrounding

African American community. Though not students at the school, Terrell and Charles "Bobo" Shaw joined the organization, coming in "from the streets to give them a semblance of what was happening," as Terrell says. The two BAG members accompanied ABC in its December 1968 building occupations and helped the organization develop a tutoring program for black children in the central city.[36]

The heated climate at the universities also allowed BAG to tap into a new network of funding and audiences, both through SDS leadership in student government and through the new black studies program. At Washington University, several SDS members became interested in supporting BAG's cultural program. Terry Koch explains that after he and several fellow SDS members were elected to student government, thereby gaining access to financial resources, they were "constantly trying to find ways to funnel that to the community. We thought, let's hire the Black Artists' Group to do some performances, and get some money into the community." With funds freed up, the group took many of its performances to the campus. Likewise, architecture students donated their time to complete a design for renovations of the BAG building.[37]

The ad hoc relationships between several of BAG's members and the student New Left opened up fresh performance opportunities. But even more useful was the university's new black studies program, which had been established mainly in response to ABC's pressure. With the program's 1969 inauguration, the school recruited the twenty-four-year-old poet K. Curtis Lyle from Los Angeles as a writer-in-residence. Like many BAG members, Lyle had experience in community arts organizations. As a founding member of the Watts Writers Workshop and one of the radical dissidents who broke away from that group with the Watts 13, his background fit easily with BAG's community focus. Lyle saw the black studies program as a "diversionary tactic" by the administration, but it did provide resources that he could direct toward experimental black artists. Though he never joined their collective, Lyle developed close friendships with BAG members such as Julius Hemphill, Oliver Jackson, and Malinké Elliott and served as an informal liaison between the collective and the university. Through the black studies program, Lyle obtained money for BAG concerts on campus, as well as importing performers like the Artistic Heritage Ensemble, a Chicago group led by trumpeter and AACM cofounder Phil Cohran. He also tapped the school's resources for projects such as *The Orientation of Sweet Willie Rollbar*, a zany experimental film that he wrote and produced with help from Hemphill and Elliott. The collaboration eventually became so close that BAG conferred with university officials about running a black studies institute for the school, though the plan never came to fruition.[38]

⇥⊖◑◐⊖⇤

While the group's members labored to create a black-oriented aesthetic and to cultivate a sense of solidarity within the black community, they also helped foster interracial arts organizations beyond the academy. Unlike several of its counterparts elsewhere in the country, the collective developed strong alliances with progressive white and multiracial groups. As actress Portia Hunt comments, "We were living in a black world and we were living in an integrated world. They coexisted, side by side." Recognition and acceptance of a multiracial world, in short, did not dilute commitment to black identity and solidarity. This cooperation was especially strong with the Human Arts Association, a loosely knit poetry and music cooperative that acted as a sort of interracial twin of BAG. Among the founders were BAG poet Ajulé Rutlin and saxophonist Jim Marshall, a white St. Louisan who had briefly attended Southwest High School. Marshall and Rutlin met in the early 1960s when both worked as activists for the city's CORE chapter. By the late 1960s, Marshall was one of several white participants in the extended network of jam sessions and poetry readings from which BAG eventually emerged. Marshall's house became a hangout for many of these musicians and poets. His wife Carol, a West Virginian studying in St. Louis, taught at MECA, where she came into contact with J. D. Parran and Malinké Elliott, and she ultimately became one of the group's most regular members.[39]

The Marshalls, Rutlin, and Charles "Bobo" Shaw formed the Human Arts Association and its performing unit, the Human Arts Ensemble, shortly after BAG's genesis. As Oliver Lake later noted, BAG's restriction to black members "was the category we had at that time, because that was a high Black Power period," but the Human Arts Ensemble "included all of us under one umbrella." While BAG outlined a vision of black nationhood through its arts presentations, the Human Arts Ensemble became a vehicle for BAG members to perform alongside white colleagues without violating the black-only membership of BAG proper. Animated by a fiercely anticommercial ethos, the ensemble dedicated itself to the "free and meaningful expression of human values," a program they counterposed to the "unrighteous, violent, oppressive environment where the dollar is god and mediocrity is exalted." More diffuse and ad hoc than BAG, the group's performing ensemble often included musicians such as Lake, Floyd LeFlore, Baikida Carroll, and J. D. Parran, as well as budding artists such as the teenage saxophonist Marty Ehrlich. Members sponsored events ranging from informal free-jazz jam sessions to more elaborate projects, such as their music and poetry cycle based on the Hopi creation myth.[40]

Rutlin expanded the personnel of the Human Arts Ensemble by drawing on his friends from poetry circles at Washington University. The revolutionary élan sweeping the campus had spilled over into the arts, galvanizing a countercultural poetry scene consisting of a shifting, interracial squad of young writers. Michael Castro, a graduate student in English, led this raucously anti-academic crowd. Though Washington University had assembled a distinguished group of writers that included poets Howard Nemerov, Donald Finkel, Constance Urdang, Mona Van Duyn, and novelists William Gass and Stanley Elkin, the group objected to what they saw as the stuffy "academic trappings" of the city's contemporary literary circuit. Like the poets in BAG and the Black River Writers, these mavericks wanted to explore poetry as a performance art, to give poetry a central place in the community, and to strengthen the art form's role "in the consciousness raising that was taking place in the turmoil of the larger culture," as Castro later put it. They shot many of their poetic fusillades toward the university's ties with the defense industry, as in Castro's "Brookings Hall Exorcism," a poem condemning the "hypocritical camaraderie of backroom politics" where "pat-hands are dealt to society's death-merchants." The young writers formalized their efforts first as the Peace-Eye Poets and later as the River Styx Poets.[41]

Their goals meshed well with those of BAG's writers, who took part in a number of joint appearances. BAG poets Ajulé Rutlin, Malinké Elliott, and Shirley LeFlore were regulars at the group's informal series of readings, scattered through apartments, churches, LaClede Town, and area campuses. The performers of BAG, the Human Arts Ensemble, and Castro's irregular groupings also took advantage of a set of alternative media outlets. All of these venues offered young, radical artists new outlets to distribute poetry chapbooks and political pamphlets, perform music and drama, and advertise shows and events for a sympathetic, if small, group of supporters. They published their works in the city's leftist underground newspapers—the *St. Louis Free Press* and its successor, *The Outlaw*—and sold chapbooks and other items at Left Bank Books, a shop opened by former members of Washington University's SDS chapter.[42]

One outlet that particularly attracted the overlapping BAG–Human Arts Ensemble crowd was the alternative community radio station KDNA, a project founded by Jeremy Lansman, a local high school dropout and radio school graduate, and financed by the West Coast alternative radio impresario Lorenzo Milam. Headquartered in a tumbledown brick house in Gaslight Square, the station took to the airwaves early in 1969 when, after years of legal wrangles, Lansman and Milam beat out a fundamentalist Christian broadcaster competing for the license. Reflecting its founders' anticommercial doctrines, KDNA served up extended monologues on social issues, a wide range of music that was ignored by mainstream media, and shows by an eclectic mix of organizations, from the John Birch Society to the Black Panthers. KDNA "returned the community to the radio studio," as Milam later wrote, and it formed a vital outlet for small-run pressings of records and live poetry and music from BAG and Human Arts Ensemble performers. Michael Castro soon organized a two-hour, bimonthly poetry and music show on

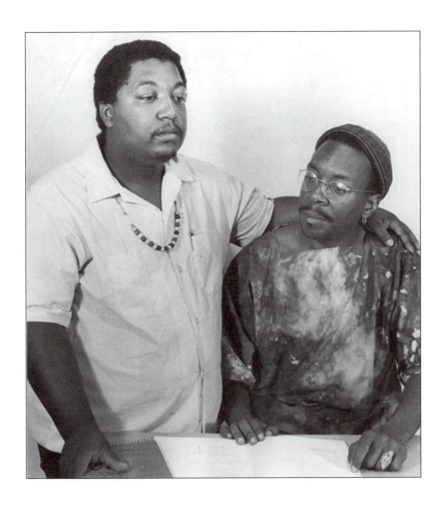

Director Malinké Elliott (left) and poet Ajulé Rutlin, here posing for a staff photographer from the *St. Louis Globe-Democrat*.

Photograph from the collections of the St. Louis Mercantile Library at the University of Missouri – St. Louis.

KDNA that ran for three years. Rutlin, Elliott, and LeFlore appeared on the show, along with musicians such as Marty Ehrlich. Ehrlich later pointed to the station's impact as a stimulus for artists, recalling that the first time he heard a Julius Hemphill record was on KDNA, and claiming that the station's free-form broadcasts "had a big influence on my own sense of how to put one's cosmology and music together."[43]

Maintaining the altitude of all this activity wasn't easy, however. Left Bank Books complained that selling radical and black-oriented materials was difficult, since police would browse around on a weekly basis, often requesting the removal of politically charged books. Meanwhile, with its frequent programming critical of U.S. foreign policy and local government corruption, KDNA managed to inflame much of the St. Louis establishment. The station faced charges that it was a front for SDS, frequent "exposés" in the conservative *Globe-Democrat*, several police raids, and detectives tailing radio hosts between the station and their homes. Following a September 1970 drug raid, KDNA had to fend off attempts by the right-wing evangelist Bill Beeny to nab the station's frequency for his expanding fundamentalist radio network. As BAG would later discover, its allies in the white progressive community would prove as insubstantial as the grant money that initially accelerated BAG's career.[44]

⊷⊫⊙ʙᴀɢ⊙⊪⊶

BAG itself was not immune to internal struggles. Contention over resources, administrative style, and gender sometimes strained relations within the group. Early on, for example, Hemphill and Elliott had come to regret their choice of Thurman Faulk as director for the AIR Program's film division. Faulk managed to recruit only two students for what turned out to be an enormously expensive program, and his constant out-of-town trips on private business—jaunts to the Gulf of Mexico to shoot training films for Mobil Oil, for instance—left little time for his St. Louis commitments. The short-lived film department accomplished few of its goals and even threatened to become a public-relations fiasco before BAG's leaders phased it out. And while the foundation grants for the AIR Program had allowed BAG to expand its own programming, the money also introduced an element of dissension within the group. Technically, the AIR Program and BAG were separate entities, but because of the substantial overlap in personnel, location, and activities, for the most part the distinction existed only on paper. With some BAG members receiving jobs and salaries through the AIR Program and others not, tensions simmered over the distribution of resources. Hemphill later commented, "It looked like the leadership was getting paid and the other participants were not, and that proved to be . . . a bone of contention, actually." In an attempt to compensate the nonsalaried artists, the group launched periodic fund-raising drives, though these met with only marginal success. And such gestures did little to assuage those BAG members who felt, as Vincent Terrell later charged, that "the lumpenproletarians were giving their services!"[45]

Notions of appropriate gender roles, too, occasionally collided with the putative egalitarian communalism of the collective. Though many nationalist organizations cast black culture as a tool for the formation of political and racial solidarity, these groups often undermined that project by consigning women to subordinate status. Part of the Black Power project's thrust involved a recovery of "black manhood" in response to the emasculating limits of a racist white society. This focus often led to the marginalization of female participants, despite the important roles that women played in ongoing civil rights and liberation struggles. Meanwhile, many participants, whatever their views on gender relations, saw the bourgeoning women's movement as specifically a white women's movement. These attitudes oftentimes sloshed over into the arts: for example, much of the Black Arts Movement's poetry valorized heroic male personae while celebrating women for procreating and nurturing roles. With the black liberation struggle represented in overwhelmingly masculine terms, many female artists felt competing tugs toward race and gender concerns and struggled to create aesthetic solutions to the conflict.[46]

The consensus seems to be divided about how much BAG exemplified these views of the sexes. Some women detected a muted discourse on gender that, while never bubbling to the surface, served to divide the group. This stemmed mainly from the primacy of BAG's all-male music component among the group's artistic departments, which produced a gendered division of artistic labor. Actress Portia Hunt feels that, in BAG, "music was kind of viewed as a male art form, and a way of liberation for black men. . . . As it stood, the musicians were valued over the other areas." And historically, women have been marginalized in a jazz world that has ignored the part that female musicians can rightly claim in the music's development. Many avant-garde musicians of the late 1960s, notably the AACM's Anthony Braxton, believed the exclusion of women to be detrimental to the art form. Still, Hunt says, BAG contained "very strong women who were supposed to support black men and were supposed to be in the background," producing a "split loyalty" among several women between race and gender issues. Of course, the lack of female musicians in BAG can be traced as well to an endemic sexism rooted in the city's musical culture, rather than specifically in the organization itself. As in most of the country, St. Louis's school bands and drum-and-bugle corps were composed overwhelmingly of boys, thus discouraging girls from developing their musical talents. These hurdles may have been even higher in St. Louis than elsewhere. Unlike a city such as Detroit, which has produced a prodigious number of nationally recognized female jazz musicians, St. Louis has produced few.[47]

As K. Curtis Lyle describes it, BAG and many of its contemporaries "were based around an art where women were not essentially empowered, and that was music." On the other hand, many members found BAG to be an empowering place for women. Shirley LeFlore saw important confluences between women's and black people's struggles for equality, commenting, "The goal of the women's movement was the same as the goal of the civil rights movement—the goal was liberation." And a number of strong and assertive female artists held leadership positions in BAG, including LeFlore, Georgia Collins, Portia Hunt, and, in the group's later years, dancer Luisah Teish and director Muthal Naidoo. This contrasts favorably with many of BAG's national Black Arts Movement contemporaries, where women were often relegated to separate spheres, far removed from the centers of planning and action. In

BAG, women were far better represented in the dance and theater components; in fact, probably no other multidisciplinary Black Arts collective had such a strong dance component. The influential presence of the PATC in East St. Louis allowed BAG to develop richer theater and dance programs than it otherwise would have had, both of which boosted women's importance within the collective. So, although the barriers to women's full participation in the group may have existed, they were lower than might be expected, given the prevailing climate. Nevertheless, rather than a coherent philosophy, BAG presented a contradictory stew of messages on gender and sexuality.[48]

BAG's progress was also monitored, if not hampered, by regular FBI scrutiny. And though the scope of the FBI's COINTELPRO activities did not become public until congressional investigations in 1976, those on St. Louis's political and cultural Left were certainly aware at the time of covert meddling from authorities. BAG's members knew that their brand of artistic agitation and their ad hoc cooperation with groups like ACTION could easily attract unwanted police attention. Baikida Carroll remembers that the group was "savvy enough to know that our artistic choices placed us under high scrutiny by the authorities." According to Vincent Terrell, the police searched BAG's Washington Boulevard building on at least two occasions. Actors such as Terrell and LeRoi Shelton suspected that plainclothes police were attending BAG's performances on a regular basis. And due to his heavy involvement with the antiwar movement based at Washington University, Malinké Elliott drew particular attention from the authorities. The shotgun that occasionally leaned beside their building's door signaled the apprehensions of several of BAG's members.[49]

Though men in BAG were sometimes hassled by police—a common occurrence for black males in that part of the city—no documentary evidence suggests that the FBI carried out direct operations against the group. Still, records show that local FBI agents did keep at least intermittent tabs on the collective, and particularly on certain of the more politically active members. The more general, systematic repression of the city's activists took a heavy psychological toll on many in St. Louis's Left, including members of BAG. This had the unfortunate consequence, at least intermittently, of creating an atmosphere of mistrust in the group, even leading some members to suspect that others were police informers. "I never did know if somebody was infiltrating the group," Shelton says; "There was no way to know! . . . There was no way for you to stand up and accuse nobody." Of course, Shelton's and Terrell's suspicions were far from paranoid, given the police and FBI harassment not only of radicals but also of moderates such as Katherine Dunham. Covert police and FBI operations against the city's black nationalists and student activists contributed to a general chilling of the political climate, stirring up fears of infiltration among targets and nontargets alike.[50]

Whatever the passing difficulties, they never undermined the organization's sense of community and solidarity. Looking back, Shirley LeFlore remembers the group as an extended family, as "our social life as well as our creative life." Over the early part of its existence, BAG had developed its notions of community and identity both through its local engagements and through its collaborative artistic development. And by the summer of 1969, BAG was fully established as a powerful and dynamic organization, busy educating children, putting on dozens of multimedia performances, and actively engaging with the surrounding neighborhoods. Though the group would last until late 1972, BAG reached its height in the years 1969 and 1970, with over fifty dancers, musicians, actors, and poets performing constantly, as well as composing, writing, teaching, and raising money. Deliberations over black identity and nationalism unfolded through the group's emphasis on community presence and programming, but BAG's various multimedia performances would also foreground such debates, bringing the discussion out of the back room and onto the public stage. In multidisciplinary shows such as *Poem for a Revolutionary Night*, writers, musicians, and actors tried to distill the politics of black identity into a strong brew of aesthetic adventurousness and social awareness—all of this squeezed out of the struggle for meaning under the peculiar pressures of everyday urban life in St. Louis.[51]

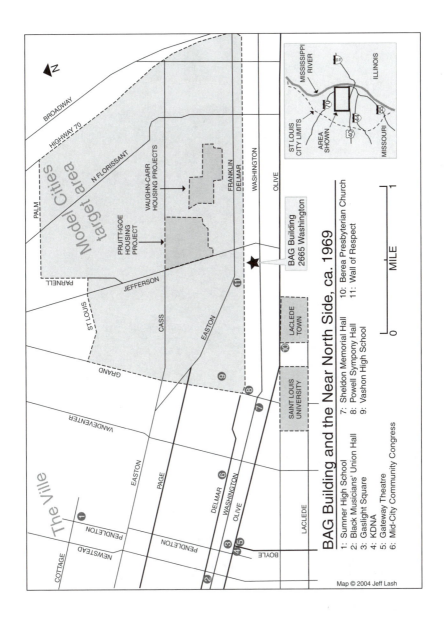

BAG Building and the Near North Side, ca. 1969

BAG Building
2665 Washington

1: Sumner High School
2: Black Musicians' Union Hall
3: Gaslight Square
4: KDNA
5: Gateway Theatre
6: Mid-City Community Congress

7: Sheldon Memorial Hall
8: Powell Sympony Hall
9: Vashon High School

10: Berea Presbyterian Church
11: Wall of Respect

0   MILE   1

Map © 2004 Jeff Lash

CHAPTER 4

"A SINGULAR EXPRESSION": BAG's MULTIMEDIA CONTINUUM

T here were few things that Malinké Elliott loved more than burrowing through the stacks at Bill Burgdorf's bookstore. An eccentric hole-in-the-wall nestled in St. Louis's Central West End, the shop had long been a magnet for the city's more bohemian intellectual community. And it was often the quirky old owner who drew Elliott's attention to the latest dramatic works from Black Arts heavyweights such as Ed Bullins and Charles Fuller. But Elliott was particularly delighted one afternoon in early 1969 when, while casually skimming the shop's poetry chapbooks, he alighted on a new collection called *Black Boogaloo*, by the Philadelphia poet Larry Neal.[1]

Though Neal was one of the leading essayists of the Black Arts Movement, Elliott knew little more than that about him. But he had been searching for a scaffold on which to build a major multimedia pageant for BAG, and the collection seemed perfectly configured for such a large-scale project. Over the next several weeks, he lent the chapbook to several of his BAG colleagues. They shared his enthusiasm for Neal's work, especially for the piece called "Poem for a Revolutionary Night." Taking this as the working title for their own multimedia spectacle, BAG's artists began crafting the dramatic scenarios, dance interludes, jazz scores, and rear-projection films that would structure the production. In retrospect, *Poem for a Revolutionary Night*, more than any other BAG production, would embody the intermingling of the arts that its founders had envisioned, a blend whose recipe was familiar but whose ingredients were singular. Although the centrality of BAG's music tends in retrospect to crowd the other arts to the margin, much of the group's vitality arose from this busy interchange among the arts, one that ended up nourishing all of them.

⇢⊱≡⊚BAG⊚≡⊰⇠

Over the four years of its existence, BAG kept up a hectic performance schedule, punctuated by major presentations combining music, poetry, theater, and dance. All the while, members attempted to hammer out a core philosophy based upon unifying BAG's various modes of expression. Elliott explains, "Our concept was that black arts in the black community should be about multiple disciplines but a singular expression." The "singular expression" voicing this ultimate, elusive goal was a collaborative and integrative approach to the various arts, one that combined them, again in Elliott's phrase, like "layers of transparencies," with no one element dominating. Even for the musicians, as saxophonist Hamiet Bluiett later remarked, the focus "was all about playing with other people. We would play along with poets, actors and painters, all moving to the same beat." And so an observer strolling into a BAG performance might witness all sorts of unusual amalgamations—juxtaposing, perhaps, a poet, a dancer, and a trumpeter; or two saxophonists, a drummer, and an actor against a backdrop created by a visual artist. At the same time, many of the artists explored disciplines other than their primary ones: poets picked up musical instruments, while musicians tried their hands at painting. Saxophonist Oliver Lake even published a collection of his poems, *Life Dance*, in 1979. Soon, all sorts of multidisciplinary organizations clustered in BAG's orbit: the Human Arts Ensemble, Ajulé Rutlin's Poetry/Music Function and its later incarnation, Children of the Sun, and Vincent Terrell's TSOCC Players, all using the group as an umbrella for raising funds, selling tickets, and attracting audiences.[2]

Such an attempt was not unique. The decade spawned a multitude of community arts organizations, many of which aimed—in theory at least—to erase or transgress the boundaries among performance disciplines such as theater, dance, poetry, and music. But BAG enacted such theories on the ground, and eventually proved to be one of the most truly interdisciplinary arts collectives to emerge from the Black Arts Movement. Far from seeming exotic or avant-garde, this interpenetration of the modes and means of the various arts was taken as a given. Indeed, many of the group's members saw the very idea of "interdisciplinarity" as a Eurocentric concept, one derived from a traditional Western division of art into discrete or even rival territories. But the relentless tendency to pigeonhole resulted in a quandary for critics: were BAG performances ballets, operas, dance dramas? And what should one call a production when painting or film was incorporated? No one seemed to know.[3]

This kind of fusion worked through and with a call to synthesize black history with present-day struggle, or, as Ajulé Rutlin wrote, "to absorb the traditions of the ancestors and to extend them in positive directions." Ideally, this multidisciplinary black aesthetic would harness traditional forms to avant-garde technique and contemporary subject matter, unifying various modes of expression into a medium that conveyed the black artistic heritage. And the philosophical glue for this fusion was the idea of the African continuum, a concept that visual artist Oliver Jackson spent much of his intellectual energy refining. Jackson saw the continuum as a set of aesthetic commonalities binding together all people of African descent; or, as he put it in a 1971 speech, as "the reflection of African peoples' sensibility in the forms and images that they create, in the institutions and constructs that they make." He rejected what he saw as the segmentation of Western culture that sharply differentiated the material and spiritual, the physical and mental—all those habits of thought that separated and marginalized. His vision summoned up a more African-derived concept of reality, one that espoused a creative interaction of form and substance. For Jackson and his BAG cohort, the African continuum functioned as a vast subterranean stream coursing beneath the foundations of all black creative expression, a source that individual artists could draw upon once they understood their own unique sensibilities.[4]

At the time, *Poem for a Revolutionary Night* must have seemed the embodiment of much of what he was talking about. Combining readings from Larry Neal's poems with a musical score written by Julius Hemphill, choreography from Georgia Collins, and a set of semi-improvised scenarios from the actors, the company crafted a work characterized by modernist fragmentation and ritualistic repetition. Like Neal's work itself, the production drew on European modernist technique to attack the majority culture—a process akin to what Houston Baker, in describing the Harlem Renaissance, calls "the deformation of mastery," a way of reconfiguring the monuments and methods of Western history into a different cultural language. Elliott conceived of the drama, as he told the *Globe-Democrat*, as "an evolutionary history of black consciousness," a sweeping narration of the freedom struggle that would range from the slave ships of the sixteenth century to the troubled central cities of the 1960s. But at the same time, he aimed to raise questions about the relationship of the arts to contemporary social and political battles. The production's opening narration somewhat opaquely set forth this crux, announcing in Neal's words: "Hover. She hovers, the Big Momma of the seas and the forest. / the Black Mother laid outstretched on the plains. Who is Her / Lover? the Black Angel with the Sword or the Poet of the / Guitar?" For Elliott, the lines seemed to evoke a gulf that the era's radical black artists straddled, pulled between violence and the arts, revolutionary engagement and cultural development, the "sword" and the "guitar."[5]

The production went on to dramatize the divergence, in which "Both compete. Each exaggerating. Each claiming dominance / over the Other." It outlined not only clashes against oppressors, but also contemporary conflicts within the black community among revolutionary militants, cultural nationalists, and mainline integrationists. For this, too, the company took its cue from the Neal work. Out of the mist drifting through the modernist urban inferno in the streets of Harlem, representative figures emerge to offer their apologia and disappear: the black establishment figure as naïve integrationist, the "Back-to-Africa" nationalist, an anonymous old man who claims that "revolutions are dull," and the enigmatic underground "contact." Like the hollow men of Eliotic fame, all are caught between "the idea and the reality," "the motion and the act." To Neal's characters, BAG added other symbolic figures: a corrupt black preacher; a despotic policeman (performed in whiteface); an idealistic young revolutionary; and the black "masses," depicted by the dancers as a collective swaying and pulsing body.[6]

The performers structured the production around these various characters rather than along a linear plot and offered a set of improvisations that could differ with each presentation. Leaning on Stanislavski acting concepts, the players carefully identified each of these character's "through lines," the underlying motivations that drive actions and emotions. But while the play laid out complex questions of tactics and goals in the quest for black nationhood, it wasn't intended to answer them in simple fashion. Though the play, like the poem, culminated in the exhortation to "let the night's death and revolution come," in fact, it raised more questions than it answered. As in Neal's poem, the only betrayal here took the form of shrinking from confrontation, reducing oneself to "the size / of a mouse" to "run out in the streets unseen." The goal was action of *some* kind, a call for unity. But what form that action, even that unity, would take was left up to the audience.[7]

After extensive rehearsals, in June 1969 BAG unveiled the production in an outdoor performance at the Pruitt-Igoe housing project. In the midst of St. Louis's public housing rent strike, more than two dozen BAG actors, dancers, and musicians descended on the complex, with spotlights, scaffolding, and several hundred chairs in tow. As dusk fell, a curious crowd of hundreds of tenants gathered to watch, with children sometimes overrunning the stage. As coda, Vincent Terrell presented *Now Hear This*, a puppet show based on the ongoing rent strike. The tenants in the audience jeered the puppets representing their City Hall opponents and applauded puppets representing the strike's leaders. In an event perfectly tailored to BAG's goal of community engagement, the performers and audience felt at one, as Hemphill later noted: "We weren't talking down to them in any kind of way. We were talking about the stuff they experienced every day."[8]

Poem for a Revolutionary Night quickly became a signature piece for the group, one that they gradually refined from the trial run at Pruitt-Igoe into an extended, improvisatory multimedia happening. Over the next few months, the group presented the show at the Gateway Theatre, University City High School, and the University of Missouri in Columbia. Nor did the performances themselves remain static. A com-

Cast members of *Poem for a Revolutionary Night*, performed in 1969.

◦─▷═▣═◁─◦

Photograph courtesy Oliver Lake.

pletely revamped version took the stage in November 1969 at the Festival of Creation, a daylong arts event at the city's high-church Episcopal Christ Church Cathedral. Trumpeter Baikida Carroll had recently taken the reins of the BAG big band following Hamiet Bluiett's departure for New York, and he was invited to create an entirely new score. In late-night sessions, Carroll remembers, he dissected the poem along with Elliott and Ajulé Rutlin, pondering audio approaches that would animate Neal's text and "propel the author's conviction of ethics and aesthetics as one principle." Carroll eventually developed a "tone-poem collage" using an ensemble of fifteen musicians.[9]

The play, like much of BAG's work, staked out that contested territory where social and artistic engagements meet. The performance art of the 1960s had challenged New Critical ideas of the "purity" of art and laid to rest notions that art should, or could, remain untainted by the social and cultural conditions surrounding its production. From the agitprop of the Bread and Puppets Theater and the San Francisco Mime Troupe to the nationalist dramas of the Black and Chicano Arts Movements, artists simultaneously recast their crafts as tools in contemporary struggles and injected a theatrical consciousness into the broader social movements with which they were associated. As BAG's artists mapped out their vision of identity through dramatic, musical, and literary vehicles, they vibrated to the nationalist energies percolating through the central city. Out of this volatile mix they distilled a set of practices that linked black expression and urban politics, projected through experiments in movement, sound, color, and line. The artistic thrust was firmly embedded in local social realities, but conflict was not merely reproduced on the stage; rather it was amplified and transformed. Strongly influenced by the essays, plays, and poetry of writers such as Malcolm X, Amiri Baraka, and Frantz Fanon, BAG productions during these years ranged from sharp satires dramatizing immediate issues of the local community to sweeping, ritualistic pageants that laid out broad visions of black survival, spirituality, and nationhood while refining ideas of African heritage.[10]

--==◎BAG◎==--

Most of these productions incubated first in BAG's theater department, and Malinké Elliott and Vincent Terrell, the collective's stage directors, represented two distinct faces of the company. Often cast as the serene philosopher, Elliott was frequently called upon as the collective's peacemaker. In his manifesto-cum-acting-manual *Black Theatre Notebook* (1970), he elaborated on key principles of the Black Arts Movement, claiming the black theater as a forum in which to establish the "legitimacy to demand and win our freedom." At the same time, he saw contemporary African American theater as a product, in equal parts, of an "African continuum [of] black perceptual experience" and the long tradition of European dramaturgy, and he aimed to yoke these heterogeneous creatures. Marshalling a broad familiarity with the texts of modernist dramatic theory, Elliott drew extensively from a divergent set of practitioners: Konstantin Stanislavski's acting approaches, Jerzy Grotowski's austere "poor theater," and Bertolt Brecht's politically charged "epic theater." To train his company's actors in dramatic and production techniques, he called on Alan and Joanna Nichols, two white performers from New York, and Maria Lexa, an actress trained in London and Paris then studying in St. Louis. Attempting to build an ensemble feeling, Elliott selected plays from a wide repertoire, sometimes looking to Africa, Europe, and the Caribbean for texts.[11]

If Elliott represented the more formal, academic impulses of the group's theater wing, then Terrell represented the troupe at its most improvisational. The tall, lean director combined an almost ceremonial courtesy with a volatile intensity. Relying on a directing method that was very much to the moment, Terrell pushed his actors to explore outside the confines of a pre-existing text. In the days leading up to a production, he dashed about town collecting props and costumes, constructing sets, and revising scripts, all the while keeping his apprehensive actors in the dark about the play aside from his deliberately sketchy instructions. At the very last minute, the baffled troupe would get their scripts, but oftentimes Terrell would feed his actors new lines during the performance, building up an initial anxiety that, ideally, would eventuate in stronger, more immediate and intense renderings of character and situation. And out of this quest for authentic emotion, Terrell sometimes sprang surprises on his cast during plays. A classic example came in a performance of his play *It Happened on the Way Here*: while LeRoi Shelton was delivering an impassioned monologue, Terrell flung a flaming pyrotechnic device onto his chest and then quickly extinguished it, startling Shelton half to death but eliciting the reaction that Terrell wanted.[12]

For both Elliott and Terrell, the composition of the theater component was key, and the company deliberately drew from a wide range of the local black community: among the actors, LeRoi Shelton was an assembly worker at the McDonnell Douglass aircraft plant, Woodie Tate a municipal pollution-control inspector, Bill Archibald a postal worker, and Pat Mountjoy a typist and clerk. One of the strongest actors was Portia Hunt, a young woman who had grown up in the public housing projects of East St. Louis. As a student at Southern Illinois University's Edwardsville campus, she had hoped to study theater and dance but was summarily brushed off by professors who told her she was only fit for comedy. Unwilling to surrender her performance ambitions, Hunt migrated to Katherine Dunham's PATC in East St. Louis to study. There, she was soon teaching dramatic techniques and eventually joined BAG. Her attitude, experience, and training exemplified what the group's directors were looking for: a person who, as Hunt puts it, "knew both lives—the streets and the arts."[13]

From the start, the group looked to some of the major works of Black Arts Movement dramatists in New York and California. Following Amiri Baraka's injunction that the new black theater "should force change, it should be change," many of these 1960s playwrights attacked Western materialism and canons of greatness, rejected the idea of art as icon, and celebrated black cultural forms—all themes that fit well with BAG's own philosophical orientation. But the group's script selections also ranged more widely among contemporary African and African American play-wrights, coming to include Baraka's *The Toilet* and *Home on the Range*, Douglass Turner Ward's *Happy Ending*, Wole Soyinka's *The Trials of Brother Jero*, and Adrienne Kennedy's *A Rat's Mass*. Their approach frequently entailed scriptless performances. Through a regimen of physical training exercises and improvisatory theater games, the actors created stock scenarios that could be mixed and matched inside any performance. They paired these improvisations with the improvisatory nature of BAG's music, aiming to wrap productions in what Elliott calls "an envelope of music," one that would infuse every part of the drama without being relegated to the background. The jazz musicians, eager to participate in this type of integrative performance work, not only added scores but frequently took on acting roles themselves. For Hemphill, Oliver Lake, and their col-

BAG DANCERS REHEARSE IN PREPARATION FOR A 1969 PERFORMANCE OF

Poem for a Revolutionary Night.

Photograph courtesy Portia Hunt.

"POINT FROM WHICH CREATION BEGINS"

leagues, the daily cooperation with artists in other media broadened their approaches to improvisation and composition.[14]

In addition to improvisations and works by established dramatists from elsewhere, BAG's actors soon began writing their own plays, developing thematic material out of issues current in the local community and also from historical subjects that dealt with the African American experience. Terrell, for instance, based scripts on the 1831 slave rebellion led by Nat Turner and on the life of the eighteenth-century black Bostonian Crispus Attucks, whose death at the hands of British soldiers presaged the start of the American War of Independence. Many productions were more sharply, even didactically, directed toward the concerns of the moment. In skits such as *The Pigs*, for example, BAG's theater department assailed the local police force for its record of brutality against black St. Louisans. The piece, as Ajulé Rutlin remembers it, narrated the experiences of a job-hunting African American man. When the character passes a police recruiting station (its sign reading "We Buy Souls") he joins the force, but he is quickly overwhelmed by his newfound sense of power and ends the piece with a homicidal shooting spree. Heeding West Coast playwright Ed Bullins's call for a black street theater in which each spectator would "have his sense of reality confronted, his consciousness assaulted," the actors often brought such dramas to public spaces of North St. Louis. "What we're after," Elliott told the *Post-Dispatch*, "is total theater in the streets."[15]

Even works by non-BAG playwrights were sometimes selected for their relevance to events in St. Louis. Ben Caldwell's one-act play *Prayer Meeting: Or, The First Militant Preacher* is a good example. The play is a call for black ministers to embrace more radical means for change, and BAG performed it while headlines were filled with news of the church reparations campaign, spearheaded locally by the Black Liberation Front and ACTION. In an attempt, as Percy Green put it, to bring "black humane revolutionary change" to local churches, activists picketed white congregations and interrupted services to demand reparations money for the Christian church's historic complicity in slavery. When local organizations of black clergy denounced the approach, ACTION quickly added black churches to the campaign, condemning their ministers for a lack of leadership on civil rights issues. BAG's staging of *Prayer Meeting* featured LeRoi Shelton, himself a member of ACTION, in the role of a black minister, and the plot revolves around a burglar rifling through the preacher's house. When the clergyman returns home, the burglar conceals himself and, pretending to be the voice of God, insists that the minister stop acting on behalf of the white establishment and instead lead his flock in militant action. Although outside the context of contemporary events Caldwell's play loses much of the power it might once have had, when the small BAG contingent produced the work during a July 1969 worship service at Berea Presbyterian Church it spoke directly to the issues of the moment.[16]

Neither did the company shy away from plays addressing sexually charged topics, often raising a clamor in the community and even within the organization. In April 1969 at the Gateway Theatre, Elliott directed Dorothy Ahmad's *Papa's Daughter*, a play that obliquely treats the issue of incest. And around the same time, Terrell staged *Clara's Ole Man* by Ed Bullins. The play focuses on the experiences of the working-class lesbian woman called Big Girl, who stymies the attempts of Jack, an urbane postal worker, to seduce her partner. For his trespasses, Jack earns himself a beating from Big Girl's friends. Bullins weaves issues of class as well as gender and race into the very language of the play, setting off Jack's carefully acquired upper-class diction against the more "natural" rhythms of the working-class heroine and her friends. More controversial productions followed, with Portia Hunt taking on topics such as abortion in her improvisations and monologues. These kinds of presentations "blew the top off the kettle," says Terrell; "we were denounced by the preachers, you name it. They said we were in there raising hell and talking foolishness." Given the conservative politics of gender and sexuality in 1960s St. Louis—in both the black and the white communities—BAG's presentations dealing frankly and explicitly with such issues were provocative and risky on every level.[17]

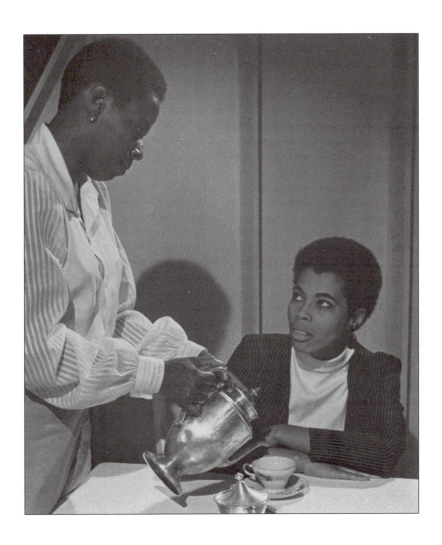

BAG actors Portia Hunt (left) and Pat Mountjoy in *Papa's Daughter*, 1969.

⟶⟦⊙BAG⊙⟧⟵

Photograph courtesy Portia Hunt.

An almost seamless connection existed as well between the word enacted on the stage and the word enacted on the page and recited in the lecture hall. Theater and poetry have always been siblings, and they claimed kin within BAG as well. But while the collective pulled in a handful of the area's young black poets, the city's literary milieu was far more diffuse than the musical or theatrical scenes. Though BAG had its own small stable of poets—Shirley LeFlore and Ajulé Rutlin chief among them—the collective's formal boundaries here seemed more permeable and shifting, as a number of writers more loosely associated themselves with the group during this period. For poetry and fiction, BAG formed merely one node among a set of overlapping centers for new black writers, which also included the Experiment in Higher Education, the PATC, and the Black River Writers group.

Writers from this network of institutions published their works in little magazines, neighborhood newsletters, student journals, and small-run chapbooks, and established venues in local churches and schools, community centers, coffeehouses, and bars. The most ubiquitous of the city's young black writers was Eugene Redmond. Though never a member of BAG, Redmond seemed to have a hand in almost every arts project based in the metropolitan area's black communities. His approach to poetics and activism resided in the relationship between what he terms "academic poets" and "poets of the street," a divide that he himself straddled. To mediate the chasm between the insular ivory tower and the politics of street and neighborhood, Redmond felt, required the establishment of "parallel institutions" embedded in the local community. With organizations such as the Rap-Write Now Creative Workshop and the Black River Writers publishing company, Redmond created an entire infrastructure for the city's black literary scene.[18]

The young writers in these St. Louis circles worked in form and subject matter similar to their Black Arts counterparts around the country—satire and exhortation, celebration of heroes and censure of enemies, evocations of black music, and romantic visions of a distant African past. To these, they fused a local flavor, an aesthetic that K. Curtis Lyle calls the "packinghouse consciousness," one bred out of the working-class vernacular of midwestern cities and raised on the blues at their most visceral level. Redolent of life in the cities of the heartland, their work distilled the peculiarities of economic and cultural life in these urban ports of call on the Great Migration. The slaughterhouses that drove the growth of cities such as East St. Louis—once second only to Chicago in the railway and animal-processing industries—gave rise to imagery such as Redmond's "sunglassed city of copper-river-smiles, pack-ing-house-hips, & rail-road-legs." The old rural existence was remain-dered in this working-class milieu, mediated by the railroads, the packinghouses and factories, the corner joints offering up jazz and blues. Out of it came an urban poetry characterized not by the Sandburgian "Hog Butcher for the World... / City of the Big Shoulders" swagger, but rather by an acute sense of the banality and brutality of the factory floor, a poetry that marched to a powerfully rhythmic language and music, underscored by city slang and the call and response of the black church.[19]

For BAG's poets, these themes frequently worked their way back to the ground bass of jazz and blues, as both model and subject. That poetry draws sustenance from music is no modern discovery, but perhaps nowhere did jazz musicians have a greater psychic impact in the 1960s than on the imagination of the poets and writers of the Black Arts Movement, many of whom cast musicians as guides or sentinels for the African American people. Believing that black music embodied, preserved, and disseminated the spirituality of black culture in the face of oppression or Western deca-dence, such poets often used language to explain and extend this musical heritage. Homages to jazz and blues greats, recurrent referencing of master musicians, mimicking of jazz syncopations, solo styles, and improvisatory schema—all became commonplaces of the poetic repertoire. Like their national counterparts, BAG's writers embraced music as a transformative art form, the touchstone of black culture, and cast African American musi-cians as "the true leaders of the Black people," in Ajulé Rutlin's words. Rutlin and Shirley LeFlore, the collective's two main poets, constantly sought out ways to blend their verse with other art forms. But the goal here was not merely to replicate the cadences or structures of jazz in the verbal medium. Ideally, in performance, poetry could intensify and accelerate the music.[20]

"I've always looked at poetry as another instrument," Shirley LeFlore has commented. She was reared in a family of writers, poets, and musicians, and for her, poetry and music were intimately intertwined. Indeed, the influences she credits sound uncannily like those of the jazz musicians with whom she worked: "I was always fascinated by words, the language spoken in my community. People in the African American community spoke in terms of the effect of song, churches, sermons. There was such an element of rhythm and repetition." When not working with BAG, LeFlore performed much of her poetic work with the Berea Messenger Singers, a female a cappella ensemble based at Berea Presbyterian Church that moved through the BAG constellation. The Messenger Singers played a strong role in LeFlore's development as a poet, allowing her to pair readings with musical styles ranging from spirituals and African chants to contemporary gospel songs and jazz arrangements. A number of BAG musicians and their AACM associates joined LeFlore in these Messenger Singers' performances, including Baikida Carroll, Charles "Bobo" Shaw, and the percussionist Famoudou Don Moye of the Art Ensemble of Chicago.[21]

Rutlin also delved into these kinds of artistic crossovers, closely linking his poetry with jazz in his own small ensembles, the Poetry/Music Function and Children of the Sun. Black music as subject and form is suggested in many of the titles in his 1971 chapbook *AJULÉ-of-the-Shadows*: "Roaches in his trumpet case," "John Coltrane," "Left Handed Music," "Sing, Then, of Piano Players." He often worked out what he called "total experience dramatizations" of his poems, as with his work "A Blacker Litany," for which he solicited musical and visual contributions from Oliver Lake and Emilio Cruz. Rutlin frequently traveled to Chicago to collaborate with the musicians of the AACM, as well as to participate in the writing workshops that Gwendolyn Brooks then offered at her home. Reviewing a reading in Chicago, *Down Beat* critic John Litweiler praised the care with which Rutlin handled the mixture of jazz with his own "exhortative expressionist" reading style, an interactive approach that drew "expressions of delight and agreement" from his audience. Rutlin later explained that his work with BAG and the AACM—

Poet Shirley LeFlore, shown here in 1976.

⊰⧉⊱

Photograph from the collections of the St. Louis Mercantile Library at the University of Missouri – St. Louis.

and particularly those musicians' push beyond traditional or easily recognizable structures—"helped me develop a really musical way of regarding the spoken word, just short of singing."[22]

Many of the BAG poetic works dealt directly with particular
social and political events, and in Rutlin's case, these ventures sometimes give the poems an ad hoc aspect that loses effectiveness outside of
its contemporary social context. When his poems filter political and
social commentary through the lens of personal issues or through music,
they retain some of their immediacy, as with the recognition of the complexity of human relations in the verse for his five-year-old, biracial son
Miles, in whose heart "The slave and the master huddle together. . . ."
Or in his tribute to Bud Powell, "Sing, Then, of Piano Players," which
employs a jagged, staccato rhythm suggestive of the bebop pianist's style:

> WATCHED HANDS; FINGERS / FLEET / FURTIVE; THE LEFT HAND
> THE RIGHT HAND SWING
> HARD OVER THE BLACK AND WHITE RHYTHM
> OF OUR NIGHTS AND DAYS
> AND HIP WAYS. . . .

Geared more toward performance than toward the printed page, Rutlin's
poetry gains by being heard on such recordings as Children of the Sun's
Ofamfa (1970) and the Human Arts Ensemble's *Poem of Gratitude* (1972).[23]

Other BAG writers took different directions. Vincent Terrell
penned a set of terse, naturalistic short stories describing the rigors of
the local neighborhood and the grind of factory life, both of which drive
his protagonists to violent acts of self-destruction. And following in the
wake of poets such as Ishmael Reed, Askia Touré, and Henry Dumas,
some of the collective's writers dipped into explorations of mysticism,
pan-African religions, and languages. Malinké Elliott, for example, frequently used surrealist imagery to treat themes such as death, desolation, and forbidden desires. In "The Dream Time," he wrote of the
"terrible secrets" whispered by "the great Phoenix, / Mother of the universe," who bequeaths to the poem's dreamer only death and "her great
murky sexuality."[24]

The city's diffuse literary scene also gave BAG's artists a number of opportunities to collaborate with poets who were not formally members of the collective, particularly the Watts Writers Workshop veterans Quincy Troupe and K. Curtis Lyle. Raised in a St. Louis family prominent in local political and athletic life, Troupe by the late 1960s was living and working in California. Though he detested his native city, feeling that the "sickness that exists there is terrifying," Troupe returned frequently to perform with musicians such as Julius Hemphill and Lester Bowie, occasionally bringing along several of his poet-colleagues from Los Angeles.[25] Lyle was a more permanent presence, and when he arrived to teach in Washington University's black studies program, he set off a new vibration in local poetry circles. Raised in the vibrant multicultural stew of Southern California, Lyle brought to St. Louis some of the flavor and cosmopolitanism of the West Coast. His poetry was undergirded by an affection for Latin American revolutionary poets such as Pablo Neruda, Octavio Paz, and Rubén Darío, and a strong interest in comparative religion, especially voudou, Sufism, gnosticism, and Kabala. After forming strong links with BAG artists, especially Hemphill, he began working with the group on a regular basis. In April 1970, the two staged an event at Washington University featuring Hemphill leading a nineteen-piece band and Lyle reading his long poem "Primeval Mother," composed for the occasion. Lyle also joined forces with BAG members for two more permanent documents: the eccentric experimental film entitled *The Orientation of Sweet Willie Rollbar*, and his collaboration with Hemphill on their 1971 album *The Collected Poem for Blind Lemon Jefferson*.[26]

The first project, strangely enough, was inspired by a Saturday-morning cartoon character. Watching *Tom Slick: Racer* on ABC, Lyle and Hemphill grew captivated by the show's crafty antagonist Sweet Willie Rollbar, "the meanest racer in racecar driving." The two reformatted the Rollbar character, using it as a pop culture stand-in for the signifying monkey of African American mythology, a trickster and unparalleled master of language and nuance. Lyle obtained funds from Washington University to plan an entire calendar of campus events revolving around this hybrid persona, before eventually drafting his film script for *The Orientation of Sweet Willie Rollbar*. Along with Hemphill and Malinké Elliott, Lyle shot a montage of unrelated scenes that veered from the farcical to the macabre to the purely bizarre. Episodes included a giant rat lecturing at the university's chapel; actors shambling down a country road in emulation of the phantasms in *Night of the Living Dead*; Baikida Carroll patrolling city streets outfitted as a gun-slinging cowboy; a bound and gagged actor being hurled from a moving Volkswagen into a vacant Pruitt-Igoe lot; and Elliott darting about the city's annual Veiled Prophet Parade sporting a robe constructed entirely from neckties. Bearing nothing akin to a legible plot, the script was glued together only by the pervasive presence of Sweet Willie Rollbar, here a devious joker, fantastic and indecipherable. The persona shifted throughout the film so that any of the characters—if possessed with charisma, survival skills, and command of language—could, in essence, embody Rollbar. With their film's brio and exuberant wit, Lyle and Hemphill aimed for a contrast with the ideological and aesthetic severity of much Black Arts Movement production.[27]

Coming off this project, Lyle and Hemphill next headed for the studio to record their *Collected Poem*. The duo album is a poetic cycle in homage to the legendary Texas-born blues singer Blind Lemon Jefferson, whose late 1920s recordings had influenced generations of blues, folk, and jazz musicians. Speaking, chanting, and half-singing the various poems, Lyle moves effortlessly between bluesy verbal riffs and fragmented images while Hemphill interpolates acerbic half-runs and crazed arpeggios on saxophones and flute. Voice and instruments echo and anticipate one another as Lyle reaches for metaphors reminiscent of what Léopold Sédar Senghor had dubbed African Surrealism, while simultaneously serving up a stew of vernacular street talk and arcane philosophy. In "Lemon's Brand-New-Shiny-Sky-Boat-Blues," for example, "the first day / the sun came out purple / circled the universe twice / swinging a black machete / beat-up the melody / and cut the thinning skin / from the earth's loins. . . ." At the same time, he spices the album with a helping of the dozens, firing repeated punch lines at "your mama" in a boisterous stream of sexual invective. Remembering Hemphill as "the ultimate collaborationist," Lyle explains the advice the older saxophonist served up during the recording sessions: "He took me aside one day and said, 'Look man, you're trying too hard.' I said, 'Well, you know man, I can't sing.' He said, 'Ray Charles can't sing!' He said, 'You just have to relax, and do what you do with confidence. . . . You believe in your poetry; *do* it that way.'" The finished product comes off very much as a pair of instruments playing off one another, Hemphill's reeds providing commentary as much as accompaniment and occasionally imitating the inflections of Lyle's speaking and chanting.[28]

The challenges posed by the new black poetry and theater riled many critics, and the nation's Black Arts poets, especially, faced constant questions over the legitimacy and quality of their work. Several writers working in these St. Louis circles anticipated such arguments, remaining particularly alive to the political implications at work in their writing and to the dangers of applying the often-alien standards of European modernism to African American poetry. Still, even practitioners such as Redmond and Troupe occasionally questioned the overt, simplified political rhetoric of some of their national colleagues. Speaking at Washington University, Troupe denounced those poets who "think that you are a stupid people, because they are saying that you cannot understand anything complex," while Redmond warned against the loss of poetic integrity in a "tradition of immediacy and transiency, political urgency, and newspaper headlines." Much of the work of BAG poets such as LeFlore and Rutlin inhabited that contested borderland between political engagement and aesthetic self-consciousness, without necessarily aiming for a negotiated settlement.[29]

⋗⟨⟩⋘

Like their counterparts in other media, many African American visual artists of the 1960s embraced forms of collective organization, inspired perhaps by groups like Romare Bearden's Spiral, founded out of concern for black identity in a white-dominated arts world, or AfriCOBRA in Chicago, established to promote local involvement and a recognition of the social responsibilities of artists. So it wasn't unusual for a group like BAG to attract a number of painters, and under the aegis of the Artists-in-Residence Program, Emilio Cruz directed a more-or-less formal visual arts department. But unlike the collective's other members, the visual artists worked in a generally non-performative medium, one that called for solitary labor rather than continual teamwork. Thus, BAG's visual arts component was perhaps the loosest of all of its divisions. Still, when not closeted away with brush and canvas, these artists assisted in all aspects of the organization's life: constructing elaborate sets for the dramatists, designing posters to advertise events, creating chapbook covers for poets, or rendering advice on visual aspects of multimedia performances. The group's painters contributed to the group's integrative approach in all sorts of ways, and several of them—especially Cruz, Oliver Jackson, and Manuel Hughes—would go on to distinguished careers in New York, California, and Europe. While in St. Louis, their work spanned a wide range of practices, from abstraction to assemblage to figurative distortion.[30]

Cruz and Jackson, as the chief visual artists associated with BAG, worked from very different premises, and these as well as differences in personality ensured a kind of edgy energy in this branch of the collective. Cruz drew on a wider variety of styles and modes, perhaps influenced by the diversity of his New York background, while Jackson's idea of the African continuum gave a sharp, clearly focused intellectual substance to his work. K. Curtis Lyle recalls that "it was almost like St. Louis was too small to have these two guys in the same town . . . [but] both of them loved Julius Hemphill, and he would be sort of the mediator. And Julius, although quite a quirky character himself, they both respected him because they loved the music." Again in this instance, [the group's musical core provided (the ground bass) upon which differences could build productively rather than canceling out one another.[31]]

Cruz came to St. Louis with a distinguished career already well advanced, and his multiplicity of influences sums up much of what BAG was all about. The painter was then forging an expressionist style that pulled from many cultures and mythologies, and he later pointed to a blend of elements in his work that included Latin American, Native

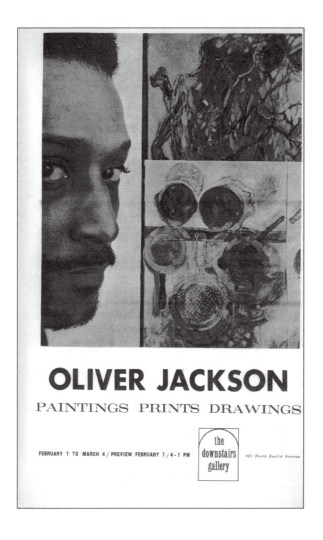

Flyer for an early exhibition by painter and BAG associate Oliver Jackson, held in 1965 at the Downstairs Gallery in St. Louis.

⟶⟩═◉ BAG ◉═⟨⟵

Courtesy Fine Arts Department, Saint Louis Public Library.

American, African, and Egyptian. For Cruz, working with the St. Louisans offered opportunities for refining a particular sense of artistic mission, a chance to "work with black people [on] our own way of saying things." As a teacher in the AIR Program, Cruz lectured at area colleges, designed mass-participation arts projects for children at neighborhood community centers, and drew on his East Coast connections in order to counsel students on careers in the arts. He describes his ongoing civil rights organizing in Missouri as "unsettling for my kind of work," disruptive to the long periods of solitude required for artistic creation. But despite his many activities, Cruz did exhibit several times during his eighteen months with the collective, capped by a one-man show of paintings and drawings at Webster College that garnered positive reviews perceptively noting the allusive quality of his work. There, he presented a series of abstractions that, in several cases, blended geometric African mask and shield motifs with brightly twisting, pop-influenced organic forms. More recently, Cruz has expanded his range of materials, as in his mid-1990s Homo Sapiens series. Here, the artist fashioned an extended series of skeletal, haunting human effigies saturated in beeswax and set in eight-foot-tall wooden panels, managing to distill, as one critic approvingly remarked, "a sense of mythic timelessness that stresses the continuity between life and death."[32]

The other eminence in the visual arts division was the local native Oliver Jackson. During the mid- and late 1960s, Jackson taught at area colleges and universities while mounting periodic displays of paintings, prints, and drawings in small downtown galleries. He was perhaps more influential within the group as a theorist rather than as a painter, and even as he moved to various parts of the country he retained a post as "artistic adviser" to BAG while returning frequently to collaborate with other members. In his own work, Jackson often stressed the "making of place" through visual media. He had begun to experiment with various visual axes on the surface of the canvas, trying to infuse a more potent energy into the free-floating space which painted and applied objects occupied. The grid became a stabilizing element, providing him with a more dynamic spatial orientation: "I . . . needed to do that in order

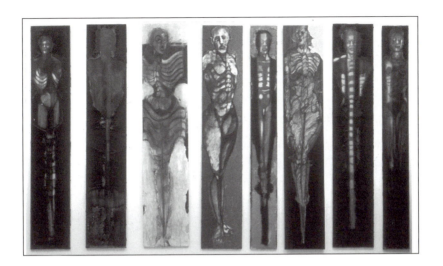

EMILIO CRUZ, FROM HOMO SAPIENS SERIES, 1990–96, CHARCOAL, BEESWAX, SAND,
AND OIL PAINT ON WOOD. FIGURES 96" x 24".

⇥≡◉≡⊙≡⊷

Reproduction courtesy Emilio Cruz.

to understand a kind of field relationship," he later said. "It was a question of mechanics, to activate the surface and to be activated in a more clear way by the canvas itself." Here, figures and colors often shifted in quasi-cinematic fashion as they moved across the grids.[33]

One of Jackson's most ambitious projects during the period was his Sharpeville series, inspired by the March 1960 massacre of peaceful demonstrators in apartheid South Africa. Composed of seven large figurative paintings, the series drew on a variety of techniques and materials, including the application of rags, ribbons, and pieces of metal scraps to the painted surface. Through recent travels to Africa, Jackson had become aware of the validity of a wider range of artistic materials, and he began to draw more heavily from the symbols and visual vocabulary of traditional African art. He explains, "As a result of thinking about the African Continuum and what's possible to use, I was thinking, 'Why can't you put rags, or why can't you put metal, on the surface with paint?'. . . When you look at the African tradition of visuals, all kinds of materials are mixed, and so I was freed." And while critics often speculate over the influence of jazz on Jackson's work, he has always tried to nuance the issue, noting that the audio and the visual are "distinct languages, but they have some things that are common. In other words, in a painting we have to take into account, literally, the two-dimensional space. . . . You have to know how to make its presence underlie the work. And musicians—it was clear how they approached the space, the space that's not yet made into music, the way they open the space, how they take the space." This attitude toward art as potential energy, as a kind of anticipatory stillness whether in the temporal or the spatial dimension, drove much of the collective's performative as well as visual work.[34]

Not all BAG visual artists leaned toward the abstract. The painter Manuel Hughes, for example, had attended Sumner High School with several of the group's musicians, and during the BAG years he seemed to be searching for his own manner of expression. Hughes frequently took his cues from Jackson, whom he described as a mentor. Unlike Jackson and Cruz, though, Hughes often chose subject matter more explicitly and recognizably tied to the particular clashes of the

Oliver Jackson, *Sharpeville II*, 1970, mixed media on canvas, 84" x 120".

—⊱⋈⊙ʙᴀɢ⊙⋈⊰—

Reproduction courtesy of the artist and Anne Kohs & Associates.

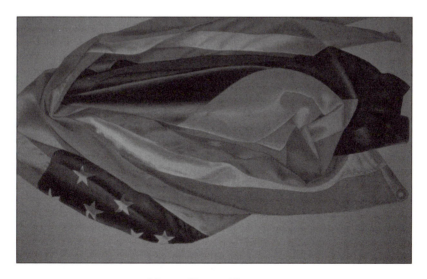

Manuel Hughes, *Flags*, 1972.

—⊱⋈⊙ʙᴀɢ⊙⋈⊰—

Reproduction courtesy Manuel Hughes.

decade. Some of his works were plotted from contemporary newspaper photographs of lynchings in the South, while in a series of paintings entitled Guardians of the Golden Thighs Hughes reached for explosive images of sexuality and race—depicting, for instance, a policeman guarding an obese white woman. In various other showings, he presented black and white sketches of African American civil rights leaders and a series of larger-than-life self-portraits bearing titles such as *Chitlin' Eater, Me Myself,* and *Nigger* that aimed to manipulate and deconstruct stereotypes. Hughes comments, "Everyone was focused on the political struggle during the late '60s and early '70s. So that was the focus for most of my work. . . . I was doing black imagery to reinforce what black people were feeling at that time."[35]

The modernist argument about the "purity" of art—often applied to music in particular—also affected critical response to the visual artists associated with BAG. And though the abstract-expressionist monopoly on critical thinking was breaking up under the assaults of pop, assemblage, and other new interests and techniques, the standards applied to these artists' work often revealed underlying assumptions based on deeply rooted suspicions about the relationship between art and social context. One local reviewer, for example, wrote of Jackson and Hughes that they are "visibly aware of their blackness in their work but also transcend it most completely in the pursuit of the purer elements of art." Interpreted this way, race and identity get left behind on the high road to aesthetic purity, and the formal elements of art serve as a kind of grand staircase out of the mire rather than as vehicles for the expression of social vision. Against this type of formalism, Jackson later offered his own view of how one should connect social engagement and aesthetics, explaining that the "responsibility of the artist is to give back—not a reflection, but a sense of clarity about the spiritual state."[36]

⊷⊨◎⊕⁂⊜⊪⊷

With its rich and varied menu of mixed-media productions, the BAG collective firmly established itself as the city's edgiest, hippest performance group, the latest word in avant-garde presentation. A few audience members apparently came along for a sort of secondhand glamour or revolutionary chic. Redmond recalls, "You could go there and dig BAG, and a lot of people were afraid not to do it, because intellectually, they wanted to appear to be on the cutting edge." As one might expect, though, even nominal allies occasionally raised disapproving eyebrows. Reviews in the city's black newspapers often seemed obsessed with the group's "profanity," and according to Oliver Lake, a poetry recitation at a community college even drew a call to the police from a spectator aggrieved by some four-letter words.[37]

Spurred, no doubt, by incidents such as these, many of the group's artists came to find St. Louis drearily provincial. But despite indignation among a few and a general indifference toward the performing arts in the local black press, the hybrid performances often drew spirited and raucous crowds, mixed in both kind and motive. Generally, the seats were filled with audiences composed of working-class and professional African Americans along with a smattering of white students and a few establishment figures. Area organizers and activists often frequented the shows, and prominent out-of-town artists passed through on occasion. Playwright and poet Sonia Sanchez once turned up to catch a staging of one of her scripts. Another night Barry Commoner, the renowned environmentalist and future third-party presidential candidate, dropped by and delivered a finger-wagging lecture over BAG's notoriously behind-schedule curtain times. Though audiences were usually at least two-thirds black, Malinké Elliott later described the performances as the only place in the city "where you had blacks and whites communing together, enjoying each other, understanding where we each were coming from."[38]

If the drama onstage was but a continuation of the larger social drama playing on the streets outside, then the goal here was to transform observers into participants in both arenas. Hoping to erase that traditional separation of spectator from stage, artists frequently gave talks or hosted discussions after presentations; at other times, poets broke from their verse to riff with the audience on recent happenings, delivering interactive and opinionated roundups of the week's headlines.

Actors also encouraged audiences to augment the drama itself, and viewers would sometimes oblige—bantering with performers on stage, spontaneously applauding, or leaving their seats to mill about in the aisles. Baikida Carroll characterizes the performances as a "gentle revolution," explaining that spectators "could lay claim by merely experiencing it from the safety of the audience perspective." But intensity rather than safety was more often the read from the stalls. One young white fan looks back on a BAG performance as "one of the most intense musical and artistic experiences I have ever had. I sat transfixed in my chair, torn between the awe of the art I witnessed and a basic response to flee. I was a white man among some very justifiably angry black artists and their audience. It was not easy to remember that I was also their audience." Many such "outsiders" combined enthusiasm and sincerity with a touch of naïveté in their readings of rage in the performances. Although the shows could sometimes leave spectators squirming in their seats, the performers aimed as much for engagement as they did for confrontation.[39]

While BAG's integrative approach to the arts may have been the group's greatest strength, ongoing tensions and competition continued to simmer among the various arts divisions. Vincent Terrell recounts that in the collective's early period "the collaboration and the camaraderie we had would supercede our differences," but as time passed, "the artistic rivalries within the group started to mushroom." Alongside intermittent aesthetic differences, members fiercely debated issues such as whether to put commercial enterprises into the BAG building, with some advocating this as a pragmatic way to pull in additional revenue, and others contending that the tactic would adulterate the purity of the collective's social and artistic mission. More often, disputes came back to questions over the degree to which the group should cooperate with white artists. For example, after Alan and Joanna Nichols had led a handful of workshops with the group's theater wing, BAG's board of directors overruled Elliott on his use of these teachers, declaring that white actors had no business training the organization's casts.[40]

Whatever passing contention there might have been within the group, it paled alongside the tensions between BAG and its funding agencies. The Inner City Arts Project had temporarily linked the collective with the agendas and resources of liberal philanthropists and the municipal government. But from the start, BAG had an ambiguous relationship to the seats of civic authority. As the decade progressed, public and private funding agencies of every kind had begun to fret over the notion that their funds were feeding the coffers of leftist, radical organizations. In a social drama played out in dozens of locations around the country, liberals hesitantly invested in Black Arts ventures, only to yank their dollars when performances took on a political edge. Likewise in St. Louis, BAG's alliance with its funding organizations grew strained. While the Artists-in-Residence Program's architects had envisioned dispatching cultural missionaries to the inner city, BAG's artists tended to cast themselves as cultural provocateurs. As time wore on, the discrepancy in motives became increasingly evident, and the awkward dance between liberal reformism and Black Arts institution building eventually broke down. "Because we never gave in," Baikida Carroll explains, the project's financial backers "labeled us 'artistic radicals' and our funding capabilities took a nosedive."[41]

Michael Newton, the local Arts & Education Council chief who had originally sold the Rockefeller and Danforth Foundations on the Inner City Arts Project, remained a strong advocate. He spent late summer 1969 trying anxiously to secure a two-year extension of the grant money that had established the program. But soon after the AIR Program's inception, the collective's brand of community involvement, its socially charged poetry and theater, and some members' direct activism had begun to alarm the philanthropists underwriting the program. The Danforth Foundation, headquartered in St. Louis and closely interknit with the city's corporate and political elites, tended to be on the receiving end of complaints. Unbeknownst to BAG's leaders, that foundation soon questioned the initiative's efficacy and goals in a flurry of internal memos. Meanwhile, as city officials in expensive suits toured BAG's building and beamed for the newspaper cameras, several of the group's leaders couldn't help but feel that the AIR Program was being used for political grandstanding, reinforcing the notions of paternalism that they sought to evade. Especially rankling for the BAG members was the fact that they were discouraged from displaying their political views in their programming. By mid-1969, neither side was finding the existing arrangement particularly congenial.[42]

Aside from their annoyance that the local Model Cities Agency had reneged on its long-standing promise to contribute funds, administrators at the Danforth Foundation had developed three related criticisms of the Inner City Arts Project, but especially of the AIR-BAG segment run by Julius Hemphill. First of all, the foundation soured on the program because, in the view of its president, Merrimon Cuninggim, working relations were not established between the AIR Program and Katherine Dunham's PATC, the other component of the overarching Inner City Arts Project. Given the constant interchange between the two organizations, Cuninggim's comment likely reflected annoyance that the AIR Program component had ended up running under BAG's jurisdiction rather than under Dunham's, as had originally been anticipated. Indeed, the funders had grown to see Dunham and the younger St. Louis artists in very different lights: a Rockefeller Foundation vice president concluded that Dunham "represents an older tradition" while Hemphill "represents a newer breed of social reform and militant action." If civic elites saw Dunham's PATC as a way to strengthen moderate forces in the face of creeping radicalism, BAG's program only set off alarm bells.[43]

Second, while BAG's performances invigorated the urban community in which the group operated, their tone and content increasingly exasperated the Danforth administrators. Dismissing Newton's glowing evaluations as "starry-eyed," Cuninggim argued that some of the productions "have been more notable for their shock value than their cultural value." One of his consultants reported that the artists were "more interested in social reform than art," citing their involvement in demonstrations and in the city's public housing rent strike. And third, the artists' focus on the black community rather than interracial programming irritated Cuninggim, who claimed that the group's concentration on black youth "is not particularly aimed at Danforth's definition of urban problems," and even tended to "exacerbate white-black relations, and increase rather than diminish tension." Though BAG's artists did attract interracial audiences and worked closely with white artists through the Human Arts Ensemble, the group's leaders strongly adhered to the Black Arts principle of focusing on their own community. But Cuninggim's criticism also shows the contradictory hurdles that had been set for the program: artists-in-residence were charged with bringing blacks and whites together in "interracial understanding," and at the same time were directed to focus their efforts on the Model Cities target area, which was over 85 percent black. The program set forth by the AIR-BAG group apparently was damned either way it turned.[44]

Following internal deliberations, in fall 1969 the Rockefeller and Danforth Foundations refused to renew the Inner City Arts Project's funding. While none of the Danforth Foundation's complaints was formally communicated to BAG's leaders, most members had their own guesses about the motivations for the cutoff of funds. Emilio Cruz, for one, notes that "the last thing, I'm sure, that they wanted me to do was the civil rights activity." The experience with the Inner City Arts Project left many participants with a bad taste in their mouths. Learning only years later of the Danforth Foundation's internal criticisms, Elliott dubbed the charge that BAG exacerbated racial tensions to be a "typical reaction of the white power-structure establishment [to] a black group which was trying to involve itself in issues of its community." In any case, with no major funding prospects on the horizon, the group quickly found itself in a precarious financial position. Meanwhile, across the river in East St. Louis, the end of the initiative forced Dunham to reduce drastically her numbers of teachers and students.[45]

By early 1970, the collective had completely run through its $100,000 of original grant money. Still, the foundation grants hadn't created BAG, and neither did the loss of the grants destroy the organization. The artists voted to continue offering free classes to the community for as long as possible, an operation that they managed to sustain, albeit at a reduced scale, until early 1972. After taking the reins as BAG's new chairman in summer 1970, Ajulé Rutlin explored alternative sources of funding, though his advances to most institutions were rebuffed. Some, such as the Ford Foundation, were reticent because of long-standing views that such funding could hinder the establishment of a long-term financial base in the local community. At other meetings, Rutlin says, "it came out that they thought we were too political, and what we were doing crossed the bar line, so to speak, from creativity and artistic work into propaganda." After losing its funding, the group had set the ambitious goal of raising $65,000 for the upcoming year, which would have allowed it to retain nineteen part-time instructors and employees. Though BAG never came close to meeting this figure, under Rutlin's leadership the organization did tap into a more informal network of financial support, cultivating ties with the local arts council, community chest leaders, and individual patrons from the black middle class. Carol Marshall of the Human Arts Ensemble dipped into her trust fund to sponsor individual projects, while the owner of BAG's building allowed the group to remain in the warehouse without paying rent.[46]

Still, 1970 proved to be a pivotal year for the organization. Many of BAG's artists began trickling out of St. Louis, slowing the group's dizzying performance schedule. With her salaried position terminated, the dance department's director, Georgia Collins, packed her bags, while Emilio Cruz, having earned a fellowship from the National Endowment for the Arts, took up a professorship at the School of the Art Institute of Chicago. And even those who hadn't been on AIR Program salaries started to leave. In a blow to BAG's theater wing, the two stage directors departed in the middle of the year. Vincent Terrell left for Boston to launch a reconfigured version of his TSOCC Players there, and his deputy in the troupe, LeRoi Shelton, followed Terrell to Massachusetts the following year. Malinké Elliott, meanwhile, was feeling increasingly bogged down by the administrative chores of his post as BAG's executive director. And as the tides of student protest crested at Washington University in spring 1970, pressures mounted on antiwar activists associated with the school, leaving Elliott more and more uneasy with the unstable political situation. When student protestors burned the campus ROTC building to the ground in May—on the day following the shootings of demonstrators at Kent State University—many feared an imminent crackdown by university and law-enforcement authorities. In the wake of these events, Elliott left the United States to study theater in Denmark and Sweden on a string of Danforth Foundation fellowships.[47]

The collapse of the funding program and the departure of many artists hit some departments harder than others. While the music department survived virtually unscathed, by spring of 1970 the visual arts department had ceased to operate, and the dance and theater departments had become nearly dormant. For a moment, it seemed that after only eighteen months of operation, the group might fold. The changes were not negative in result, however. In fact, the dispersion of artists from the St. Louis area allowed some of BAG's members to extend their performance network. By 1970, Oliver Jackson, Eugene Redmond, and Quincy Troupe had all taken teaching positions in Ohio, and several of the group's artists traveled to Oberlin College and Ohio University to visit their friends and give performances. Back in St. Louis, BAG's close ties with the PATC kept the depleted dance and theater departments afloat, and an influx of new talent soon re-energized the collective. Shortly after Georgia Collins's departure, the dancer Luisah Teish (originally Cathy Allen) took over BAG's dance department, while the director Muthal Naidoo headed up the theater wing. These recruits brought new flavors and directions to the collective and proved the organization's resilience.[48]

Teish's artistic inspiration came not from the professional ballet world of the older Collins, but rather from her interests in Afro-Caribbean and West African religious rituals, dance traditions, and cultural lore. During her childhood in New Orleans and her high school and college days in California and Oregon, she had delved into the black voudou traditions of Haiti and Louisiana. It was Katherine Dunham's close ties with Haiti that attracted Teish to East St. Louis for study, and the PATC's large number of Haitian artists allowed her to immerse herself in the dance and religious practices of the black Caribbean. Shortly after arriving in the area, Teish also joined St. Louis's Temple of Amun-Ra, a worship center established in 1919 by Paul Nathaniel Johnson, the founder and prophet of the Fahamme sect. A black religious order focused on racial uplift, Fahamme claims to reveal the sacred truths of ancient Egypt, Ethiopia, and Arabia, teaching that the black "Kamites" who founded these civilizations are the oldest race and are the true progenitors of Islam, Hinduism, and Christianity. In the late 1960s, St. Louis's tiny Fahamme temple functioned as a cultural as well as religious center, offering a food service program, martial arts training, and a Fahamme newspaper. When Teish migrated across the Mississippi River to become BAG's new choreographer and dance teacher, she reoriented the dance company's aesthetic, weaving in strands of mysticism, Egyptology, and her own versions of African rituals.[49]

But ritual could be effective only if it connected the transcendent to the commonplace, African roots to American branches. From her encounters with voudou and Fahamme, Teish distilled ideas about the ways that the histories, rituals, and mythologies of the African diaspora could integrate with family and community life in the here and now. Seeing BAG as a potential vehicle for her theories, she inserted elements of spirituality and religious ritual into the group's arts programming, hoping to wipe away the sharp dividing lines between the sacred and the secular. This kind of work served as a prelude and catalyst for Teish's later career as a writer, folklorist, and ritual consultant in Oakland, where she founded the School of Ancient Mysteries and Sacred Arts Center. In her time with BAG, Teish foregrounded issues of gender, as well. As a student-activist at Reed College in Portland, she had reacted strongly against men who "decided that my most important job was to have babies and teach those babies African culture." Consequently, she injected a strong feminist consciousness into BAG's dance wing, derived in part from her readings of pan-African religions and mythology. Later, she explained her attempts to highlight "women's natural power"— claiming that her work "involves reclaiming symbols of that forgotten power and integrating them into my rituals." And she tried hard to overcome the strictly gendered conception of dance that made it difficult to recruit men for her company, contending that "the idea that it is unmanly to dance is absurd. Brothers must stop adopting attitudes that are not based or useful in our culture."[50]

Under Teish's lead, the dormant BAG dance troupe was reactivated, first as the Primitive Dance Group and more permanently as the Omawali Dance & Drum Ensemble. It quickly recruited several dozen

Raised in New Orleans and Los Angeles, Luisah Teish moved to
East St. Louis to study dance with Katherine Dunham. She coordinated BAG's
Omawali Dance & Drum Ensemble beginning in 1970.

Photograph, 1970, courtesy Portia Hunt.

dancers and ten percussionists and again began regular performances and weekly classes for the community. Taking seriously the goal of nurturing young artists, the company brought many high school students into its fold. Like the musicians, the dancers occasionally ventured outside the city for collaborations with artists such as Pharaoh Sanders, Leon Thomas, and AACM saxophonist Kalaparusha Maurice McIntyre. Though still an integral part of BAG, the Omawali Ensemble became semiautonomous, with strong ties to the PATC. The troupe leaned heavily on the technique that Katherine Dunham had codified from her own anthropological research into Caribbean dance. To this, the dancers added a strong dose of improvisation, along with the angular contours of Martha Graham's modern dance technique and movements derived from karate and yoga. Writing for a local magazine, Teish contrasted the style with ballet, explaining that "it allows for total freedom of movement, and a fiery, flowering grace and beauty." The dancers frequently recruited BAG's musicians to create jazz improvisations that matched their own choreography, costumes, and masks, all of which heightened the sense of theatricality for which they were striving.[51]

The Omawali group emphasized percussion as well, adding a contingent of drummers, headed by Billy Ingram, to the BAG family of ensembles. The percussionists took up the jembe, a West African drum originally used to accompany dancing in precolonial village contexts. The jembe had vaulted into prominence in the United States through a series of hit recordings by the Nigerian drummer Babatunde Olatunji, and the Omawali drummers used the instrument to provide rhythmic accompaniments paired to the pace of the dancers. The presence of Senegalese drummer Mor Thiam as a resident artist at the PATC provided the ensemble's percussionists the opportunity to study with a jembe master. Thiam later observed that, beginning with his first concert at Forest Park, his drumming "sent a message to militant leaders" who began incorporating Thiam into their events. Likewise, the Omawali drum contigent drew in politically active St. Louisans such as Kalimu Endesha, who several years later helped found the local grassroots Organization for Black Struggle. One of the most popular dances developed under Teish was *Chaka*, a work narrating the life of the nineteenth-century South African warrior who forged a Zulu empire. Performed at the BAG building with A. J. Dickerson, Sr., in the title role, *Chaka* excited audiences with its volatile combination of ritual dance, virtuosic drumming, and violent hand-to-hand combat, culminating in a spectacular death scene.[52]

While Teish revived the dance department, the drama workshop reaccelerated under the direction of Muthal Naidoo, the only non–African American ever to join the collective. A South African woman of Indian ethnicity, Naidoo emerged from a vibrant Indic theater movement that sprang up in the city of Durban during the early 1960s. The nation's apartheid regime, although most brutal toward black South Africans, also imposed racially discriminatory policies on those of Indian descent, and so Naidoo and her colleagues forged their community theater projects under constant pressures from ruling-party functionaries. Along with writers and actors such as Ronnie Govender and Welcome Msomi, she had founded the Durban Academy of Theatre Arts, though that company split when its multiracial audiences attracted hostile attention from the authorities, ultimately leading to stricter enforcement of the country's apartheid laws. Undaunted, Naidoo and Govender went on to form the seminal Shah Theatre Academy, which performed modern and original works, fostered indigenous dramatists, and helped to establish the cultural boycott. In 1965, Naidoo migrated to the United States on a Fulbright scholarship to earn a doctorate in drama at Indiana University in Bloomington. After directing that university's Black Theatre Workshop, she was hired by Katherine Dunham in fall 1969 to develop a theater component at the PATC.[53]

Unable to round up enough actors to form a permanent drama contingent in East St. Louis, Naidoo joined BAG at Portia Hunt's behest at the end of 1969. Following the departure of Elliott and Terrell, she took over the group's drama workshop, renaming it the Black Experience Theatre. Naidoo saw strong consonances between the St. Louis artists' struggles and her own experiences under apartheid. "My friends at BAG and I had suffered the same kinds of damaging discrimination, and we needed to empower ourselves," she explains. And her background developing community theater in Durban jibed well with the tenets of BAG.

In an interview with the *Post-Dispatch*, she scoffed at actors who "perform little flighty plays which have nothing to do with anything real," arguing that her St. Louis troupe emerged "from the community" and presented dramas "related to its existence and needs." Under Naidoo, the company treated themes with local resonance, as in its improvisational theater piece *Project Slavery*, which excoriated the government neglect behind unhealthy living conditions at the city's public housing projects. Still, as the only member of BAG who was not black, Naidoo felt that she would be unable to convey the African American experience. Instead of writing her own scripts, she relied on group improvisations and encouraged the actors to create their own plays. She also built on the syncretic impulses already at work in the group by adapting European forms and structures to the demands of the African American heritage, as Elliott had done before her. By developing subthemes acted out behind the performance, her actors worked to make the unconscious explicit in what Portia Hunt calls "a meta-analysis, a performance inside a performance."[54]

This second wave of artists rejuvenated the collective. After the lull in activities, the reformatted Black Artists' Group kicked off a new weekend series at their recently redecorated building in September 1970, playing to large and enthusiastic crowds. Teish led the dance department, Ajulé Rutlin's Children of the Sun delivered poetry and a "survey of recent news from the papers and streets," and BAG's musicians joined in a memorial to John Coltrane. As the centerpiece of the program, Naidoo directed Portia Hunt in the one-woman play *Sister Son/ji*, by Sonia Sanchez. The short but demanding role called for the actress to transform herself from an old woman to her younger self, and onward through several phases of life. By the end of the play, she has come full circle, commenting along the way on issues of gender in the black community, the explosive quest for black independence from the majority white culture, and the rejection of integration as a useful goal. Hunt's rendering of the role was an immediate success, and she reprised her performance in a variety of venues through the metropolitan area.[55]

The new series marked the start of a sustained burst of activity. Through late 1970 and most of 1971, Teish and Naidoo maintained an

Muthal Naidoo, who cofounded the Shah Theatre Academy in Durban, South Africa, and later became director for BAG's drama workshop in St. Louis.

Photograph by Ted Dargan/ © 1970, St. Louis Post-Dispatch.

impressive pace of dance and theater performances. Among their many collaborations, they adapted portions of *The Autobiography of Malcolm X* into an improvisational dance-drama; revived *Clara's Ole Man*, adding a psychological element where characters performed with superego "masks" removed; and presented works such as Ben Caldwell's *Mission Accomplished* and Wole Soyinka's *The Trials of Brother Jero*, both of which treat the theme of religious exploitation and its palpable effects on the community. Their events often doubled as benefits for organizations such as the pacifist American Friends Service Committee and the St. Louis Committee on Africa, a group working to foster cultural ties among black people around the world.[56]

As the theater and dance troupes brought their performances into the city's public spaces, they further blurred the lines between performance and protest, arts and agitation. And this impulse meshed well with Naidoo's investigations into the improvisational comedy of *commedia dell' arte*. Under her direction, the acting company adapted the stock characters and topical satire of *commedia* to a series of guerrilla theater presentations in St. Louis. They would first prepare a basic scenario at their Washington Boulevard headquarters, before moving out unannounced to locations around the city. On the Fourth of July holiday in 1970, for example, the actors and dancers planned a piece called "The Declaration of Independence," intended to point out the discrepancies between the egalitarian language of that document and the realities of the black experience in the United States. Participants began the sketch with chains on their limbs to represent the period of slavery, but by the end had wrapped those same chains around their heads as a symbol of a "psychological slavery" that still persisted. In another skit, actors donned white cloth masks and impersonated eighteenth-century revolutionaries battling British soldiers during the American War of Independence. "The idea," Naidoo remembers, "was to show that slavery had not ended, and the pursuit of life, liberty, and happiness was the prerogative of white people."[57]

The group first tested these sketches at the Saint Louis Zoo in Forest Park, popping up seemingly from nowhere to stage the pieces before a startled crowd. They then headed east to a more symbolic location—downtown's Old Courthouse, a former slave market and the site where Dred Scott had unsuccessfully petitioned for his freedom in 1846. On the eastern steps of the courthouse, looking down over the Mississippi River, the troupe repeated its street plays as part of a "Love and Unity Rally" organized by members of ACTION. Following a set of speeches demanding economic justice, a small group of observers listened to poems that Eugene Redmond declaimed through a bullhorn and watched sketches and interpretive dances from the BAG contingent. The group's final play ended with the actors flinging the American flag to the ground as a symbol of oppression, while reporters and photographers clustered round. The BAG performers drew applause and laughter from the crowd assembled on the steps and, as the *Post-Dispatch* reported, "bewildered stares from passing motorists."[58]

For a short while, this flurry of performances almost matched the pace maintained during BAG's height in 1969. But by 1971, it became more and more apparent that the center could not hold. As time passed, the Black Artists' Group as a formal organization moved from axis to circumference. The numerous offshoots that it had spawned—the Omawali Ensemble, the Black Experience Theatre, the Human Arts Ensemble, Children of the Sun, the various musical groups—began operating more independently, and members devoted increasing amounts of energy to these spin-off projects. Two of the collective's key members, Julius Hemphill and Oliver Jackson, pursued just such a project in BAG's later years. Along with the poet Michael Harper, a Brooklyn native who had recently attracted national notice for his collection *Dear John, Dear Coltrane*, they created the group the African Continuum to pursue a multimedia agenda outside the confines of BAG. Though short-lived, the trio drew on talent from BAG and the PATC to present one of the richest large-scale performance events of the period, the Images: Sons/Ancestors concert held at Powell Symphony Hall in February 1971.[59]

If the Images performance marked one of the high points for the St. Louis artists, then BAG's Song for a Fallen Warrior concert later that year seems, in retrospect, to have presaged the group's dissolution, though no one then could have known that it would be one of the last major presentations. The collective's multimedia festivals often had centered on specific events of the day, and in September 1971 these culminated in a memorial celebration honoring George Jackson, the Soledad Brother who had been slain the previous month by white prison guards at California's San Quentin State Prison. Many in the Black Power Movement cast Jackson's life as heroic and his death as sacrificial. In a program intended, as they announced, to "give honor to our great hero-warrior," Oliver Lake, Baikida Carroll, and Lester Bowie joined the Berea Messenger Singers in the Jackson tribute at BAG's Washington Boulevard building. Interspersed with the musical offerings, Ajulé Rutlin delivered an overview of Jackson's life and writings, a biting critique of the American prison system, and a poem dedicated to Jackson's memory and his enormous psychic impact on the movement. "Your legend reached us slowly," Rutlin intoned, "rumbling across the heavy air breaking / ominously like The florid thunder / of the troubled western skys." With only several dozen spectators in attendance, the artists must have been presenting the selections as much for themselves as for their audience. As the program drew to a close, the musicians gathered their instruments and moved into the street to serenade the neighborhood.[60]

Over a bustling four years filled with countless collaborations, multimedia productions, classes, and exhibitions, the group's artists developed an evolving set of aesthetic practices that sometimes jostled against and occasionally even contradicted one another. But at their best, they created an atmosphere in which it was possible to explore the range of artistic media, while often achieving the "sense of clarity about the spiritual state" that Jackson later urged. Even as they attracted the ire of civic elites, the group's members maintained a constant and creative engagement with the surrounding neighborhoods of North St. Louis. And yet, fair or not to this remarkable range of activity across the arts and to the complexity of the organization as a whole, BAG's music would always be its most striking calling card to the outside world.[61]

Muthal Naidoo (center) directs a 1970 rehearsal for *Volunteered Slavery*, a BAG adaptation of materials from *The Autobiography of Malcolm* X. Portia Hunt (right) plays a white woman trying to lure Malcolm away from Laura, played here by Frank Scott and Pat Mountjoy.

⤙⟶⟩⊜⟨BAG⟩⊜⟨⟵⤚

Photograph by Ted Dargan/ © 1970, St. Louis Post-Dispatch.

CHAPTER 5

CREATIVE ADAPTATION: NEW SOUNDS, NEW INSTITUTIONS

In February 1972 Julius Hemphill lifted up his alto sax in a local St. Louis studio like an explorer might pick up his pen to write: reliving the journey past and plotting out the route ahead. His Images: Sons/Ancestors concert twelve months earlier had marked an essential stage in Hemphill's expedition, a watershed event where "all that I had learned along with others there came to a culmination." For the Images event, Hemphill's friend Donald Suggs, an oral surgeon and avid collector of African art, had loaned several artworks from the Dogon ethnic group of West Africa. These pieces fascinated Hemphill, and in the weeks following the concert, he began to research the cosmology, religions, and cultures of the region. Paging through a magazine on African art, Hemphill came across an article describing Dogon dance ceremonies, performed for funerals and death anniversaries using large wooden painted masks. While Hemphill had no intention of trying to reproduce Dogon music, he was attracted by what he thought of as the "static" quality of the accompaniment to the dances, a repetition that induces changes in the participant or observer rather than in the music. Hemphill named the record *Dogon A.D.*, in reference to the Dogon people's "adapted dance," in which they had progressively adapted ceremonies for presentation to Western visitors, altering the costumes and appropriating elements of European choreography. He later explained his gesture as "a small contribution toward their control of their stuff," staking out a vision of cultural ownership and authenticity in Africa that paralleled BAG's mission in the United States.[1]

The recording date seemed headed for disaster, however, when several musicians skipped the session. Three other musicians did turn up: trumpeter Baikida Carroll, drummer Philip Wilson of the AACM, and Abdul Wadud, a cellist Hemphill had met while performing at Oberlin College. Such is the serendipity of art that, despite the depleted

JULIUS HEMPHILL, 1969.

Photograph courtesy Portia Hunt.

"POINT FROM WHICH CREATION BEGINS"

lineup and some malfunctioning recording equipment, the four musicians produced an almost accidental classic. On the title track, Hemphill layers harmonically dense improvisational sorties over Wilson's terse, rocking 11/16 beat and Wadud's unrelenting arco cello riff, himself alternating between brawny, driving blues riffs and startling flares into overblown squeaks, whinnies, and overtones that wriggle eel-like across the accompaniment. The young Carroll, his conceptual influence moored in the modal work of Freddie Hubbard and other post-bop trumpeters, adds short explosions, muted drones, unexpectedly truncated phrases, and insistently repeated notes. On "The Painter," an homage to Oliver Jackson, Hemphill picks up his flute to exhibit a more lyrical, chamberlike side, following a taut, bop-ish head with gauzy, minimalist explorations of sound. With its deft integration of avant-garde practices and jazz tradition, the record marks the culmination of three-and-a-half years of careful experimentation.[2]

But even after all his efforts through the BAG collective, Hemphill could find no outlets for the distribution of his music. So he did what the group had done all along: made his own way without a map. He started his own record label, Mbari Records, and sat in his LaClede Town house hand-addressing dozens of sample copies to radio stations and music magazines. Through the 1970s, the hard-to-find LP acquired cult status through the more progressive reaches of the jazz world, earning esteem among a wide swath of critics and musicians.

In a sense, that February day in the studio, with the malfunctioning equipment and the truant musicians, stands proxy for the individual creative energy released and replenished by BAG. The *Dogon A.D.* project turned out to be emblematic of the collective's musical program, embodying both an economic and an aesthetic rejoinder to the era's social and musical challenges. By releasing the album on his own Mbari Records, Hemphill extended the logic of the BAG collective, responding to the economic impasse facing black experimentalists by creating an outlet that bypassed an often indifferent record industry. And with the music on *Dogon A.D.*, Hemphill and his sidemen documented BAG's ongoing mission to unite a diverse range of black musical forms into a medium that critic Robert Palmer later called a "multiplicity of incantations, symbols, and ritual actions which express . . . the unity of one world of black culture." Through both their institution-building and their musical forays, the organization's musicians crafted an aesthetic that lived in dynamic interaction with the social settings and musical traditions in which they were embedded.[3]

⇥ ❂ BAG ❂ ⇤

Soon after its genesis, the collective had pulled in the city's A-list of young, black, progressive musicians. With fourteen musicians as formal members and about twice that number as frequent participants, the group offered "a chance to work out all our musical fantasies," as Oliver Lake later explained. Players banded together in all manner of combinations for specific projects, while the BAG big band—conducted successively by Hamiet Bluiett and Baikida Carroll—provided a center of gravity, a space for members to congregate and share ideas on a weekly basis. And whatever the fare on offer at BAG, it had nourished an impressive growth spurt in the collective's young musicians, most of them now in their late twenties. But as they flexed their individual and group muscles, the strength and agility of their music was being played out in a steadily emptying stadium. The broad-based national popularity of jazz had entered a long slide in the mid-1960s, and with record contracts drying up and decent gigs becoming more elusive, Hemphill, Lake, and their circle must have been dismayed at the especially gloomy prospects for experimental jazz. The choice was stark: either give up the game or reach new listeners. To do the latter, BAG's musicians first had to confront the deepening economic challenges faced by jazz musicians in general.[4]

Over the course of the decade, national audiences for the music had begun to evaporate. Musicians looked around to see performance venues shutting their doors and album sales declining. For one thing, changes in the state of America's urban neighborhoods worked to the detriment of a live performance–based music like jazz. The urban renewal of the 1950s had flattened scores of mixed-use black neighborhoods that once hosted vibrant club scenes, from San Francisco's Fillmore District

TRUMPET SECTION AT A BAG BIG BAND REHEARSAL, C. 1969.

Photograph courtesy Baikida Carroll.

to Detroit's Paradise Valley to St. Louis's Mill Creek Valley. On its heels, the urban evisceration, rush to the suburbs, and departure of the black middle classes of the 1960s further drained away potential clientele for local music clubs. Meanwhile, following John Coltrane's untimely death in 1967, the jazz record business entered a slump that would last through the mid-1970s. Competition from other musics and media ripped away at jazz's market segment, as young white listeners gravitated to album rock and young black listeners to funk, soul, and Motown. Bigger labels, which had slowed their recording pace for jazz in general, grew particularly skittish about signing avant-garde musicians and cultivated increasingly conservative catalogues. Even Impulse Records, which had great success with Coltrane's challenging late-period output, experienced mostly dismal sales with the tenor star's former sidemen, a track record that seemed to confirm executives' presumption that innovative black music simply wasn't salable.[5]

This retreat to placid familiarity accelerated with a new corporate consolidation of the jazz record business. While the music had once been documented almost entirely by small- and medium-size independent labels, in the late 1960s and early 1970s large companies such as Warner and Columbia entered the jazz market and tightened their control over the retail, promotion, and distribution systems, leading to the demise of many small independents. Meanwhile, they encouraged the ongoing shift to a star system, cultivating a few well-known names while the majority of musicians were increasingly ignored. This chilly climate would thaw for a moment in the mid-1970s, with a few experimentalists (notably Anthony Braxton) receiving major label support and European labels picking up some of the slack from defunct American independents. But for a time in the late 1960s, free-jazz musicians newly entering the scene couldn't be blamed for predicting a long ice age.[6]

The racial dynamics, as well, of the jazz business clogged the aesthetic innovations of experimental black artists and, in turn, mobilized the development of artistic collectives. Entrenched white control over clubs, festivals, booking agencies, radio stations, record companies, and the music press emphasized the jazz world's racial stratification of worker and management. Many musicians chafed against the market logic that, they felt, transformed the musician into a commodity. Ornette Coleman summed it up succinctly: "In jazz, the Negro is the product. . . . So if it's me they're selling—if I'm the product—then the profits couldn't come back to me, you dig?" In this, Coleman echoed the attitudes of many in the business. Stories of musicians exploited and swindled by their record companies have circulated in the jazz community almost since the music's very inception. But following the urban unrest of the 1960s, many of these companies soured particularly toward artists who closely identified their music with black nationalist principles, viewing such a connection as suspect on both economic and political grounds.[7]

Thus, a new generation of black musicians felt hedged about by everyone from record companies to club owners, shut out from the venues and media they needed and denied the aesthetic freedom central to their art. More and more musicians woke up to the fact that these conditions could only negatively affect the growth of the art form itself. Whatever the source of the evaporation of audiences, jazz artists of the mid- and late 1960s could not ignore it. When, from the vantage point of the late 1970s, trumpeter and composer Donald Byrd charged that black musical creativity had been "stunted by non-aesthetic policy," with artistic direction prescribed to an ever-greater degree by "non-creators," he only voiced what a handful of jazz musicians had realized over a decade earlier: that some sort of extra musical intervention was needed.[8]

Unfazed by these ever-growing hurdles, black avant-garde jazz musicians of the mid- and late 1960s saw new modes of social and economic organization as potential bridges over the abyss of aesthetic extinction. Inspired by the theses of the Black Arts Movement, many musicians sought to lift their music out of exploitative or indifferent environments and to return it to the local black communities from which it sprang. And if this agenda was only partially realized in extending the new music to individual black communities, it was more fully realized in the dozens of musical cooperatives and musician-owned record labels that sprang into existence across the nation. Seeking to bypass the traditional club environments and record distribution systems, the core of avant-garde musicians that founded collectives through the decade pioneered cooperative business practices, created performance and recording outlets that remained firmly under musician control, and brought their music directly to inner-city churches, schools, industrial buildings, and community centers. Each of these ventures served up its own unique blend of black-nationalist guiding principles, community programming, and doctrines of self-determination and economic autonomy.

Several determined musicians had anticipated the Black Arts collectives of the late 1960s, and the decade's young musicians didn't hesitate to stand on the shoulders of their predecessors. In the mid- and late 1950s, Charles Mingus's Jazz Workshop and Sun Ra's Chicago-based Arkestra had developed new forms of cooperative business practices. And in 1961, pianist and composer Horace Tapscott had founded the Pan Afrikan Peoples Arkestra and the Underground Musicians Association (UGMA) in Los Angeles—both as efforts to provide "a cultural safe house for the music" and to address the local working-class community. In the early and mid-1960s, the movement gathered steam with several well-publicized attempts in New York to organize collectives and festivals outside corporate media and bookings structures. The 1964 October Revolution in Jazz, an insurgent festival headlined by new musicians who were shunned by mainstream venues and record labels, demonstrated the obstinate grace with which the new music was kept alive. The festival's progeny included the short-lived, multiracial Jazz Composers Guild and, on its heels, the Jazz Composers Orchestra Association.[9]

These New York efforts, though sporadic and of only mixed success, still presaged what was to come. A more permanent model emerged with the 1965 formation of the decade's most successful and influential musical collective, the AACM in Chicago. The aim of the enterprise, as AACM saxophonist Joseph Jarman later explained, "was to allow us the opportunity to perform; but to perform with dignity, with pride, without humiliation, without limitation." The collective's young musicians aimed to change the status of the black musician from entertainer to not only artist, but also teacher, curator, and mythologist in the black community. Sidestepping the corporate promotional machinery by launching its own concerts, venues, and publishing arm, the Chicago venture soon became the prototype for jazz musicians of all stripes around the country. By the early 1970s, even many artists who walked more traditional musical paths had adopted strategies of forerunners such as the UGMA and the AACM. In New York, for example, the Collective Black Artists (CBA) provided pooled business services for musicians, while the Jazz and People's Movement, more attuned to the experimental, tried to open up television to black jazz artists, pressing its position by disrupting tapings of popular talk shows. Through these and dozens of other collectives, cooperatives, and advocacy groups sprinkled through American urban centers, musicians strived to recover direct control over black musical labor and to reassert the primacy of the musician in determining aesthetic guidelines and directions.[10]

⋯⟩⊙⟨⋯

This collectivism rippling through the nation's urban jazz communities had inspired BAG artists such as Oliver Lake, Julius Hemphill, and Baikida Carroll to carry out a similar musical program in St. Louis. But while avant-garde musicians around the country responded to economic challenges with broadly similar tactics, each individual locale posed unique problems, ones that varied depending on the local audience base and club scene, the degree of access to mainstream media outlets, and the particular racial politics of the distinct local music worlds. In St. Louis, the adverse conditions that sparked the collective movement were not just replicated but amplified. Here, for one, the racial stratification that plagued the jazz world was especially acute. The musicians' union actually limited opportunities for African Americans, while a conservative club scene seemed to have no room for BAG's vanguardist commitments. Meanwhile, the city offered BAG's members virtually none of the promotional apparatus—record labels, music press, attentive critics, or radio play—that was at least fleetingly available to avant-gardists in less isolated centers such as New York, Chicago, or Los Angeles.

This state of affairs was the residue of conditions that had endured for decades in St. Louis. In general, the city's black musicians had only two main outlets for employment: through the gigs controlled by the local musicians' union, and on the club scene. And the city's discriminatory union structure exacerbated conditions for black musicians working in any style. St. Louis had a long and ignominious history of union discrimination: through the Second World War, local unions barred black workers from trades ranging from machinists to firefighters to the construction industry. In the music world, even as fifty white chapters of the American Federation of Musicians (AFM) merged with their black counterparts over the course of the 1950s and 1960s, St. Louis and a few other stragglers maintained parallel, segregated AFM chapters until 1971. The city's black musicians had suffered decades of abuse at the hands of the white Local 2, even losing their own union charter during the Depression after Local 2 filed spurious complaints with the AFM national office. Once they regained an AFM charter as Local 197, black musicians fervently defended their union prerogatives. Nevertheless, while the black union controlled some gigs, Local 2's exclusive agreements with the advertising industry and many live-music venues kept African Americans from auditioning for these jobs.[11]

Under orders from the exasperated AFM national office, the two chapters finally did merge in 1971. But even though Local 2 had previously reserved the choicest work for its own members, paradoxically, the eventual integration of the chapters even further limited employment opportunities for the city's black musicians. For one, African Americans were informally shut out of many jobs that their own Local 197 had previously controlled. At the same time, a number of small black-owned music clubs foundered in the face of competition from the larger white-owned venues that could now hire black musicians. And in the wake of the merger, Local 197's union hall—a central node for the city's black musical culture—was sold, a loss that struck a blow at the heart of the local jazz community. When black representation on the new union board was almost entirely purged in the next general election, it seemed to confirm that African American musicians would continue their long indenture in St. Louis's musical world.[12]

BAG's musicians were alive to the racist underpinnings of the segregated union structure. Hemphill later commented, "I didn't join no segregated institutions voluntarily. I spit on them first. So the union didn't exist as far as I was concerned." The club scene, however, offered little more solace. During the early 1960s, of course, BAG's musicians had cut their teeth in the city's clubs, playing bebop, hard bop, or backing bandleaders such as Oliver Sain and Albert King. And at the decade's end, hard-bop combos, organ trios, and national touring acts could still draw healthy audiences at local nightspots such as Fat States, the Riviera, the Moose Lounge, the West End Waiters' Club, Helen's Black Eagle Lounge, and, across the Mississippi River, the Blue Note, the Peppermint Lounge, and the Vets Club. But these days were drawing to a close. The marquees had begun to flicker at most of the city's jazz spots, their power cut by the suburban flight and inner-city decline that would largely extinguish the local club scene over the ensuing decades.[13]

At the same time, a club-going public reared on R&B or bebop had little patience for BAG's musical departures. As Eugene Redmond points out, "They couldn't play in conventional places, in joints, because people would go to hear 'Straight, No Chaser,' they'd want to hear a Miles tune; you know, they wanted to hear *their* jazz, however you do it." So for avant-garde artists like Lake and Hemphill, appearing in St. Louis's struggling clubs meant that their music was constantly hedged about by the restrictions of budget-conscious proprietors. Hemphill later reflected on the difficulties in finding an adequate forum to test out new ideas: "This kind of stuff didn't go over in a nightclub. . . . They wanted to sell some beer, or sell some scotch or something. So they said, 'Look, don't play all those long, unknown pieces and stuff. We want some regular songs, hit parade–type songs played so we can keep turning over this . . . drink charge.'" The way forward seemed blocked in every familiar direction. The two-punch combination of declining jazz audiences and conservative, market-driven tastes of local club owners left musically adventurous artists reeling.[14]

Rather than surrendering their avant-garde musical interests in favor of more salable styles, or giving up on St. Louis entirely to try their luck as unknowns in New York, BAG's musicians had turned to the social and economic advantages of a collective format. And their attempts to overcome these economic hurdles were necessarily rooted in a program to redefine the position of the black musician in the broader American social landscape. African American jazz musicians, as musicologist Ingrid Monson notes, have long labored under a set of stereotypes presenting them as "untutored, instinctual, nonverbal, and immoral rather than knowledgeable." On top of this was layered an assortment of often-apocryphal legends painting the black jazz player as an alcoholic, drug-addicted womanizer. Building on the Black Power Movement's conservative notion of personal responsibility, the black musical collectives of the 1960s actively sought to erase these derogatory images. The AACM, for example, adopted a strict code of conduct for its members—part of an attempt, as cofounder Muhal Richard Abrams then noted, to regain for black musicians "the level of esteem which was handed down from past cultures." Although the St. Louisans—always a bit looser with their organization—didn't adopt a formal set of rules, they were acutely attuned to racist notions of the black musician and worked hard to counteract them. Baikida Carroll recalls a series of guiding tenets among BAG's musicians, among them: "Carry yourself with dignity and command respect. Our presence represents the hope and possibilities of a proud future. We are Aesthetic Diplomats."[15]

While the group's poets and actors looked to Black Arts Movement organizations such as Amiri Baraka's Spirit House for inspiration, BAG's musicians adopted an artistic strategy learned from the AACM. Following that collective's blueprint, BAG constructed a dynamic program of musical institution-building, designed around three major initiatives. First, and most crucially, BAG's artists resituated their music and redefined the traditional spaces for jazz performance. In discarding the customary club gigs to establish their own performance venues, they eluded aesthetic restrictions and cultivated an inner-city listenership whose ears would otherwise have remained deaf to their brand of music. Second, by initiating reciprocal activities with other like-minded collective organizations, they helped to create a broad, supportive network of experimental musicians through the Midwest. And finally, by starting their own record labels in the collective's final days, several of BAG's musicians tried to create an alternative cultural space for their music, one in which they could at least partly escape the commercial pressures threatening to squeeze the life out of the music.

The first part of this agenda required decoupling their music from the economic engine of the jazz club. Governed by commercial considerations that subordinated music to the marketplace, clubs often reinforced a notion of the jazz musician as entertainer rather than artist.

OLIVER LAKE (LEFT) AND BAIKIDA CARROLL IN A DUO CONCERT, C. 1973.

Photograph courtesy Baikida Carroll.

Weary of competing against clattering utensils and patrons' chitchat, or chafing under artistic restrictions from proprietors, many of the period's musicians had harsh words for the club environment. Charles Mingus, for example, frequently railed at chatterbox audience members, while Ornette Coleman argued that the club scene revolved around "whiskey and fucking" rather than music. Archie Shepp, meanwhile, underscored the racial dynamics of the scene, poignantly referring to jazz clubs as "crude stables where black men are run until they bleed." Musicians further down the celebrity scale had an even harder time solving an economic equation that kept new musical styles out of clubs. After being fired by a Chicago cocktail lounge because his rapt listeners weren't downing enough drinks, AACM saxophonist Roscoe Mitchell sternly complained, "The music is not a sideline for other people's folly."[16]

BAG's musicians wanted to foreground their own artwork, and only a change in venue, it seemed, could make that possible. It was outside the traditional club system, and in spaces that they themselves controlled, that the artists felt they could achieve the greatest degree of recognition and autonomy. Again they took their cue from the AACM, which itself had jettisoned nightclub gigs in favor of a concert format "without the constraints of the general business community," as Joseph Jarman later put it. The St. Louis musicians developed a demanding concert schedule at venues such as the Gateway Theatre, the Circle Coffee Shop, Berea Church, and Webster College's Loretto-Hilton Theatre. And on the weekends, BAG's own Washington Boulevard building operated as an alternative to the nightclubs. In these kinds of settings, the accepted club-going conventions could be overturned. For instance, performances were freed from the traditional divisions into fifty- or sixty-minute sets, allowing the musicians to explore other formats, such as suites, extended compositions, or crossovers with other art forms. And with frequent daytime performances at their own venues as well as at schools, universities, and community centers, the BAG musicians could separate the music from its association with spaces that were often seen as illicit and libidinous. The goal, however, wasn't a stuffy sit-on-your-hands type of experience. Listeners at the BAG building could bring along their own bottles and purchase ice and soda on arrival, and crowd reaction was often vocal and even raucous. Nevertheless, the music stood front and center as the collective pursued its agenda of "putting black music in a spot that people could come and see," as BAG saxophonist James Jabbo Ware explains.[17]

The musicians welcomed multiracial audiences, but did so in settings where black artistic authority was acknowledged. In turning their backs on the city's conventional jazz performance spots, BAG's musicians took control of their own musical labor and learned important lessons in self-determination. But there was also a more symbolic significance to the new performance venues. By bringing their uncompromising musical aesthetic into elite arts spaces such as Sheldon Memorial Hall, the City Art Museum in Forest Park, and Powell

Symphony Hall—in several cases over a chorus of resistance—BAG's musicians overturned a patronizing critical tradition that had long interpreted jazz through an anthropological lens, contrasting its supposedly instinctual, folk, or primal qualities with the refined intellectualism of European art music. In challenging the association of canonical artistic greatness with exclusive venues, they reinforced the idea that black music was an artistic achievement of the highest order, no less than that of Euro-American composers and concert artists, and deserved recognition as such. With these shifts in location, the musicians changed the traditional modes of jazz performance in a manner consistent with their ideological program, an agenda they would continue in later years when many of them adopted Manhattan's performance lofts as home for their music.[18]

As well as reorienting the performance space, the musicians also participated in reciprocal exchanges with other midwestern musicians' groups. New York's concentration of large independent jazz labels traditionally sucked musicians out of cities with no recording industries, but for a brief time, the midwestern alliances helped to deactivate the gravitational pull toward the East Coast or Europe. These collaborations served the dual purpose of broadening audiences and seeding new musical ideas. Although the musical collective movement blossomed on the coasts, by the late 1960s the Midwest had developed a thriving (if mostly underground) avant-garde music scene, with the St. Louis and Chicago cooperatives at the helm. Detroit, too, had always been a hothouse for jazz musicians, and in the 1960s, a number of local players were banding together into musical cooperatives, some interracial and others nationalist in orientation. This mix included the Creative Musicians Association, John Sinclair's Detroit Artists Workshop, and Tribe, an organization formed by black musicians such as Phil Ranelin and Wendell Harrison, which sponsored concerts and published a magazine covering issues ranging from colonialism in Angola to police brutality in Detroit. The individual avant-garde musical communities of St. Louis, Detroit, and Chicago were knitted together loosely by a series of concerts organized by the AACM. In addition, several members of

BAG and the AACM made appearances at musician-run institutions in the Motor City, particularly the Strata Concert Gallery, a performance space founded by Tribe trumpeter Charles Moore, and Artists Workshop concerts held at Wayne State University.[19]

Other collectives participated in somewhat ad hoc fashion, but the link was always strongest between BAG and the AACM. Two AACM members—Lester Bowie and drummer Philip Wilson—had attended Sumner High School and frequently returned to St. Louis to visit and play with their old classmates. Several times a year, too, local music aficionados could trek down to the Gateway Theatre or BAG's Washington Boulevard headquarters to check out new sounds from other Chicagoans such as Roscoe Mitchell, Joseph Jarman, and Henry Threadgill. Oliver Lake typically coordinated these exchanges, inviting AACM members for events ranging from impromptu concerts to elaborate festivals such as BAG's May 1970 Celebration to the Living Spirit of Malcolm X. And the excitement the Chicagoans brought to St. Louis was palpable. "Man, when they came to BAG, the place was full and it was jumping," recalls Karl Evanzz, a frequent audience member for the visits.[20]

Meanwhile, three hundred miles to the north, BAG was getting some much-needed publicity while carving out a reputation among the AACM's small but loyal circle of fans. BAG members regularly dropped in on the group's weekly rehearsals at the Abraham Lincoln Center, a six-story settlement house on Chicago's South Side, and musicians from the two groups often appeared on joint concert programs in the city. And the respect went both ways between the two collectives. Lester Bowie recalled that when the St. Louisans first appeared with the AACM, "the Chicago guys were kind of chesty—'Hey, we got this down.'" But after Lake and his colleagues unpacked their horns, "They were walking all over the AACM cats! . . . It just kind of shocked everyone to realize just how great musicians are wherever they happen to be from." By way of their northern travels, Lake and Hemphill gained a small degree of access to the promotional apparatus that St. Louis lacked, picking up a complimentary write-up in the Chicago-based *Down Beat*, the nation's top-circulating jazz magazine. The reciprocal concerts also allowed the group to craft relationships with Chicago musicians that would prove fruitful when the two collectives later reassembled in Europe and New York.[21]

These initiatives were well suited to developing a local, even regional, listenership. But with each passing year, the musicians grew more frustrated at their inability to break into a wider national jazz market. In a mid-1970s position paper, BAG poet Ajulé Rutlin indignantly denounced the "master racists who control the recording industry," the "tyrannical studio controls that limit the scope of an artist's creativity," and the "slave contracts" that exploited musicians' poverty. Whether one views his rhetoric as overheated or dead-on accurate, for BAG's musicians, finding recording opportunities became their most crucial and pressing problem. Larger labels—even with a relatively low break-even point on LPs at about 2,500 in sales—viewed the music being produced by BAG as financially prohibitive. So here, too, the solution involved circumventing rather than working within the entrenched system.[22]

But when it came to releasing their own music, the St. Louis musicians were at a particular disadvantage. The AACM, too, was located outside the nexus of jazz promotional machinery in New York, but members of that collective had managed to tap into Chicago's existing recording industry, reaching a small national audience in the process. A key figure in bringing the AACM to wider attention, ironically, had played a major role in St. Louis's traditionalist jazz circles during the 1950s. Bob Koester, the founder of Delmark Records, had started his label on a shoestring during his college days at Saint Louis University, recording traditional jazz groups and forgotten country-blues singers, sometimes using a local police detective to help track down artists. After moving to the Windy City in 1958, he captured an impressive slice of the Chicago blues scene, including classic albums by the likes of Sleepy John Estes, Junior Wells, and Magic Sam. Although Koester's tastes in jazz ran toward the traditional, he allowed a young employee, Chuck

Nessa, to sign the twenty-two-year-old Roscoe Mitchell and his sextet in 1966 for the groundbreaking album *Sounds*. The record sold only around 1,200 copies in its first year, but even so, this and subsequent releases vaulted the AACM's musicians into the North American jazz press. On both Delmark and Chuck Nessa's own label, Nessa Records, AACM musicians released a spate of records in the late 1960s and early 1970s, including Anthony Braxton's *Three Compositions of New Jazz* and *For Alto*, Joseph Jarman's *Song For*, Lester Bowie's *Numbers 1 & 2*, and Muhal Richard Abrams's *Levels and Degrees of Light*.[23]

Despite their best efforts, however, BAG's musicians found no such outlet for their own work. On one trip to Chicago, Oliver Lake tried to convince Nessa to buy several of his tapes for release on Delmark Records, but since Delmark's limited resources were tied up in other projects, Nessa had to refuse. With even sympathetic avenues like Delmark seemingly closed, the only other route was to challenge the record label heavyweights in their own arena. Starting their own record labels tallied perfectly with BAG artists' agenda of controlling their own labor and performances. Of course, jazz musicians for decades had mounted sporadic efforts to take control of the recording and sales of their own music. In 1952, Charles Mingus and Max Roach had waded into the business with their own Debut Records, followed by musicians such as Dizzy Gillespie, Duke Ellington, and Lennie Tristano. But it wasn't until the mid- and late 1960s that independent, musician-run record labels proliferated. While ventures by established artists such as Sun Ra, Betty Carter, Carla Bley, Mike Mantler, Charles Tolliver, and Stanley Cowell received the greatest degree of distribution, their efforts were mirrored in dozens of tiny, regional labels that sprang up across the country. Fueled by the same impulses that drove the establishment of musicians' collectives, young avant-gardists developed eclectic and often adventurous catalogs, sidestepping the aesthetic timidity of many larger labels and avoiding the strictures of commercially geared contracts.[24]

Determined to reshape the marketplace to their own program and needs, BAG musicians started two record labels in the early 1970s. Julius Hemphill moved first, forming his own Mbari Records in early

1972 as a way to "challenge the record production thing" and circumvent the traditional road to profit making. He gathered donations of money and materials from local supporters in order to release two records from St. Louis: his collaboration with poet K. Curtis Lyle on *The Collected Poem for Blind Lemon Jefferson* and his own *Dogon A.D.* Managing to cut the albums on a miniscule budget, he pressed a thousand copies of each—waylaid only momentarily when a Cincinnati company refused to duplicate the *Collected Poem* master because of a few bawdy lines in Lyle's poetry. Hemphill had begun his label with high hopes, planning to inaugurate a series of films, publications, and lectures under the Mbari Records umbrella. But like many other musicians-turned-entrepreneurs, he soon learned that the game of selling records only begins with cutting the master. "We were a little out of our league; we didn't really have resources to do that," he ruefully remembered. In his view, the critical establishment—"the people that get behind the product there and push it or kill it"—made it impossible for a venture like Mbari Records ever to succeed financially.[25]

Many of the musicians in the BAG/Human Arts Ensemble circle shared Hemphill's biting disdain for the arbiters of taste at the major labels and jazz magazines. On the heels of Hemphill's Mbari experiment, BAG drummer Charles "Bobo" Shaw and Human Arts Ensemble cofounders Jim and Carol Marshall tried to mount their own challenge to the established record companies. Calling their venture Universal Justice Records, the three musicians hoped to counterbalance the overwhelming influence they felt was exercised by corporate media outlets. Universal Justice, they confidently announced, would bypass "the gangsters, mind molders, and soul destroyers in the main offices of New York" and eliminate "interfering obstacles between the source of sound and the ear that hears it." Sinking a good deal of their personal funds into the label's projects, they released six albums, featuring grab-bag combinations of musicians from BAG, the Human Arts Ensemble, and Ajulé Rutlin's Children of the Sun.[26]

While few of its records recouped the initial investments, Universal Justice did experience greater success than Mbari Records, in part because its founders developed a good bit of public relations acumen. Most important, they found a sympathetic ally in New Music Distribution Service, an initiative by the Jazz Composers Orchestra Association in New York. Acting as a clearinghouse for avant-garde jazz and modernist classical music, New Music Distribution strongly encouraged unknown artists to put out their own music. Shaw and the Marshalls circulated their label's records through the distributor, which also provided them with lists of radio stations and magazines that were sympathetic to new music from unknown artists. Starting with small runs of five hundred copies per album, Universal Justice advertised in *Down Beat* magazine and began filling orders from around the United States, Japan, and Europe. Having a record label, no matter how small, as an outlet for their work propelled several of the St. Louis musicians into the national jazz press. The Human Arts Ensemble's *Whisper of Dharma* garnered a generally positive review in *Down Beat*, with Oliver Lake singled out for an approach that "bristles with power, emotion, and invention." The most popular Universal Justice record, the Human Arts Ensemble's *Under the Sun*, acquired something of an underground national reputation, and eventually several thousand were pressed.[27]

Still, the Mbari and Universal Justice ventures were, at best, a mixed success. Founded in the early 1970s while BAG was already disintegrating, neither of the labels lasted for longer than a few years. The Universal Justice catalog, in particular, was of uneven quality, ranging from the infectious *Under the Sun* to several forgettable releases. Meanwhile, the draining administrative work—negotiating pressing deals, searching for distributors, placing advertisements, collecting royalties—distracted the artists from their creative work. And, though artistically satisfying, the labels did not give the St. Louisans much traction in the wider marketplace, nor did they develop the distribution networks necessary to provide a viable alternative to the major labels. But copies of the small-run records did make their way, slowly and quietly, around North America and Europe, helping the unknown artists build reputations among a small, diffuse group of connoisseurs and serving as calling cards when several of them eventually headed for New York. These experiments with self-produced records and artist-owned labels reconfigured the musicians' relationship to the means of production, creating a cultural space that, in the short term at least, partially insulated the music from marketplace pressures.

Whatever the outcome in terms of commercial success, BAG's musicians identified and addressed important questions about the control of black musical labor and the degree to which outside forces should dictate aesthetic choices. By cultivating new performance venues for experimental black music, creating networks of mutual support with the Chicagoans and other midwesterners, and founding their own record labels, they developed an enthusiastic local audience base and altered the existing set of economic relations surrounding the music. As J. D. Parran notes, through these moves he and his cohort carved out empowering roles as "musician-educators" and "cultural ambassadors." They also picked up a set of promotional skills and organizational savvy that would allow them to establish a place for their music in the equally underground avant-garde music scene of mid-1970s Manhattan. While the institutions they founded in St. Louis were short-lived, for a brief moment these initiatives opened up alternative spaces for a new generation of musicians to develop and disseminate their craft.[28]

⇢⊶⊙BAG⊙⊷⇠

Responses to economic hurdles were only half of the story, though. True, BAG's efforts at musical institution-building were aimed at refiguring the social position of the African American musician. But at the same time, through their music itself they outlined a vision of artistic freedom that could work in tandem with ideas of social and cultural liberation and, in doing so, address specific economic and artistic conditions faced by black experimentalists.

The collective's musicians stepped into the jazz scene during a period in which the art form was evolving at a bewildering pace. Over the course of the 1960s, new techniques and styles proliferated so quickly as to obliterate any comfortable notion of linear, evolutionary development. In past decades, a code of informal conventions had governed the ways improvised jazz solos were structured, all layered neatly over the stable rhythms and recognizable harmonic cycles that even the iconoclastic beboppers had left substantially intact. By the late 1950s, however, musicians such as Miles Davis and John Coltrane were discarding bebop's cyclic cadences in favor of static chords overlaid with modal scales. And when Ornette Coleman stormed the ramparts of the New York jazz scene in 1959, he opened up new channels with his freedom from orthodox chord patterns, using jagged phrasing and a highly individualized sense of melody to drive the harmony in unexpected directions.

The early 1960s output from musicians such as Coleman and Coltrane ignited a series of radical and exhilarating changes for jazz, ones characterized by an astounding diversity of approaches. Suddenly, it seemed that every rule existed to be broken, every convention to be turned on its head. Coleman's work may have retained a reliable rhythmic pulse, but new jazz musicians of the 1960s soon dismantled even this familiar structural principle, making timekeeping a matter of artistic preference rather than necessity. As traditional techniques were abandoned, it seemed to many observers that mere anarchy was loosed upon the jazz world. With harmonic and rhythmic certainties upended, jazz listeners must have felt themselves adrift in an ocean of sound with no land in sight, no anchor to stay them—a feeling akin to that elicited by early abstract expressionism. Just as viewers had to interpret experiments in color, line, and volume rather than the representation of familiar objects, so listeners needed to become attuned to the elemental properties of sound itself, a strategy presaged by Luigi Russolo's "Art of Noises" and developed by classical composers such as John Cage from at least the early 1950s. Free-jazz musicians' collage-like soundscapes could jump from lyrical minimalist passages to furious atonal blasts, protracted rubato introspections to unfettered, cacophonous swing. Various artists reached back to the traditions of collective improvisation from the music's earliest days, erased conventional distinctions between soloists and accompanists, expanded the range of instruments with everyday objects and found sounds, and questioned even the value of playing "in tune" using a bevy of extended techniques.

With a sometimes-messianic fervor, practitioners and sympathetic critics began describing aesthetic goals with new phrases and metaphors, all centered on radical artistic individuality and freedom from every constraint. Jazz writer Gary Giddins points to Coltrane's 1965 *Ascension* album as a culmination—jazz at the end of its tether—and, simultaneously, a new starting point for groups like the AACM. With its roaring waves of sound and obliteration of rhythmic and harmonic conventions, *Ascension* set the stage for musicians like those in the AACM to strike off in new directions, reorganizing the sounds that Coltrane had unlocked from the strictures of tradition. Early albums by AACM musicians were characterized by a delicacy and use of silence that contrasted with Coltrane's crowded density of sound. Like their Chicago comrades, BAG's musicians pulled from a host of traditions to cultivate an aggressively modernist aesthetic, constantly striving to "make it new," in Ezra Pound's famous dictum. The new music may have mystified the untutored ear, but aficionados could hear the various nuances that distinguished these musical siblings from one another. For his BAG cohort, Oliver Lake noted, much of the free music emanating from New York seemed frantic and haphazard, so they tried to find new ways to balance freedom and openness with structure and organization. While their techniques, by themselves, were not completely original, the St. Louisans distilled and expanded avant-garde practices that had circulated with increasing regularity over the course of the decade.[29]

There was never a completely homogenous or unified BAG "sound," but certain similarities anchored their music. In a set of interchangeable combo lineups and in the BAG big band, players developed a strong interest in group, rather than purely individual, conception and pioneered unusual instrumental combinations that frequently dispensed with a standard rhythm section. In an effort, as Lake said, to exploit the "colors of sound," he and his BAG colleagues created imaginative relationships of timbre, density, and dynamics, often abandoning a strong sense of forward motion in favor of diffuse, atmospheric soundscapes, layered over bass pedal points and etched with intricate contrapuntal lines. But at any moment, pungent blues shouts, hellbent bebop runs, or impish instrumental arguments could puncture these austere surfaces, startling and delighting audiences by their contrast and humor. They augmented their sonic arsenal with an array of nonstandard instruments— whistles, gongs, chimes, bicycle horns, harmonicas, rattles, gourds, scrapers—to create coloring effects of vague rhythmicality, contributing to the soundscape effect. And on their own instruments, they drew liberally from the full catalog of extended techniques, integrating multiphonics, pitch bends, microtones, harmonics, and residual tones into their music—all allowing them to extend the jazz lexicon and explore a range of emotions, from the sentimental to the sardonic. At its most inventive, their music evaded stylistic boundaries, sliding seamlessly from military marches to funk hooks to free-form blowing sessions.[30]

"Eclectic" was the default term that many journalists fell back on when trying to describe the new midwestern sounds under development by AACM and BAG musicians: it covered all the bases without exercising the intellect. But what might have seemed random or miscellaneous to the casual listener was actually a canny, if not always explicitly articulated, set of organizing principles. Taking its cue from the AACM, BAG developed a musical mission dominated by two over-arching goals: reuniting artificially separated black musical forms into an integrated and socially engaged whole; and developing a freedom of source that continually erased accepted boundaries between "high" and "popular," "classical" and "jazz," Western and non-Western.

For the midwestern collectives, the various labels that observers slapped onto the music—"free jazz," "avant-garde," "the New Thing"— seemed not only inadequate to capture the diversity of the music's latest evolutions, but also an imposition from the record and critical industries, intended to contain and confine rather than explain and extend. Julius Hemphill, for instance, scoffed at the terms, citing a long history of freedom in improvised music to argue that "free jazz" and "avant-garde" were commercial words, not musical descriptions. But for many activist musicians of the 1960s, even the term "jazz" was suspect. More than merely a prickly quibble over terminology, the lexical dispute dramatized the word's potential to denigrate and exoticize the music of African

FLOYD LEFLORE (LEFT) AND JULIUS HEMPHILL.

Photograph courtesy Oliver Lake.

Americans, or to shift credit away from the music's progenitors. The AACM rejected that restrictive term in favor of its own, more expansive formulation—"Great Black Music: Ancient to the Future"—a phrase that mandated "the authority to determine who and what is great," in trombonist George Lewis's description.[31]

The Great Black Music motto became the philosophical lynchpin for the embryonic Art Ensemble of Chicago, an outgrowth of the AACM. The Chicagoans envisioned Great Black Music as a tree, Lester Bowie later explained, with black musical forms such as blues, gospel, and jazz as its roots, all merging into a single trunk before expanding into many branches in their own work. The project implicit in the motto was, in part, a reunification, a search-and-rescue mission in which musical explorers restore the orphaned forms of black music to their true extended family. These various forms, however, were not moldy artifacts for display, but resources for a vanguard style and method. With their elaborate costuming the Art Ensemble dramatized in somewhat histrionic form the dual nature of the musical impulses at work. Several adopted African-derived masks and face paint to signal an allegiance to African cultural roots and to foreground ceremonial aspects of the music, while Bowie himself donned a white lab coat that, as he said, "stands for research" and situates "the stage as my laboratory." In melding a wide-ranging compendium of black musics into a decidedly experimental aesthetic, the group worked, as historian Robin D. G. Kelley suggests, to reframe the African diaspora from "the 'counter' modern" to "the very center of modernity."[32]

BAG's musicians resonated to their Chicago colleagues' exercise in naming. While not rejecting the term "jazz" per se, they applauded the concepts behind the Great Black Music banner. "It's all one big hook-up," Oliver Lake later said, explaining his goal to encompass "the whole scope of styles that black people have evolved." BAG's musicians occasionally borrowed the Great Black Music designation for their own events, though in press releases they more often referred to their work simply as "new forms of black expression." In crafting a musical aesthetic, Lake and his cohort turned their sights on an artificial, commercially

imposed separation among various forms of black music, one exacerbated by record companies' desire to aim products at rigidly differentiated segments of the potential audience and even to control specific
designations in record-store bins. Soul, country blues, gospel songs, New
Orleans jazz, bebop, and a plethora of other styles all have deep roots
in the African cultures that were transplanted to the Americas, yet
increasingly the fragmentation of styles and audiences chafed against
that heritage. Baikida Carroll later expressed discouragement with those
who "tend to think that there is only one type of thing that can come
out of one people's music," while Lake complained that "words have
been used to separate and catalogue and divide, and consequently they
divide the people from listening to the music."[33]

For Lake and his colleagues, music was the ultimate repository
of black history, tradition, and consciousness but could only truly connect with listeners when these commercially imposed musical divisions
were set aside. Lake laid out this idea of dispersion and reunification
early on in his poem "Separation," a work that he frequently performed
several years later in New York's loft venues:

> . . . DIXIE; AND, BE-BOP, SOUL, RHYTHM & BLUES, COOL SCHOOL,
> SWING, AVANT-GARDE, JAZZ, FREE JAZZ, ROCK, JAZZ-ROCK
> WHAT KINDA MUSIC U PLAY? "GOOD KIND"
> ARETHA FRANKLIN & SUN RA IS THE SAME FOLKS
> MILES & MUDDY WATERS SAME . . .

As the poem suggests, the boundaries among these various musical cat-
egories fade in the face of an underlying unity of source.[34]

This fusion shone through in the BAG musicians' approach to
composition and improvisation. They commingled an amazing range of
motifs from black musical culture—snatches of jazz standards, testimo-
nial preaching, spirituals, gospel hymns—and resituated them in an
ironic blend that a later reviewer dubbed "a hyper-referential jam session." If the group's artists worked at the place where tradition met innovation, then their music was also fueled by a combination of local,
national, and international resources. BAG shaped an experimental
free-jazz aesthetic while looking in at least three directions for inspira-

tion. As a starting point, they retained a strong allegiance to local styles of popular music and a keen appreciation for jazz history, anchoring their art form in St. Louis's musical watershed and remaining connected to yet not tethered by "tradition." From this base, they developed an internationalist vision, one that could assimilate a wide range of non-Western artistic influences into a spiritually oriented musical project. And finally, many of them drew from the innovations of twentieth-century European concert music, embracing an experimental, modernist ethos that, nonetheless, remained grounded in a black musical continuum.[35]

This aesthetic approach began with the decidedly local. The St. Louisans matured in a city at least sporadically alive with an evolving African American musical tradition, and they acknowledged a debt to this regional heritage. BAG's musicians maintained an engaged, if somewhat ambivalent, relationship with the styles they had absorbed during the early 1960s playing backup parts on songs such as Little Milton's "I'm a Lonely Man" and Ike and Tina Turner's "It's Gonna Work Out Fine." This background continued to thread through their sounds, and while drawing on Ornette Coleman's "harmolodic" chiaroscuro and the frenetic forays of energy music, the artists frequently dipped into the riff-based rhythm-&-blues canon that had dominated their musical upbringings. In fact, some of them remained active on the local popular music circuit even after BAG's inception. Lake and Hemphill, for instance, worked together several nights a week in a rhythm-&-blues quintet fronted by the guitarist James Bonner, and the collective's musicians once even split a concert bill with the Detroit vocal soul group the Superlatives. Meanwhile, Baikida Carroll recalls taking blues gigs in East St. Louis "where I knew I was going to play from nine o'clock to four in the morning and make only fifteen dollars—but I needed the fifteen dollars to get through the week!" The immediate impetus may have been economic necessity, but the payoff was a free-jazz vocabulary firmly grounded in the blues.[36]

And though BAG's mavericks saw much of the local music scene as dowdy and derivative, they often invited older black musicians to perform as guests, treating them as elders and mentors. Some of the city's straight-ahead musicians scoffed at the young experimentalists, but others supported their approaches. Marty Ehrlich recalls attending a jam session at Lake's house in the early 1970s: "This legendary St. Louis bebop drummer, this guy named Sonny Hamp, came by and played," he recounts; "I was very impressed, because at that point I thought the 'out' guys didn't play with the beboppers. But I remember, at the end, Sonny and Oliver hugging each other and saying, 'Man, it was really great, we've got to play together more.'" In fact, an interloper stealing into a BAG rehearsal was almost as likely to find the artists winding their way through bebop changes as engaged in a free-form blowing session.[37]

Even St. Louis's isolation from the coastal centers abetted this unique synthesis. Although they hailed from various regions of the country, the musicians associated with Ornette Coleman and John Coltrane formed a movement based firmly in New York. Record producer Chuck Nessa suggests of Chicago what could be said of St. Louis as well, that the AACM musicians' very remoteness from these New York jazz circles presented an opportunity for advancement, allowing them to "step back and reflect on the scene, and not worry about . . . having to try to out-blow Albert Ayler tomorrow night in a loft." The jazz scholar Ekkehard Jost extends the distinction, noting that the vicissitudes of competition in New York drove a struggle for individuality, while in Chicago, AACM musicians renounced claims to personal fame and their music took on a collective, group-oriented sound. Members of the two collectives also traced their musical development to some of the more ephemeral aspects of urban life in the Midwest. Lester Bowie in 1967 remarked that "it is frantic enough in Chicago to give the music its meaning, but there's still enough time to relax and see what's going on," and Lake later echoed that thought, commenting that because St. Louis was "not very rushed . . . , we had a chance to sit back and relax and create." While musicians in New York often navigated frenzied calendars of rehearsals and gigs, their counterparts in the slower midwestern cities could count on stable rosters of collaborators, allowing them durable workshops to practice writing for big bands, specific ensembles, dramatic performances, and the like.[38]

Local and global buttressed one another in BAG's most experimental work. The city's musical traditions, its social pace and organization, may have acted as a foundation, but from this base the St. Louis
musicians looked outward to develop a more international musical
vision. Seeing much of the Euro-American tradition as contrived and
artificial, BAG artists and their Human Arts Ensemble comrades often
spoke of a "primitive" music, drawn from non-Western contexts, that
might reinvigorate a stale Western musical paradigm. Perhaps stimulated by the Middle Eastern, Indian, and African folk musics that were
frequently broadcast on KDNA, they investigated a variety of world
musical cultures, reaching for what Hemphill called "the 'natural' sounds,
the primitive sounds of man." Especially within the confines of the
Human Arts Ensemble, various artists surveyed Native American cultures, embraced Eastern spiritual precepts, or composed pieces referencing Sufi religious expressions and Gobi Desert landscapes. Occasionally
these explorations were undertaken with an almost anthropological attitude, but usually, the goal wasn't authenticity. More often, the musicians
looked to such elements as part of a quest to augment the spiritual dimen-
sions of their work.[39]

BAG and Human Arts Ensemble musicians frequently employed
both new melodic materials and an expanded range of instruments
elicited from non-Western musical cultures. On their composition
"Lover's Desire," for instance, Charles "Bobo" Shaw and Jim Marshall
borrowed a lilting Afghan folk song from one of the Smithsonian
Folkways series of recordings. The two used the melody as the basis for
an extended free-jazz and rock jam that they eventually recorded on
Under the Sun, with an ensemble that included J. D. Parran, Lester Bowie,
and Marty Ehrlich. The biggest cache of new instruments, meanwhile,
appeared when the Human Arts Ensemble's Jim and Carol Marshall
returned from a journey through India and Nepal in 1971. Shipping
home a large batch of Eastern instruments, the Marshalls introduced
their friends in BAG to a selection of Tibetan trumpets as well as to the
nagaswaram, a raucous oboe-like instrument indigenous to southern
India. On "Whisper of Dharma," the musicians put the new instruments

to good use, at one point laying down extended bass drones on the nagaswaram while sax lines intertwine in melismatic fashion amidst a sea of chanting, rattles, and bells.[40]

In BAG itself, however, nowhere was this internationalist bent more pronounced than in their turn to Africa, real or reimagined, for inspiration. Following in the footsteps of predecessors such as Duke Ellington, Dizzy Gillespie, John Coltrane, and Randy Weston, a range of black jazz musicians in the late 1960s continued to celebrate the continent, acknowledging contemporary artistic debts to African cultural roots. Regional groups such as Detroit's Griot Galaxy, retracing the arc of Sun Ra's Solar Arkestra, blended science-fiction references with visions of precolonial Africa into a mix that has been dubbed "Afrofuturism." Oftentimes the continent could serve as palimpsest, to be reinscribed to suit contemporary needs in America. The St. Louis musicians, like their colleagues in the visual arts, poetry, and drama, looked to Africa as both font of spirituality and symbol of freedom, stressing their own participation in a diasporic, pan-African continuum of musical expression. This attention to Africa worked hand-in-hand with the traditions of the local black music scene as the group elaborated the idea of an extended black aesthetic archive, one that stretched outward from the clubs of East St. Louis and girdled the globe.[41]

These Afrocentric impulses infused many of their performances in more explicit fashion. Some BAG members adopted bold, African-inspired stage attire; others collaborated with the set of West African artists that Katherine Dunham had recruited to the area; and still others, particularly Hemphill, researched specific groups such as the Dogon for themes and inspiration. And the musicians often attempted to evoke the continent with assortments of reed and wooden flutes and whistles, hand drums, bells, and rattles. In his 1971 composition "Africa," for instance, Lake and his ten-strong ensemble lay out one particular vision of the continent. Over a strictly repeating 6/8 bass vamp, they conjure up a primal, teeming rain forest—a sonic stew that bubbles over with cawing bird noises, hand drums, panting, and growls as quartal harmonies in the horns emerge.[42]

The task of creating and sustaining a unified musical aesthetic, grounded in black American musical traditions yet open to new aesthetic directions, was sometimes also aided by the incorporation of European modernist techniques. While not accepting the primacy of the European concert-music tradition, musicians such as J. D. Parran and Oliver Lake kept up a lively dialogue with St. Louis's classical music world. And during the late 1960s, the city was alive with interest in newly composed classical music. It boasted at least a handful of composers whose music had received national attention—among them, Robert Wykes, Arthur Custer, and John Perkins—and new work was staunchly supported by several local universities, the symphony, and the New Music Circle, an organization that worked to convey the classical avant-garde from academe into the wider community. Several of BAG's artists kept one foot in this world, primarily through close associations with the city's academic music departments.[43]

Such connections often abetted a playful experimentalism that appropriated techniques of contemporary Euro-American composers. By drawing on everyday objects and homemade instruments, BAG's musicians paralleled innovations of composers such as Henry Partch and John Cage, and with their graphic scores and open-ended notational systems, they mirrored some of the experiments of 1950s New York School composers such as Cage, Morton Feldman, and Earle Brown. Many of the period's avant-garde jazz musicians drew from the languages of European modernists such as Arnold Schoenberg, Karlheinz Stockhausen, and Pierre Boulez, and likewise, these musical idioms provided a fresh set of resources for BAG's budding composers. With their composer-centered ethic and interest in modernist technique, the St. Louisans seemed intent on erasing the divisions between high and popular art.[44]

These interests often seeped into compositions, but sometimes stimulated more formal partnerships. The group's closest ties to local classical circles came through the distinguished modernist composer Arthur Custer. Previously known mainly as a serialist, by the late 1960s Custer was reaching for a wider range of musical devices, including prerecorded tape and found objects. The extreme fluidity of boundaries in musical influence and collaboration was strikingly illustrated in Custer and Hemphill's 1969 joint composition "Songs of Freedom, Love and War," commissioned as centerpiece for the New Music Circle's tenth-anniversary "Catalytic Celebration." In one of the most unlikely intersections of the BAG years, Custer and Hemphill recruited as their partner a local rock band called the Guise, itself a spin-off from the minor pop chart-maker Bob Kuban and the In-Men. Under Custer's baton, the Guise and Hemphill's jazz ensemble joined a chorus of fifty-five singers and a twenty-piece orchestra, all presenting a kaleidoscopic work that wove together snatches of syncopated percussion, electric rock, chanted texts, and poems by Malinké Elliott. Over the loudspeakers, prerecorded vignettes obliquely commented on the destruction being wrought in Vietnam and strife on the streets of American cities. The musicians drew a diverse crowd that ranged from smartly dressed symphony-goers to teenage Guise fans to some of BAG's black urban constituency. Dubious in conception and rather sloppy in execution, their stylistic synthesis played to tepid reviews. Still, as Hemphill's first large-scale composition, "Songs" prepared him for commissions in later decades from ensembles such as the Arditti String Quartet and the Richmond Symphony Orchestra.[45]

BAG's musicians opened up the jazz archive by bounding among earlier styles and genres, reaching to African musical traditions while infusing their music with cutting-edge invention. But despite their relentless performing schedule, the collective's musicians left few documents of the sounds they were experimenting with during their early days in St. Louis. The Mbari and Universal Justice record labels were founded too late in BAG's lifespan to capture anything like a unitary, evolving body of work. In several cases, the St. Louis albums were a last-minute attempt to get something on tape, by players with one foot out the door. Still, musicians such as Lake, Hemphill, Bluiett, and Carroll would continue to build on the BAG foundation during the 1970s, as they developed prolific recording careers in New York. In drawing on a range of African, African American, and European modernist themes and techniques, the BAG musicians worked to confirm their art's axial position at the intersection of modernist and postmodernist performance practices.

This hybrid approach was deeply colored by the imperatives of the black liberation struggle which had so thoroughly penetrated the musical world by the late 1960s. Infused with the nationalist ideas sweeping African America, musicians in styles ranging from Motown, soul, and hard bop to the farthest reaches of the avant-garde struggled to bring greater political relevance to their work. Of course, jazz musicians responded to these currents in all sorts of different ways. But as the civil rights, antiwar, and student movements each took up musical genres that they felt exemplified their ideological directions, a number of radical intellectuals gravitated to free jazz, in particular, as a vehicle for new and revolutionary impulses, as an art form that uniquely reflected social consciousness and that acted as protest on personal, aesthetic, and social levels. Amiri Baraka, for instance, incorporated free jazz into his political program, bringing musicians such as Archie Shepp, Sun Ra, and Albert Ayler to his arts centers in Harlem and Newark. Following Baraka's analysis, a growing cadre of critics saw strong consonances between the thundering language of black militancy and the audacious reverberations of free jazz, sounds that the Marxist critic Frank Kofsky famously dubbed "a repudiation of the values of white middle-class capitalist America." Although terms such as "liberation" and "freedom" had become watchwords for the jazz world in a more specialized musical sense, many interpreted the quest for freedom from aesthetic constraints as just one expression of a more generalized demand for freedom emanating from the Black Power Movement.[46]

Musical collectives such as the AACM and BAG, with their nationalist cultural programming and community orientation, seemed perfectly aligned to position their music in this sort of framework. But of the many critical debates and controversies surrounding free jazz, one of the sharpest centered on the relationship between social and sonic symbolism. Despite the temptation to pair the liberated sounds of free jazz with calls for social and political liberation, the new music's messages—unlike those of the new black poetry or theater—were intrinsically nonverbal. Even as a host of critics and musicians pointed to the

Black Power Movement as the ground on which free jazz stood, others of the period's musicians checked their politics at the door when it came time for the gig, expressing annoyance at what could at times appear to be a hijacking of their own musical expressions.

Like so many other musical groups of the day, BAG was of at least two minds regarding these debates. Although Hemphill mused in a 1970 interview that "unsatisfactory conditions" could affect "your very breathing, let alone your music," the collective's musicians more often denied an explicit connection between the sounds that emerged from their instruments and the sociopolitical winds buffeting the nation. In fact, while stressing their deep commitment to a black aesthetic, they more often saw their artistic work as operating alongside, but not directly with or within, the political thrust of the moment. Decades later, Lake maintained that he "never really thought of [my music] as political. If it makes a political statement, then it does, but I don't consciously think about, 'I'm going to do this political thing.'" In the late 1970s, Hamiet Bluiett put it more starkly, commenting, "I'm not interested in talking about sociology. . . . I'm a musician. The music comes first." And, speaking of the AACM in 1972, Lester Bowie made the same distinction between aesthetic and political realms, saying that the Chicago collective "was purely musical" and "never really had a political orientation." For the musicians of BAG, racial identity was inherent and not always or explicitly political.[47]

Such comments may reflect an attempt to insulate their music from a corps of commentators who heard in every note a denunciation, in every downbeat a call to arms. Oftentimes, the collective's musicians made efforts to evade critical tactics that might overdetermine artistic possibilities and even listeners' responses. The commitment to black identity took different forms and encompassed various strategies, and the goal here was recasting this identity on a cultural plane, rather than retailing explicitly political statements on the skirmishes of the day. By celebrating music's spiritual qualities and its ability to unite, BAG's musicians aimed to draw sharp contrasts with the unadorned material- ism of the business realm and the harsh divisiveness of politics. And by bridging the musical boundary lines that Lake found so objectionable, they attempted to craft a black aesthetic that might transcend a mere reflection of the social universe.

That is not to say, though, that the group's musical program couldn't sometimes work in concert with the goals of their allies in nationalist political organizations. Sharing the critical agenda of a community-based black art, members often put their musical offerings at the service of radical causes in St. Louis. And, ranging farther afield, in May 1969 Oliver Lake transported his quartet to Yale University for a three-day Festival of Revolutionary Culture, a Malcolm X memorial topped off with a searing address from Black Panthers chairman Bobby Seale. Through these types of crossovers, the musicians suggested broad consonances between their own aesthetic program and the agendas of black-nationalist political groups, even while stressing that the music itself was not to be read as overtly political in nature. Sociologist Paul Gilroy has pointed to music's power as a tool for "organizing consciousness" in black struggles, and at such events, the goals of freedom and autonomy on aesthetic and social levels seemed at least temporarily aligned.[48]

And, whether staking out roles as archivists of the African continuum through their musical explorations or working to instruct and mobilize area residents, the artists never denied their connection to the city's black community. In 1970, Lake explained, "We try to make our music relevant to everyday life, day-to-day existence," noting that even the groans, screams, and yowls that his group frequently inserted into their performances "are aimed at relating to the lives of black people." As part of this task of local engagement and awareness-building, BAG's musicians often drew on a set of extramusical practices that could encompass the ritual, the ceremonial, and the theatrical. The St. Louisans enlisted the collective's visual artists and dramatists to construct ritualistic performance environments, replete with elaborate sets, lighting schemes, and costumes, and at Lester Bowie's suggestion, they began staging all-night concerts that culminated at dawn with sunrise ceremonies on the sidewalks of Washington Boulevard. Lake, Hemphill, and their colleagues also adopted a quick-witted brand of theatricality that was

THREE SAXOPHONISTS CONVERSE OUTSIDE THE BAG BUILDING.
LEFT TO RIGHT: JAMES JABBO WARE, JULIUS HEMPHILL, AND THE AACM'S ROSCOE MITCHELL.

Photograph, c. 1969, courtesy James Jabbo Ware.

thoroughly embedded in the local. Skits and pantomimes punctuated many of the musical presentations, often swerving from slapstick humor to fragmented absurdism to biting social commentary. Reviewing a Lake Art Quartet performance in Chicago, for example, *Down Beat* labeled trumpeter Floyd LeFlore "the group's character actor"—after a musical skit in which LeFlore, who then worked a day job at an employment service, riffed caustically on the arcane codes used to classify jobseekers' skills and places of residence.[49]

The St. Louisans' dream of an experimentalist yet community-based black music was a laudable but often elusive goal. Ironically, given many of its musicians' claims to speak about and for the black community, hostile critics often pointed fingers at free jazz as the primary cause for the decline in jazz's commercial viability. As the story goes, new musicians of the 1960s produced a stubbornly alienating elitism, a music that didn't swing, one whose angry atonalisms or arid abstractions progressively estranged all but a small circle of cognoscenti. Of course, this version of jazz history ignores changes in America's urban fabric, the rising commercial power of other musical genres, and the fact that there were, indeed, many more traditional musicians playing during the late 1960s and 1970s. Meanwhile, collectives like BAG and the AACM, far from turning their backs on a broad-based black listenership, placed local engagement among their highest priorities. Nonetheless, BAG's cadre of avant-garde musicians did face enormous and eventually insurmountable difficulties in developing a strong local audience base.

Negative reactions to the collective's theatrical or poetic offerings were most often grounded in offended political or moral sensibilities, but negative reactions to BAG's music component usually came back to aesthetic distaste, pure and simple. As the musicians flouted the conventions that governed the city's club scene, local listeners reacted with ambivalence and occasionally even ridicule. So while some concerts drew large and appreciative crowds, at other times audiences would simply evaporate over the course of a show. Eugene Redmond, a frequent audience member at BAG concerts, tells stories of listeners driven from the hall: "You'd sit there, and you'd look around and there'd be like five people left." A black weekly captured these sentiments, gleaning from one performance that "not all black music is rhythmical, nor is it even listenable." In a more outlandish example, concert organizers at a local college once mocked the Lake Art Quartet by surreptitiously projecting cartoons onto the wall behind the performers, eliciting giggles from the audience and exasperation from the BAG musicians.[50]

Some members shrugged off the intermittent slings and arrows of hostility, feeling that the St. Louis audiences "just didn't know what was happening," as J. D. Parran later charged. For others, suggestions that their musical approaches were too esoteric, too impenetrable, for most listeners never failed to irritate. Shortly after leaving Missouri, Lake protested that it was "ridiculous" to claim that the new styles weren't commercially viable: "The music *is* commercial," he insisted; "It could be, if people were exposed to it." Despite the interventions of community music groups like BAG and the AACM, the low level of radio play and support from major record labels consigned new styles to the margins in most cities, St. Louis included. When *PROUD Magazine*, a new local publication for the city's black community, interviewed Hemphill and Lake in summer 1970, the two saxophonists spoke in some detail about their thorny relationships with audiences. For his part, Hemphill dismissed those who were uncomfortable with his music as "people who have no real Black awareness." Meanwhile, Lake expressed frustration that audiences "think they have to *do* something at a concert, tap their feet, or feel a rhythm. They can't just listen." He described a somewhat adversarial approach, geared toward jolting audiences into attention: "[W]e almost force a kind of atmosphere and people don't seem to like it. We force them to listen to us." The group's aesthetic highlighted particular tensions between participatory and more reserved audience interaction styles that would continue to emerge over the ensuing decade.[51]

Ambiguities and contradictions sometimes surrounded BAG's interactions with audiences, its experiments with new aesthetic forms and methods, and its approaches to economic challenges. But however difficult it proved to build and sustain an audience base, the forays into collective modes of organization allowed musicians a space in which to develop innovative individual styles and approaches. And the BAG musicians not only opened up a space in which to further their own careers. Along with their colleagues in musical collectives around the country, they also proposed a fresh set of answers to debates over black artistic labor, economic relations in the jazz world, and the connections between new approaches to music making and individual neighborhoods and communities. By the mid-1970s, BAG and its sister collectives around the country would have left in their wake questions about the very notion of what the art form was and what it could become.

BAIKIDA CARROLL IN CONCERT, C. 1973.

Photograph courtesy Baikida Carroll.

CHAPTER 6

POINTS OF DEPARTURE: EUROPEAN INTERLUDES

As the Black Artists' Group sank its roots into the community, several of the founders had begun to envision their collective as something of a permanent institution, one that could survive the departure of any particular set of members. The organization, they predicted, would continue to strengthen and mature over the years, acting as a vital forum for succeeding generations of young African American artists. Unfortunately, this wasn't to be. In retrospect, Julius Hemphill ruefully admitted that "there was no backup. No younger people had come in who were trained, who were going to see what the job was. . . . We hadn't cultivated them; that's a mistake we made." By late 1971, BAG's tenure in St. Louis was drawing near to a close, and within a year the beleaguered organization would disappear from the city entirely. The early 1970s would see many of its artists scattering across the country and the world, with clusters forming a musical arts colony in Oregon, setting up shop as a working ensemble out of Paris's American Center, developing their acting skills in Sweden, hurtling back and forth to St. Louis for occasional studio sessions and concerts, and making their first forays into the New York City jazz world.[1]

To many members, the decline and eventual dissolution of their organization seemed to coincide with the end of a political moment. Formed at the intersection of Black Arts nationalism and liberal urban reform efforts, the group began to crumple at precisely the time when both of these thrusts were dissipating. Around the country, the scores of Black Arts collectives that had blossomed only a few years earlier were withering, even as campus protest subsided, the New Left fractured amidst sectarian infighting, and the Black Power Movement's flagship political organizations staggered under the combined weight of government repression and internal divisions. BAG's conservative home city dramatically registered this change in tenor. "Once the political possibilities of the '60s started to dampen," painter Oliver Jackson asserts, most St. Louisans "had no interest in a serious black cultural thrust that was as individuated and as clear about its origins" as BAG. Meanwhile, the much-publicized failures of the Community Action and Model Cities programs had convinced many voters that there could be no effective governmental solution to urban poverty. The toothless version of the War on Poverty that survived through the first Nixon administration provided few resources for the myriad community groups that had once drawn on public support. In St. Louis, as the local Model Cities Agency limped toward its 1974 extinction, the foundations, arts agencies, and municipal bodies that had formerly been so eager to sponsor inner-city, neighborhood-based initiatives like BAG grew increasingly cool toward such projects.[2]

If the shifting political landscape provided a less congenial climate for an institution such as BAG, this period was also characterized by several more specific factors internal to the organization, all of which undermined its longevity. These included cumbersome disputes among artistic departments, the group's inability to cultivate new sources of funding, a torrent of key participants spilling out of St. Louis, and a frustrating lack of wider recognition combined with a plummeting local audience base. In earlier days, although tensions may have roiled the group, and battles to obtain funding and administer the program may have strained the organizers' creative energies, the artists' solidarity and single-minded focus had kept the ship afloat. But though the group's leaders steered their vessel nimbly, the craft was eventually springing leaks left and right.

First of all, by 1971 aesthetic and ideological disagreements among the group's artistic divisions had escalated, bringing to light more fundamental, underlying questions of purpose. Artists in the various departments had developed divergent, if often overlapping, ideas about what the organization's mission should be, differences that had always remained unsettled but now emerged into full view. For some members, BAG was principally an artists' guild, intended to foster careers by leveraging influence with promoters, venues, or record companies. For others, the group above all represented the cultural front in local political struggles, a vehicle for an aggressive brand of agitprop. And for still others, BAG's chief focus was as a community education project, a kind of grassroots rejoinder to the War on Poverty. Of course, these various agendas could work in concert, but in the collective's final months, they were jostling more often than coinciding. Poet Ajulé Rutlin, for instance, ended up squaring off against a set of newcomers who "wanted it to be *totally* political," while the musicians sometimes found themselves accused of being more interested in their professional careers than in the collective's social mission. As ideological and interpersonal disputes cascaded through the group, the atmosphere grew increasingly toxic.[3]

During BAG's first three years, the artists had managed to work around these kinds of conflicts, but negotiation and accommodation became far trickier once the organization's scope was limited by a lack of financial resources. St. Louis never provided enough material support to sustain the group. Bills began to pile toward the ceiling. And the owner of BAG's building, who had allowed the artists to use the space for a nominal fee, eventually sold the warehouse to a large real estate company, which was soon demanding a hefty rent. At the same time, sloppy accounting practices, though not malicious in intent, contributed to a general sense that money was floating around yet no one knew where it was going. With the group's coffers depleted, mistrust and anger mounted over the allocation of diminishing resources, once even leading, as Rutlin remembers, to "an uproar that almost conflagrated into some real physical contact." Frictions culminated when—in what was probably the biggest blowup of the BAG years—the other artists expelled Julius Hemphill from the group. As funding began to run dry, members had refused Hemphill's demand for a salary of $150 per week to continue his administrative duties. Some accused him of mishandling funds. Finally, as Hemphill later recounted, at a membership meeting the artists "voted me out of the organization, and requested that I not use the facilities in any way. So I said okay, you know, and I resigned from everything, and I stopped going." The expulsion of Hemphill provoked fury from many of his friends in the musical wing.[4]

While these internecine dramas transpired, key members in dance and theater began filtering out of the group. Following the first wave of departures in late 1969 and 1970, BAG had managed to plug the holes by attracting new leaders—notably choreographer Luisah Teish and drama director Muthal Naidoo—from Katherine Dunham's PATC. But the second wave of departures permanently crippled the collective's dance and drama wings. For her part, Teish had grown disillusioned with the whole St. Louis scene, and particularly with the sexism she often detected within the city's radical black arts and political circles. Teish was also finding little respect in St. Louis for her explorations of voudou and other non-Western religious traditions, claiming in her autobiography that she had been "accused of being counterrevolutionary and told that my visions were fantasies." Unhappy with the social situation, in late 1971 Teish relocated to the San Francisco Bay Area, and BAG's Omawali Dance & Drum Ensemble gradually faltered in the wake of her exit. Meanwhile, the theater division faced even greater depopulation. In the collective's final days, Naidoo, the only non–African American member, had begun to sense that "not being racially African became a problem as some members . . . were moving the group towards a more exclusive understanding of what it meant to be black." Feeling increasingly unwelcome, Naidoo resigned from BAG in early 1972 to take up a teaching post at Washington University. Shortly thereafter, actress Portia Hunt, a pillar of the company, left the United States to join a theater project that Malinké Elliott had established in the north of Sweden.[5]

Others left not out of dissatisfaction, but simply out of an urge to seek new experiences elsewhere. The artists' ranks were further depleted in 1971, when a contingent of the Human Arts Ensemble moved its operations from the gritty urban setting of St. Louis to the bucolic hills of Creswell, Oregon, a small village ten miles south of Eugene. There, based around a set of large trailers on a mountainside just outside Creswell, Jim and Carol Marshall set up an informal creative arts colony. Residents and visitors spent their time in meditation and constant outdoor rehearsals, occasionally arranging concerts and other musical events just up the road in Eugene. The project became an alternate center of gravity for members of the BAG/Human Arts Ensemble circle, with performers such as Ajulé Rutlin, saxophonist Luther Thomas, and bassist Arzinia Richardson spending extended periods of time in Oregon throughout the early 1970s. The Marshalls' dream of creating a permanent artists' colony in Creswell was never realized. But for a short time, the serene outpost gave several of the performers an opportunity to play out the more ascetic, reflective, and spiritual impulses at work in the Human Arts Ensemble.[6]

Back in St. Louis, the collective's last months must have been dispiriting. The new mood contrasted sharply with the dynamism and energy that had propelled the group through its first three years. As spring arrived in 1972, it seemed as if BAG's music wing was the only artistic division whose lineup remained at least somewhat intact. Even for the musicians, though, difficulties had multiplied. Through sheer grit and persistence, the organization's jazz players were becoming increasingly well known throughout the Midwest. Still, after almost four years of operation as a collective, their efforts to reach a national audience, or even a wider local listenership, had proved disappointingly unfruitful. Outside of a small underground arts audience, most St. Louis jazz listeners had never expressed much interest in the types of music played by BAG, and by the early 1970s even these small crowds had started tailing off. "Things were going great," trumpeter Floyd LeFlore later lamented; "And then, you know, all good things in St. Louis must come to an end, and it seemed like we didn't get the audience support. Sometimes we would be playing to empty rooms." As for local press coverage, members could count on one hand the number of articles that had bothered to discuss their music. However strong their aesthetic assertions, it could often feel as if they were shouting into a void of disregard or outright hostility. Oliver Lake, in particular, concluded that the group had accomplished all that it could while in Missouri. "We'd played just about everywhere in that tri-state area round St. Louis," he explains, "and we were saying to each other, 'Let's break out of this circle.'"[7]

Like Lake, many of the musicians had begun to peer beyond the St. Louis horizon, even if it wasn't quite clear what paths were open to them. The traditional route for the jazz musician, a move to New York City, still seemed an uncertain prospect. Instead, the BAG musicians had as catalyst the example of their comrades in the AACM, who had first turned not to the East Coast but to Europe. For the Chicago cooperative, too, the usual story for avant-garde artists had obtained: critical praise combined with popular indifference, leading to an economic impasse. The demands of the jazz marketplace often collided with the AACM's ideological and aesthetic convictions, and to several members, who were working day jobs while playing for the same handful of listeners week after week, the group's musical program was beginning to look impossibly utopian. By the late 1960s, even Lester Bowie—one of the few AACM members making his living entirely from music—doubted the feasibility of further artistic or financial progress in the Midwest: "We had gotten as far as it was going to go in Chicago."[8]

The European continent, by contrast, was host to an increasingly well-developed free-jazz scene, and opportunities there seemed at least marginally better. Fortuitously, the Chicagoans had on hand a series of enthusiastic letters from the French drummer and promoter Claude Delcloo, pledging that if they relocated to Europe he would arrange concerts for them. So in May 1969, just as BAG was hitting full stride in St. Louis, the first AACM delegation—saxophonists Roscoe Mitchell and Joseph Jarman, trumpeter Lester Bowie, and bassist Malachi Favors—left Chicago's South Side for Paris, shipping across the Atlantic a Volkswagen van and their mammoth collection of over five hundred instruments. Once there, they assumed for the first time their iconic name, the Art Ensemble of Chicago, and set up living and rehearsal space at a country house in Saint-Leu-la-Forêt, a small town twelve miles outside of Paris. Within a year, they had added to their group an acquaintance from Detroit, the twenty-three-year-old drummer Famoudou Don Moye, who brought to the ensemble the vast assemblage of homemade, conventional, and non-Western instruments that he dubbed "sun percussion." Shortly after the Art Ensemble's departure from Chicago another AACM progeny, the Creative Construction Company, composed of saxophonist Anthony Braxton, violinist Leroy Jenkins, and trumpeter Leo Smith, joined their colleagues in France.[9]

While the latter group was not quite as warmly received—perhaps, as Braxton suspected, because they lacked a rhythm section—it took only days for the Art Ensemble of Chicago to electrify Parisian audiences. Often beginning concerts shrouded in darkness, declaiming statements on pride, heritage, and Great Black Music from the wings, the group left critics at once baffled and elated. With their flamboyantly theatrical stage presence, their invocations of African ancestors, and their experimentalist stew of black musical styles, the players sent sharp reverberations through the city's jazz scene. The Art Ensemble's performances stoked French enthusiasm for theatricality and spectacle, rite and ritual—one that was reinforced the following year when Sun Ra brought to the country his astonishing medley of dancers and musicians, light and slide shows, ancient African motifs and futuristic space-age dramaturgy. Eagerly embraced by local listeners, the Chicago musicians recorded numerous albums and film soundtracks while in France and appeared in dozens of live and televised concerts. Meanwhile, they were cordially received by American bebop players of an older generation who made their homes in Paris.[10]

Journalists and fans interpreted the Art Ensemble as fiercely aggressive, as the musical manifestation of a turbulent and uncompromising black-nationalist sentiment in the States. This supposition may have thrilled Paris's intellectual, critical, and student communities, but it only alarmed skittish French authorities, whose reception was not nearly as congenial. The dwindling tolerance of the country's police agencies—aftermath of the May 1968 student revolt—had resulted in increased monitoring of foreigners and, even in some cases, deportation of African Americans who participated in political activities. Although the Art Ensemble's members steered clear of overt political entanglements in France, the group's reputation still elicited unease from officialdom. After about a year in the country, Lester Bowie recounted, a commentator discussing the group on Radio Luxembourg "portrayed us as revolutionaries, damn-near Black Panthers," not neglecting to inform listeners that "yes, by the way, they live in Saint-Leu-la-Forêt." Local authorities must have tuned in to the broadcast as well, for shortly thereafter, according to Bowie, the Art Ensemble was expelled from France. Undeterred, the group packed its instruments into a convoy of trucks and crisscrossed the continent from the Mediterranean to Scandinavia, often living in improvised campsites and performing prolifically to euphoric applause.[11]

The Art Ensemble returned to the United States exultant over the European reception of their music, but ambivalent at the prospect of going back to the familiar Chicago grind. Instead, Lester Bowie, Roscoe Mitchell, and Don Moye headed for St. Louis to relax, regroup, and collaborate with their Missouri friends. Bowie and his family bought a house from BAG's Arzinia Richardson, while Mitchell and Moye moved into the organization's Washington Boulevard warehouse, unloading their mountains of instruments into the upstairs loft quarters formerly occupied by Emilio and Pat Cruz. The BAG building and the Gateway Theatre might have lacked the allure of Paris's Théâtre du Lucernaire and Vieux Colombier, but the Art Ensemble musicians' presence in Missouri for those few summer months in 1971 prompted a minor spurt of renewed interest on the part of St. Louis audiences. More important, however, were the glowing reports of opportunities in Europe that they carried along with them. Although the trip had not been without its problems—Bowie, for instance, complained of being ripped off by French record companies—the Chicagoans strongly urged Lake, LeFlore, and several others to abandon their St. Louis efforts and relocate to Paris. "Just get there—you'll work," Bowie exhorted his dubious colleagues. In a jazz world where gaining public recognition was often, as one journalist put it, "a matter of where you play, not how you blow," the grass was looking decidedly greener next to the Seine than it did on the banks of the Mississippi.[12]

Accordingly, when Oliver Lake shepherded a ten-piece ensemble into a local recording studio in summer 1971, he had larger plans for the project. The album they recorded—*NTU: Point from Which Creation Begins*—would not only be the saxophonist's first as a leader, it was also intended as the musicians' ticket out of St. Louis.

Far and away the collective's shrewdest businessman, Lake planned to use the record as the basis for an extended European tour with the entire ensemble. By the time of the studio date, Lake had digested the influences of Eric Dolphy, one of his most important models, and was carving out angular sonic figures with a newly biting and acerbic tone. Propelling his improvisations with a dexterous command of the full range of the alto, he frequently combined wild, bluesy riffs with madcap intervallic leaps, sometimes anchoring the listener with phrases reminiscent of his bebop hero, Jackie McLean. The album that Lake's ensemble recorded showed off several aspects of his musical work with BAG. On the composition "Electric Freedom Colors," for instance, the group lays down a choppy, pointillistic soundscape that dissolves into an overdriven guitar solo, the musicians adding groans, grunts, and moans processed through studio distortion. At the same time, they demonstrate their ability to play in more explicitly tonal styles, as on Baikida Carroll's "Tse'lane," a pretty bossa nova held together by Lake's flute.[13]

Soon after the recording session, however, the floor fell through on Lake's plan. The small St. Louis label that was to issue the LP went out of business, leaving the tapes to gather dust for five years before they were finally released. This turn of events must have been a bitter disappointment. By early 1972, with no record in hand and several of the ten musicians unwilling to travel abroad, it seemed that Lake's plan would be unworkable. Still, even without the advantage of an album as calling card, Lake and several of his colleagues were determined to escape the deteriorating situation within BAG and to pursue new audiences elsewhere. Lake began mailing tape versions of his record to critics and booking agents in Western Europe, hoping to lay some kind of advance groundwork for concert and recording opportunities across the Atlantic. As bandmates for his prospective move, Lake signed up four others of the collective's leading musicians: trumpeters Baikida Carroll and Floyd LeFlore, drummer Charles "Bobo" Shaw, and the teenage trombonist Joseph Bowie, who had graduated from high school only months before.[14]

SAXOPHONIST AND BAG COFOUNDER OLIVER LAKE, SHOWN HERE IN A 1971 PUBLICITY SHOT
FOR HIS ALBUM *NTU: Point from Which Creation Begins.*

-»│═◉BAG◉═│«-

Photograph courtesy Oliver Lake.

At the organization's Washington Boulevard headquarters, the quintet fine-tuned its sound in marathon rehearsal sessions—making do without lights since BAG could no longer pay its electricity bills. To finance the transatlantic journey, Lake and his combo embarked on a bout of heavy gigging around town, sold off fixtures from the collective's building, and traded on BAG's local reputation to scrounge up a few tiny grants. Eventually they were able not only to finance their own passage, but also to bring along two vans for driving to the French provinces for gigs. On October 6, the quintet completed unfinished business in St. Louis, recording *Whisper of Dharma* along with saxophonists J. D. Parran and Jim Marshall. Ten days later, Lake and his family of five, along with Carroll and LeFlore, arrived in New York and boarded the S. S. *France* en route to Le Havre via Southampton, with Shaw and Bowie trailing close on their heels. For a short time, their remaining comrades tried to carry on the collective's dwindling artistic program in Missouri. But the five musicians' departure for Europe, coming four years and two months after BAG's inaugural performance of Genet's *The Blacks*, marked the formal end of the Black Artists' Group as a St. Louis institution.[15]

→⇒◎BAG◎⇐←

In decamping for Paris, the quintet of BAG musicians replicated the transatlantic journey of half a century's worth of African American musicians, visual artists, and writers. Since the early decades of the century, black migrants from the United States had often remarked that racial boundaries seemed somewhat more permeable in France, allowing a welcome freedom from constant reminders of their position in America's racial hierarchy. The years following World War II, especially, saw a vast wave of African American artists—figures such as Richard Wright, James Baldwin, Chester Himes, and Romare Bearden—relocate to France in what historian James Hall calls "a dramatic collective demonstration of dissatisfaction, if not disaffection." And the resurgence there of a heady pan-Africanism combined with the vision of colonialism's impending demise made the nation's capital not only a destination in itself, but also an entrepôt between the United States and newly independent African nations. Once in France, many of these émigrés formed links with leaders and theorists from the colonial world, as well as attracting the admiring attention of contemporary French intellectuals such as Jean Genet, Simone de Beauvoir, and Jean Paul Sartre. Rooted in the arts, but including expatriates working in many professions, the city's African American community was at once tightly knit and cosmopolitan.[16]

Moreover, from the days of Montmartre's vibrant interwar jazz scene onward, the French capital had always seemed particularly amenable to the American jazz musician. Even a partial list of those who made the city their temporary home would be a long and distinguished one. By the early 1960s, the image of the African American jazz artist marginalized at home but fêted in Paris had become a compelling legend, inspiring many to undertake the journey themselves. Unlike the older Paris discovered by Josephine Baker or Coleman Hawkins, by mid-decade the city had become both fashionable and expensive, confronting recent immigrants with greater challenges to make ends meet. Still, a vibrant musical community remained. Dozens of clubs featured French and international talent, and the city welcomed a constant infusion of newcomers that included artists such as Donald Byrd, Dexter Gordon, Steve Lacy, and Archie Shepp. Mid-1960s appearances by Ornette Coleman and Albert Ayler had ignited French interest in the art form's latest currents, and writers for the nation's leading music publications judiciously reported on many of the most noteworthy free-jazz events, so often ignored in the American music press. Despite the occasional difficulties faced by African American migrants in the wake of France's 1968 student uprisings, in the early 1970s the Parisian jazz scene still seemed to capture that elusive combination of critical acclaim and popular applause.[17]

With its broad networks of expatriates, noisy political commotion, and highly animated arts circles, the city seemed to hold promise for the St. Louis musicians, even if they did disembark with no name recognition, no booked engagements, and virtually no album releases to their credit. The group's initial place of residence in France—a dilapidated farmhouse just outside Rouen—was "really a drag," Floyd LeFlore says, "because it was like living in the sixteenth century," so the quintet quickly rented a house in Cressley, south of Paris, near the end-of-the-line Metro station at Saint-Remy-les-Chevreuse. Once settled, the BAG musicians drew on a list of contacts provided by their Chicago colleagues and, as LeFlore relates, "things started happening just like that." The promoters who had worked with the Art Ensemble proved happy to arrange a few preliminary concerts, to introduce the musicians to Parisian jazz audiences. The St. Louisans' first engagement, a televised concert, was an anticlimax: while the musicians were already in the midst of setting up their equipment, the show was canceled due to a French TV strike. Brushing off this false start, the ensemble instead made its debut at the Grand Palais on the Champs-Elysées as part of the inaugural Festival d'Automne, a citywide festival of contemporary arts.[18]

Perhaps unsure of how audiences would react to their highly theatrical performance approaches, in this first concert the BAG musicians refrained from adding their usual complement of grunts, hoots, and snatches of dialogue to the instrumental music. Instead, they opted for what one reviewer dubbed an "obstinate impassability," a stage presence marked by a "mask" style of seriousness. They must have been reassured, though, by the listeners' delighted reactions, for in their second concert they returned to more familiar approaches. Here, they melded vocalizations with an almost vocal style on their horns, both enhancing their rapport with the audience and informing the way that the instruments were heard.[19]

In Paris, the musicians carried on in developing the unusual instrumental combinations that had been one of their hallmarks in the United States. It was by necessity that they had developed their ability and fondness for playing without a standard rhythm section, for their entire St. Louis collective contained only one bass player, Arzinia Richardson. Hence, far from an unexpected or daunting move, the group's journey to France without the customary rhythm complement only provided new opportunities for creating fresh instrumental textures. The ensemble's bass-less lineup could sometimes even further free up the time; at other moments, it forced the musicians to develop innovative timekeeping roles on their own horns, disrupting the more rigidly defined instrumental responsibilities of the traditional jazz ensemble. Once in Europe, the BAG contingent also followed the model set by Anthony Braxton's 1968 album *For Alto*, the first for solo saxophone, by exploring the various possibilities inherent to solo or duo horn concerts.

Adrift at first, it didn't take long for the BAG veterans to integrate themselves into the thriving Parisian arts scene. They soon established an informal home base at the American Center for Students and Artists, a cultural organization at 261 Boulevard Raspail in the city's fourteenth arrondissement. Founded in the late nineteenth century, over the course of the 1960s the American Center had become a bustling focal point for expatriate dancers, writers, painters, and musicians, as well as a hangout for American countercultural figures, draft refugees, and radical intellectuals. At the center, the musicians discovered a ready-made version of the kind of vibrant, multidisciplinary artistic hub they had dreamed of creating in St. Louis. Here, Parisians and American émigrés could mingle while attending art exhibitions, benefits for civil rights causes in the United States, panel discussions featuring an eclectic assortment of writers and thinkers, or political speeches by figures such as James Baldwin and Jean Genet. But it was for the jazz avant-garde that the institution formed a particularly powerful center of gravity, hosting concerts by the likes of Marion Brown, Steve McCall, Frank Wright, and Archie Shepp from the mid-1960s onward. With its disciplinary diversity and its constant flurry of performance activity, the American Center proved an ideal locus of operations for the St. Louisans during their Paris tenure.[20]

Drawing on connections made at the center, the quintet busied itself with a packed schedule of performances, from routine club dates to major festivals. As Joseph Bowie explains, traveling "as an intact unit gave us a lot of advantages. We were a group already, with material, so it wasn't too difficult to market ourselves in the creative jazz scene which was flourishing in Europe at that time." Shows followed one after another at a range of venues, including the Cinéma le Palace, the Théâtre de la

THE BAG QUINTET WARMING UP BEFORE A PERFORMANCE IN PARIS, 1972. LEFT TO RIGHT:
CHARLES "BOBO" SHAW, JOSEPH BOWIE, FLOYD LEFLORE, BAIKIDA CARROLL, OLIVER LAKE.

-->=◉BAG◉=<--

Photograph courtesy Baikida Carroll.

Cité Universitaire, and the state broadcasting authority. In 1973, the American Center granted artist-in-residence positions to Oliver Lake and Anthony Braxton, and there the two arranged a series of duo reeds concerts. When not booked in Paris, the BAG ensemble traversed Western Europe, performing a number of times in Belgium and the Netherlands and opening for the fusioneers of Weather Report at the Châteauvallon Jazz Festival. In another attempt at self-production, they later released tapes of a spring 1973 performance at the Grand Palais as the LP *In Paris*. The only album ever released under the BAG name, the record garnered little attention, though London's *Jazz Journal*

International remarked that it "can be recommended to free freaks without reservation."[21]

The European jazz circuit seemed to allow for more fluid, relaxed interactions than were possible in the aggressive, highly competitive New York environment. Playing at festivals alongside Americans such as Don Cherry, Cecil Taylor, and Wayne Shorter, the unknown Missourians made valuable connections that would later help ease their transition into the New York musical milieu. "They hadn't heard us," Baikida Carroll later explained, "and when we'd come off the stage they would be elated." Members also found the city's existing free-jazz community to be warmly welcoming. They collaborated on occasion with U.S. emigrants such as Steve Lacy and Alan Silva and shared concert bills with the reedman and French free-jazz pioneer Michel Portal, who encouraged musical cross-fertilization between American and European players with his shifting improvisational group the Michel Portal Unit.[22]

Two musicians, in particular, more regularly joined the BAG quintet on concert dates. The first of these was Dominique Gaumont, a twenty-year-old guitarist, born just outside Paris of parents from French Guiana. A fervent devotee of Jimi Hendrix, Gaumont brought to the group an aggressive electric style that tallied perfectly with the interests of drummer Charles "Bobo" Shaw and trombonist Joseph Bowie, both of whom had always incorporated heavy funk and rock elements into their playing. Gaumont formed his own trio with Shaw on percussion, but ended up playing with the BAG ensemble so often that the French magazine *Jazz Hot* interviewed him as a sixth member of the group. It was Shaw who introduced Gaumont to members of Miles Davis's fusion band after that group's 1973 appearance in France. In the young guitarist's playing, Davis heard an "African rhythmic thing" that appealed to him, and several months later he called on Gaumont as sideman for his own *Dark Magus* and *Get Up With It* albums.[23]

Meanwhile, in the forty-five-year-old Bartholomew "Bazzi" Gray—a dynamically eccentric poet and singer, and a contributor on Archie Shepp's *Attica Blues*—the BAG musicians found a willing partner for crossovers with theater and spoken word. Impresario as well as musician, Bazzi Gray busily worked to organize a series of multimedia performance events in Paris. Often, Gray contrived these occasions as artistic dialogues between African and black American performers, and he sometimes drew on the BAG ensemble—for example, at a fall 1973 Black Arts Festival at the American Center and again for his mini-festival "Ceremonies for an Old Face," held at the Théâtre du Ranelagh in April of that year. The latter show was strikingly reminiscent of BAG's multimedia spectacles in St. Louis, interspersing contemporary jazz and Gray's idiosyncratic vocals with rhythm and blues, African dance and percussion, a vocal chorus, and a film from a Cameroonian director. Lake's seven-year-old son Gene pitched in on drums. The BAG contingent, though now shorn of its dance, drama, and poetry components, still embellished musical pieces with impromptu theater sketches, using them as "attention-getters," in Lake's description. During one performance, the puckish Gray leapt onstage to add to the St. Louis ensemble's music his trademark holler, "Where is that drivin' music, man?"—to which the instrumentalists fired back strings of scat scales, distorted scraps of jazz standards, and shouted phrases: "What's going on? Night time is the right time! The blues, the blues!" Decentered from their familiar geographic and musical contexts, such catalogs of allusions must have seemed a kaleidoscopic brand of postmodern performance art—a compendium, as one reviewer admiringly remarked, of "referential tatters."[24]

The presence of Lake and company in the French capital set off a minor critical buzz, even if the reception was less rapturous than that accorded to the Art Ensemble three years earlier. "There were some lean times," LeFlore recalls, "but once again, we had an audience. Once again, we had that stimuli where we could put our stuff out there." Given the group's impressive array of nonstandard instruments, its highly thematic and compositional approach to improvisation, and its broad scope of black musical styles, comparisons with the Art Ensemble were inevitable. "Since the Art Ensemble of Chicago passed through Paris, things have changed," noted critic Philippe Carles; "The memory, the reference is difficult to erase." Critics familiar with the Chicago musi-

BAG MUSICIANS IN PARIS, WINTER 1973.

⟶⟢◉⟣⟶

Photograph courtesy Baikida Carroll.

cians were eager to discern similarities and differences between the two ensembles, one noting that they shared "the same disciplined work ethic," another detecting a "politics of exchange" among their membership. Carles made clear, however, that the two cadres of musicians did not produce a monolithic body of work. The St. Louisans "cleanly distinguish themselves from those from Chicago," he commented, most notably in "their use of relationships between sound and silence, breath and music."[25]

The immediate attention from critics and listeners seemed again to confirm the wisdom of the move from Missouri. In contrast to the cold shoulder from the St. Louis arts press, here the ensemble's concerts

"POINT FROM WHICH CREATION BEGINS"

elicited savvy and approving appraisals from a small set of discerning critics, including a feature article from the longtime dean of French jazz writers, Maurice Cullaz. Reviewers lauded the group's "inventive power," the blues that was always "legible between the lines," the musical discourse "that is violently heterogeneous and never resolved." Several astutely noted the ensemble's diversity of sonic resources, culled from the African American musical archive and at once cited, manipulated, and resituated into a freshly inventive brew. Meanwhile, as Lester Bowie had promised, the audiences too proved enthusiastically receptive, and the St. Louis quintet in return admired their knowledgeable new fans. "We were amazed by the French audience," Shaw told *Jazz Hot* in summer 1973; "People seem to concentrate and participate completely. We feel that our music is really accepted without reservation."[26]

While Lake, Carroll, and their ensemble navigated the currents of the Parisian music scene, elements of BAG were also regrouping far to the north. The lure of new experiences outside of the United States had already drawn Malinké Elliott to the continent, and after leaving St. Louis in mid-1970, he studied under a string of artists at the forefront of contemporary European theater—first with the Italian-born director Eugenio Barba at Denmark's Odin Teatret drama laboratory, and then at the National Mime School in Stockholm, Sweden. Once settled in Stockholm, Elliott again crossed paths with his friend Maria Lexa, an actress who had briefly helped him train the original BAG troupe in St. Louis, and shortly thereafter he joined a drama company assembled by Lexa and her partner, the Swedish director Ingemar Lindh. Under Lindh's lead, Elliott and the small band of actors founded the seminal Institutet för Scenkonst, or Institute for Scenic Art, a theater workshop that matured into an influential international center for the education of actors and directors. The project offered Elliott the perfect opportunity to delve into the modernist continental traditions that he had only begun to unpack in St. Louis. Building on the innovations of theorists such as Jerzy Grotowski and Etienne Decroux, the institute's actors developed unpredictable performances characterized by a highly improvisatory physical technique and a strong dose of audience participation.[27]

As part of its national decentralization policies, the Swedish government soon assigned to Lindh's company the task of establishing a regional theater school in the sparsely populated north of the country. Just outside the small city of Östersund, the institute developed its headquarters at an old, disused schoolhouse, and participants traveled into the city to teach acting classes. From his base in Östersund, Elliott set about the task of reassembling a contingent of his BAG colleagues. Answering Elliott's entreaties, two members of BAG—actress Portia Hunt and actor/costume designer Darryl Harris—joined him in 1972 at the Institutet för Scenkonst, both serving as instructors and actors. The following winter, Julius Hemphill too flew across to Sweden. Having rounded up a handful of his old associates, Elliott, along with his wife Mary, the three other BAG alumni, and several young Swedes, formed his own troupe, a company called Sällskapet Sol, or Fellowship Sun. With modest stipends from the government, the five St. Louisans and their native partners embarked on several tours of the tiny villages in the country's snowy northern regions, drawing audiences of only dozens and lodging in the homes of sympathetic spectators.[28]

The four BAG artists brought to Sweden a taste of the improvisatory dramatic styles they had cultivated during earlier years in St. Louis. Hemphill and Mary Elliott backed performances on flute and bassoon, basing their music on Hemphill's *Dogon A.D.* project, while Harris and Malinké Elliott improvised various series of short sketches. Along with the new European techniques he was researching at the institute, Elliott infused his own troupe's productions with references to African American culture and, more specifically, the black church. The pieces, Hemphill observed later, were greeted with some puzzlement by the small Swedish audiences that showed up: "They didn't know what the hell he was talking about—you know, Baptist Church. . . . We had an interesting show, but people kept scratching their heads. Malinké was preaching, 'I'll take my text from bla bla bla. . . .' We had a bit of a cultural barrier, because the people didn't quite understand the references we were making."[29]

After several months with Sällskapet Sol, in April 1973 Hemphill borrowed the Swedish group's elderly Volvo, barreled through Germany along the autobahn, and tracked down the BAG quintet at their house south of Paris. Apparently, all was forgiven and forgotten regarding Hemphill's expulsion from BAG. He spent about ten days with his former colleagues, performing a set of informal concerts at the American Center.[30]

⇢⟾⟾◉BAG◉⟽⟽⇠

All was not bliss in Paris, however. The worldwide recession and oil crisis of the early 1970s pounded the French economy especially hard, and, accordingly, the slump upset the financial balancing acts of more than a few expatriate artists. Life for African American musicians in Paris grew more precarious as the decade wore on, a situation dramatized by the extinction of a host of jazz clubs that had flourished during the prosperous 1960s. True, the reception for their music was gratifying, but by the time the BAG ensemble had arrived on the scene, some of the novelty on both sides—European and African American—was wearing a bit thin. Lester Bowie came to believe that European listeners' enthusiasm for the Art Ensemble was not necessarily by virtue of a greater sophistication or erudition, but rather because the music's potential for consciousness-raising was less threatening in Europe than in the United States. The basis of French appreciation, too, was at times grounded in partial or even mistaken assumptions about the groups' ideology, with some listeners hearing in the music solely alienation and anger rather than the unbroken legacy of African American musical culture. While an earnest but sometimes naïve enthusiasm for black resistance in the United States had generated a vogue for the Black Arts nationalism of musical groups like the Art Ensemble and BAG, even this fascination turned out to be rather ephemeral. By the time the St. Louisans arrived, the initial shock had worn off. As Oliver Lake later noted, BAG entered the city "right at the end of that cycle. Things were just beginning to slow down by the time I arrived."[31]

Although their European travels had provided a congenial respite from the pressures and anonymity of artistic life in St. Louis, after several years abroad the BAG musicians began filtering back to the States. Hemphill's performances with Sällskapet Sol had been an artistic boon but a financial debacle. Penniless after three months in Sweden, he finally asked his wife Lynell to mail him a return ticket to the States. Meanwhile, after a little over a year in France Floyd LeFlore had grown homesick, and, with a baby daughter back in Missouri, he soon left for the States, followed shortly thereafter by Joseph Bowie and Charles "Bobo" Shaw. Lake and Carroll lingered in Paris through 1974, presenting duo saxophone/trumpet concerts and forming a working ensemble with American avant-gardists Peter Warren and Oliver Johnson, while Lake reprised a familiar St. Louis role by serving as solo accompanist for a Parisian dance company. Finally, feeling that Parisian opportunities had been at least partially exhausted, the two packed their bags for the return voyage, Lake in fall 1974 and Carroll the following year.[32]

While BAG's expatriate members developed their artistic careers abroad, back in Missouri the remnants of the group had almost entirely disintegrated. In 1973, Ajulé Rutlin returned home from travels through Oregon, Africa, and the American Southwest only to find that there was "no building, and no money, and no inspirational theme." The few alumni still in St. Louis surely must have found the period following the group's dissolution frustrating, for the volatile energy that BAG had released onto the local arts scene was not replicated by any other collective organization.[33]

Through the 1970s, remaining members tried to recapture some of the intensity and vigor of earlier years—Rutlin with his new poetry and music group Sources of Creativity, Floyd LeFlore and J. D. Parran with their band Third Spirit in Circuit, and others with various configurations of the Human Arts Ensemble. Paradoxically, though BAG had disappeared from the city, the early 1970s proved a fruitful period for recordings in St. Louis. The young saxophonist Luther Thomas, in particular, took on a leading role, forming funkier editions of the Human Arts Ensemble that fused uninhibited energy-music romps with elements drawn from the abstract, polyrhythmic electric collages then being released by Miles Davis. As musicians bounced back and forth to the city from their travels abroad, old faces reunited in various lineups for a handful of albums, as on the live 1973 recording *Funky Donkey*, where Thomas fronts an eleven-piece version of the Human Arts Ensemble that vibrates the interior of Berea Church with propulsive funk and Latin vamps overlaid with gusts of freewheeling collective improvisation. For a few years, new projects from the Human Arts Ensemble did fill some of the artistic vacuum left by BAG, although without a building or a formal organizational structure the group never became a center of gravity in the same sense that the original collective had been.[34]

The spectacular flowering of the Black Arts Movement was short-lived, and very few of the community arts groups that had been forged in its crucible lived on past the mid-1970s. The most notable exception, perhaps, is the AACM, which by 1971 had attracted a large second wave of members—artists such as trumpeter Malachi Thompson, percussionist Kahil El' Zabar, and saxophonists Douglas Ewart and Chico Freeman. Over the next several decades, the organization would continue to be rejuvenated by fresh cohorts of young musicians, and to this day it maintains a schedule of free classes on Chicago's South Side. And although the Black Arts organizations of the 1960s eventually faded from the nation's urban neighborhoods, the decade's numerous musical collectives, in particular, provided inspiring models of community engagement and economic self-sufficiency for emergent artists of the 1970s and 1980s. Within a few years of BAG's demise, critic John Litweiler later observed, "any number of music-producing cooperatives had appeared, some to thrive, others to disappear, from California to Connecticut and also in Europe."[35]

Perhaps, had its founders struggled on in St. Louis, BAG could have managed to survive like its sister collective in Chicago. Or maybe with a better organizational structure and a more generous program of funding, younger artists might have been trained to take the place of those who moved on to opportunities elsewhere. More likely, however, the emergence of the Black Artists' Group was part serendipity, a unique convergence of personalities seeking an artistic voice adequate to the social dislocations of their time. Indeed, several participants had always seen the collective's dissolution as inevitable and believed that their group had fully served its purpose during its four years of life. "BAG was an evolutionary process, and so I never lamented [its] passing," says Malinké Elliott. "BAG was merely a seed that allowed so many of us to develop out into the world community of arts." Former members also extended the creative spirit that had launched the organization, continuing to collaborate on a frequent basis long beyond BAG's St. Louis heyday. But when the musicians returned from Paris, it wasn't to their old home that they looked, but to New York.[36]

CHAPTER 7

GOING OUT LIVE: BAG AND THE NEW YORK LOFT SCENE

On a Friday evening in May of 1976, crowds jostled outside an unmarked warehouse on a side street just north
of Manhattan's SoHo district. From the gray, deserted
streetscape outside, a passerby would have little idea that some of avant-
garde music's leading lights were congregating to record an impressive,
near-encyclopedic document of contemporary jazz. Inside, sound engineers scrambled to make last-minute mike adjustments as sidemen for
bands led by Philip Wilson, David Murray, and others tuned up their
horns. Over the course of two successive weekends, twenty-eight ensembles would bustle through the loft building—dubbed Studio Rivbea by
proprietors Sam and Bea Rivers—laying down tracks in competition
with a noisy air conditioner while engineers clambered up and down
ladders trying to capture all the music on tape. The recording session
turned out to be a virtual who's who of New York's recent émigrés from
St. Louis and Chicago. Eleven of the festival's twenty-eight bands were
led by BAG or AACM personnel, including St. Louisans Oliver Lake,
Julius Hemphill, Hamiet Bluiett, and Charles "Bobo" Shaw, along with
their associates from the Chicago collective such as Roscoe Mitchell
and Anthony Braxton. The festival exemplified the ways in which black
musicians from BAG and the AACM, by the mid-1970s, had claimed
a dominant role in the city's creative music scene.[1]

Studio Rivbea's proprietor, the fifty-five-year-old saxophonist
Sam Rivers, was a veteran of the jazz circuit's trenches, with extensive
credits as a leader and as sideman to Miles Davis, Charles Mingus, and
others. Rivers and his wife Bea had made their home in a loft north of
SoHo for the past eight years, and since 1970 had been hosting performances and rehearsals, developing the site as a major center of new,
improvised music. In the days before the May 1976 festival, Rivers
and his friends canvassed the district, pasting makeshift flyers on the

ubiquitous boarded-up windows and peeling walls lining the streets. The do-it-yourself mentality that BAG and the AACM had pioneered in the Midwest was echoed in the underground music scene that New York's avant-garde musicians had come to embrace, whether reluctantly or enthusiastically, in the 1970s.

Small, independent labels such as Survival Records and India Navigation had managed to document a few of the New York avant-garde's performances, but up to this point the new music scene in the city's lofts still represented jazz music's worst-publicized innovation. The recording that emerged from Studio Rivbea's festival-cum-recording session, a five-LP release entitled *Wildflowers: The New York Loft Jazz Sessions*, introduced many listeners for the first time to midwestern artists such as Julius Hemphill and Oliver Lake. However, what in retrospect looks like an extraordinary all-star session was, at the time, an almost everyday occurrence in the industrial loft buildings of Lower Manhattan. So what brought these innovators from cities on the Mississippi or Lake Michigan or the Seine, or even from the Upper East Side, to the industrial bleakness of Lower Manhattan's manufacturing districts in the first place? How did their diverse styles of art music, with their compositional complexities and challenging improvisations, especially those born and bred in St. Louis, take root and thrive amidst the detritus of a manufacturing quarter in decline?[2]

The drama had already been played out in BAG's relationship with its alma mater—brought up in St. Louis, but finally loosening if not cutting those ties. The search for expanded musical opportunities had taken key members of BAG and the AACM to Europe, a quest that continued when both collectives began to regroup in New York during the early 1970s. And the philosophy of self-determination that they had cultivated in the Midwest dovetailed with similar impulses among resident New York players. By the time of their arrival, the city was overflowing with new, unknown performers and progressive musical ideas but lacked outlets for most of these players to present their work and build reputations. Of established clubs, only Sweet Basil and Storyville booked new jazz regularly, while major nightspots such as the Village

Vanguard, the Blue Note, and the Cotton Club typically opted for big-name stars, fusion, or older bop-oriented styles, all of which more easily filled seats than could free-jazz improvisers and other experimentalists. In response, dozens of musician-proprietors developed an extended circuit of Lower Manhattan loft venues as an alternative to the clubs, circumventing the bottleneck clogging the flow of new work into the marketplace. Describing this trend several years later, *Down Beat* critic Chuck Berg enthused that performers had "eliminated the middlemen of the music biz," commanding their own destinies in spaces "unfettered by commercial considerations." The arrival of so many BAG offspring in New York demonstrated once again the close relationship between artistic experiments and the social and physical spaces in which they are developed.[3]

The St. Louis and Chicago musicians entered the city's music scene in several waves, and the first to arrive were baritone saxophonists Hamiet Bluiett and James Jabbo Ware. After only thirteen months with BAG in Missouri, Bluiett had migrated directly to New York in September 1969, and his remarkable reading skills and range on the baritone quickly made him a prize member of many ensembles. Within weeks, Bluiett was sitting in with the likes of Sam Rivers, Pharoah Sanders, McCoy Tyner, and Elvin Jones. In 1972, Bluiett was invited to join the band of the bassist and composer Charles Mingus, and during his two-year tenure with the group, the saxophonist went through a period of intense turmoil and growth. In addition to working for a famously cantankerous bandleader, and "terrified to come" to New York in the first place, he was quickly becoming aware of the consequences of the adventuresome music he had chosen to play. As he later explained, he had developed "serious emotional problems" stemming from the tension between breaking musical conventions and satisfying audiences. Left "tormented" by negative reactions from listeners, for Bluiett the pressure grew so intense that he began skipping rehearsals and concerts. Finally, after discovering from an old interview that even the great John Coltrane had experienced similar trepidations over audience reactions, he coined the phrase "samurai baritone man" to describe a new, fearless attitude that he had adopted.[4]

Soon publications such as *Down Beat* had dubbed Bluiett "the most important baritone player to come along since Harry Carney"—the illustrious Ellington band member who had pioneered the instrument's use. His growing self-confidence combined with his versatility of styles made the "samurai baritone man" an indispensable player on the city's loft scene. At Bluiett's urgings, Ware also abandoned St. Louis for New York, there finding a musical home with Sam Rivers's rehearsal band and an income by gigging with Latin ensembles. Pursuing a long-standing dream to lead his own big band, he soon began assembling the Me, We and Them Orchestra, an ensemble that survives to this day. "You needed a day job in St. Louis," Ware remembers, "but when I first stepped into New York I could make a living at my trade, and I was in heaven." Shortly thereafter, several AACM members assembled in New York when saxophonist Anthony Braxton convinced AACM comrades Richard Davis and Muhal Richard Abrams, both still living in Chicago, to form a New York–based group with him. Ever since the death of Coltrane in 1967, many in the city's jazz avant-garde had felt that the scene was in a holding pattern, and they welcomed the new ideas and energy that the midwesterners brought with them.[5]

Opportunely, this New York migration coincided with the availability of large, open floors previously used for light industry as spaces for both living and performance. Of course, Manhattan's industrial loft buildings had been used sporadically by jazz musicians since at least the 1920s. Most famously, until the mid-1960s painter David X. Young's Flower District loft had hosted late-night jam sessions by a roll call of legends, musicians such as Bill Evans, Thelonious Monk, and Miles Davis. Free-jazz players of the 1960s also mounted occasional loft concerts, and Amiri Baraka opened his Cooper Square home to such events. It was only in the early 1970s, however, that lofts were adopted wholesale as performance venues, as jazz musicians sought out new spaces that evaded the seemingly stagnant or exploitive environment of the city's mainstream clubs. Here, the relationship between the arts and the city's physical spaces worked in both directions: the availability of low-rent lofts stimulated new musical directions, while the presence of these artists in industrial lofts spurred changes in the uses of Manhattan's built environment.[6]

The flowering of this particular musical community came at a moment of instability in the real estate market, when the city's loft buildings were poised between two successive uses: the old light industry and new, high-end housing. The trend toward converting industrial lofts for artistic purposes had accelerated during the early 1960s in SoHo, a Lower Manhattan district containing late-nineteenth-century building stock serving millinery, textile, and related industries. The area's manufacturing firms had been on the wane since World War I, and by the late 1950s, many of the remaining tenants appeared marginal and unstable. Numerous buildings sat boarded up or had been razed for parking lots. Meanwhile, a vigorous construction boom on SoHo's borders created an atmosphere of uncertainty about the district's future, which depressed rents, encouraged owners to defer maintenance, and spurred viable manufacturers to relocate. Although the territory south of Washington Square was seldom traversed by connoisseurs, cut-rate prices made it possible for low-income visual artists to move in. Early pioneers lived under spartan conditions, yet for those willing to forgo creature comforts, the cavernous lofts and huge freight elevators served an impulse toward creation on a grand scale, one derived in part from the minimalist, pop, and Fluxus movements. Once SoHo's first galleries opened their doors in 1968, a flood of performance artists, filmmakers, painters, and sculptors poured into the district. The area began to run on two parallel schedules: the nine-to-five timetable of industrial production, with the clatter of machinery percolating through artists' lofts; and the irregular rhythms—swelling to a crescendo on Saturdays—of art showings, crowded galleries, and '60s-style "happenings."[7]

However fashionable, the terrain was extremely unstable for artists. Those who moved to SoHo in the early 1960s had been living there in violation of zoning codes prohibiting residential use. In an attempt to legalize arts uses of the lofts without opening the area to a flood of conversions for the general public—which would presumably amplify price pressures on the area's remaining industry—a 1964 law allowed artists to live in SoHo's industrial buildings legally if they registered as artists with the city. But, lacking funds to bring buildings up to residential code, the area's artists did not enroll en masse. For landlords, who often colluded in this continuing violation, illegal residential conversions were potentially more profitable than industrial uses or making legal conversions. The more unscrupulous landlords sometimes leased space to artists illegally, and after they had performed improvements to make the space livable, would promptly alert building inspectors in order to have the illegal tenant evicted. Meanwhile, the continuing loft conversion process fueled fears among planners and critics that a flood of development would sound the death knell for remaining manufacturing.[8]

Musicians discovered the area several years later than the city's visual artists. The ethos of self-determination espoused by the jazz avant-garde meant little in practice without a physical environment under artists' direct control, so for them, too, the city's lofts held distinct advantages. They were spaces for both living and performing; were large enough to accommodate decent-sized audiences; and were located in industrial areas with few residents, allowing for noisy rehearsals at all hours of the night. And as the 1970s dawned, the process of deindustrialization was accelerating. From 1969 to 1975, Manhattan's manufacturing sector lost an average of 25,000 jobs per year—triple the average for the preceding twelve years—which left over a third of the borough's industrial lofts vacant. This transformation, however grim for workers and small businesses, did make it easy and inexpensive for jazz musicians to carve out new venues in SoHo and its adjacent districts. As the drummer and club owner Rashied Ali remarked, "Back in the '60s, you could get a loft for next to nothing—just to watch the building for a cat who didn't want to brush the bums off his doorstep." Spacious, cheap, and in the heart of America's jazz capital, the lofts fit the bill remarkably well, something that the former BAG musicians would leverage as they arrived on the New York music scene.[9]

The forerunner, though, was saxophonist Ornette Coleman. After moving into the fourth floor of an aging warehouse on SoHo's

Prince Street, Coleman had transformed the ground-floor storefront into a lively performance venue that he dubbed Artists House. Over the years of Coleman's residency on Prince Street, he encouraged a wide array of musical and dance performances: players from around the world lived for various stretches in the building, and leading lights of the experimental jazz and contemporary classical movements visited and performed. The communal atmosphere that developed inside the raw, unfinished spaces of Coleman's venue set the tone for the lofts to follow, and on the heels of Artists House, a spate of jazz performance lofts opened in the early 1970s. The gritty urban terrain where they set up shop had more in common with hole-in-the-wall clubs of yesteryear— or even with BAG's erstwhile headquarters on Washington Boulevard in St. Louis—than with the borough's new, upscale supper clubs.[10]

Two of the area's most important venues—Studio Rivbea and the Ladies' Fort—shared their digs with visual artists and light industry on adjacent blocks of NoHo's Bond Street. Rivbea's proprietor, Sam Rivers, had come up empty-handed in his hunt for a suitable location in Harlem. So he leased space on Bond Street and, in 1970, began presenting an extraordinary concert series in the building's spacious basement, even as manufacturers churned out cardboard boxes and novelty hats in the floors overhead. The studio swiftly became the epicenter of Manhattan's avant-garde jazz world, with *Down Beat* dubbing Rivers himself the "Warlord of the Lofts." Enthused a critic for *Coda* magazine, "Sam and Bea have converted their pad into a sounding board for creative music," describing crowds perched on folding chairs or sprawled on the floor, the performers and aficionados strolling and conversing between sets. Only a year later, Rivbea's dynamic atmosphere was duplicated just down the street at the Ladies' Fort. The Fort was run by Joe Lee Wilson, a gospel-influenced singer from Los Angeles who had opened the venue with funds from a winning horse bet. Along with several buddies, Wilson combed Manhattan streets in search of discarded carpets and furniture and hired the area's nocturnal graffiti artists to festoon his building's exterior with ancient Egyptian motifs and faces of musicians such as Billie Holiday. Soon thereafter, the Ladies' Fort was hosting both straight-ahead and free musicians, though Wilson recalls the biggest crowds for free jazz: "The further out it was, it seemed like the bigger the audiences for the shows."[11]

Within a few years, an entire grassroots performance circuit had emerged, spreading out from SoHo and adjacent districts into Chelsea, the Bowery, Gramercy, and beyond. Adventuresome listeners could catch shows at Jazzmania, with its overstuffed sofas and living-room ambiance; at Ali's Alley, a dingy SoHo building converted by Rashied Ali into a club and recording studio for his own Survival Records; at Environ, with its stark, white-walled interiors and impressive eleventh-floor view; at Studio We, 501 Canal, Sunrise Studio, and more than a dozen other venues. Here, audiences found a new kind of space for jazz listening, one that differed markedly from the nightclub or auditorium. For one thing, the fluid divisions between areas for living and performance, for audience and player, encouraged a more informal, egalitarian relationship among spectators and musicians. Environ's proprietor, pianist and sculptor John Fischer, explained this phenomenon to *The New York Times*: "People come to these lofts and they don't have to buy drinks or sit wedged in at a tiny table. So there's a freedom and a give-and-take between performers and audiences that you don't find in clubs or concert halls." And while the loft performances—as elsewhere in the jazz community—tended still to be male-dominated affairs, one female reviewer pointed out that unaccompanied women could frequent Studio Rivbea without encountering "the traditional attitudes . . . concerning women who go to hear jazz alone." Finally, many of the proprietors combined their music programs with other arts: for instance, sculpture and painting exhibitions at Environ, jazz-dance amalgams at Jazzmania, and Sunday poetry at the Ladies' Fort. Quite fortuitously, these had been the very attributes that BAG had sought to create in its own St. Louis operation.[12]

The communal atmosphere in the lofts was summed up in the title of Ornette Coleman's jubilant 1970 album *Friends and Neighbors*. By mid-decade, with musicians from around the world migrating to New York, the loft scene was bursting with what one reviewer called "a staggering amount of interchanging combinations of players, composers, and arrangers." Rather than dominated by a menu of a few big names, the new scene served up a mélange of shifting groups and personnel. Jazz events in the lofts could veer from casual jam session to polished concert and back again, and often the distinctions between performance and rehearsal seemed to disappear. Pundits saw the music as having the potential to re-energize a moribund jazz scene. As Hamiet Bluiett commented, "The critics who were going to the different halls . . . were bored. They came downtown where we were playing in the different lofts, and they began jumping up and down."[13]

<hr />

It was into this environment that the St. Louisans swept when a second wave of BAG alumni joined Bluiett and Ware in the early 1970s. Coming off his theater work in Sweden, Julius Hemphill spent the summer of 1973 in St. Louis, but felt he had "rather exhausted the possibilities" that the city could offer. In September, the saxophonist borrowed three hundred dollars from a local arts patron and bought a ticket for New York, where his wife Lynell had recently taken a position at Brooklyn College. Several members of the BAG quintet in Paris followed close on his heels. In France, the eager reception by audiences had stoked the musicians' enthusiasm for fresh challenges, and the thought of trying once again to drum up audience support and critical notice in Missouri seemed grim. Despite the previous decade's proliferation of regional cooperatives and record labels, in the jazz world of the 1970s, Manhattan still loomed just as imposingly as in Saul Steinberg's iconic New Yorker cartoon, with the rest of the country dwindling into a few dots on the horizon. Just before leaving Paris, Oliver Lake had conferred with Anthony Braxton and Baikida Carroll, mulling over the decision to return to potential obscurity and poverty in the United States. But, understanding New York's centrality in the jazz world—"the businessmen have it set up that way," he remarked—Lake with some reluctance made the move in September 1974, followed later by Carroll.[14]

The alternative arts community that had developed in the city's industrial buildings created a host of opportunities for these newcomers, and they were soon networking with musicians on the Lower East Side, leading bands at lofts and galleries, and participating in black cultural festivals. Lake studied meditation and comparative religion in his spare time, while Carroll supplemented his income playing backup studio work for funk albums and directing a big band at Queens College. Bluiett continued to be the most prolific of the collective's alumni on the burgeoning loft scene, organizing a series of big band workshops and presentations of his own music at Environ as well as writing for and directing a group he called the Hamiet Bluiett Free-Form Telepathic Instrumental Choir Workshop.[15]

Another transplant was the Human Arts Ensemble, now in a new incarnation headed by percussionist Charles "Bobo" Shaw and trombonist Joseph Bowie. After relocating from Paris to New York, the two had developed close friendships with Ellen Stewart, the director of the La MaMa Theatre, one of the city's leading incubators for experimental drama. In spring 1974, Stewart offered Shaw the use of the East Third Street building housing her Children's Workshop Theatre. Along with Bowie, the drummer took up residence there and quickly transformed the theater into a hub for the new jazz sounds buzzing through Lower Manhattan. When a young bassist named John Lindberg was evicted from his apartment across the street, Shaw invited him to move in, and Lindberg watched as the Children's Workshop Theatre evolved into an "all-day, all-night hangout and rehearsal hall. . . . Anyone might be there at any time—you just never knew." At their East Village center, Shaw and Bowie organized music workshops and classes for area children, opened their doors to round-the-clock rehearsals, put on Sunday morning "free-jazz church services," and started a hugely popular concert series featuring almost exclusively the new, edgy performers who worked in the various lofts, including Hamiet Bluiett, Julius Hemphill, Abdul Wadud, and Lester Bowie.[16]

Using the Children's Workshop Theatre as their geographic base, Shaw and Bowie reactivated the Human Arts Ensemble with a fresh cast of musicians. Gone were founding members from the group's late-1960s incarnation such as Ajulé Rutlin and James Marshall. Instead,

THE HUMAN ARTS ENSEMBLE IN A 1978 PERFORMANCE AT COLUMBIA UNIVERSITY.
LEFT TO RIGHT: JOHN LINDBERG (BASS), LUTHER THOMAS (ALTO SAX),
CHARLES "BOBO" SHAW (DRUMS), GEORGE LEWIS (TROMBONE), JAMES EMERY (GUITAR),
LESTER BOWIE (TRUMPET), PHILIP WILSON (PERCUSSION).

Photograph courtesy James Emery.

Shaw and Bowie assembled a shifting company that included St. Louisans Luther Thomas and Marty Ehrlich on reeds, Ohio and Michigan natives James Emery and John Lindberg on guitar and bass, and occasionally the AACM veterans George Lewis, Lester Bowie, and Philip Wilson. Though shorn of the poetry element that was so integral to the group's earlier embodiment, the Human Arts Ensemble developed a newly eclectic repertoire, ranging from mid-1960s modal swing to high-energy free jazz to three-chord electric rock. Powerfully motivated by Miles Davis's 1970s rock and fusion albums, Shaw formed the bedrock of the ensemble with his skill in weaving emphatic funk and Latin grooves into a free and expressive aesthetic. Later in the decade, the group took on two successful European tours, traversing the continent from Sicily to Norway—hamstrung only by Shaw's penchant for impulsively firing musicians in midjourney. This cross-genre work with the reformatted Human Arts Ensemble spurred Joseph Bowie in 1978 to form his most recognized group, Defunkt, an ensemble that melded danceable funk bass riffs, a jagged, hard-edged horn section, and strident, energy-charged lyrics with elements of punk rock and free jazz.[17]

Looking back, Oliver Lake explained that through the 1970s, the Black Artists' Group continued to exist "in a spiritual sense" through ongoing collaborations among its alumni in New York. Although the collective had ceased to be, here its musical wing continued a ghostly afterlife, functioning not as a formal organization, but rather as a broad network of allies who had shared a powerful artistic and social experience in St. Louis. Still, two themes remained constant from the organization's four-year tenure in the Midwest: constantly seeking out methods to circumvent the established route to marketplace success, and developing a musical aesthetic that worked in tandem with a variety of other artistic mediums. Regarding the first, the artists' formative years in St. Louis had given them valuable training in artistic institution-building, and they put these skills to use once again in New York. As Hemphill explained, in the early days "it was like starting from scratch, *inventing* the loft scene, really. There was no such thing until some people . . . came to town who had had experience in putting on stuff and seeing it bear fruit." While the midwestern émigrés cooperated with a set of partners from around the country, it was undeniable that the Chicago and St. Louis musicians injected the loft scene with a heady dose of fresh energy.[18]

Indeed, the self-production techniques that BAG's members had pioneered in St. Louis were almost as necessary in their new home. For although their efforts slowly earned them growing recognition among a small circle of cognoscenti, more often than not, the mainstream press and club-going public paid little heed to the new music being generated in the city's loft buildings. Critic David Jackson in 1975 lamented that Hemphill and Lake "are just two of many musicians . . . who are playing some mind-blowing music that's mostly being heard by the walls or a small group of devotees . . . who try to stay on top of the situation." So by necessity, the loft musicians' do-it-yourself mentality extended to arranging their own concerts and promoting them through word of mouth, advertisements in small-circulation papers such as *The Village Voice* and the *SoHo Weekly News*, and with handbills posted in the vicinities of the various lofts. Despite the usually small numbers, listeners were generally enthusiastic, attracted by nominal admission charges and the opportunity to hear fresh and stimulating, if often unknown, performers. From their Missouri years, BAG's musicians also drew upon a wealth of experience in acquiring grant money, a crucial talent in a decade during which government, academic, and philanthropic support was becoming central to the survival of the jazz art form. Lake explicitly connected these efforts in New York with BAG's ethos of self-determination in St. Louis, explaining that in both settings, "We didn't sit around and wait for someone to hire us. We went and got the place, we printed the posters, we put up the posters, we rehearsed the band. We became supermen in a way."[19]

Attempting to overcome this lack of audience and protest the exclusionary policies of the established jazz festivals, avant-garde musicians and loft proprietors had soon initiated a flurry of alternative festivals in the lofts, either confined to a single venue or ranging citywide. Since 1960, when Charles Mingus had staged an insurgent festival in protest against the exclusive and stodgy Newport Jazz Festival, independent, musician-produced festivals had become increasingly common. The loft jazz festivals had their beginnings when Newport director George Wein, cast by many avant-gardists as a chief antagonist, shifted his event to New York City in 1972. Angered by Wein's exclusion of experimental performers, musicians such as James DuBois, Archie Shepp, Rashied Ali, and Juma Sultan crowded into the Bowery's Studio We loft and there laid the groundwork for a counterfestival. In opposition to Newport, they organized the New York Musicians' Festival, using Artists House, Studio Rivbea, and sixteen other sites. By the following year, their festival had expanded to include 220 events, and soon almost all of the loft venues were organizing annual or biannual festivals. Oftentimes marathons lasting weeks on end and featuring astoundingly diverse lineups of avant-garde artists, they included the Tin Palace's Festival Fire pairing new and established musicians, the annual April Jazz Festivals at the Ladies' Fort, Studio WIS's New Music Festival, and Environ's Spring Solo Festival. These alternative festivals drew wider attention to the music and soon became a staple of the Manhattan creative music scene.[20]

Amid all this activity, the St. Louisans' commitment to expanding black audiences and challenging discriminatory conditions for African American musicians never waned. Although the jazz scene in the lofts was, for the most part, an interracial affair, the black cultural nationalism embraced by musicians of the 1960s survived in the New York music world of the 1970s. In the lofts, Sam Rivers argued, the music "is based on a lifestyle and that is black." At the same time, various New York institutions—among them the Jazz & People's Movement, the Black Artists for Community Action, and the Black Order of Revolutionary Enterprise—mirrored the work of forerunners such as BAG and the AACM by striving to overcome marketplace hurdles in order to promote an assertive and distinctive black identity in the jazz world. For several of BAG's members, the Collective Black Artists (CBA) served as a key vehicle for cooperative action. Spearheaded by the bassist Reggie Workman, the CBA was born in Chelsea's Studio WIS loft in 1970, and soon after they arrived in New York, Hamiet Bluiett and James Jabbo Ware joined the group. Unlike the Chicago and St. Louis collectives, the CBA as an organization held no particular aesthetic allegiance to experimental music, instead embracing artists working in a broad range of styles. But like its midwestern precursors, the CBA did focus strongly on economic issues for black musicians and on refurbishing the often denigrated or discounted African American musical tradition. Immediately after joining, Bluiett appeared along with Herbie Hancock, Freddie Hubbard, and others at a well-attended Black Solidarity Festival coordinated by the CBA, and he brought several St. Louis colleagues to the city for a seminar sponsored by the organization. Through the mid-

1970s, BAG alumni such as Bluiett and Ware worked steadily to build the CBA, and Bluiett eventually took a position on the group's seven-member executive board.[21]

Persistent labors to expand opportunities bore fruit, and audiences for new music swelled as the decade progressed. The loft scene reached its pinnacle of popularity in 1976 and 1977, with a flurry of feature articles in the mainstream press and a crest in the number of performance sites and alternative festivals. In 1976, four of the lofts—Environ, Jazzmania, the Ladies' Fort, and Sunrise Studio—banded together to put on the first New York Loft Jazz Celebration, and the next year their festival featured thirty concerts crammed into a three-day, round-the-clock musical marathon. For a brief moment, it wasn't unusual to witness stretch limousines gliding up to the various loft venues, lines snaking around the block, and jazz critics and industry scouts flocking to the shows. One reviewer colorfully remarked that Studio Rivbea's front rows were now filled by "record exec types who only lack gold medallions dangling on their exposed chests to complete the image." And by the mid-1970s, the BAG and AACM musicians had established themselves as integral members of New York's flourishing creative music community, anchoring the loft concerts and recording prolifically. Robert Palmer, music critic for *The New York Times*, pronounced in 1976 that the midwesterners "have rendered the clamorous playing characteristic of much of New York's jazz avant-garde all but obsolete with their more thoughtful approaches to improvisational structure and content."[22]

Through it all, the kinds of multimedia productions central to BAG in its heyday continued to exercise a hold on former members, as they expanded on the integrative aesthetics at work in the collective's earlier days. Once in New York, Oliver Lake worked as accompanist for the Merce Cunningham Dance Company, and his 1977 album *Life Dance of Is* evolved from a dramatic piece involving two actresses, original poetry, and music. Likewise, Baikida Carroll began crafting scores for a variety of theatrical productions, and he trekked back to St. Louis with Hemphill in order to revive a large multimedia show, *Coontown*

Bicentennial Memorial Service, for which the two had written music years before. And other artists who had emerged from the collective's cauldron were drawn into the circle again when Hemphill, Bluiett, Malinké Elliott, and several AACM veterans traveled to Chicago in 1976 to collaborate on *Musical Homage to Ants and Other Symbiotic Creatures*, a conceptual theater piece written by former BAG painter Emilio Cruz. A story recounted by the poet Quincy Troupe strikingly illustrates the collective's distinctive approach to blending different artistic forms into a single, seamless tapestry. When Troupe accepted a call for a big-band concert that Bluiett was organizing at a Manhattan church, Bluiett placed the poet in the saxophone section rather than in front of the band. Surprised by this configuration, Troupe asked the leader: "'How am I going to know when to read?' Bluiett told me, 'I'm going to point at you. I don't know when it's going to be.' That meant you had to drop right in like a musician. You couldn't have a poem ready, because you don't know what he's going to play. Usually you had to make it up at first, and then go into something you know. He points at you and—bang! Whatever the music is, wherever the tempo is, you had to drop in right there and do it." The idea here was to obliterate rather than enshrine the conventional distinctions among various performance mediums.[23]

Julius Hemphill remained the collective's chief organizer of multimedia performance events. Ever since his return from Sweden, the saxophonist had been collaborating with Malinké Elliott whenever he could on such theatrical presentations. In New York, the two popularized an original and idiosyncratically personal concept of the "audio-drama" in the city's galleries and lofts. Mounting improvisational dramatic pieces with names like *Obituary: Cosmos for Three Parts* and *Twilight Boogie*, the two drew on a set of unorthodox spaces for their work—venues such as Ornette Coleman's Artists House, a Chelsea music loft known as the Brook, and the Peace Church in Washington Square, with its massive pipe organ and restrooms plastered with leftist graffiti.[24]

The piece that attracted the most notice, however, was an audio-drama originally dubbed *Ralph Ellison's Long Tongue*, with Hemphill culling his title from an aphorism that he often heard as a child—"laying a tongue on somebody"—meaning that "an elder had given an upstart a good dose of wisdom." To the saxophonist, that phrase could equally well summon up "the versatility of the saxophone, and its endless ability to dispense wisdom." In its original version, the show borrowed text from Ralph Ellison's novel *Invisible Man* and, in particular, from the section where the unnamed protagonist delivers a disillusioned and fatalistic monologue at the funeral of the recently murdered Brotherhood leader Tod Clifton. The inaugural performance, a 1978 show at the Corcoran Gallery in Washington, D.C., featured Elliott improvising on the Ellison monologue in various voices—a preacher, a professor, a carnival barker, a street person, an activist—while Hemphill "tried to proceed with the rhythm of spoken language" in his accompaniment, often mirroring each syllable with a specific musical note. Elliott used the *Invisible Man* source materials, he remembers, to craft loosely structured, gallows-humor commentaries on both political apathy in the black community and the persistent repression of African Americans who attempted to "assert their manhood." Though reviewers criticized the initial presentation as "elliptical" and "verbose," the two artists continued to rework and expand their audio-drama over the next thirteen years, eventually attracting funding from the National Endowment for the Arts and other nonprofit arts agencies.[25]

Within a few years, the concept had evolved into an entirely new show. In a 1981 presentation at the Kitchen, a leading SoHo venue for experimental jazz and contemporary classical music, Hemphill and Elliott solicited poetic readings from their St. Louis friend K. Curtis Lyle and integrated dancers as well as rear-projected snippets from their decade-old experimental film *The Orientation of Sweet Willie Rollbar*. By then, they had dropped the *Invisible Man* underpinnings in favor of a fictional nightclub setting, where successive generations of jazz musicians mingled and rehearsed while Elliott, in the role of the club's cynical and irritable janitor, tries to goad them out the door. Here, in a series of dialogues and monologues, the musical history of jazz was employed as a lens through which to recount the postwar transformation of African American politics and culture. Later in the decade, the show took on a greater degree of historical and geographic specificity when it was revived as *Long Tongues: A Saxophone Opera*. Choosing as their setting the Crystal Caverns—a prominent black club in Washington, D.C., that had remained permanently shuttered after that city's 1968 riots—Hemphill and Elliott presented a series of meditations on the evolution of the jazz art form. The pit band summoned up the musical styles of performers who had passed through the Caverns over the decades, while actors evoked the club as a vibrant node for cultural innovation, examining the music's relationship with landmark civil rights events and the social geography of Washington's black neighborhoods. In his saxophone opera's final incarnation, a lavish 1990 staging at New York's Apollo Theater, Hemphill yet again expanded on these themes, delivering an intergenerational exchange between the Crystal Caverns' fictional curator and two materialistic young rappers in which the curator encourages the disaffected youths to claim the long black musical heritage as their own.[26]

⇥•≡⊙ఴ◖≡•⇤

Busy establishing themselves through scores of self-produced loft concerts and multimedia experiments, for BAG's New York cadre, the next career move involved finding opportunities to place their work before a wider national listening public. But after the decidedly mixed success of their own St. Louis record companies, cutting and selling albums no longer seemed an enterprise that so easily lent itself to self-production. With the Universal Justice and Mbari labels, Charles "Bobo" Shaw and Julius Hemphill had managed to develop only extremely limited distribution networks, and while several of their albums—especially the Human Arts Ensemble's *Under the Sun* and Hemphill's *Dogon A.D.*—had become underground classics in musicians' circles, apart from new-music connoisseurs, the record-buying public remained mostly oblivious. So once they arrived in New York, the BAG musicians retained little interest in the mundane, day-to-day tasks necessary for keeping their own labels up and running, and they quickly sought out opportunities to put old albums back onto the market with a minimum of hassles. Because of the reputations that several of the BAG artists had established in Paris, the longtime record producer Michael Cuscuna had become aware of their work and was eager to meet the musicians upon their return to the United States. Cuscuna was then heading up the British Freedom label, distributed domestically by Arista Records, and he offered to buy a handful of old masters, giving several of the out-of-print Mbari and Universal Justice records a second life by reissuing them on Freedom. Still, despite the St. Louis musicians' newfound success on the New York loft circuit, the old Human Arts Ensemble records were among the least popular in the Freedom catalog, selling fewer than 2,400 copies each over a period of several years. At around 4,000 copies in sales, Hemphill's *Dogon A.D.* reissue proved only slightly more popular, boosted in part by extensive play on college radio.[27]

However, most of the BAG musicians soon began recording new material at a prolific pace, reaching wider audiences with a spate of album releases throughout the mid- and late 1970s. While a few of the city's AACM transplants, notably the Art Ensemble of Chicago and Anthony Braxton, had signed long-term deals with major labels such as Atlantic Records and Arista, the St. Louisans found locating attractive record contracts somewhat more difficult than did their Chicago counterparts. Still, a few small New York labels did offer contracts to some of the leading musicians on the loft circuit, even if these outlets lacked extensive distribution networks and advertising budgets. For example, India Navigation, founded in 1972 by a moonlighting corporate lawyer, recorded important avant-garde artists such as Hamiet Bluiett—many of them live in the loft venues. And as minor European labels continued to assume the role once played by their defunct American counterparts, companies such as Italy's Black Saint Records provided a congenial home for performers such as Lake and Hemphill.[28]

Through the 1970s, BAG alumni recorded a set of extraordinary albums that represented the maturation of many of the concepts first cultivated at their St. Louis headquarters. Three months after Lake's move to New York, he recorded *Heavy Spirits*, his first LP for Arista Records, incorporating many modernist classical influences. From live concerts in 1976 and 1977, Hamiet Bluiett issued his albums *Endangered*

Species and *Birthright*, the latter a solo baritone recording containing tributes to Brooklyn, Illinois, and many of the teachers and family members who had helped to launch his career. And with *Coon Bid'ness*, Hemphill delivered a set of compositions that adapted free-jazz solo techniques to a blues and R&B sensibility, remaining constantly informed by the cadences of the black church.

By the mid-1970s, Lake, Hemphill and their BAG comrades had been working for over a decade to find and foster settings where they could get a hearing—from early days at the Circle Coffee Shop and elaborate programs at the BAG center to their barnstorms across Western Europe and the bustle of the Manhattan loft scene. Now legendary among a small group of musical insiders, they nevertheless remained frustrated at the lack of wider attention for their music. Oliver Lake pursued his critique, developed during his years with BAG, of a capitalist media and music industry that ended up controlling or even muffling black creativity. He maintained his contention that while in African American communities the musician functions as "the one who takes the word, gives messages, or inspires people to do other things," the nation's system of commercial media outlets acts in the opposite direction, squeezing artistic creation into a carefully structured hierarchy. Since the unexpected, the serendipitous, or the experimental is less easily commodified, this closed system works only to stifle the aesthetic imagination. "The more docile and trained they keep the masses," explained Lake, "the less trouble." The next phase in three of the BAG artists' careers was yet another attempt to break out of that suffocating musical and economic paradigm. It took the form of one of the most innovative and lasting ensembles to emerge from the BAG collective: the World Saxophone Quartet, a group that existed in one form or another from 1976 to the present and garnered at least some of the wider critical acclaim that had always eluded the St. Louisans. Despite that larger audience, Lake later explained that, just as with BAG, the World Sax Quartet was yet another effort to "protect artists' rights and encourage self-empowerment."[29]

Three of the four group members were BAG alumni: Oliver Lake, Julius Hemphill, and Hamiet Bluiett. They had first showcased a four-sax piece sans rhythm section on Anthony Braxton's album *New York Fall '74*, but since unusual instrumental combinations had been BAG's bread and butter and were staples on the loft-scene menu as well, they apparently thought no more about the concept over the next two years. Then in summer 1976, Edward "Kid" Jordan, an altoist who had spent the summer playing the loft circuit, booked the three BAG saxophonists for a December concert at Southern University in New Orleans, where he chaired the music department. For that show, the three St. Louisans filled out their ensemble with the young tenor saxophonist David Murray, a former protégé of drummer and critic Stanley Crouch at Pomona College and a rising star on New York's loft scene. In New Orleans, the quartet was met by a rapturous response from a primarily black audience, one that ranged from infants to senior citizens. "We hit," Bluiett later narrated, "and the energy of the music was so out and everybody dug it. . . . Kids were just running around like a wagon train and nobody said anything to them." And just as intriguingly, as Hemphill noted, the performers elicited "as good a reception *without* any kind of rhythm [section] as we did *with* it." The four musicians decided to push the concept further. They prepared to launch a more permanent career, first as the New York Saxophone Quartet, and then—after discovering the name was already taken by a classically oriented group—as the Real New York Saxophone Quartet. Finally, under threat of legal action, the foursome "decided to give them New York" and settled instead on the more ambitiously titled World Saxophone Quartet—en route, as Hemphill wryly put it, "to being the Intergalactic Saxophone Quartet."[30]

Several months later, in February 1977, the quartet made its New York debut at the Tin Palace, a grungy East Village club sitting just a block north of punk-rock mecca CBGB's and directly under the loft apartment that Murray shared with Crouch. Despite the recent proliferation of art lofts and music clubs, the Lower East Side was still decidedly mixed in its commerce and population. The Tin Palace's proprietor, a poet and former merchant seaman named Paul Pines, described his venue in an autobiographical novel as "an oasis in badlands that stretched between Fourteenth and Canal," a club that he had spent years "defending . . . against the pissers, hawks, drifters and winos who spilled out of the men's shelter on Third Street." The music spilling out of the Palace door was emphatically outside the middlebrow comfort zone as well, and on any given night one might find the likes of Charles Mingus, Cecil Taylor, or Barry Altschul filling the club's seats or perched on its small bandstand. In short, everything about the Palace was auspicious for the daring swerve from the conventional that traversed the stage that February night. Taking the platform in front of a packed house, the four-man ensemble opened with a flute quartet and moved to an all-sax lineup before adding a rhythm section for the second set. It was the first set, though, that caught the critics' attention. To many listeners, an ensemble composed of four saxophones and no rhythm section appeared an oddly truncated approach to jazz, a rehearsal that seemingly began before all the players had arrived. But like it or not, the lineup dramatically forced musicians and their audiences to find new ways to articulate and imagine rhythm, and eventually to redefine what even constituted a jazz ensemble.[31]

Given the range of individual players and groups ultimately influenced by the World Sax Quartet, it is easy to overlook the tremendous amount of flak directed at the group's novel configuration. Was it a gimmick? reviewers and listeners asked. When would the group relent and add a standard rhythm section? At a few performances, incredulous audience members strolled past the stage pantomiming drums or bass, and at least one owner of an eminent New York jazz club insisted that the group add a rhythm section before he would book them—a demand the group flatly refused. At the time, Hemphill observed, he was "galled" by the hidebound thinking that provoked such reactions, feeling it was "absolutely ridiculous to think that meaningful music could not be made unless certain elements were present. . . . So that alone was an inspiration to me to prove them wrong." The group's stubborn confidence was at least indirectly rewarded when one after another single-instrument ensemble sprang up in the World Sax Quartet's wake, projects that later included Bluiett's own Clarinet Family and Baritone Nation. Within a few years, a wide body of listeners had come to concur with *The New*

York Times assessment of the quartet as "probably the most protean and exciting new jazz band of the 1980s."[32]

The World Sax Quartet used thick, weighty textures to conjure up an immense variety of black musical styles and forms. Their sound plumbed the well of gospel, blues, New Orleans swing, rhythm and blues, bebop—all strained through the mesh of a distinctly modernist musical vocabulary and technique. And over time, its members developed increasingly compelling ways of fusing experimentalism with tradition and intense, ferocious propulsion with subtle, restrained elegance. A number of reviewers, however, noted the sometimes unassimilated alternations of virtuosic solos on the group's first recording, the 1977 live album *Point of No Return*, and David Murray retrospectively described the World Sax Quartet's first two years as "star wars, cacophony. . . . We were trying to blow each other away." Subsequent releases, especially beginning with their third album, *W.S.Q.*, and continuing through 1980's *Revue* and 1981's *Live in Zurich*, found the ensemble's players working more and more intentionally as an ensemble rather than as individual virtuosos, layering the tonal ranges of their instruments and playing off solos dramatically against the interventions of other members.[33]

Hemphill was often mistakenly seen as the band's leader, probably because he was its most prolific composer. In fact, all of the members constructed charts for the quartet, though Hemphill did provide the lion's share of the compositions. His rapid maturation as a composer took the form of lush, Ellingtonian harmonies that dissolved into ethereal solo passages, and part-writing that often evoked chamber music, with harmonies simultaneously suggesting the acidic bite of the blues and the carefully mapped dissonances of a Bartok string quartet. The effect on the group was stimulating: the intricately complex compositions, Bluiett remembers, forced them sometimes to rehearse ten or twelve hours a day in order to execute the treacherous section passages precisely. Still, only about a fifth of the group's repertoire was composed prior to performance; the rest of the music was frequently improvised within broad frameworks dictating voicings, solo lengths, and so on.

HAMIET BLUIETT
baritone saxophone, flute

JULIUS HEMPHILL
alto & soprano saxophones

OLIVER LAKE
alto & soprano saxophones, flute

DAVID MURRAY
tenor saxophone, bass clarinet

HAMIET BLUIETT, JULIUS HEMPHILL, OLIVER LAKE, AND DAVID MURRAY, PICTURED ON THE BACK COVER OF THEIR 1979 ALBUM *STEPPIN' WITH THE WORLD SAXOPHONE QUARTET*.

This type of extended collective improvisation was made possible by each member's almost telepathic awareness of his bandmates' proclivities, a skill at least partially traceable to the long partnerships established in their erstwhile St. Louis collective.[34]

A distinctly theatrical bent to performance also harked back to the days of BAG. The World Sax Quartet often donned tuxedoes for concerts, suggesting not only the seriousness of their endeavor but also the surrendering of individual personality to the identity of the group. And yet their approach to playing was never somber, and performances could be filled with buoyant onstage repartee. One contemporary reviewer described a concert opener this way: "From stage right at New York's Public Theatre comes a honking, infectious vamp figure that calls forth visions of dancers, blues bands and endless nights walking the bar. The World Saxophone Quartet comes bopping out to a unison step, looking armed and dangerous in their natty tuxedoes." With their powerfully driving rhythmic approach, the group often elicited intensely visceral responses from listeners. "I think if people don't move, there is something wrong," Bluiett commented; "If I don't want nobody to move, I'll go play at a mausoleum." And as in the BAG years, the quartet was keen to cultivate a wider black audience for their music. In a 1979 interview, Hemphill cited African American listeners' "intimacy with the music that we play"—an "awareness and exuberance" that derived from the embedded nature of the music in black communities—as reason that black audiences were "like home ground" for the quartet. Even as audiences for early performances usually turned out to be at least 85 percent white, the ensemble's members continued to cite the mostly black audience for their inaugural New Orleans show as the most exciting and satisfying they had played for.[35]

Given the highly conservative aesthetic turn in the jazz world of the 1980s, the World Sax Quartet's commercial success came to appear somewhat astounding. A number of their recordings on the Black Saint label sold well, their performances and albums elicited solid reviews in major papers and magazines, and they were in constant demand not only at small clubs but also on some of the most prestigious festival stages in the United States, Europe, and Japan. Critical acclaim, a degree of popular success, and a vehicle for musical innovation that seemed built for the long haul—all were goals that extended back to the first glimmerings of BAG in 1968. And when they released *The World Saxophone Quartet Plays Duke Ellington* in 1986 on Elektra Nonesuch, their first American label, the album broke through to a wide jazz-listening public, selling more copies in the United States in its first ten days than had any of their previous six albums worldwide. But paradoxically, the group's greatest commercial success also surfaced latent tensions, revealing the polarity between Hemphill's structured arrangements and the others' pull toward the more highly improvisational. Oddly, this wasn't helped by even the good reviews. As Hemphill put it, "I was getting too much credit. I always told interviewers we all contributed, but people had the perception that I was the leader because I wrote the bulk of the music. And that didn't sit well." More serious were disagreements over choice of projects and the artistic direction of the band, and these led ultimately to Hemphill's expulsion from the group in 1989, a parting of ways that seemed uncannily reminiscent of his ejection from BAG eighteen years earlier.[36]

<hr/>

As the 1970s progressed, the loft scene that had propelled many artists into the limelight began to transform. While musicians had been eager to create the loft performance opportunities in the early years of the decade, the prospect of eking out a living through unsteady loft gigs slowly began to lose its appeal. Those who had once anchored the scene could be seen less and less frequently in the city's loft venues. Meanwhile, the mixed and sometimes incommensurate uses of Lower Manhattan's industrial buildings—visual art, music, residence, and manufacturing—eventually led to conflicts among the district's inhabitants. While the SoHo of the 1960s was generally deserted at night, by the mid-1970s the neighborhood's increasingly residential character meant that late-night jam sessions were likely to elicit complaints. In Ornette Coleman's case, for example, the constant rehearsals at Artists House led to ongoing battles with neighbors over sound levels. The saxophonist was first evicted from the ground floor; following several court battles, he finally threw up his hands and deserted Artists House in frustration. And paradoxically, even as residents such as Coleman were driven out by noise complaints, other musicians and visual artists were forced to relocate by a proliferation of ear-splitting late-night disco dance clubs.[37]

But the loft movement's success was apparent in the expanding number of new, nonloft concert venues for innovative jazz musicians. Avant-garde players such as Oliver Lake appeared at Carnegie Recital Hall, Alice Tully Hall, and New York University's New Music Showcase. Meanwhile, the New Jazz at the Public series, which ran at Joe Papp's Public Theater on Lafayette, mixed established names—players such as Sun Ra, Archie Shepp, and Anthony Braxton—with relative unknowns. The series soon became the premier showcase for the city's avant-garde jazz community, with various concerts released on record or broadcast over National Public Radio, and it offered a prominent forum for BAG offspring such as Oliver Lake and his quartet, Baikida Carroll and his Ring septet, and Julius Hemphill's twelve-piece ensemble to cultivate a growing public for the music's new directions. "Avant-Garde Jazz Climbs out of the Loft," proclaimed a 1979 *Washington Post* headline—the reviewer asserting that wider exposure and new venues were transforming experimental artists into "full-fledged members of the popular music community." To the pioneers who had forged the loft scene in the early 1970s because there was simply nowhere else to play, the striking number of venues for new music—lofts, concert halls, clubs, theaters—seemed remarkable. The exodus of the loft scene's leading lights for higher-paying, more prestigious venues was an escape made possible, ironically, by the very success of the lofts in introducing a favored few artists to the broader public.[38]

Although some stalwarts slipped into an undeserved obscurity in the aftermath of the loft scene's zenith, for the St. Louisans this alternative music circuit had acted as a springboard to wider appreciation. But regrettably, by 1978 the city's loft scene itself was in decline, and within two years it would vanish almost entirely. For many players, the strain of constant hustling to find and fill venues had taken a toll, sapping energies away from rehearsing and composing, and ultimately making the unremitting calendar of loft performances difficult to sustain. These venues, too, never did supply enough opportunities for all the city's struggling artists to display their work. But several factors led more directly to the end of the decade's loft jazz era. In addition to the gradual exodus of the scene's highest-profile artists, the loft community was severely destabilized by rising prices of industrial buildings due to real estate speculation and residential conversions; by the escalating costs for performing in lofts as musicians were increasingly required to rent spaces by the night; and by squabbles among loft proprietors, mostly over the economic terms under which performers would use the venues.[39]

Experimentalist musicians had claimed their tenuous position in the inhospitable terrain of the city's jazz world in large degree through their ability to capture a slice of real estate. But as the municipal government gradually legalized residential use of Manhattan's industrial buildings, a period of rapid and intense gentrification ensued, with landlords and speculators happily displacing commercial businesses and artists alike. In 1975, the city began offering tax abatements and exemptions to owners and developers converting manufacturing buildings to residential use, and the following year, TriBeCa and other districts were rezoned to permit general residence. In a city that had seen little apartment construction over the preceding decade, residential loft conversions were "essentially the only game in town," as one urban planner noted, "and developers were hot to play." And ironically, the press coverage that had accompanied the artists eventually worked to price them out of the area by attracting an image-conscious, upper-income residential population. With conversions proliferating even as the manufacturing sector stabilized dramatically, the city's industrial-space vacancy rate plunged from 35 percent in the mid-1970s to 5 percent by 1980. The crunch for space and spiraling rents contributed to an increasing dispersion of the loft performance facilities, as new jazz lofts opened farther north in Manhattan than ever before, chased outward by the expanding circle of rising prices centered on SoHo. By the early 1980s, artists of all kinds were abandoning the borough, driven to Brooklyn, Hoboken, Jersey City, and even farther afield.[40]

It wasn't surprising, then, that the loft jazz scene grew increasingly institutionalized, and perhaps more rigid, during the late 1970s. Loft performance space was now a hot commodity for artists, and the relaxed, communal music venues of the early part of the decade were being supplanted by more formal, professionally managed sites that leased their space to performers rather than hiring them. While playing in the lofts had never been a lucrative proposition for jazz musicians, the new climate, with by-the-night rentals and a lack of guaranteed pay from proprietors, meant that musicians could actually lose money on a show with a poor audience turnout. As Hemphill grimly explained, "We practically had to pay to play. By the time we ran off some handbills and got somebody to distribute them, maybe rehearsed, maybe not, you could get fifteen, twenty, thirty people to show up. . . . You maybe had to rent the space from somebody. Sometimes if they provided the space, then they'd get a percentage of whatever proceeds occurred. And there was no kind of money to be made."[41]

At the same time, many musicians were feeling increasingly typecast by the "loft jazz" label. The majority of observers imprecisely used the term to designate a specific musical style rather than a type of venue, casually conflating the avant-garde jazz community with the trend toward performing in converted industrial spaces. In fact, however, experimentalist musicians used all sorts of venues—churches, lofts, theaters, and colleges—while the lofts themselves frequently hosted bebop, swing, and Latin players. In response, several of the most visible musicians, primarily émigrés from the St. Louis and Chicago collectives, appeared in the press to discuss their reservations about the "loft jazz" pigeonhole and the economics of the scene in general. Hamiet Bluiett, for example, fumed in *The New York Times* that mid-1970s publicity had "convinced some of the people who ran the lofts that they should be getting more out of it. . . . Now I find a lot of the lofts want to have a kind of sharecropping system: they want the musicians to split profits above $200, or something like that." To some proprietors, such negative comments in the media reflected only ingratitude for the opportunities that musicians had been afforded. Jazzmania manager and clarinetist Mike Morgenstern, for instance, argues that a cadre of players wounded the scene by deciding "to bite the hand that originally fed them, and be quoted in all the jazz magazines saying they were against 'loft jazz,' there was no such thing as 'loft jazz,' [and] that they were being exploited by being asked to work off the door." In any case, such tensions over media practices, musical categories, and financial conditions could simmer to the surface at any given moment—especially in a milieu where the life-giving oxygen of media coverage was in such short supply.[42]

As the loft scene peaked in popularity in 1977, disagreements over proper economic practices touched off bitter quarrels among proprietors. The concept of by-the-night loft rentals appalled Sam Rivers, a longtime advocate of guaranteed compensation. Rivers himself paid performers at Studio Rivbea a flat fee, and he objected to loft owners who booked musicians in exchange for the money taken at the door, arguing that this practice undercut musicians' ability to demand a salary from nightclub owners. Other proprietors found this criticism rather hypocritical, since Studio Rivbea alone among the loft venues received subsidies from the state arts council and the National Endowment for the Arts. The less charitable dismissed the Rivbea scene as "welfare jazz." Escalating feuds culminated in July 1977 with the infamous "War on Bond Street," when Studio Rivbea and the Ladies' Fort planned competing festivals for the same week. Stanley Crouch, the organizer of the Ladies' Fort festival, had booked many of the same musicians as Studio Rivbea, and Rivers issued an ultimatum that those appearing in the rival festival would be scratched from his own lineup. Since Crouch's festival guaranteed participants only the door money, a few performers acquiesced, although others defied Rivers's demand. After three days of mediocre audiences, Rivers abruptly canceled his festival, decrying "hasty duplications . . . by imitators" and a "lack of cooperation by some of the musicians." The divisive affair left the lofts "wracked by disunity," as *The New York Times* reported, and ended with irate musicians duking it out on the sidewalks of Bond Street.[43]

⇢⇥⊙✦⊙⊜⇤←

The progenitors of BAG had cultivated an art form inextricably tied to the spaces of urban America. But not for the first time in the collective's history had commercial indifference, bureaucratic entanglements, and alternate civic priorities united to undermine the synergy between environment and art. Of course, civic elites have long cast the arts—especially large-scale cultural facilities—as a means to revitalize depressed urban areas, while artists themselves, who do not wield such power, commonly find themselves in search of urban spaces that are amenable in both price and design to their professions. However, by the early 1980s in New York, a cacophony of competing interests drowned out the music, as a range of factions sought to define and control how the city's loft spaces would be used. Various municipal offices wanted either to preserve the industrial base or to raise property tax valuations; community groups called for stable, viable neighborhoods; manufacturing unions and firms demanded security for established industrial uses; construction unions and developers insisted on new building; the real estate industry aimed for a continuing rise in prices; and artists sought the ongoing availability of low-rent spaces. In the end, artists blamed urban planners for allowing developers access to areas such as SoHo and TriBeCa. The instability of real estate uses that had initially made this jazz performance circuit possible finally made it untenable when the economic terrain shifted once more.[44]

For BAG's musicians, though, the loft scene had unlocked the New York City music world, giving them entrée to larger audiences and the standing to pursue groundbreaking projects such as the World Saxophone Quartet in increasingly prestigious venues. The hard work of circumventing the established record companies and clubs that they had begun in St. Louis paid off, as the avant-garde of the 1970s solidified its hold on at least a small sector of the listening public during the difficult years of the 1980s. The contrast between the jazz scene in the loft venues and the conventional fare of New York's more expensive mainstream clubs demonstrated yet again the importance of "space" to aesthetics, not just in the metaphorical sense of a cultural or social space for risk-taking, adventurous art, but in the concrete sense of physical space—buildings, districts, neighborhoods—where economically marginal but culturally valuable artistic creation can take place. For a brief moment, a convergence of physical, financial, and aesthetic forces opened the loft districts of Lower Manhattan to the creation of something rich and strange.

EPILOGUE

Almost two decades after the Studio Rivbea sessions, and only twelve months before his untimely death at age fifty-seven, Julius Hemphill spoke with Katea Stitt, daughter of the legendary saxophonist Sonny Stitt. During this oral history for the Smithsonian Institution, Hemphill insisted: "People keep looking rearward for the tradition. The tradition in this music is forward, forward! Not what you did last week, but *this* week." In defining the past not as a fund of dead memories to relive nostalgically but rather as a springboard to innovation, Hemphill identifies a crucial attribute of the entire BAG experiment and experience. So when in 2001 Harvard's Fogg Art Museum sponsored a collaborative tribute to Hemphill, it is not surprising that BAG associates Marty Ehrlich and Oliver Jackson took on the task, and also that they collaborated to create a space filled with images and sound—painting, sculpture, music. Their goal was not to look "rearward," as Jackson and Ehrlich explained, but to "create an homage to him, something that has a particular ambience," a space "where the different elements interact so the [visitor] will be drawn into a resonant relationship with both music and painting." This kind of shared exploration across established boundaries speaks to the forward-looking spirit of the Black Artists' Group, and the musicians' foray into the New York loft scene had been just one more example of that vigorously innovative orientation. From their immersion in St. Louis's black musical heritage to their early networking in the city's black clubs and on the rhythm-&-blues scene, from their first multimedia productions to their new set of spaces at LaClede Town and ultimately their own building, from St. Louis to New York—those associated with BAG combined restless experimentation with a sense of origins and tradition.[1]

Admittedly, retrospect makes all things seem to cohere. The ephemeral burns away; the accidental disappears to reveal the essential form that had been hidden from the contemporary eye. But the history of BAG resists such idealizing, not least because the organization itself was so protean. A few constant themes, however, do emerge from BAG's repertoire: arts as a potent method of community engagement, institution-building as a response to the social and economic forces rending the fabric of urban life, and an aesthetic vision focused on black heritage and tradition in the context of new forms and techniques. As Oliver Lake told *Down Beat* in 1975, "BAG was an incredible organization, full of raw energy. It was creative stimulus for all the artists involved. We were voluntary specimens in an experiment to present culture as both an exclusive creation of the people and a source of creation, as an instrument of socio-economic liberation." Lake's claim positions community as source and subject of an art that both reflects and challenges the culture that gives rise to it.[2]

The organization's history suggests ways that a collaborative and community-based approach to creativity can energize both artist and audience. In particular, its experience tells us about the potential links between the arts and individual neighborhoods, social struggles, and efforts at a particular kind of institution-building. Like so many of the 1960s community arts organizations, BAG sought to make the arts accessible to local people as audience members, while at the same time developing a forum for wider participation. In another sense, the group took the arts as a means to address and engage with indigenous issues, creating a space in which aesthetic creation both reflects and speaks to the traditions and concerns of the surrounding area. It claimed the arts as part of the fabric of life in a given locale, not external to or privileged over the quotidian, but in continual dialogue with it.

This interplay suggests the arts as one forum for a kind of public discourse that often eludes us today. Shirley LeFlore locates the complex nature of BAG's collective orientation in its dual allegiance to collaborative and individual expertise. The St. Louis organization, she says, "reached some of the goals that it didn't even know it had: the collective voice; a place to be somebody; a place to develop your craft. Because ultimately, whether it's the Black Arts Movement or the human arts movement, artists need a place to work on their craft. And not just art for the sake of art, but art that can be appreciated, art that can be shared."

Whether in poems and plays generated by pressing civil rights concerns, performances that thrust the arts into the middle of local events, or venues that grounded the organization's energies in the city's individual neighborhoods, BAG's impetus derived from a dynamic relationship with the St. Louis community. And while that community encompassed a number of intersecting circles, it was centered in the north side black populace with which the group tried to connect both by its social activism and by its choice of location for its base. Here, the community was creative engine as well as passive recipient, something Hemphill pointed out many times: "This ain't out of a conservatory. This is out of the neighborhood. That's where my impetus comes from."[3]

Community involvement, of course, does not guarantee creativity and innovation, in fact sometimes works against them, as any group tries to perpetuate its more conservative norms and values. BAG's art in its most experimental and radical form may have been increasingly inaccessible to an uninitiated audience, but the collective's members worked to overcome this aesthetic distance by grounding themselves in the concerns, the struggles, and even the streets of North St. Louis. This commitment to building artistic institutions embedded in the local continued on in the work of BAG alumni long after the group's demise. In Tucson, Arizona, Ajulé Rutlin founded a performance and production unit called Eneke-the-Bird in 1977, with Oliver Lake on the board of directors, an effort to present challenging and underappreciated artists to audiences there. And in 1985, Lake and Lester Bowie teamed up with pianist Cecil Taylor to establish the Musicians of Brooklyn Initiative, an attempt to boost employment opportunities for musicians and to cultivate public appreciation for known and unknown artists working in America's indigenous music. A number of the artists associated with BAG even found themselves back where they had begun their careers. After sixteen years teaching elsewhere, for example, Eugene Redmond returned to East St. Louis in 1985 to lend his artistic vision to local struggles once again, and he was eventually named that city's poet laureate. In the 1980s, Shirley LeFlore founded the Creative Arts & Expression Laboratory in St. Louis, an organization built from the BAG blueprint as a means to foster young poets and creative writers. And more recently, Hamiet Bluiett left New York in 2002 to make Brooklyn, Illinois, once again his "home base for the world."[4]

The Black Artists' Group emerged during a time when social pressures and historical transition collided with the stability of a particular place and its traditions. Its luck was to draw in a set of individuals with the skills to register the tremors of that collision of forces, to negotiate for a brief time the divide between the communal and the individual talent. Social and cultural instability can often create a space for aesthetic innovation. Musically, the fault line between traditional and experimental forms of jazz had not yet opened so wide that it could not be bridged. Theater was negotiating a wobbly balance between the demands of avant-garde form and those of social engagement. The long reign of abstract expressionism over the American art scene had been challenged by new departures from its austere strictures. In this context, BAG tapped into an opportune ambivalence about artistic subject and style. The group was energized, in turn, by like-minded innovators just outside the tight circle in St. Louis. Baikida Carroll observed this synergistic interplay in a comment about music that, in fact, shrewdly describes the organization's entire project: "The miracle of the AACM and the Black Artists' Group, existing in different cities as they did, is that we were all searching for something, philosophically, to keep the world of improvised music perpetuated." Rooted in the local, the St. Louisans drew also upon regional and national sources of artistic energy to fuel their creative journey. And, as the group's aftermath demonstrates, they did not cease from exploration.[5]

In all of this the organization was exemplary, perhaps, rather than influential, as evidenced by its peculiar absence from conventional histories of its home city. Today, the building that housed the cooperative for its brief career sits vacant, the surrounding storefronts even more derelict, the streets emptier than they were thirty-five years ago. And however many projects its members have undertaken or awards they've received in the years since, the group itself still remains just about as underground as it was during its four years of existence in its abandoned warehouse on Washington Boulevard. Yet though many former members have gone on to national and international recognition, even those who continue to labor in relative obscurity still draw on the BAG spirit. Whether one is absorbing the sounds of Oliver Lake at Carnegie Hall or Jerome "Scrooge" Harris at the tiny Delmar Lounge in St. Louis, the BAG experience still undergirds the approach to creation and performance. The astonishing richness of the Black Artists' Group deserves recognition as a unique and engaging effort to strike a note that would resonate to the social and cultural vibrations of its time.

ACKNOWLEDGMENTS

Shuffling in from a light rain to a small, upstairs art gallery in St. Louis several years ago, I witnessed an absorbing performance that mingled a puppet show with poetry and contemporary jazz. The program notes told me that the bandleader, Floyd LeFlore, was a founding member of the seminal Black Artists' Group. The show and the BAG acronym stuck in my head, and Mary Seematter of Washington University later encouraged me to explore the collective's history. I'd like to acknowledge her kind and expert help. For their mentorship over recent years, I also want to thank the following teachers: Les Back, Chris Becker, Annette Burkhart, Michael Denning, Rockwell Gray, Robert Hughes, Roland Jordan, William Lenihan, Hugh Macdonald, Angela Miller, Ingrid Monson, Linda Presgrave, John Szwed, Sue Taylor, Fran Tonkiss, and Conevery Bolton Valenčius.

This project was made possible by the many people who shared memories, dug old papers out of attics, passed along faded chapbooks, and supplied other one-of-a-kind items. I'd especially like to thank Suzy Frechette, Charlie Rose, and Evan Spring for providing assistance and materials. I gratefully acknowledge permission to reprint portions of Katea Stitt's 1994 interview with Julius Hemphill: © The Jazz Oral History Project Collection, Archives Center, National Museum of American History, Smithsonian Institution, and America's Jazz Heritage, supported by the Lila Wallace–Reader's Digest Fund. In consideration of future researchers, transcripts of the interviews conducted for this book have—when permission was granted by the interviewee—been placed at the Missouri Historical Society Library and Research Center and at the Special Collections of Washington University in St. Louis.

Several of my interviewees kindly consented to read portions for accuracy. Though they may differ with my account in places, I hope they feel that it does a small measure of justice to their accomplishments. I appreciate the assistance from teachers and friends who insightfully commented on draft segments: among them, Amanda Ciafone, Michael

Denning, Daniel Gilbert, Dolores Hayden, Ellen Ketels, Eric Rosenstock, John Szwed, Sue Taylor, and Logan Wall. I also thank Jeff Lash, who expertly constructed the map, and K. Curtis Lyle, for his guidance and good humor. My father, Mark Looker, has gone far beyond the call of duty in reading, commenting on, and discussing this project with me, and I am deeply grateful for his help. Naturally, all errors and shortcomings are mine alone. My most important acknowledgment goes to my parents Karri and Mark, and my sister Anna for their unflagging support.

APPENDIX:
BAG MEMBERSHIP LIST, 1970

BOARD OF DIRECTORS

EXECUTIVE COMMITTEE

Chairman	Mr. Julius Hemphill
Executive Director	Mr. Malinke Kenyatta
Treasurer	Mr. Oliver Lake

Artistic Advisor	Staff Secretary
Mr. Oliver Jackson	Marian Hill

MEMBERS

Cathy Allen
Liz Carpentier
Georgia Collins
Emilio Cruz
Pat Cruz
Roswell Darby
Robert Edwards
Carl Flowers
Stanley Hanks
Darryl Harris

Ricky Curtis
Julius Hemphill
Portia Hunt
Malinke Kenyatta
Oliver Lake
Floyd LeFlore
Pat Mountjoy
Muthal Naidoo
J.D. Parran
Victor Reef

Carl Richardson
Charles W. Shaw
LeRoi Shelton
Joseph Steward
Bensid Thigpen
James Ware
Valerie Williams
Bakida Yaseen

AT LARGE

Ajule Menelek

REPRODUCED FROM BHG, "BLACK ARTIST'S GROUP: PROPOSAL FOR A NEW THEATRE,"
UNPUBLISHED TRANSCRIPT, 1970, AT MISSOURI HISTORICAL SOCIETY

Discography:

TITLE: *Ofamfa*

ARTIST: Children of the Sun

RECORDED: St. Louis, fall 1970

TRACKS: *1.*) Sweet street song
2.) Uu-twee
3.) After Jeremiah's wed
4.) Sounds of Scorpio
5.) 'Trane song
6.) Rent man
7.) A little Tom is a dangerous thing
8.) Echoes (O Suzanna)

PERSONNEL: Ishac Rajab (trumpet); Floyd LeFlore (trumpet, small instruments); Oliver Lake (soprano, alto, flute, poems, small instruments); Arzinia Richardson (bass, small instruments); Rashu Aten [Carl Davis] (conga, small instruments); Vincent Terrell (cello); Ajulé Rutlin (poetry, arrangements, small instruments, drums)

RELEASED: c. 1971, Universal Justice Records, UJ 101 (LP)

NOTES: Universal Justice Records promotional materials read: "Music/Poetry from live performances at the Black Artists' Group Center, St. Louis, Mo. Recorded during the Fall Concert Series of 1970, featuring the Children of the Sun and poet Ajulé Rutlin's arrangements of eight selections from the repertoire. The theme: Spiritual Ecology."

TITLE: *The Collected Poem for Blind Lemon Jefferson*

ARTIST: K. Curtis Lyle and Julius Hemphill

RECORDED: St. Louis, 1971

TRACKS:
1.) Lemon's Holy Blues
2.) Lemon's Warm Life Blues
3.) Lemon's at the Shore of the World Blues
4.) Lemon's Etched in Halved Moons Blues
5.) Lemon's Comin on Strong Blues
6.) Lemon's Born at a Bad Time under a Lemon Sign Blues
7.) Lemon's Revised Birdman Blues
8.) From Sun to Sun Blues
9.) Devil Got My Woman Blues
10.) Lemon Dance
11.) Lemon's Easy Riding Skyboat Too Late Earth Moving Blues or a Dozen Different Blues
12.) Lemon's Brand New Shiny Skyboat Blues
13.) Lemon's Whistle Blowin Heart Pealin Blues
14.) Lemon's New World Blues
15.) Lemon's Fixin to Die Blues
16.) Lemon's New Shot between Planets Blues
17.) Lemon's Last Ditch Harmonize My Black Mule Blues
18.) Lemon's New Everclear Blues
19.) My Own Blues

PERSONNEL: K. Curtis Lyle (vocals); Julius Hemphill (saxophones, flute); Malinké Kenyatta [Malinké Elliott] (vocals on track 17)

RELEASED: 1972, Mbari Records, 5002 (LP)
2002, Ikef Records, IKEF 05 (CD)

TITLE: *NTU: Point from Which Creation Begins*

ARTIST: Oliver Lake

RECORDED: St. Louis, 1971

TRACKS:
1.) Africa
2.) Tse'lane
3.) Electric Freedom Colors
4.) Eriee
5.) Zip

PERSONNEL: Oliver Lake (alto, soprano, flute, small instruments); Baikida E. J. Carroll (trumpet, small instruments); Floyd LeFlore (trumpet, small instruments); Joseph Bowie (trombone, small instruments); Richard Martin (guitar); John Hicks (piano); Clovis Bordeaux (electric piano); Don Officer (electric bass); Charles "Bobo" Shaw (drums); Don Moye (conga)

RELEASED: 1976, Arista-Freedom, AL 1024 (LP)

TITLE: *Red, Black and Green*

ARTIST: Solidarity Unit, Inc.

RECORDED: St. Louis, 18 Sept. 1970

TRACKS: *1.)* Something to Play On
2.) Floreo
3.) Beyond the New Horizon

PERSONNEL: Charles Wesley Shaw, Jr. [Charles "Bobo" Shaw] (percussion); Richard Martin (guitar); Oliver Lake (alto, flute); Floyd LeFlore (trumpet); Joseph Bowie (trombone); Carl Richardson [Arzinia Richardson] (bass); Clovis Bordeaux (piano); Danny Trice (conga); Baikida Yasseen [Baikida Carroll] (trumpet); Kada Kayan (bass)

RELEASED: 1972, BAG Live Concert Series (LP)

TITLE: *Dogon A.D.*

ARTIST: Julius Hemphill

RECORDED: St. Louis, Feb. 1972

TRACKS: *1.)* Dogon A.D.
2.) Rites
3.) The Painter

PERSONNEL: Baikida Yasseen [Baikida Carroll] (trumpet); Julius Hemphill (alto, flute); Abdul Wadud (cello); Philip Wilson (drums)

RELEASED: 1972, Mbari Records, 5001 (LP)
1977, Arista-Freedom, AL 1028 (LP)

TITLE: *Coon Bid'ness*

ARTIST: Julius Hemphill

RECORDED: St. Louis, Feb. 1972 (track 5); New York, 29 Jan. 1975 (tracks 1–4)

TRACKS: *1.)* Reflections   *4.)* Skin 2
2.) Lyric   *5.)* The Hard Blues
3.) Skin 1

PERSONNEL: Tracks 1–4: Julius Hemphill (alto); Black Arthur Blythe (alto); Hamiet Bluiett (baritone); Abdul Wadud (cello); Barry Altschul (drums); Daniel Ben Zebulon (congas). Track 5: Julius Hemphill (alto); Baikida E. J. Carroll (trumpet); Hamiet Bluiett (baritone); Abdul Wadud (cello); Philip Wilson (drums)

RELEASED: 1975, Arista-Freedom, AL 1012 (LP)
1995 (as *Reflections*), Freedom, 741012 (CD)
1996, Black Lion, 760217 (CD)

NOTES: Track 5 recorded at the *Dogon A.D.* sessions in St. Louis.

TITLE: *Poem of Gratitude*

ARTIST: Human Arts Ensemble

RECORDED: St. Louis, Oct. 1972

TRACKS:
1.) Introduction
2.) Out to Lunch
3.) Sophisticated Lady
4.) Imagination 1
5.) Imagination 2
6.) Imagination 3
7.) Funny Things
8.) Poem of Gratitude
9.) Strange Autumn Tree Shapes
10.) Upbeat Feeling
11.) God Bless the Child

PERSONNEL: Ajulé Rutlin (tenor radong, vocals, drums, small instruments); Luther Thomas (tenor, tenor radong, small instruments); James Marshall (alto, tenor radong, small instruments); Carol Marshall (vocals, bass radong, small instruments)

RELEASED: 1972, Universal Justice Records, UJ-102 (LP)

TITLE: *Whisper of Dharma*

ARTIST: Human Arts Ensemble featuring C. Bobo Shaw

RECORDED: St. Louis, 6 Oct. 1972

TRACKS: 1.) Whisper of Dharma   2.) A World New

PERSONNEL: Charles "Bobo" Shaw (drums, small instruments); Joseph Bowie (trombone, congas, small instruments); Oliver Lake (tenor, soprano, flute, small instruments); James Marshall (alto sax, radong, wooden flutes); J. D. Parran (tenor, soprano, bass clarinet, small instruments); Floyd LeFlore (trumpet, small instruments); Gene Lake (drums, small instruments); Baikida E. J. Carroll (gong, small instruments)

RELEASED: 1972, Universal Justice Records, UJ 103 (LP)

1977, Arista-Freedom, AL 1039 (LP)

TITLE: *In Paris, Aries 1973*

ARTIST: Black Artists' Group (BAG)

RECORDED: Paris, spring 1973

TRACKS:
1.) Echoes
2.) Something to Play On
3.) Re-Cre-A-Tion
4.) OLCSJBFLBC

PERSONNEL: Baikida E. J. Carroll (trumpet, flugelhorn, bass, log, cowbells); Floyd LeFlore (trumpet, voice); Joseph Bowie (trombone, conga); Oliver Lake (saxophones, flute, marimba, mud drum); Charles "Bobo" Shaw (drums, percussion)

RELEASED: 1973, BAG, 324 000 (LP)

TITLE: *Under the Sun*

ARTIST: Human Arts Ensemble

RECORDED: St. Louis, July 1973

TRACKS: *1.)* A Lover's Desire   *2.)* Hazrat, the Sufi

PERSONNEL: Lester Bowie (trumpet); Marty Ehrlich (alto, tin flute); Carol Marshall (vocal, small instruments); James Marshall (alto, wooden flute, punji, small instruments); J. D. Parran (bass clarinet, soprano, flute, piccolo, harmonica, small instruments); Victor Reef (trombone); Charles "Bobo" Shaw (drums); Butch Smith (bass); Abdallah Yakub (percussion, small instruments); Alan Suits (tamboura); Vincent Terrell (cello)

RELEASED: 1973, Universal Justice Records, UJ 104 (LP)
1975, Arista-Freedom, AL 1022 (LP)
1996, Freedom (Japan), TKCB-70329 (CD)

⟶⟫═◉⟨BAG⟩◉═⟪⟵

TITLE: *Funky Donkey, Vols. 1 & 2*

ARTIST: Luther Thomas Human Arts Ensemble

RECORDED: St. Louis, fall 1973

TRACKS: *1.)* Funky Donkey
2.) Una New York
3.) Intensity

PERSONNEL: Luther Thomas (alto), Lester Bowie (trumpet); Joseph Bowie (trombone); Charles "Bobo" Shaw (drums); J. D. Parran (reeds); Floyd LeFlore (trumpet); Harold "Pudgey" Atterbury (trumpet); Abdella Ya Kum (percussion); Rocky Washington (percussion); Marvin Horne (guitar); Eric Foreman (electric bass)

RELEASED: 1977, Creative Consciousness Records, CC-1001T (LP)

2000, Atavistic/Unheard Music Series, UMS/ALP 215 (CD)

NOTES: Live recording of a concert at Berea Presbyterian Church, St. Louis.

⟶⟫═◉⟨BAG⟩◉═⟪⟵

TITLE: *Banana: The Lost Session, 1973*

ARTIST: Luther Thomas Human Arts Ensemble

RECORDED: St. Louis, 1973

TRACKS: *1.)* Three Seven
2.) B Natural
3.) Headhunter
4.) Banana
5.) Out
6.) B Natural (alternate take)

PERSONNEL: Luther Thomas (alto, piano, slide whistle, finger chimes); James Marshall (alto, tenor, soprano, flutes, small instruments); Abdullah Yakub (alto horn, small instruments); Carol Marshall (voice, accordion, small instruments); Charles "Bobo" Shaw (drums)

RELEASED: 2002, Atavistic/Unheard Music Series, UMS/ALP 227 (CD)

AUTHOR INTERVIEWS

Aten, Rashu (Carl Davis)

Bowie, Joseph

Carroll, Baikida

Castro, Michael

Cruz, Emilio

Cruz, Patricia

Cuscuna, Michael

Dickerson, A. J., Sr.

Dudley, Carl

Ehrlich, Marty

Elliott, Malinké Robert

Emery, James

Emrick, Michael E.

Gaillot, Philippe

Green, Percy

Harris, Jerome "Scrooge"

Holder, Kendrick

Hughes, Manuel

Hunt, Portia

Jackson, Oliver

Koch, Richard "Terry"

Krasne, Margo T.

LeFlore, Floyd

LeFlore, Shirley Bradley

Lexa, Maria

Lindberg, John

Loewenstein, Carol (Carol Marshall)

Lyle, K. Curtis

Major, Alvin

Marshall, James

Mason, Keith Antar

Morgenstern, Mike (Mo Morgen)

Murray, Nicholas

Naidoo, Muthal

Nessa, Chuck

Osby, Gregory

Parran, J. D.

Pines, Paul

Pratter, S. Jerome

Ranelin, Phil

Redmond, Eugene

Ries, Stan

Rose, Charles E.

Rutlin, Ajulé

Sargent, Peter

Sayad, Elizabeth Gentry

Shelton, LeRoi

Terrell, Vincent

Troupe, Quincy, Jr.

Ware, James Jabbo

Wilson, Joe Lee

Where permission was granted by the interviewee, transcripts of these interviews have been placed at the Missouri Historical Society Library and Research Center and at the Special Collections of Washington University in St. Louis.

Key to Abbreviations in Notes

MHS   Library and Research Center, Missouri Historical Society,
               St. Louis.

WHMC   Western Historical Manuscripts Collection,
               University of Missouri, St. Louis.

SCSL   Special Collections, Saint Louis Public Library.

FASL   Fine Arts Department, Saint Louis Public Library.

WUSC   Special Collections, Washington University,
               St. Louis, Missouri.

FFA   Ford Foundation Archives, New York, New York.

NYPL   New York Public Library, New York, New York.

ICAP-RAC   Inner City Arts Project, Record Group 1.2, Series 200R,
               Box 289, Folders 2719-2722, Rockefeller Foundation Archives,
               Rockefeller Archive Center, Sleepy Hollow, New York.

COINTELPRO   FBI Counter-Intelligence Program, File no. 100-448006,
               Federal Bureau of Investigation, Washington, D.C.

NOTES

INTRODUCTION NOTES

[1] "Black Arts Concert Feb. 26," *St. Louis Post-Dispatch*, 7 Feb. 1971; "African Continuum," *PROUD Magazine* 2, no. 3 (Mar. 1971): 16–21, MHS; program for the African Continuum, Images: Sons/Ancestors, Powell Symphony Hall, St. Louis, MO, 26 Feb. 1971. Thanks to Anne Kohs & Associates of Portola Valley, CA, for providing the program. Musicians playing at the Images concert included Willie Akins, Zak Diouf, Julius Hemphill, John Hicks, J. D. Parran, Ishaq Rajab, Victor Reef, Mor Thiam, Abdul Wadud, and Philip Wilson.

[2] Program for Images: Sons/Ancestors; Julius Hemphill, interview by Katea Stitt, 26 and 27 Mar., 14 Apr. 1994, tape 3 of 4, transcribed by Evan Spring and Conrad Bauer, Jazz Oral History Project Collection, Archives Center, National Museum of American History, Smithsonian Institution, Washington, DC. I am grateful to Evan Spring for drawing my attention to Hemphill's Smithsonian Institution oral history and providing me with the transcription. Where I quote from the oral history in this book, I generally follow the Spring and Bauer transcription, although in several instances I have used alternate punctuations and sentence divisions.

[3] Dana L. Spitzer, "Powell Hall Brings Glitter Back to Grand," *St. Louis Post-Dispatch*, 9 Feb. 1968; Eugene Redmond, "Indigenous Struggle Pays Off," *FOCUS/Midwest* 6, no. 41 (1968): 43; Jackson, author interview.

[4] Hemphill, interview by Stitt, tape 3 of 4; program for Images: Sons/Ancestors; Michael Harper, *History Is Your Own Heartbeat: Poems by Michael S. Harper* (Urbana: University of Illinois Press, 1971), 77–95. See also Michael Harper's poem "Audio," which describes the Images event, in *Songlines in Michaeltree: New and Collected Poems* (Urbana: University of Illinois Press, 2000), 327–28. For commentary on the influence of Oliver Jackson's visual art on Michael Harper's poetry, see Michael Antonucci, "Cryptic Cartography: The Poetry of Michael S. Harper and the Geo-Poetic Impulse" (Ph.D. diss., Emory University, 2000), 220–22, 259–61.

[5] On Black Arts Movement critiques of the Harlem Renaissance, see, for example, Larry Neal, "The Black Arts Movement," in *The Black Aesthetic*, ed. Addison Gayle, Jr. (Garden City, NY: Doubleday, 1971), 273.

[6] J. D. Parran, "The St. Louis Black Artists' Group (BAG): Improvisation in an Unbroken Continuum," unpublished essay presented at the symposium Improvising across Borders, University of California–San Diego, Apr. 1999, 3, on file with author.

[7] Howard Nemerov, "Thirteen Ways of Looking at a Skylark," in *Figures of Thought: Speculations on the Meaning of Poetry* (Boston: David R. Godine, 1978).

CHAPTER ONE NOTES

[1] *The Mississippi: River of Song,* dir. John Junkerman (Washington, DC: Smithsonian Institution, 1999).

[2] William Cronon, *Nature's Metropolis: Chicago and the Great West* (New York: W. W. Norton & Co., 1991), 296–303; William Howland Kenney, "Just before Miles: Jazz in St. Louis, 1926–1944," in *Miles Davis and American Culture,* ed. Gerald Early (St. Louis: Missouri Historical Society Press, 2001), 26.

[3] Parran, "The St. Louis Black Artists' Group," 3. On the Luca Conservatory of Music, founded in 1888, see John Cleophus Cotter, "The Negro in Music in St. Louis" (M.A. thesis, St. Louis: Washington University, 1959), 131–32, 156–57n40.

[4] Katherine T. Corbett and Mary E. Seematter, "No Crystal Stair: Black St. Louis, 1920–1940," *Gateway Heritage* 8, no. 2 (Fall 1987): 12; Harriet Ottenheimer, "The Blues Tradition in St. Louis," *Black Music Research Journal* 9, no. 2 (Fall 1989): 135–43; Miles Davis with Quincy Troupe, *Miles: The Autobiography* (New York: Simon & Schuster, 1989), 34; Kenney, "Just before Miles," 25–26, 29. For decades, one of the primary venues for employment of black dance bands was the racially segregated riverboats, which hosted excursions for individuals and social groups on the Mississippi River. Through the 1920s, 1930s, and 1940s, ten- to twelve-piece dance bands performed in the spring and summer on these boats. Racial segregation on riverboats ended only in 1969. Ibid.

[5] Ottenheimer, "The Blues Tradition," 143–44; Chuck Berry, *Chuck Berry: The Autobiography* (New York: Harmony Books, 1987), 25, 94. The most successful local independent record label was Bobbin' Records, founded by an area radio station owner who recorded artists like Little Milton Campbell, Albert King, Oliver Sain, and Fontella Bass. But even Bobbin' Records could only keep afloat for five years, folding in 1962.

[6] Ottenheimer, "The Blues Tradition," 144–45; Berry, *Chuck Berry,* 89; Tina Turner with Kurt Loder, *I, Tina: My Life Story* (New York: William Morrow, 1986), 44–45, 51–52; *The Mississippi: River of Song,* "Part Two: Midwestern Crossroads"; Oliver Sain, interview by Doris Wesley, n.d., in "Lift Every Voice and Sing" oral history project, sl 609, folder 76, WHMC; Davis with Troupe, *Miles,* 38.

[7] David Jackson, "Profile: Julius Hemphill, Oliver Lake," *Down Beat* 42, no. 12 (19 June 1975): 32; Howard Reich, "Trumpeter Lester Bowie, Force in Avant-Garde Jazz," *Chicago Tribune,* 10 Nov. 1999; David Wild, "Bluiett, Hamiet," in *The New Grove Dictionary of Jazz,* ed. Barry Kernfield (London: Macmillan Press, 1988), 130–31; Bluiett quoted in Mary Ann French, "Setting the Record Straight: Slaves Died at This Plantation, Now Jazz Is Master," *The Washington Post,* 3 Sept. 1995, p. G1.

[8] Paul F. Berliner, *Thinking in Jazz: The Infinite Art of Improvisation* (Chicago: University of Chicago Press, 1994), 24; Harper Barnes, "Jazz Threads through Life of Oliver Lake," *St. Louis Post-Dispatch Everyday Magazine,* 14 Feb. 1993; Olakunle Tejuoso, "The Jazz Connections: Interview with Lester Bowie," *Glendora Review: African Quarterly on the Arts* (Nigeria) 2, no. 2 (1997): 78; "Floyd LeFlore to Perform 'Ritualistic Revival,'" *New Music Circular* 4, no. 3 (Jan. 1996): 1, MHS; David Parker, "Floyd LeFlore Interview," *Cadence* 18, no. 6 (June 1992): 11; Fred Jung, "A Fireside Chat with Baikida Carroll," Jazz Weekly, *www.jazzweekly.com,* May 2001.

[9] Sandra Schoenberg and Charles Bailey, "The Symbolic Meaning of an Elite Black Community: The Ville in St. Louis," *Missouri Historical Society Bulletin* 33, no. 2 (Jan. 1977): 97–98; Amy Stuart Wells and Robert L. Crain, *Stepping over the Color Line: African-American Students in White Suburban Schools* (New Haven, CT: Yale University Press, 1997), 31, 36–37.

[10] John A. Wright, *Discovering African-American St. Louis: A Guide to Historic Sites* (St. Louis: Missouri Historical Society Press, 1994), 75; Schoenberg and Bailey, 98–101; Wells and Crain, 153–54. See also Charles Bailey, "The Ville: A Study of a Symbolic Community in St. Louis" (Ph.D. diss., Washington University, 1978).

[11] Schoenberg and Bailey, 97; Cotter, 214–16; Wright, 80. Tina Turner narrates her time at Sumner High School in Turner with Loder, 12, 43–44. Also alumni of Sumner High are former congressman Bill Clay, comedian and activist Dick Gregory, and tennis star Arthur Ashe.

[12] Philippa Jordan and Rafi Zabor, "Lester Bowie: Roots, Research, and the Carnival Chef," in *The Jazz Musician*, eds. Mark Rowland and Tony Sherman (New York: St. Martin's Press, 1994), 55; "David Hines," in *Sweet, Hot and Blue: St. Louis' Musical Heritage*, ed. Lyn Driggs Cunningham and Jimmy Jones (Jefferson, NC: McFarland & Co., 1989), 88–89; Parker, "Floyd LeFlore Interview," 12; David Jackson, "Profile: Julius Hemphill, Oliver Lake," 32; Bob Rusch, "Speaking with Oliver Lake," *Cadence* 2, no. 5 (Feb. 1977): 5.

[13] Lester Bowie, radio interview with Terri Gross, *Fresh Air*, National Public Radio, 3 Nov. 1989, rebroadcast 29 Dec. 2000; John Fordham, "Lester Bowie: Bold Improviser at the Cutting-Edge of Jazz," *The Guardian* (UK), 11 Nov. 1999; Tejuoso, 74; Ekkehard Jost, *Free Jazz* (New York: Da Capo Press, 1994 [1974]), 166; Reich, "Trumpeter Lester Bowie"; Jordan and Zabor, 55–57; Lincoln T. Beauchamp, Jr., "Lester Bowie Interview," in *Great Black Music: Ancient to the Future*, ed. Beauchamp (Chicago: Art Ensemble of Chicago Publishing, 1998), 38.

[14] Ware, author interview; J. D. Parran, curriculum vitae, c. 1999, on file with author; Peter Danson, "Baikida Carroll," *Coda* no. 192 (Oct. 1983): 12; Carroll, author interview.

[15] Baker quoted in Berliner, 26–27; Danson, 12; Carroll, author interview; Ware, author interview; Dean C. Minderman, "Jazz Man: Hamiet Bluiett Understands the Yin and Yang of Saxophone," *Riverfront Times* (St. Louis), 26 Nov. 2003, p. 60; Charlie Rose, author interview; Charlie Rose, personal communication to author, 4 Feb. 2004. On Elwood Buchanan, see also Davis with Troupe, 30–31. Local 197's union hall was located at 4414 Delmar Boulevard. On the Riviera, located at 4460 Delmar Boulevard and owned by the local politician Jordan Chambers, see Davis with Troupe, 8–9. In the late 1960s, the Riviera still hosted jazz, as well as rallies held by the city's black nationalist organizations. See Frank Leeming, Jr., "Cassius Clay Star Attraction at Muslim Affair Here," *St. Louis Post-Dispatch*, 22 May 1968; and "Liberators, SNCC Form An Alliance," *St. Louis Post-Dispatch*, 9 Nov. 1968.

[16] Hemphill, interview by Stitt, tape 1 of 4; Harper Barnes, "Visit to St. Louis Stirs Memories of '60s for Julius Hemphill," *St. Louis Post-Dispatch*, 9 Apr. 1989, p. 3E; Chip Stern, "The Hard Blues of Julius Hemphill," *Musician, Player and Listener* no. 25 (June/July 1980): 46; "Julius Hemphill: Noted Musician and Composer," *St. Louis Post-Dispatch*, 4 Apr. 1995. On John Carter and the Fort Worth music scene, see Norman C. Weinstein, *A Night in Tunisia: Imaginings of Africa in Jazz* (Metuchen, NJ: Scarecrow Press, 1992), 83, 166–68.

[17] Berliner, 56–57, 355; Hemphill, interview by Stitt, tape 2 of 4; Bill Smith, "The Oliver Lake Interview," *Coda* no. 147 (May 1976): 4; Jordan and Zabor, 56, 68. "The whole school was locked in a desperate attempt to middle-class bag everyone," Hemphill later said of Lincoln University, recalling the rules banning jazz practices and requiring coats and ties in the cafeteria on Sundays. Olivia Skinner, "Jazz Is His Bag," *St. Louis Post-Dispatch*, 18 Feb. 1970. See Donald Byrd's criticisms of the reluctance of some historically black colleges and universities to embrace African American musical forms, in Ursula Broschke Davis, *Paris without Regret: James Baldwin, Kenny Clarke, Chester Himes, and Donald Byrd* (Iowa City: University of Iowa Press, 1986), 111–12.

[18] Bill Smith, "Lake Interview," 4; Hemphill, interview by Stitt, tape 2 of 4; Jordan and Zabor, 56, 68.

[19] Parker, "Floyd LeFlore Interview," 12; Jordan and Zabor, 55–56; Richard B. Woodward, "Four Saxmen, One Great Voice," *The New York Times Magazine*, 12 Apr. 1987, p. 47.

[20] Skinner, "Jazz Is His Bag"; BAG, "Black Artists' Group: Proposal for a New Theatre," unpublished typescript, 1970, p. 16, MHS; Hemphill, interview by Stitt, tape 2 of 4. Defending an unauthorized absence from his post, Hemphill recalls telling an officer, "I feel like I'm a second-class citizen defending a way of life largely denied to me, so I might as well be a second-class soldier." Ibid. Though Hemphill used the Nation of Islam materials in an attempt to be discharged from the service, he never actually joined the organization.

[21] Danson, 13.

[22] Bill Smith, "Lake Interview," 4; Skinner, "Jazz Is His Bag"; "Julius Hemphill: Noted Musician and Composer," *St. Louis Post-Dispatch*, 4 Apr. 1995; Hemphill, interview by Stitt, tape 2 of 4; Barnes, "Visit to St. Louis"; Parker, "Floyd LeFlore Interview," 12; Parran, "The St. Louis Black Artists' Group," 1. Oliver Lake and Julius Hemphill left Lincoln University without finishing their degrees, and both later returned to complete their studies— Hemphill graduating in spring 1967, and Lake in spring 1968.

[23] Turner with Loder, 92; Hemphill, interview by Stitt, tape 2 of 4; Skinner, "Jazz Is His Bag"; Carroll quoted in Danson, 13; Hemphill quoted in Roger Riggens, "An Introduction to Julius Hemphill," *Coda* no. 150 (Aug./Sept. 1976): 24.

[24] Danson, 13; Jung, "Fireside Chat, with Baikida Carroll"; Hemphill, interview by Stitt, tape 2 of 4; Skinner, "Jazz Is His Bag"; Parker, "Floyd LeFlore Interview," 13; Terrell, author interview. James Jabbo Ware has similar memories of the reactions from older musicians: "They didn't pay us no attention. They thought we was a bunch of wild animals, not real musicians. [They said,] 'Ah, you can't play. I don't know what you're doing! And look at your hair. What's all that hair for?'" Ware, author interview.

[25] Reich, "Trumpeter Lester Bowie"; Ottenheimer, 146.

[26] John Litweiler, *The Freedom Principle: Jazz after 1958* (New York: William Morrow and Co., 1984), 173–84; John B. Litweiler, "The Free Jazz Movement: New Music in Chicago," *FOCUS/Midwest* 6, no. 41 (1968): 26; Alyn Shipton, *A New History of Jazz* (New York: Continuum, 2001), 804. On decline of musical life in Chicago, see Shipton, 805.

[27] Jordan and Zabor, 59–60; Lester Bowie, "Fresh Air"; Tejuoso, 77.

[28] Parker, "Floyd LeFlore Interview," 12; Bill Smith, "Lake Interview," 3; Hemphill, interview by Stitt, tape 2 of 4; Parran, "The St. Louis Black Artists' Group," 2.

[29] Bill Smith, "Lake Interview," 4; Barnes, "Life of Oliver Lake"; Harris, author interview. A videocassette copy of JAZZOO is held at the Saint Louis Public Library.

[30] Parker, "Floyd LeFlore Interview," 15; Ajulé Rutlin, curriculum vitae, c. 1986, on file with author; Rutlin, author interview.

[31] Gary L. Carlson, "A History of Resident Professional Theatre, St. Louis, Missouri" (M.A. thesis, Pennsylvania State University, 1975), 67, 75–77, 97–98, MHS; Ethel Louise Pitts, "The American Negro Theatre: 1940–1949" (Ph.D. diss., University of Missouri, 1975), 33, 37; Sally Forth, "History of the Persona Players," unpublished typescript, 1975, in Afro-Americans in St. Louis Collection, sl 36, folder 3, WHMC.

[32] Elliott, author interview. Robert Elliott took on the name Malinké Kenyatta, and sometimes went by combinations such as Robert Kenyatta or Malinké Robert Elliott; in this book, I refer to him in the most commonly used version, as Malinké Elliott.

[33] Metropolitan Educational Center in the Arts, "End of Project Report, 1967–1970," 1–2, 25–26, sl 48, WHMC; Pamela Niehaus, "MECA—New Spirit in Saint Louis," *Greater Saint Louis Magazine*, Nov. 1968; Robert K. Sanford, "Arts Go to Schools," *St. Louis Post-Dispatch*, 26 July 1968; Michael Newton and Scott Hatley, *Persuade and Provide: The Story of the Arts and Education Council in St. Louis* (New York: Associated Councils of the Arts, 1970), 167–69; Redmond, "Indigenous Struggle Pays Off," 41; Norman Lloyd, summary of interview with Arthur Custer, 19 Jan. 1968, ICAP, folder 2720, RAC. The Harlequin Players were known in New York as the Second Story Players and won an Obie Award in 1967.

[34] Malinké Elliott, audiotaped comments sent to author, Feb. 2001; John Brod Peters, "All-Negro Cast in 'The Blacks,'" *St. Louis Globe-Democrat*, 2 Aug. 1968, p. 2N; Durgin quoted in Elise Cassel, "Black Theaters Train Players for Acting Jobs," *Watchman-Advocate*, 13 Aug. 1968, in "Negro Scrapbooks," MHS. Russell Durgin was then chairman of the English department at St. Louis Country Day School.

[35] Vincent Terrell, author interview; Terrell, telephone conversation with author, 28 Feb. 2004.

[36] Shelton, author interview.

[37] Hughes, author interview; Harper Barnes, "Out of Diversity, LaClede Town," *St. Louis Post-Dispatch Sunday Pictures Magazine*, 2 Nov. 1969, pp. 2–7; Ron Fagerstrom, *Mill Creek Valley: A Soul of Saint Louis* (St. Louis: privately published, 2000), 22, MHS; JoAnn Adams Smith, *Selected Neighbors and Neighborhoods of North Saint Louis and Selected Related Events* (St. Louis: Friends of Vaughn Cultural Center, 1988), 33; Wells and Crain, 56–57.

[38] Ramin Bavar, "LaClede Town: An Analysis of Design and Government Policies in a Government-Sponsored Project" (M.Arch. thesis, Washington University, 1995), 79, 83; John M. McGuire, "Farewell to Utopia: LaClede Town Was a '60s Vision or an Urban Paradise," *St. Louis Post-Dispatch*, 12 Feb. 1995, p. 1D; A. J. Cervantes with Lawrence G. Blochman, *Mr. Mayor* (Los Angeles: Nash Publishing, 1974), 68–69; Floyd LeFlore, author interview. See also Ellen Perry Berkeley, "LaClede Town: The Most Vital Town in Town," *Architectural Forum* 129, no. 4 (Nov. 1968): 57–61, which gives a different racial breakdown than Bavar's: 60 percent white, 30 percent black, and 10 percent nonwhite foreign residents.

[39] Bavar, 83–84; Barnes, "Out of Diversity"; McGuire, "Farewell to Utopia"; Miyoshi Smith, "An Interview with Julius Hemphill," *Cadence* 14, no. 6 (June 1988): 14.

[40] Shelton, author interview; Parran, author interview; Redmond, author interview; Dudley, author interview; Hunt, author interview; Murray, author interview; Barnes, "Life of Oliver Lake"; Nell Gross, "Instant Folk Art," *St. Louis Globe-Democrat*, 15 Oct. 1967, in "Theaters & Movies Scrapbook," vol. 4, MHS; Redmond, "Indigenous Struggle Pays Off," 42–44; Parran, author interview. Despite the attention lavished on the Circle Coffee Shop, it was never profitable and closed in Nov. 1968: see "Town Talk," *Mill Creek Valley Intelligencer*, Dec. 1968/Jan. 1969, p. 2, MHS. On the Viet Rock debut in New York, see Walter Kerr, "Viet Rock," *The New York Times*, 11 Nov. 1966. On the 1967 Viet Rock performance in St. Louis, see the forthcoming memoir (untitled as of yet) by Nick Murray, a white Washington University graduate student in the cast.

[41] Fagerstrom, 22; JoAnn Adams Smith, 14; Dudley, author interview; Dudley, curriculum vitae, 1969, on file with author; Ernest Calloway, "A Case for Carl Dudley," *St. Louis Sentinel*, 1 Feb. 1969, p. 6; "Church to Live 'Welfare' Style," *St. Louis Sentinel*, 29 Nov. 1969, p. 9. Not surprisingly, Berea drew scrutiny from the FBI, which noted in 1969 that Dudley "has supported militant and leftist activities in St. Louis area for the past several years. Meetings have been held at his church . . . by ACTION and other organizations." Dudley, FBI records, on file with author.

[42] Shirley LeFlore, author interview; Hunt, author interview; Dudley, author interview; Shelton, author interview.

[43] "Afro Talent Style Revue Set for Sept.," *St. Louis Sentinel*, 31 Aug. 1968, 4. Similar efforts were made in the 1970s, such as the mural "The Emergence of Pride," executed in 1976 on the JeffVanderLou News Building at 2953 Martin Luther King, Jr. Boulevard by the Creative Coalition, a group of African American muralists led by Kenneth Calvert. See records on "The Emergence of Pride" in On the Wall Productions Records, box 2, folder 3, MHS.

[44] Eva Cockcroft, John Pitman Weber, and James Cockcroft, *Toward a People's Art: The Contemporary Mural Movement* (Albuquerque: University of New Mexico Press, 1998 [1977]), 5–8, 11, 178–81; Jeff Donaldson, "The Rise, Fall and Legacy of the Wall of Respect Movement," *International Review of African American Art* 15, no. 1 (1998): 22–26; D. H. Melhem, *Gwendolyn Brooks: Poetry and the Heroic Voice* (Lexington: University Press of Kentucky, 1987), 178–81.

[45] "Local Militants Paint New 'Wall of Respect,'" *St. Louis Sentinel*, 15 June 1968, pp. 1–2; "Koen Says He Was 'Framed,'" *St. Louis Sentinel*, 6 July 1968, p. 8; "Afro Talent Style Revue Set for Sept." The Wall of Respect sat at the intersection of Leffingwell and Franklin Avenues.

[46] Terrell, author interview; Harris, author interview; "Oliver Lake Quartet to Give Concert," *St. Louis Sentinel*, 7 Dec. 1968, p. 4; biographical note in Ajulé Rutlin, *AJULÉ-of-the-shadows* (St. Louis: privately printed, 1971); Eugene Redmond, "Wedge Wall, Huge Hand," in *Sentry of the Four Golden Pillars* (East St. Louis, IL: Black River Writers, 1970), 11–3. On the vandalism of the Wall of Respect, see "Zulus Offer $500 Reward," *St. Louis Sentinel*, 25 Jan. 1969, p. 12.

[47] Megan Conway and Joseph M. McMahon, "Jean Genet: 1910–1986," in *French Novelists, 1930–1960: Dictionary of Literary Biography*, vol. 72, ed. Catherine Savage Brosman (Detroit: Gale Research, 1988), 184.

[48] Cassel; John Brod Peters, "All-Negro Cast in 'The Blacks,'" *St. Louis Globe-Democrat*, 2 Aug. 1968, p. 2N; Elliott, audiotaped comments.

[49] Peters, "All-Negro Cast."

[51] Jean Genet, *The Blacks: A Clown Show*, trans. Bernard Frechtman (New York: Grove Weidenfeld, 1960); Peters, "All-Negro Cast."

[51] Hemphill, interview by Stitt, tape 3 of 4. Durgin took a less visible role in BAG's affairs after a dispute with one of the cast members over payment for the show. Hunt, author interview; Terrell, author interview; Elliott, author interview.

[52] Elliott, audiotaped comments; S. Jerome Pratter, letter to Michael Newton, 16 June 1969, on file with author; "Old and New Afro Music BAG Blends," *St. Louis Sentinel*, 31 Aug. 1968, p. 2; "Lectures, Films, Demonstrations 1968–69," unpublished calendar, Saint Louis Art Museum Archives. Jerry Pratter, a University of Michigan Law School graduate, had just arrived in St. Louis when Hemphill, Lake, and Elliott requested his help with incorporating BAG. He then continued to lend the group legal advice. Pratter later was a founding partner with Team Four in St. Louis. Pratter, author interview.

[53] "Old and New Afro Music."

Chapter Two Notes

[1] U.S. Census data; Tim O'Neil, "St. Louis' Racial Picture at King's Death Had a Much Different Look," *St. Louis Post-Dispatch*, 29 Mar. 1998; Jon C. Teaford, *Cities of the Heartland: The Rise and Fall of the Industrial Midwest* (Bloomington: Indiana University Press, 1993), 211–16; Cervantes quoted in "We Just Can't Make It Any More," *U.S. News & World Report* 64, no. 26 (24 June 1968): 62. For a more booster-ish take, see "The New St. Louis: A Swinging Town," *St. Louis Globe-Democrat Sunday Magazine*, 17 May 1970, pp. 4–17. By 1970, the city was 41 percent black, up from 18 percent black in 1950. At the same time, the suburbs of St. Louis County remained over 95 percent white in 1970. Through the 1960s, real estate agents conspired to keep the suburban County segregated, refusing to show blacks houses in white neighborhoods while steering whites away from University City, and complaining to small firms that disregarded this unwritten code. See "Segregation Practices Here Barred," *St. Louis Globe-Democrat*, 17–18 Jan. 1970; the *Jones v. Mayer* case, 392 U.S. 409, 88 Supreme Court 2186; and *Hearing before the United States Commission on Civil Rights, St. Louis, January 14–17, 1970* (Washington, DC: U.S. Government Printing Office, 1971).

[2] Robert A. Beauregard, *Voices of Decline: The Postwar Fate of U.S. Cities* (Cambridge, MA: Blackwell, 1993), 189, 210; Eric Sandweiss, *St. Louis: The Evolution of an American Urban Landscape* (Philadelphia: Temple University Press, 2001), 233–34; O'Neil, "St. Louis' Racial Picture"; Al Delugach, "Area Has Nation's Worst Case of Negro Joblessness," *St. Louis Globe-Democrat*, 14 Feb. 1968, p. 6D; Lana Stein, *St. Louis Politics: The Triumph of Tradition* (St. Louis: Missouri Historical Society Press, 2002), 96–97, 139. From 1960 to 1965, after the Mill Creek Valley demolition, the city cleared another 12,000 housing units for renewal projects and highways. In the late 1960s, 1,500 to 2,000 low-income families were displaced each year. Wells and Crain, 56–57.

[3] Robin D. G. Kelley, "Dig They Freedom: Meditations on History and the Black Avant-Garde," *Lenox Avenue* no. 3 (1997): 18; Lorenzo Thomas, *Extraordinary Measures: Afrocentric Modernism and Twentieth-Century American Poetry* (Tuscaloosa: University of Alabama Press, 2000), 119; Michel Oren, "The Umbra Poets Workshop, 1962–1965: Some Socio-Literary Puzzles," in *Belief vs. Theory in Black American Literary Criticism*, eds. Joe Weixlmann and Chester J. Fontenot (Greenwood, Fla.: Penkevill Publishing, 1986), 177–223; James G. Spady, *Larry Neal: Liberated Black Philly Poet with a Blues Streak of Mellow Wisdom* (Philadelphia: PCInternational, 1989); Elliott, audiotaped comments.

[4] Ron Karenga, "Black Cultural Nationalism," in *The Black Aesthetic*, ed. Addison Gayle, Jr. (Garden City, NY: Doubleday, 1971), 32; Samuel A. Floyd, *The Power of Black Music: Interpreting Its History from Africa to the United States* (New York: Oxford University Press, 1995), 185; William L. Van Deburg, *New Day in Babylon: The Black Power Movement and American Culture, 1965–1975* (Chicago: University of Chicago Press, 1992), 181–83; Mike Sell, "The Black Arts Movement: Performance, Neo-Orality, and the Destruction of the 'White Thing,'" in *African American Performance and Theater History: A Critical Reader*, ed. Harry J. Elam, Jr., and David Krasner (New York: Oxford University Press, 2001), 56.

[5] Thomas, *Extraordinary Measures*, 204; Anne Walmsley, *The Caribbean Artists Movement, 1966–1972* (London: New Beacon, 1993); Lorraine D. Hubbard, "Black Theatre Canada: A Decade of Struggle," *Polyphony: The Bulletin of the Multicultural History Society of Ontario* 5, no. 2 (Fall/Winter 1983): 57–65; Paul Gilroy, *The Black Atlantic: Modernity and Double Consciousness* (Cambridge, MA: Harvard University Press, 1993).

[6] Rolland Snellings (Askia Touré), letter to Larry Neal, 2 June 1967, Neal Papers, Schomburg Center for Research in Black Culture, NYPL; Eugene Redmond, *Drumvoices: The Mission of Afro-American Poetry — A Critical History* (Garden City, NY: Anchor Books, 1976), 330, 381–88; Susanne E. Smith, *Dancing in the Street: Motown and the Cultural Politics of Detroit* (Cambridge, MA: Harvard University Press, 1999), 10–11, 111–13, 174, 291n68; Don D. Bushnell and Kathi Corbera Bushnell, *The Arts, Education, and the Urban Sub-culture: The National Survey of the Performing Arts for Minority Youths* (Santa Barbara, CA: The Communications Foundation, 1969), 48–49, 164; Shraine L. Newman and Margaret Ford-Taylor, *Karamu House, Inc.: 75th Anniversary* (Cleveland: Karamu House, 1991); "A City Arts Survey: The Arts in Detroit," *Negro Digest*, Nov. 1962.

[7] Ernest Patterson, *Black City Politics* (New York: Dodd, Mead & Company, 1975), 36–39; Ernestine Patterson, "The Impact of the Black Struggle on Representative Government in St. Louis, Missouri" (Ph.D. diss., Saint Louis University, 1968), 28–29; Lawrence Harvey Boxerman, "St. Louis Urban League: History and Activities" (Ph.D. diss., Saint Louis University, 1968), 166, 170–72; Timothy Bleck, "Nonmilitant Negro Groups Making Progress Quietly," *St. Louis Post-Dispatch*, 19 Sept. 1968. See also James C. Brown, "Rooks and CORE Try to Disrupt Groundbreaking," *St. Louis Argus*, 24 May 1968, pp. 1, 4; and Urban League executive director Walter E. Douthit, quoted pseudonymously in William B. Helmreich, *The Black Crusaders: A Case Study of a Black Militant Organization* (New York: Harper & Row, 1973), 138.

[8] O'Neil, "St. Louis' Racial Picture"; Teaford, 222; Dennis R. Judd and Robert E. Mendelson, *The Politics of Urban Planning: The East St. Louis Experience* (Urbana: University of Illinois Press, 1973), 13, 26–27, 78; Harold R. Piety, "Revolution Comes to East St. Louis," *FOCUS/Midwest* 6, no. 42 (1968): 14; G. Louis Heath, "Corrupt East St. Louis: Laboratory for Black Revolution," *The Progressive* 34, no. 10 (Oct. 1970): 24–27; Rosellen Cohnberg, "East St. Louis: Poverty on a Rampage," *FOCUS/Midwest* 8, no. 51 (1970): 10–12. Historian Robert Self argues that the Black Power Movement in many northern and Pacific Coast cities was also rooted in "the political-economic geography of the new city-suburb conglomerations," offering "a critique of the whole of metropolitan development since World War II." Self, "'To Plan Our Liberation': Black Power and the Politics of Place in Oakland, California, 1965–1977," *Journal of Urban History* 26, no. 6 (Sept. 2000): 759–60. On black nationalism and municipal politics, see also Komozi Woodard, *A Nation within a Nation: Amiri Baraka (LeRoi Jones) & Black Power Politics* (Chapel Hill: University of North Carolina Press, 1998).

[9] Pat Lee Woods, "Crime and the Administration of Justice in a Selected Black Community: Survey of Police Behavior in East St. Louis, Illinois" (M.A. thesis, Sacramento State College, 1974), 2, 17–23, 39–43. On the Warlords of East St. Louis, see Piety, 14; FBI file on "The Warlords," no. 157-HQ-10581; "The Police War against Activists in Kansas City, East St. Louis, Chicago, etc.," *FOCUS/Midwest* 6, no. 44 (1968): 5, 17. On the Black Egyptians, see Betty J. Lee, "Black Egyptians: New Directions in Leadership," *PROUD Magazine* 1, no. 1 (1970): 16–18, MHS. On Black Culture, Inc., see Heath, 24–27; Piety, 15; Kenneth W. Thompson, summary of interviews with Arts & Education Council officials, 21 Mar. 1968, folder 2720, ICAP-RAC. On national conferences hosted by these groups, see Piety, 17, and "Negro Groups to Hold Parley in E. St. Louis," *St. Louis Globe-Democrat*, 18 Feb. 1969, p. E1. Often rivals, the three groups formed a string of tenuous alliances, though these eventually crumpled over ideological disputes: see Elin Schoen, *Tales of an All-Night Town* (New York: Harcourt Brace Jovanovich, 1979), 40; Heath, 24–27; Special Agent in Charge (SAC), Springfield, IL, Field Office, letter to Director, FBI, 2 Sept. 1969, COINTELPRO. On infiltration, see Director, letter to SAC, Springfield, IL, Jan. 1969, in "The Warlords," file no. 157-HQ-10581, Federal Bureau of Investigation, Washington, DC.

[10] Gregory J. Conroy, "EBR Writers Club: Still Activists after All These Years," *The Observer* (Southern Illinois University–Edwardsville), 20 Mar. 2001; Redmond, *Drumvoices*, 400; Linda Lawson, "Poet Eugene Redmond: Weaving Life's Rhythms into Words," *St. Louis Times*, Mar. 1996, pp. 22–23, in Redmond file, MHS; "Poet Laureate of East St. Louis Constantly Moving," *West End Word* (St. Louis), 23 Jan. 1986, MHS; Redmond, author interview; Eugene Redmond, "Sacred Place" and "Smoke and Fire," in Redmond, *Sentry of the Four Golden Pillars*, 4–5, 11–13; Eugene Redmond, *A Tale of Time & Toilet Tissue* (East St. Louis, IL: Black River Writers, 1969). One publication that emerged from the Rap-Write Now Creative Workshop is *Sides of the River: A Mini-Anthology of Black Writings*, ed. Eugene Redmond (East St. Louis, IL: Black River Writers, 1969). On Leon Thomas and East St. Louis, see Damian Lazarus, "Leon Thomas: It's My Life I'm Fighting For," *Straight, No Chaser* (UK) no. 33 (Autumn 1995): 30.

[11] The Grace Hill settlement house was located on the Missouri side of the river, in a near north side neighborhood known as Murphy-Blair. On the Experiment in Higher Education (EHE), founded in 1966: Redmond, author interview; Piety, 14; "SIU: Experiment in Higher Education," *PROUD Magazine* 1, no. 2 (Feb. 1970): 16–17, MHS; "100 Get Another Chance in SIU 'Experiment' Plan," *St. Louis Sentinel*, 1 Mar. 1969, p. 16; EHE brochure, 1968, on file with author. On IMPACT House: Piety, 14; Redmond, author interview; Redmond, "Indigenous Struggle Pays Off," 44; "IMPACT Director Arrested on Rape Charge," *St. Louis Globe-Democrat*, 28 Aug. 1968; "IMPACT Head to Stay Despite Rape Charge," *St. Louis Post-Dispatch*, 29 Aug. 1968, in "Crime and Low-life Scrapbook," vol. 2, MHS. IMPACT House was the physical location for the program Innovative Methods of Progressive Action for Community Tranquility, founded in 1967.

[12] Redmond, author interview. On the Zulu 1200s, see Timothy Bleck, "Black Liberators Represent Type of Militancy Unknown in St. Louis before This Summer," *St. Louis Post-Dispatch*, 17 Sept. 1968, in "Negro Scrapbooks," MHS; "Afro Talent Style Revue Set for Sept.," *St. Louis Sentinel*, 31 Aug. 1968, p. 4; "Black Feud Is Denied," *St. Louis Sentinel*, 16 Nov. 1968, pp. 1, 8. On the Mid-City Community Congress, see Donald Kornblet, "In Search of the Model City: Fighting for the 'Goodies,'" *FOCUS/Midwest* 5, no. 38 (1967): 30–31; and "African Ark on a River of Soul: Open House Theme," *St. Louis Argus*, 15 Jan. 1971, p. 11A. The "1200" in "Zulu 1200s" represents the Arabic numeral form of the Roman numeral MCC, also the acronym for Mid-City Community Congress, reflecting the group's early origins in the congress.

[13] Biographical notes on Charles Koen taken from Timothy Bleck, "Negro Militants Make Proposal to Businessmen," *St. Louis Post-Dispatch*, 23 Aug. 1968; Bleck, "Black Liberators Represent"; "Both Sides of the Story: Militants Versus 'Negro Radio,'" *St. Louis Argus*, 28 June 1968, pp. 1, 4; Piety, 17; Charles Koen, unpublished interview transcript, 4 Oct. 1968, in Free Lance Archives, series 3, box 7, folder 40, WUSC; Helmreich, 37–38. Before Koen came to St. Louis, he spent seven semesters studying ministry at McKendree College in Lebanon, Illinois, then briefly worked at a Job Corps Center in Kentucky, set up Cairo's Illinois Migrant Council School, and served as coordinator for the Black Economic Union. Koen's "colonial analysis" of black urban poverty followed that of Stokely Carmichael and Charles V. Hamilton, *Black Power: The Politics of Liberation in America* (New York: Random House, 1967), 16–31. In Helmreich's *The Black Crusaders*, a study of the Black Liberators, the author refers to organizations and individuals with pseudonyms in order to protect members from police agencies. I identify the "Crusaders" as the Liberators with Helmreich's permission, and noting that previous authors have already identified many of the pseudonyms in public sources.

[14] Helmreich, 36, 49, 54–55, 104–05, 130–31; "Black Feud Is Denied"; Bleck, "Negro Militants Make Proposal"; Edward W. O'Brien, "Militants Tied to Extortion Plot, St. Louis Officer Tells Senators," *St. Louis Globe-Democrat*, 26 June 1969; "Pamphlets Attack Hearnes," *St. Louis Post-Dispatch*, 24 Oct. 1968; "Liberators, SNCC Form An Alliance," *St. Louis Post-Dispatch*, 9 Nov. 1968; Robert Boczjiewiez, "Department of Labor Investigating CEP," *Metro-East Journal* (East St. Louis, IL), 16 Jan. 1969. On the Black Liberators' symposium series, see "Lester to Speak For Liberators," *St. Louis Sentinel*, 18 Jan. 1969, p. 13. In addition to their office at 2810 Easton Avenue (now Martin Luther King Boulevard), the Liberators used the facilities of St. Stephen's Episcopal Church, a south side congregation headed by the white minister William Matheus, himself a member of ACTION.

[15] Timothy Bleck, "Black Liberators Represent"; "To the Brink," *St. Louis Sentinel*, 21 Sept. 1968, p. 6; "ACLU to Sue Police Dept.," *St. Louis Post-Dispatch*, 13 Sept. 1968; "Protest at Home of Mayor," *St. Louis Post-Dispatch*, 14 Sept. 1968; "Bill Clay Sends Request for Probe to Atty. General," *St. Louis Argus*, 20 Sept. 1968, p. 1; "Lucas Police Station Fired on after Black Liberator's Arrest," *St. Louis Post-Dispatch*, 16 Nov. 1968. Koen resigned as leader of the Black Liberators in February 1969 and was replaced first by Leon Dent, then by twenty-four-year-old Atlanta native Yusuf Shabazz. Though the group's official statement explained that Koen was replaced "for his personal safety," Shabazz claimed there would be "no more one man-rule," and Dent later denounced Koen as an "Uncle Tom." See "Chuck Koen, Black Liberators Part," *St. Louis Sentinel*, 8 Feb. 1969, p. 3; and "Cochran Protest Rally Held," *St. Louis Sentinel*, 20 Sept. 1969, pp. 1, 8. In a disconcerting twist, Shabazz later testified in court that he had been an "undercover agent" for the police, though the police denied this. See "Shabazz Suffered, Is Bitter," *St. Louis Sentinel*, 21 June 1969, pp. 1, 8; "Black Militant Found Guilty in Money Case," *St. Louis Post-Dispatch*, 17 Sept. 1970, p. 3E; and "Mission Shabazz," *St. Louis Sentinel*, 17 Oct. 1970, p. 6. On the 1975 prison death of Leon Dent, see the Deverne Calloway Papers, addenda 1929-1989, sl 551, box 4, roll 23, series 3, folder 290, WHMC.

[16] Special Agent in Charge (SAC), St. Louis Field Office, letters to Director, FBI, 29 Oct., 22 Nov. 1968, 24 Jan., 14 Feb., 26 Feb. 1969, and Director, letters to SAC, St. Louis, 6 Nov. 1968, 30 Jan., 28 Feb. 1969; all COINTELPRO. See also "Black Feud Is Denied." For general studies of COINTELPRO, see Ward Churchill and Jim Vander Wall, *The COINTELPRO Papers: Documents from the FBI's Secret Wars against Dissent in the United States*, 2nd ed. (Cambridge, MA: South End Press, 2002); and Nelson Blackstock, *COINTELPRO: The FBI's Secret War on Political Freedom* (New York: Monad Press, 1975).

[17] Jesse Todd, "The Black Defenders Talk to the Community," typescript speech, 1969, Eda Houwink Papers, series 3, box 3, folder 18, MHS; correspondence regarding the Black Defenders' Community Variety Store, in ibid.; Jerry W. Venters, "Black Defenders Do Own Thing—Quietly," *St. Louis Post-Dispatch*, 23 Dec. 1968; Gerald J. Meyer, "Inside Black Militants' GHQ," *St. Louis Post-Dispatch*, 22 Mar. 1970; "Heavily Armed Blacks Seized," *St. Louis Post-Dispatch*, 18 May 1970, p. 1A; "Black Nationalists Plan to Build West End Houses," *St. Louis Sentinel*, 24 Oct. 1970, p. 1; "Black Nationalists Seek Legal Aid Funds," *St. Louis Sentinel*, 20 Feb. 1971, p. 13; "Black Patriots Sponsor Weekly Breakfast Program," *St. Louis Argus*, 22 Jan. 1971, p. 7A. In the early 1970s, St. Louis was also home to a small chapter of Amiri Baraka's Congress of Afrikan People, which organized celebrations of Marcus Garvey's birthday, campaigned against police brutality, and operated an "Afrikan Free School." See Clarence Lang, "'Forward Still': The Development of Black Radical Insurgency in St. Louis, 1940–1990" (M.A. thesis, Southern Illinois University, 1997), 137–39.

[18] For examples of rhetoric on "outside agitators," see "Stop Guerrilla War in St. Louis!" *St. Louis Globe-Democrat*, 6 Sept. 1968; and Mayor Cervantes's comments in "Two Top Black Power Leaders Fined $500 Each," *St. Louis Post-Dispatch*, 9 Sept. 1968. The priorities of the *Post-Dispatch* are made clear in an exchange where a black reader complained to the newspaper's managing editor, Evarts Graham, that an article on the Black Nationalists' cultural center emphasized "white anxieties and projections." Graham replied that the intended audience was "our white readers," and that speaking to those readers "requires a white interpretation to be credible, not more black rhetoric." Evarts Graham, letter to Eda Houwink, 25 Mar. 1970, Eda Houwink Papers, series 3, box 3, folder 18, MHS. On media representations, see also Percy Green, "Black Militant Is a 'White' Name," *St. Louis Sentinel*, 15 Mar. 1969, p. 21.

[19] August Meier and Elliott Rudwick, CORE: A Study in the Civil Rights Movement 1942–1968 (New York: Oxford University Press, 1973), 65, 93–94; Mary Kimbrough and Margaret W. Dagen, Victory without Violence: The First Ten Years of the St. Louis Committee of Racial Equality (CORE), 1947–1957 (Columbia: University of Missouri Press, 2000); Ernest Patterson, 31–33; Denny Walsh, "Pro-Communists Heavily Infiltrate CORE Leadership," St. Louis Globe-Democrat, 27 Dec. 1963.

[20] Meier and Rudwick, 132, 237, 258, 308–13, 367–70, 385; Jules B. Gerard, "Jefferson Bank Dispute Rocks St. Louis," FOCUS/Midwest 5, no. 36 (1967): 13, 16; John MacGuire, "Banking on a Dream," St. Louis Post-Dispatch, 6 Nov. 1988, pp. F1, F12; Ernest Patterson, 92–93, 99–111, 119; Stein, 131–32; Ernestine Patterson, 43; Green quoted in Gerald J. Meyer, "Percy Green's Tactic: Stir Public Outrage," St. Louis Post-Dispatch, 12 July 1970. On the Jefferson Bank episode, see also news clippings in Black History Project Collection, sl 201, box 2, folder 36, WHMC.

[21] Thomas M. Spencer, The St. Louis Veiled Prophet Celebration: Power on Parade, 1877–1995 (Columbia: University of Missouri Press, 2000), 114–17; George Lipsitz, A Life in the Struggle: Ivory Perry and the Culture of Opposition (Philadelphia: Temple University Press, 1988), 84; Ernest Patterson, 137–39; Percy Green, interview by Doris Wesley, 5 Dec. 1996, in "Lift Every Voice and Sing" oral history project, sl 609, folder 38, WHMC; Samuel Slade, "Why Basie Missed Veiled Prophet," St. Louis Sentinel, 5 Oct. 1968, pp. 1, 10; Peggy Swanson, "Black Veiled Prophet Ball," St. Louis Post-Dispatch, 24 Sept. 1968; "Black Veiled Prophet Ball to Feature Katherine Dunham," St. Louis Argus, 20 Sept. 1968, p. 20; Jean Ehmsen, "Fourth Annual Black Veiled Prophet Afro Festival," St. Louis Post-Dispatch, 23 Dec. 1970. On FBI harassment of ACTION, see Spencer, 135, and Special Agent in Charge (SAC), St. Louis Field Office, letters to Director, FBI, 5 Mar. and 19 June 1970, COINTELPRO.

[22] Meier and Rudwick, 312–13, 385, 418; "CORE Moves toward Phasing Out Whites," Evening Star (Washington, DC), 5 July 1967, p. A2; "Black Power," FOCUS/Midwest 5, no. 33 (1967): 7; "Floyd McKissick: Angry Man at Reception," St. Louis Sentinel, 27 Apr. 1968, pp. 1–2; "CORE Adopts a Constitution Backing Black Power," The New York Times, 17 Sept. 1968; L. Virgil Overbea, "Roy Innes Tells Core, No Integration for Him," St. Louis Sentinel, 21 Feb. 1970, p. 1; "CORE Announces Grand Opening of Standard Station," St. Louis Argus, 27 June 1969, p. 3A; "CORE's Boycott of Busch Finds Support in Government Action," FOCUS/Midwest 8, no. 52 (1970): 5; "CORE Boycott Effective in Area; Anheuser-Busch Hollers Unfair," St. Louis Argus, 14 Aug. 1970, p. 1A. On internal controversy over CORE's aborted 1969 jobs campaign directed toward a soft-drink firm, see "Hanky Panky," St. Louis Sentinel, 4 Oct. 1969, p. 6; "CORE Confronts All St. Louis Soda Bottlers," St. Louis Argus, 27 June 1969, p. 3A.

[23] Rutlin, author interview; Carroll, author interview; Harris, author interview; Shelton, author interview; Terrell, author interview; Shirley LeFlore, author interview; photo caption to "Leaders Call Mar. the 'Last Chance,'" St. Louis Sentinel, 22 June 1968, p. 1. Many musicians of BAG would see this extended narration of political activism and the Black Power Movement in St. Louis as relevant to BAG's genesis in only the most tangential way, if at all. But, on the other hand, many BAG actors and writers—Terrell and Elliott among them—now cast such context as absolutely essential in understanding the collective. Departing from the usual narrative of BAG as a primarily musical collective that drew its inspiration mostly from the AACM, they describe BAG as a Black Arts Movement organization that drew more heavily from the intellectual and social paths of institutions such as Black House, the Black Arts Repertory Theatre, and Spirit House. The highly divergent interpretations of BAG that its former members hold today point to a richness and diversity in the organization's life that the standard accounts sometimes miss.

[24] Lake quoted in Peter Madden, "Creative Collectivism: A Study of the AACM, BAG, and the CAC" (senior honors thesis, University of Michigan, 1996), 24; Malinké Elliott, telephone conversation with author, 2 Feb. 2004.

[25] Joyce Aschenbrenner, *Katherine Dunham: Reflections on the Social and Political Contexts of Afro-American Dance*, Congress on Dance Research Annual XII, ed. Pat A. Rowe (New York: Congress on Dance Research, 1981), 11–12; Joyce Aschenbrenner and Carolyn Hameedah Carr, "The Dance Technique of Katherine Dunham as a Community Rite de Passage," *Western Journal of Black Studies* 13, no. 3 (Fall 1989): 139; Lynne Fauley Emery, *Black Dance: From 1619 to Today*, 2nd ed. (Princeton, NJ: Princeton Book Company, 1988), 252, 256; Mary A. Renda, *Taking Haiti: Military Occupation and the Culture of U.S. Imperialism, 1915–1940* (Chapel Hill: University of North Carolina Press, 2001), 20; John O. Perpener III, "African American Dance and Sociological Positivism during the 1930s," *Studies in Dance History* 5, no. 1 (Spring 1994): 28.

[26] Michael Denning, *The Cultural Front: The Laboring of American Culture in the Twentieth Century* (London: Verso, 1997), 308, 311; Constance Valis Hill, "Katherine Dunham's 'Southland': Protest in the Face of Repression," in *Dancing Many Drums: Excavations in African American Dance*, ed. Thomas F. DeFrantz (Madison: University of Wisconsin Press, 2002), 289–316; Lynne Fauley Emery, 257; Dunham quoted in Aschenbrenner and Carr, 139.

[27] Newton and Hatley, 194; Eugene B. Redmond, "Cultural Fusion & Spiritual Unity: Katherine Dunham's Approach to Developing Educational Community Theatre" [1976], in *Kaiso! Katherine Dunham, An Anthology of Writings*, ed. VéVé A. Clark & Margaret B. Wilkerson (Berkeley: Institute for the Study of Social Change, University of California, 1978), 265–66, MHS; James Haskins, *Katherine Dunham* (New York: Coward, McCann, & Geoghegan, 1982), 123–25, 128; Katherine Dunham, letter to W. McNeil Lowry, Ford Foundation, 11 June 1969, in Katherine Dunham file, GEN 69 (HA), FFA; Norman Lloyd, summary of interview with Katherine Dunham, 19 Jan. 1968, Folder 2720, ICAP-RAC; Aschenbrenner, *Katherine Dunham*, 7.

[28] Niehaus, "MECA"; Newton and Hatley, 197; Haskins, 126, 131; Aschenbrenner, *Katherine Dunham*, 62; Redmond, "Indigenous Struggle Pays Off," 42; Redmond, "Cultural Fusion & Spiritual Unity," 266; Katherine Dunham, "Performing Arts Training Center as a Focal Point for a New and Unique College or School" [1970], in *Kaiso! Katherine Dunham, An Anthology of Writings*, ed. VéVé A. Clark & Margaret B. Wilkerson (Berkeley: Institute for the Study of Social Change, University of California, 1978), 261–63, MHS.

[29] Aschenbrenner and Carr, 140; Redmond, "Indigenous Struggle Pays Off," 42; Redmond, "Cultural Fusion & Spiritual Unity," 267–68; Dunham quoted in Bushnell and Bushnell, *The Arts, Education, and the Urban Sub-culture*, 152; Michael Newton, letter to Norman Lloyd, appendix C, 15 Aug. 1969, Folder 2722, ICAP-RAC; "Katherine Dunham Group to Present Program at Webster," *St. Louis Sentinel*, 20 July 1968, p. 4. Taylor Jones, III, was one of the St. Louis CORE members jailed for the 1963 Jefferson Bank demonstrations, and by the time of his death, he was CORE's chairman for the ten-state midwestern region.

[30] Dunham quoted in Bushnell and Bushnell, *The Arts*, 152; "Katherine Dunham Is Jailed 3 1/2 Hours Following Protest," *The New York Times*, 30 July 1967; Haskins, 133; Norman Lloyd, summary of interview with Katherine Dunham, 20 Sept. 1968, Folder 2721, ICAP-RAC.

[31] Dunham quoted in Bushnell and Bushnell, *The Arts*, 23n1. Dunham's views on poverty and the arts are clarified in a 1965 document, where she casts her proposed cultural enrichment center as a way toward "improving the individual self-image, and through this, uplifting the community's view of itself as a step towards breaking the poverty cycle." Katherine Dunham, Southern Illinois University Community Action Proposal, 3 Aug. 1965, Folder 2719, ICAP-RAC.

[32] Director, FBI, letter to Special Agent in Charge (SAC), St. Louis Field Office, 14 Apr. 1969, with attachment "Blackboard," and SAC, St. Louis, letters to Director, 26 May and 3 June 1969, COINTELPRO.

[33] Charles H. Smith & Leland C. DeVinney, summary of interviews with Dunham and Lawrence Howard, 19–20 Mar. 1969, Folder 2720; Katherine Dunham, letter to Lawrence Howard (vice president, Danforth Foundation), 24 Jan. 1969, Folder 2721; Norman Lloyd, summary of interview with Dunham, 8 Feb. 1968, Folder 2720; Lloyd, summary of interview with Dunham, 16–17 July 1969, Folder 2722. All in ICAP-RAC

[34] Michael B. Katz, *The Undeserving Poor: From the War on Poverty to the War on Welfare* (New York: Pantheon Books, 1989), 16–23, 37. On these ideas and their role in the War on Poverty, see Nicholas Lemann, *The Promised Land: The Great Black Migration and How It Changed America* (New York: Alfred A. Knopf, 1991), 118–219; and Alice O'Connor, *Poverty Knowledge: Social Science, Social Policy, and the Poor in Twentieth-Century U.S. History* (Princeton, NJ: Princeton University Press, 2001), 124–36, 158–65.

[35] Becky Jenkins, forward to Bushnell and Bushnell, *The Arts*, v-vii; Frances Fox Piven and Richard A. Cloward, *Regulating the Poor: The Functions of Public Welfare*, 2nd ed. (New York: Vintage Books, 1993), 288; Don D. Bushnell, "Black Arts for Black Youth," *Saturday Review*, 18 July 1970, pp. 43–44.

[36] Charles M. Haar, *Between the Idea and the Reality: A Study in the Origin, Fate and Legacy of the Model Cities Program* (Boston: Little, Brown and Co., 1975), 25, 89, 143, 157; Kornblet, 32; "Ghetto Power Base Urged by Bourgeois," *St. Louis Post-Dispatch*, 17 Feb. 1968; Leonard Richards Howard, "A Comparison of the Model Cities Programs of St. Louis and Kansas City, Missouri" (Ph.D. diss., University of Missouri, 1972), 63, 152–53, 166–67; "Negro Leaders Protest Slur," *St. Louis Sentinel*, 20 July 1968, pp. 1, 8; Robert Jacob Kerstein, "The Political Consequences of Federal Intervention: The Economic Opportunity Act and Model Cities in the City of St. Louis" (Ph.D. diss., Washington University, 1975), 164, 179, 189. On jockeying between residents and the political machine in East St. Louis, IL, over control of Model Cities appropriations, see Judd and Mendelson, 25–26, 149. For analysis of the political effects of the War on Poverty in St. Louis, see Robert J. Kerstein and Dennis R. Judd, "Achieving Less Influence with More Democracy: The Permanent Legacy of the War on Poverty," *Social Science Quarterly* 61, no. 2 (Sept. 1980): 208–20.

[37] Michael Newton, letter to Norman Lloyd, 4 Dec. 1967, Folder 2719, ICAP-RAC; Lloyd, summary of interview with Mrs. George Hoblitzelle, 19 Jan. 1968, Folder 2720, ICAP-RAC; Newton and Hatley, 192. The original study, funded by the Missouri State Council on the Arts, was conducted by Russell and Rowena Jelliffe, founders of Cleveland's Karamu Foundation, and refined by local consultants.

[38] Rockefeller Foundation, Staff Newsletter, Oct. 1964, p. 1, and Norman Lloyd, curriculum vitae, c. 1972, personnel files, Rockefeller Archive Center, Sleepy Hollow, NY; Danforth Foundation, "The Urban Program of the Danforth Foundation: The First Three Years," (St. Louis: Danforth Foundation, 1971), MHS; Danforth Foundation Board of Trustees, meeting minutes, 6–8 Jan. 1968, quoted in Merrimon Cuninggim, *Private Money and Public Service: The Role of Foundations in American Society* (New York: McGraw-Hill, 1972), 136, 185. The Danforth Foundation no longer retains records on the Inner City Arts Project. All surviving records on the initiative are held at the Rockefeller Archive Center, Sleepy Hollow, NY

[39] Michael Newton, "Unity—For What Purpose?" *FOCUS/Midwest* 6, no. 41 (1968): 9; Newton, letter to Lawrence C. Howard, 14 Mar. 1968, and Rockefeller Foundation, appropriation no. RF68036, 3 Apr. 1968, both in Folder 2720, ICAP-RAC; Kenneth W. Thompson, summary of interviews with Arts & Education Council officials, 21 Mar. 1968, Folder 2720, ICAP-RAC; A. Donald Bourgeois, letter to Norman Lloyd, 1 Apr. 1968, Folder 2720, ICAP-RAC. Damage in St. Louis from firebombs and looting following the King assassination was unofficially estimated at $30,000, a tiny amount relative to other cities. Gina L. Henderson, "The Civil Rights Movement in St. Louis, 1954–1970: A Socio-Historical Perspective" (senior history thesis, Washington University, 1980), 68–69, sl 187, WHMC. The sense of foreboding was heightened, though, by the St. Louis Police Board president's public criticisms of the Detroit police for not using force more promptly to quell that city's 1967 riot. "Fr. Cervantes Says Unified Rule Can End Strife," *St. Louis Post-Dispatch*, 25 Sept. 1967, p. 3C. On police planning for response to urban disorders, see also Jules B. Gerard, "St. Louis Police Plays Politics with Law," *FOCUS/Midwest* 6, no. 40 (1968): 15–23.

[40] Daniel Widener, "'Something Else': Creative Community and Black Liberation in Postwar Los Angeles" (Ph.D. diss., New York University, 2003), 197–243; Lyle, author interview; Troupe, author interview. The Watts Writers Workshop and the Watts 13 included the poets K. Curtis Lyle and Quincy Troupe, both of whom would later collaborate with BAG. Troupe remembers his growing weariness with the patronizing stance of white audiences, who formed an important financial base for the Watts Writers Workshop through readings at Los Angeles–area universities, recalling that they often brought preconceived notions of an "authentic" black poet: they "wanted you to be complaining, talking about how bad the whites folks were, and [saying] that you wanted to burn down the city and kill some white folks." Ibid.

[41] Norman Lloyd, summaries of interviews with Katherine Dunham, 19 Jan. 1968 and 8 Feb. 1968; Michael Newton, letter to Lawrence C. Howard, 14 Mar. 1968; all in Folder 2720, ICAP-RAC. For criticism of "compensatory enrichment," see, for example, Bushnell, "Black Arts for Black Youth," 43.

[42] Kenneth W. Thompson, summary of interviews with Arts & Education Council officials, 21 Mar. 1968, Folder 2720, ICAP-RAC. The Arts & Education Council did recognize at least some of these problems, declaring it "foolish to think of Summer programs as merely some kind of stopgap device to prevent civil disorders," and pointing to a year-round commitment to its clientele. Arts & Education Council of Greater St. Louis, "Summary of Summer Programs Funded in 1968," Fall 1968, Folder 2721, ICAP-RAC.

[43] Michael Newton, letter to Norman Lloyd, 25 Mar. 1968; Budget Draft of Artist-in-Residence Program & Cultural Enrichment Center; and Kenneth W. Thompson, summary of interviews with Arts & Education Council officials, 21 Mar. 1968, all in Folder 2720, ICAP-RAC; text of statement by Mayor A. J. Cervantes, Folder 2721, ICAP-RAC; "Two Foundations Give $100,000 for Cultural Development," *St. Louis Argus*, 24 May 1968, p. 21; Robert K. Sanford, "Arts Go to Schools," *St. Louis Post-Dispatch*, 26 July 1968; "Bold Wisconsin and St. Louis Grants Establish Precedent," *FOCUS/Midwest* 6, no. 41 (1968): 37; *Wall Street Journal* quoted in Newton and Hatley, 181.

[44] Terrell, author interview; Elliott, author interview; Skinner, "Jazz Is His Bag"; Norman Lloyd, summary of interview with Michael Newton, 2 June 1969, Folder 2722, ICAP-RAC; "MECA Director Announces Appointment of Hemphill, Hicks," *St. Louis Argus*, 8 Nov. 1968, 11A. See 1967-68 issues of the *Model City Voice* at MHS. Vincent Terrell was Hemphill's assistant editor at the newspaper.

[45] Norman Lloyd, summary of interview with Katherine Dunham, 20 Sept. 1968, Folder 2721, ICAP-RAC; "Black Artistic Experience," flyer for BAG Open House, 15 Mar. 1969, Folder 2722, ICAP-RAC; Hopkins, "'AIR-BAG' Training Center,": 4–5, MHS.

[46] "Emilio Cruz," in *Ten Negro Artists from the United States: First World Festival of Negro Arts, Dakar, Senegal, 1966* (New York: United States Committee for the First World Festival of Negro Arts, 1966); Emilio Cruz, author interview; Pat Cruz, author interview; Emilio Cruz, personal communication to author, 12 Dec. 2003; Michael Newton, letter to Norman Lloyd, 13 Aug. 1969, Folder 2722, ICAP-RAC; Hopkins, "'AIR-BAG' Training Center,": 4–5, MHS.

[47] Ronald M. Radano, *New Musical Figurations: Anthony Braxton's Cultural Critique* (Chicago: University of Chicago Press, 1993), 90; Emilio Cruz, author interview; Carroll, author interview. Scholar Eric Porter makes a similar point about outside financing for the Collective Black Artists (CBA) of New York, writing, "Because such government and corporate intervention stemmed, in part, from fears over urban uprisings and radical activism, it can be seen as diffusing the radical or transformative potential of activist arts groups such as the CBA." Eric Porter, *What Is This Thing Called Jazz?: African American Musicians as Artists, Critics, and Activists* (Berkeley: University of California Press, 2002), 223–24. The AACM's stance, however, remains murky: while Radano explains that the AACM "stood decidedly against accepting grants from formal institutions," member Joseph Jarman indicated in 1972 that the collective had unsuccessfully applied to a number of agencies for support. See "Art Ensemble of Chicago: Great Black Music!" *Ann Arbor Sun*, 18 Aug. 1972, pp. 8–9.

[48] Leo B. Hicks, "Progress Report of the Inner-City Art Project," Dec. 1968, Folder 2721, ICAP-RAC; Inner City Arts Project summary, Folder 2722, ICAP-RAC; Lyle, author interview; Redmond, author interview; Newton and Hatley, 196; Redmond, "Cultural Fusion & Spiritual Unity," 269. On Thiam's recruitment, see "Conversations with Mor Thiam," *The Voice of African Music: A Newsletter of the St. Louis African Chorus* 5, no. 1 (Winter/Spring 1998): 2. For PATC participation in nationalist events, see "Blacks Present Stokely," *St. Louis Sentinel*, 31 Aug. 1968, pp. 1, 8; John Brod Peters, "'Black Hip Session' in Lafayette Park," *St. Louis Globe-Democrat*, 29 July 1968; "Hip Session Features Afro Music and Militant Poetry," *St. Louis Sentinel*, 7 Sept. 1968, p. 10; Peggy Swanson, "Black Veiled Prophet Ball," *St. Louis Post-Dispatch*, 24 Sept. 1968; "Lester to Speak for Liberators"; "James Foreman to Speak at Black Liberators' Seminar," *St. Louis Argus*, 3 Jan. 1969, p. 19; Michael Newton, letter to Norman Lloyd, appendix C, 15 Aug. 1969, Folder 2722, ICAP-RAC.

[49] Hemphill, interview by Stitt, tape 2 of 4; Norman Lloyd, summary of interview with Michael Newton, 2 June 1969, Folder 2722, ICAP-RAC; Leo B. Hicks, "Progress Report of the Inner-City Art Project," Dec. 1968, Folder 2721, ICAP-RAC; Fred Onovwerosuoke, "Mor Thiam: Maverick Drummer Extraordinaire," *The Voice of African Music: A Newsletter of the St. Louis African Chorus* 5, no. 1 (Winter/Spring 1998): 2.

[50] Carroll, author interview.

CHAPTER THREE NOTES

[1] The map, prepared in 1969, can be found in BAG, "Black Artists' Group: Proposal for a New Theatre," unpublished typescript, 1970, 3, MHS.

[2] Newton and Hatley, 195; "AIR-BAG Performances: July 1968–July 1969," Folder 2722, ICAP-RAC; "Oliver Lake: B.A.G.," promotional brochure, c. 1971, on file with author; Shirley LeFlore, author interview; Malinké Kenyatta (a.k.a. Robert Elliott), *Black Theatre Notebook* (St. Louis: privately published, 1971), 6, MHS.

[3] Thomas, *Extraordinary Measures*, 144; Mance Williams, *Black Theatre in the 1960s and 1970s: A Historical-Critical Analysis of the Movement* (Westport, Conn.: Greenwood Press, 1985), 119; Kenyatta, *Black Theatre Notebook*, 3.

[4] Terrell, author interview; Elliott, author interview.

[5] Hemphill, interview by Stitt, tape 3 of 4; Hunt, author interview; Elliott, author interview. On debates over closing the building to whites: Ware, author interview. On debates over whites in casts and audiences: Shelton, author interview. The inclusion of a white member in the AACM had been extremely divisive, leading some members to quit the organization. See Porter, 213–14. BAG's only exception to its membership policy came with the arrival of Muthal Naidoo, as narrated in the following chapter.

[6] Danny Kathriner, "The Rise and Fall of Gaslight Square," *Gateway Heritage* 22, no. 2 (Fall 2001): 34–37, 43; Dan Koden, "Gaslight Square: A Personal Study" (student paper, Washington University, 1966), 1, MHS.

[7] Kathriner, 40–41; Koden, 2–6; Jon Dressel, "Gaslight Square Ain't What She Used to Be," *St. Louis Globe-Democrat*, 3–4 Feb. 1968, in "Hotels, Taverns, and Restaurants Scrapbook," vol. 2, MHS; Redmond, "Indigenous Struggle Pays Off," 44; "The Exit in Gaslight Square in for Face Lift," *St. Louis Argus*, 23 May 1969, p. 6B. The Exit Coffee Shop eventually left Gaslight Square in May 1969.

[8] Kathriner, 33; Carlson, 67, 75–76; Leo B. Hicks, "Progress Report of the Inner-City Art Project," Dec. 1968, folder 2721, ICAP-RAC; Michael Newton, letter to Norman Lloyd, 13 Aug. 1969, 10, Folder 2722, ICAP-RAC; Hemphill, interview by Stitt, tape 2 of 4. The PATC extension site in St. Louis was coordinated by Jacqueline Redmond, sister of the poet Eugene Redmond.

[9] Rutlin, author interview; "Black Artists Group Presents Concert Mar. 9," *St. Louis Argus*, 7 Mar. 1969; "BAG Sponsors Concert, Open House," *St. Louis Sentinel*, 8 Mar. 1969, p. 4;

"AIR-BAG Performances: July 1968–July 1969," folder 2722, ICAP-RAC; Hemphill, interview by Stitt, tape 2 of 4.

[10] Norman Lloyd, on-site evaluation, 16–17 July 1969, folder 2722, ICAP-RAC; Pat Cruz, author interview; Emilio Cruz, author interview; Hemphill, interview by Stitt, tape 3 of 4.

[11] Emilio Cruz, author interview; Parker, "Floyd LeFlore Interview," 13; Hemphill, interview by Stitt, tapes 2 and 3 of 4; St. Louis City Directory, 1969, MHS.

[12] Emilio Cruz, author interview; Pat Cruz, author interview; Joseph Bowie, author interview; Shirley LeFlore, author interview; John Brod Peters, "Negro Artists Open New Training Center," St. Louis Globe-Democrat, 15 Mar. 1969; Parker, "Floyd LeFlore Interview," 13–14; "BAG Sponsors Concert," 4; Michael Newton, letter to Norman Lloyd, 13 Aug. 1969, and "Black Artistic Experience," flyer for BAG Open House, 15 Mar. 1969, both in folder 2722, ICAP-RAC. While an accurate statement of the group's beliefs, this phrase was taken directly from Inner City Arts Project planning documents prepared by philanthropic executives.

[13] Jackson, author interview; Elliott, audiotaped comments.

[14] Hemphill, interview by Stitt, tape 3 of 4; Harris, author interview; Carroll, author interview.

[15] Carter quoted in Weinstein, 83; George E. Lewis, "Singing Omar's Song: A (Re)construction of Great Black Music," Lenox Avenue no. 4 (1998): 72–73; Litweiler, The Freedom Principle, 173–84; Rutlin, author interview. Joseph Jarman later described the AACM school as the collective's most successful feature "because all these poor, black children that didn't have anything going on were given the opportunity to express themselves and direct their energies into a positive thing without being controlled by all the bullshit going down in the white power-structure educational system of this country." Jarman quoted in "Art Ensemble of Chicago: Great Black Music!" Ann Arbor Sun, 18 Aug. 1972, pp. 8–9.

[16] Michael Newton, letter to Norman Lloyd, 13 Aug. 1969, and "Class Enrollment of Artist-in-Residence," typescript, c. 1969, both in Folder 2722, ICAP-RAC; Hopkins, "'AIR-BAG' Training Center,": 4–5, MHS; "Culture through AIR for Inner City," St. Louis Sentinel, 19 July 1969, 10; Harris, author interview; Carroll, author interview; Phil Hulsey, "St. Louis," Down Beat 37, no. 15 (6 Aug. 1970): 42; Elliott, audiotaped comments; Hemphill, interview by Stitt, tape 2 of 4; Rutlin, author interview. During this period, Rutlin took the name Ajulé Menelek (replacing his birth name of Bruce Rutlin), drawing the first part of the name from the language developed by the children in his class exercise. Ibid.

[17] Redmond, "Indigenous Struggle Pays Off," 42; Howard, 179–80, 188; "Culture through AIR for Inner City"; Hemphill, interview by Stitt, tape 3 of 4; Carroll, author interview; Sargent, author interview. The BAG school was not unprecedented in the area. A tutoring and arts center called Sophia House, started by the Jesuit seminarian Dennis O'Brien of Saint Louis University, had opened in 1967 near Pruitt-Igoe, serving mostly male youngsters, all of them African American. After the collapse of his Sophia House program, O'Brien in 1970 founded "Logos: An Urban School," a high school for troubled youngsters, in a refurbished tool-and-die shop at 3325 Washington Boulevard. Unlike Sophia House, Logos attracted mostly white youths. Like so many other institutions, Logos eventually moved to the suburbs, buying an unused elementary school building in Olivette in 1982. "Sophia House: Bright Hope for Youth," *PROUD Magazine* 1, no. 4 (Apr. 1970): 22–25, MHS; Redmond, "Indigenous Struggle Pays Off," 42–43; author conversation with former Logos teacher Kyle Radcliffe, 18 Nov. 2003.

[18] Wells and Crain, 56–57; Lee Rainwater, *Behind Ghetto Walls: Black Families in a Federal Slum* (Chicago: Aldine Publishing Company, 1970), 8, 104; Model Cities director A. Donald Bourgeois quoted in Kornblet, 29; Terrell, author interview. For arguments that structural racism was responsible for Pruitt-Igoe's failure, see Elizabeth Birmingham, "Reframing the Ruins: Pruitt–Igoe, Structural Racism, and African American Rhetoric as a Space for Cultural Critique," *Positions* no. 2 (1998). Oliver Jackson had already worked at Pruitt-Igoe in summer 1967, coordinating Project Uhuru, an arts training course for twelve- to sixteen-year-olds "aimed at self-discovery." Redmond, "Indigenous Struggle Pays Off," 44–45.

[19] "Bowie, Joseph," in *The New Grove Dictionary of Jazz*, ed. Barry Kernfeld (London: Macmillan Press Ltd., 1988), 140; Paulo Hewitt, "Debunking the Funk," *Melody Maker*, 13 June 1981, 18; Joseph Bowie, author interview; Osby, author interview.

[20] Thomas quoted in I. B. Skovgård, "Luther Thomas in Denmark," *Jazz Special* (Denmark), First International Edition (2002), 95; Ehrlich, author interview; Gene Santoro, "Marty Ehrlich," *The Nation* 262, no. 10 (11 Mar. 1996): 34; Karl Evanzz, personal communication to author, 25 Nov. 2003. For more on Karl Evanzz, see his memoir, tentatively titled *Malcolm's Son*, forthcoming 2006. While Luther Thomas was a student at Webster College in St. Louis, he became acquainted with John Zorn, who studied classical music at Webster in 1971 and 1972. But Zorn explains that, counter to certain myths, he did not collaborate with the BAG musicians while he was at Webster College, other than attending a handful of their concerts, nor was he a member of the Human Arts Ensemble. Zorn, telephone conversation with author, 21 May 2002. And though Marty Ehrlich formed close friendships with BAG members such as Malinké Elliott, contrary to popular belief he was never a member of BAG, and he explains that he never attended a formal BAG concert until after the group's dissolution in 1972.

[21] Sue Ann Wood, "Reviving Their African Heritage," *St. Louis Globe-Democrat*, 5 July 1969.

[22] Elliott quoted in Robert Adams, "Black Artists' Goal Is Art That Tells It Like It Is," *St. Louis Post-Dispatch*, 13 Apr. 1969; Hemphill quoted in "Black Artists' Center to Offer Free Classes," *St. Louis Post-Dispatch*, 13 Mar. 1969; Pat Cruz, author interview.

[23] Elliott quoted in Wood, "Reviving Their African Heritage"; Parker, "Floyd LeFlore Interview," 14.

[24] Norman Lloyd, on-site evaluation, 16–17 July 1969, Folder 2722, ICAP-RAC; "Culture through AIR for Inner City"; Emilio Cruz, personal communication to author, 18 Jan. 2004; Green, author interview; Emilio Cruz, author interview; Pat Cruz, author interview. On BAG performances at benefits and events for civil rights groups, see Green, author interview; "Zulus Offer $500 Reward"; BAG, "Black Artists' Group: Proposal for a New Theatre"; "CORE Plans Black Culture Extravaganza," *St. Louis Argus*, 14 Feb. 1969, p. 16; "Shon McGowan and BAG to Appear at Annual Bug-a-Loo," *St. Louis Argus*, 2 May 1969, p. 7B; "AIR-BAG Performances: July 1968–July 1969," Folder 2722, ICAP-RAC. Emilio Cruz also notes that he participated with Percy Green in a dialogue with the U.S. attorney's office over hiring discrimination at the McDonnell Douglas Corporation. Cruz, personal communication to author, 18 Jan. 2004.

[25] Rutlin quoted in Wood, "Reviving Their African Heritage"; Elliott quoted in Adams, "Black Artists' Goal"; Hemphill, interview by Stitt, tape 3 of 4. For example, Dolan Chappell, a Black Liberators captain, commented, "Whoever heard of starting a revolution with writing poetry? You can write poetry *after* the revolution's over but you can't make one *with* it." Chappell quoted pseudonymously in Helmreich, *The Black Crusaders*, 94 (emphasis in original). These sentiments were expressed by national leaders like Stokely Carmichael, for example, who wrote, "We have to say, 'Don't play jive and start writing poems after Malcolm is shot.' We have to move from the point where the man left off and stop writing poems." Carmichael, "We Are Going to Use the Term 'Black Power' and We Are Going to Define It Because Black Power Speaks to Us" [1966], in *Black Nationalism in America*, ed. John H. Bracey, Jr., August Meier, and Elliott Rudwick (Indianapolis: Bobbs-Merrill, 1970), 472.

[26] Anders Corr, *No Trespassing! Squatting, Rent Strikes, and Land Struggles Worldwide* (Cambridge, MA: South End Press, 1999), 155; Lipsitz, *A Life in the Struggle*, 148–49; Cervantes, *Mr. Mayor*, 54; Charles Kimball Cummings, "Rent Strike in St. Louis: The Making of Conflict in Modern Society" (Ph.D. diss., Washington University, 1976), 2, 404–05, 411, 422, 453, 474. For many public housing residents on welfare, rents ate up over 60 percent of their benefits and had been increasing dramatically over the past several years. From 1965 to 1967, rent increases ranged from 16 to 32 percent, depending on the tenant and the project. Ibid., 352–53, 401–02.

[27] Lipsitz, *A Life in the Struggle*, 149; Cummings, 149, 429, 463–64, 473.

[28] Miyoshi Smith, "Interview with Julius Hemphill," *Cadence* 14, no. 6 (June 1988): 14; Kenneth W. Thompson, summary of interviews with Merrimon Cuninggim and Gene Schwilk, 16–18 Sept. 1969, Folder 2722, ICAP-RAC; Emilio Cruz, personal communications to author, 13 and 19 Jan. 2004; Hemphill, interview by Stitt, tape 3 of 4; Terrell, author interview; Emilio Cruz, author interview. On Goldman, see "Sister Cecilia Says She Faces Ouster as Nun," *St. Louis Sentinel*, 5 July 1969, p. 4; Harry J. Cargas, "There Will Be a New Form of Christianity," *FOCUS/Midwest* 8, no. 52 (1970): 12–15.

[29] Pat Cruz, author interview.

[30] Corr, 156; Lipsitz, *A Life in the Struggle*, 164. On the aftermath of the rent strike, see Daniel J. Monti, *Race, Redevelopment & the New Company Town* (Albany: State University of New York Press, 1990), 44–50.

[31] Van Deburg, 10, 61; Redmond, author interview; "Directory of Black Owned Business," 1970, in Afro-Americans in St. Louis Collection, sl 36, folder 12, WHMC; Robert L. Joiner, "Only Black Book Store in City May Be Closing," *St. Louis Post-Dispatch*, 14 Mar. 1971; Pat Rice, "The AFRO Boutique," *St. Louis Post-Dispatch*, 30 July 1970; "CORE Sponsors Classes in Negro History," *St. Louis Argus*, 23 Feb. 1968, p. 2; "House of Umoja," *Model City Voice* 1, no. 2 (24 July 1968): 3, MHS; "Black Light Cultural Center to Open Sunday," *St. Louis Sentinel*, 14 Feb. 1970, p. 9.

[32] Redmond, author interview; "'Heads Up' Premieres: KMOX-TV," *St. Louis Sentinel*, 14 Dec. 1968, p. 4; Jack Bernstein, "Project Becomes Show," *St. Louis Post-Dispatch*, 14 Mar. 1969; "Music Store Ripped," *St. Louis Sentinel*, 3 Jan. 1969, p. 1; supplement to "Directory of Black Owned Business," 29 July 1970, in Afro-Americans in St. Louis Collection, sl 36, folder 12, WHMC; Joiner, "Only Black Book Store." The *Argus* claimed, for example, that if natural hair "is to serve as an identification of some sort of cultural revolution then it is not in the best interests of the Negro goals." "The Natural Look," *St. Louis Argus*, 5 Jan. 1968, p. 12. See also "Teachers Put Down Afro Culture," *St. Louis Free Press*, 18 Oct. 1968, p. 5, in Underground Newspaper Collection, microfilmed by Bell & Howell, Wooster, Ohio. The bookstores also faced outside opposition: the Black Smith Shop, for example, struggled to stay in business after a raid in which police claimed to have found marijuana and "subversive books." Joiner, "Only Black Book Store."

[33] Lang, 111–12; John Willson, "St. Louis University: Apathy Distinguishes Students, Faculty, and Administration," *FOCUS/Midwest* 7, no. 45 (1969): 37–39; "Black Students at SLU Take Over Dean's Office," *St. Louis Argus*, 2 May 1969, pp. 1, 14; "'I Am a Man,'" *St. Louis Sentinel*, 3 May 1969, p. 8; "Fontbonne Black Sisters Rise," *The Outlaw* 1, no. 8 (4 Nov. 1970): 14, MHS; "Forest Park College Is Open, Quiet," *St. Louis Sentinel*, 4 Oct. 1969, p. 1.

[34] Gorden F. Andrus, "Washington University: Students Trigger Reform," *FOCUS/Midwest* 7, no. 45 (1969): 32–34; Norman Pressman, "Blacks Occupy Campus Police Office," *Student Life* (Washington University), 6 Dec. 1968, pp. 1, 6; Fred Faust, "Thursday Night: Whites Take Brookings," *Student Life* (Washington University), 9 Dec. 1968, p. 2; Association of Black Collegians, "Black Manifesto," unpublished typescript, Dec. 1968, held at AFAS Office, Washington University; "Washington University and the Defense Establishment," unpublished typescript, c. 1970, in Daniel I. Bolef Collection, series 6, box 1, WUSC; Brendan Watson, "Background to the ROTC Burning: Activism at WU, 1964–1970," *Student Life* (Washington University), 17 Apr. 2001. On tensions between Washington University's SDS and ABC chapters, see Ernestine Cofield, "Inside College USA," *St. Louis Sentinel*, 14 Dec. 1968, p. 1. On charges that the administration acceded quickly to the ABC demands in order to suppress more effectively the SDS demands, see "Student Unrest and Political Progress at Washington University," *FOCUS/Midwest* 7, no. 45 (1969): 34–36.

[35] Koch quoted in Rebecca E. Klatch, *A Generation Divided: The New Left, the New Right, and the 1960s* (Berkeley: University of California Press, 1999), 141–42; biographical note to Bob Elliott, "Fire and Ice," *Free Lance* 6, no. 1 (Sept. 1967): 6, WUSC; "WU Student Fined $500, Gets 6 Months," *St. Louis Globe-Democrat*, 22 Apr. 1970, p. 5H; "Holder Put under Psychiatric Study," *St. Louis Globe-Democrat*, 5 May 1970, p. 3A; Malinké Elliott, telephone conversation with author, 23 Feb. 2004; Vincent Terrell, telephone conversation with author, 28 Feb. 2004; Murray, author interview; Holder, author interview.

[36] Terrell, author interview; photo caption to "Some on Faculty Back Dissidents on ROTC," *St. Louis Post-Dispatch*, 28 Mar. 1970.

[37] Koch, author interview; Parran, "The St. Louis Black Artists' Group," 4–5; Emrick, author interview. On SDS members' election to student government, see Devereaux Kennedy, interview by Lisa Salt, 20 Apr. 2001, unedited transcript, Washington University Liberation Front Reunion Archive, WUSC. As J. D. Parran notes, "Student activity money [for BAG] became generally available at the colleges with the advent of the student political protest movement." Parran, "The St. Louis Black Artists' Group," 4–5. The proposal for the BAG building renovation was developed by architecture students Michael E. Emrick and Dennis Bolazina through Washington University's Community Design Workshop and can be found in BAG, "Black Artists' Group: Proposal for a New Theatre." Since BAG's funding from the Rockefeller and Danforth Foundations was curtailed before the design was completed, it was never put into effect.

[38] Lyle, author interview; "King Symposium Focuses on Black Music This Weekend," *Student Life* (Washington University), 28 Mar. 1969, p. 11; handwritten attachment to Richard C. Sheldon, memo to files, 12 Aug. 1970, GEN 70 (HA), Black Artists' Group, FFA.

[39] Hunt, author interview; Rutlin, author interview; Marshall, author interview; Loewenstein, author interview.

[40] Rusch, "Speaking with Oliver Lake," 3; liner notes to Human Arts Ensemble, *Under the Sun* (Universal Justice Records, UJ-104, 1973; rereleased Arista/Freedom, AL 1022, 1975); Marshall, author interview; Loewenstein, author interview; Rutlin, author interview; Michael Castro, author interview; Ehrlich, author interview. Members of the Human Arts Ensemble recorded many of their early rehearsals, and these recordings are now being digitally remastered by poet and participant Jay Zalenka for distribution over the Internet. The poem for the Hopi event was written by Michael Castro.

[41] Michael Castro, "The Origins of River Styx," in *Seeking St. Louis: Voices from a River City, 1670–2000*, ed. Lee Ann Sandweiss (St. Louis: Missouri Historical Society Press, 2000), 851–54; Michael Castro, "Brookings Hall Exorcism," in *Ripple* (St. Louis: Hard Times Press, 1970), on file with author; Castro, personal communication to author, 23 July 2001; Castro, author interview.

[42] Joiner; Koch, author interview; Castro, author interview; Clay Claiborne, Jr., interview by Lisa Salt, 20 Apr. 2001, unedited transcript, Washington University Liberation Front Reunion Archive, WUSC. Incomplete runs of the *St. Louis Free Press* and *The Outlaw* can be found at MHS. Some of the missing issues are contained in the Underground Newspaper Collection, microfilmed by Bell & Howell, Wooster, Ohio.

[43] Jeannette E. Roach, "KDNA—for the Entire Community," *Greater St. Louis Magazine*, Aug. 1969, 16–19; "KDNA-FM on the Air at 102.5," *FOCUS/Midwest* 7, no. 45 (1969): 7; Lorenzo Wilson Milam, *The Radio Papers: From KRAB to KCHU—Essays on the Art and Practice of Radio Transmission* (San Diego: MHO & MHO Works, 1986), 108–09; Harper Barnes, "Kooky KDNA: Long Gone, But Legacy Lingers," *St. Louis Post-Dispatch*, 3 July 1983; "KDNA 102.5 mHz," *St. Louis Journalism Review* 28, no. 200 (Oct. 1997): 8; Red Wilford, "Radio Station KDNA FM and Its Bag of Tricks," *St. Louis Argus*, 26 Oct. 1972, p. 10A; Ehrlich, author interview; Castro, "The Origins of River Styx," 853–54; Castro, author interview. Also see unprocessed KDNA files, which include the station's newsletter *Fat Chance*, at SCSL. Tapes of several of these Human Arts Ensemble broadcasts survive: see KDNA/KDHX Radio Tapes, 1965–1992, sl 536, box 4, tape 115, and box 9, tapes 299, 302–3, WHMC.

[44] Koch, author interview; Joiner, "Only Black Book Store"; Eric Zoeckler, "Police Censoring Books at Some County Stores," *St. Louis Post-Dispatch*, 9 Apr. 1970; Marguerite Shepard, "'Underground' Media Have a Few Surprising Connections," *St. Louis Globe-Democrat*, 21 Jan. 1972; "KDNA 102.5 mHz," 8; Lorenzo W. Milam, *Sex and Broadcasting: A Handbook on Starting a Radio Station for the Community*, 3rd ed. (Saratoga, CA: Dildo Press, 1975), 344–46; Milam, *The Radio Papers*, 109; "Evangelist Bill Beeny Seeking License of KDNA," *St. Louis Post-Dispatch*, 3 Jan. 1971, and "FCC Denies Bid by Evangelist for FM Station," *St. Louis Globe-Democrat*, 9 Mar. 1971, both in Bill Beeny folder, box 35, Group Research Archive, Rare Book and Manuscript Library, Columbia University, New York, NY. Lansman claimed that the drugs were planted, and the charges were later dropped. Although KDNA fended off Beeny's license grab attempt, which the FCC rejected in February 1971, listener donations never surmounted the station's red ink. After the station closed in 1972, staff fanned out to community broadcasters such as Atlanta's Radio Free Georgia (WRFG), KOPN in Columbia, MO, and stations in Pittsburgh, Madison, Dallas, and Columbus. Meanwhile, the nonprofit corporation Double Helix, created in KDNA's wake, founded the St. Louis radio station KDHX, which captured some of the old KDNA ethos and remains on the air today.

[45] Michael Newton, letter to Norman Lloyd, 13 Aug. 1969, folder 2722, ICAP-RAC; Elliott, author interview; Hemphill, interview by Stitt, tape 3 of 4; Terrell, author interview.

[46] Van Deburg, 298; Karen Jackson Ford, *Gender and the Poetics of Excess: Moments of Brocade* (Jackson: University Press of Mississippi, 1997), 22, 176, 191–92.

[47] Hunt, author interview. On Braxton's gender critique, see Porter, 283–84. A few examples of female jazz musicians produced by Detroit over the past few decades might include: Geri Allen, Dorothy Ashby, Bess Bonnier, Betty Carter, Regina Carter, Alice Coltrane, Marian Hayden, Sheila Jordan, Gayelynn McKinney, Shahida Nurrulah, Eileen Orr, Della Reese, Terry Pollard, Alma Smith, Angie Smith, Ursula Walker, Kim Weston, and Pamela Wise.

[48] Lyle, author interview; Shirley LeFlore, author interview.

[49] Carroll, author interview; Terrell, author interview; Shelton, author interview; Holder, author interview.

[50] Shelton, author interview; Terrell, author interview. In response to the author's Freedom of Information requests for files on BAG, the FBI initially claimed that it had no materials. In an 18 Nov. 2003 response to the author's appeal of this finding, the Department of Justice's Office of Information and Privacy explained that FBI records on BAG had been unearthed and released nine pages of documents (all newspaper clippings). The Office of Information and Privacy's codirector further explained: "The Black Artists' Group is not the subject of a St. Louis Field Office main file; however, it is mentioned briefly seven times in five files, the subjects of which are other individuals or organizations. . . . I have determined that this information is not appropriate for discretionary release."

[51] Shirley LeFlore, author interview; Shipton, 824.

Chapter Four Notes

[1] Larry Neal, *Black Boogaloo: Notes on Black Liberation* (San Francisco: Journal of Black Poetry Press, 1969); Elliott, author interview. Burgdorf's was located at 4744 McPherson Avenue.

[2] Elliott, audiotaped comments; Bluiett quoted in John Kille, "St. Louis Jazz, Remembering," *Sauce Magazine* (St. Louis) 3, no. 1 (Jan. 2003): 24; Oliver Lake, *Life Dance* (Cooper Station, NY: Africa Publishing Co., 1979).

[3] Elliott, audiotaped comments; Jackson, author interview.

[4] Ajulé Rutlin, "The Black Artists' Group: As a Tree," unpublished typescript, c. 1971, on file with author; Jackson, author interview; Oliver Jackson, "Political Stance and the African Continuum," speech at Washington University in St. Louis, 22 Mar. 1971, archive tape no. 71-13, WUSC; "Jackson Explains Pan-African Unity," *Student Life* (Washington University), 26 Mar. 1971, p. 5.

[5] Houston Baker, *Modernism and the Harlem Renaissance* (Chicago: University of Chicago Press, 1987), 66; Elliott quoted in Wood, "Reviving Their African Heritage"; Larry Neal, "Libations for Olorun," in Neal, *Black Boogaloo*, 4–5; Elliott, author interview.

[6] Elliott, author interview; Elliott, telephone conversation with author, 2 Feb. 2004; "BAG Presents 'Poem' Drama Sat. and Sun.," *St. Louis Sentinel*, 24 May 1969, p. 6; Larry Neal, "Poem for a Revolutionary Night," in Neal, *Black Boogaloo*, 47–49.

[7] Elliott, author interview; Neal, "Poem for a Revolutionary Night," 47–49.

[8] "'Poem' Drama First in Series Planned by BAG," *St. Louis Sentinel*, 14 June 1969, p. 12; "BAG and AIR to Entertain in Pruitt-Igoe," *St. Louis Sentinel*, 21 June 1969, p. 10; Hemphill, interview by Stitt, tape 3 of 4; Terrell, author interview.

[9] "Christ Church Cathedral Festival of Creation Set," *St. Louis Sentinel*, 1 Nov. 1969, p. 9; Danson, 14; Carroll, author interview; Elliott, author interview.

[10] Parran, "The St. Louis Black Artists' Group," 2; Claudia Orenstein, "Agitational Performance: Now and Then," *Theater* 31, no. 3 (2001): 139–151; Yolanda Broyles-González, *El Teatro Campesino: Theater in the Chicano Movement* (Austin: University of Texas Press, 1994).

[11] Kenyatta, *Black Theatre Notebook*, 7, 13; Newton and Hatley, 195; Lexa, author interview; Elliott, author interview; Elliott, audiotaped comments; Richard Alan Nichols, personal communication to author, 9 Mar. 2004; "MECA Workshop Openings Still Available," *St. Louis Argus*, 22 Jan. 1971, p. 2A; Jerzy Grotowski, *Towards a Poor Theatre* (New York: Simon and Schuster, 1970 [1968]), 211–18; "AIR-BAG Performances: July 1968–July 1969," folder 2722, ICAP-RAC.

[12] Terrell, author interview; Vincent Terrell, telephone conversation with author, 28 Feb. 2004; Elliott, author interview; Malinké Elliott, telephone conversation with author, 23 Feb. 2004.

[13] Michael Newton, letter to Norman Lloyd, 13 Aug. 1969, 11, folder 2722, ICAP-RAC; Portia Hunt, curriculum vitae, c. 2001, on file with author; Bleck, "Black Liberators Represent"; Hunt, author interview; "Rehearsing Part," *Metro-East Journal* (East St. Louis, IL), 13 Oct. 1971; "Theatre," *PROUD Magazine* (May/June 1972): 32, MHS. By 1971, Hunt was teaching acting techniques for BAG's theater component as well as serving as coordinator for a federally funded job training program in East St. Louis.

[14] Sell, 58; Geneviéve Fabre, *Drumbeats, Masks and Metaphor: Contemporary Afro-American Theatre*, trans. Melvin Dixon (Cambridge, MA: Harvard University Press, 1983), 101; LeRoi Jones, "The Revolutionary Theatre," *Liberator*, July 1965, pp. 4–6; Elliott, audiotaped comments; "Culture through AIR for Inner City"; "Two Plays by Blacks to Be Given Friday," *St. Louis American*, 3 June 1971. Hemphill, interview by Stitt, tape 3 of 4, later spoke of the multimedia performances' influence on his musical sensibility, saying, "I really came alive under these kind of new circumstances here."

[15] Rutlin, author interview; Terrell, author interview; Ed Bullins, "A Short Statement on Street Theatre," *The Drama Review* 12, no. 4 (Summer 1968): 93; Elliott quoted in Adams, "Black Artists' Goal." These scripts by Terrell were entitled "Right, Reverend Nat Turner" and "From These Shores, or Good Olde Crispus." On police brutality in St. Louis, see coverage in the black press, especially "Police Blasted on Civil Rights," *St. Louis Sentinel*, 10 May 1969, p. 1; and Lipsitz, *A Life in the Struggle*, 118, 129–30. On sporadic efforts to recruit more black officers to the force, see Eugene J. Watts, "Black and Blue: Afro-American Police Officers in Twentieth-Century St. Louis," *Journal of Urban History* 7, no. 2 (Feb. 1981): 132–36, 142–46, 158.

[16] "Culture through AIR for Inner City"; Robert Hughes, "Prayer Meeting," publication unlisted, Aug. 1969, in Black Artists' Group file, FASL; Ben Caldwell, "Prayer Meeting: Or, The First Militant Preacher," in *Black Theatre USA: Plays by African Americans, 1847 to Today*, ed. James V. Hatch and Ted Shine (New York: The Free Press, 1996); Green quoted in "Black Sunday Demands," *St. Louis Sentinel*, 14 June 1969, p. 7. For the daily newspapers' reportage of the local church reparations campaign, see "Negro Scrapbooks," MHS. See also "ACTION Accuses Black Ministers of Misleading Flocks," *St. Louis Argus*, 5 June 1970, p. 1A. For background on Jimmy Rollins, leader of the Black Liberation Front, see Dana L. Spitzer, "Jimmy Rollins Is Back in St. Louis (Temporarily)," *The New Republic*, 1 June 1968, pp. 15–16. On concurrent housing demonstrations at the St. Louis Cathedral, see Lipsitz, *A Life in the Struggle*, 152, 161.

[17] Shelton, author interview; Terrell, author interview; Hunt, author interview; "AIR, BAG Open House Saturday," *St. Louis Sentinel*, 15 Mar. 1969, p. 7; "Black Artists Line Up Shows for Two Months," *St. Louis Sentinel*, 19 Apr. 1969, p. 4; "Black Open House Sat.," *St. Louis American*, 13 Mar. 1969; Dorothy Ahmad, "Papa's Daughter," and Ed Bullins, "Clara's Ole Man," both in *The Drama Review* 12, no. 4 (Summer 1968): 139–41, 159–71; Peter Bruck, "Ed Bullins: The Quest and Failure of an Ethnic Community Theatre," in *Essays on Contemporary American Drama*, eds. Hedwig Bock and Albert Wertheim (Munich: Max Hueber Verlag, 1981), 129–30. Theater scholar Samuel A. Hay dubs *Clara's Ole Man* "the first scripted non-homophobic play in African American theatre." Hay, *Ed Bullins: A Literary Biography* (Detroit: Wayne State University Press, 1997), 137.

[18] Eugene Redmond and Jabari Asim, "Conversation: Eugene Redmond and Jabari Asim," in *The Furious Flowering of African American Poetry*, ed. Joanne V. Gabbin (Charlottesville: University Press of Virginia, 1999), 93; Elliott, author interview. For an overview of African American poets working in the St. Louis area during the mid- and late 1960s, see Redmond, *Drumvoices*, 320, 394, 398–99, 400–401. A sample of Redmond's performance style can be heard on his recording *Blood Links and Sacred Places* (Black River Writers LP 110-13, 1973; rereleased Ikef Records, IKEF01, 2002). Redmond's writing frequently revolved around people and places of the local community, as in his collection *River of Bones and Flesh and Blood* (East St. Louis, IL: Black River Writers, 1971), which contains poetic odes to Henry Dumas, Jerome "Scrooge" Harris, Taylor Jones III, and the Grace Hill settlement house. In 1969, Redmond left East St. Louis for a string of teaching posts in Ohio, California, Holland, and Nigeria, though he returned frequently to the area.

[19] Lyle, author interview; Eugene Redmond, "We're Tight, Soul-Tight—Like Lincoln Nights," in *African American Literature*, ed. Keith Gilyard and Anissa Wardi (New York: Pearson Longman, 2002), 724–27. See Fahamisha Patricia Brown, *Performing the Word: African American Poetry as Vernacular Language* (Piscataway, NJ: Rutgers University Press, 1999).

[20] Thomas, *Extraordinary Measures*, 136; Porter, 194–95; Sascha Feinstein, *Jazz Poetry: From the 1920s to the Present* (Westport, Conn.: Greenwood Press, 1997); Bruce Rutlin, "Oliver Lake," *St. Louis Free Press*, 29 Nov. 1968, p. 4, MHS. For Redmond, music was the "most shared experience" and "most vital commodity" among African Americans, and he dubbed poetry "music's twin." Redmond, *Drumvoices*, 422. This long tradition of pairing jazz with poetry was somewhat unique in St. Louis of the late 1960s. River Styx founder Michael Castro gives BAG credit for that, and particularly recalls Shirley LeFlore as a pioneer locally in bringing together poetry and music into a dynamic performance. Castro, author interview.

[21] Shirley LeFlore, author interview; Major, author interview; LeFlore quoted in Mary Lindsley, "Beyond Boundaries: Poet, Scholar Is Comfortable in Classroom or Carnegie Hall," *The Current* (University of Missouri–St. Louis), 26 Feb. 1998, p. 1; Berea Presbyterian Church, "75th Anniversary Souvenir Program," 25 Mar. 1973, in Freedom of Residence Committee records, sl 590, folder 65, WHMC. The Messenger Singers were directed by Alvin Major, a Texas-born graduate student in music at Washington University.

[22] Rutlin, author interview; Ajulé Rutlin, curriculum vitae, c. 1986, on file with author; Ajulé Rutlin, *AJULÉ-of-the-Shadows* (St. Louis: privately published, 1971), on file with author; "'Blacker Litany' to Open Summer Ready June 15," *St. Louis Sentinel*, 14 June 1969, p. 12; "Pulitzer Prize Winning Poet on Radio Show," *St. Louis Sentinel*, 7 June 1969, p. 6; John Litweiler, "Oliver Lake/Julius Hemphill," *Down Beat* 36, no. 12 (12 June 1969): 34–35. "Children of the Sun" was Rutlin's appellation for all people of African descent, and he created the ensemble bearing that name by adding three dancers to the poets and musicians of his Poetry/Music Function.

[23] Ajulé Rutlin, "Sing, Then, of Piano Players" and "Brooding Cherub, Miles," in *AJULÉ-of-the-Shadows*; Human Arts Ensemble, *Poem of Gratitude* (Universal Justice Records, TS73-38, rec. Oct. 1972). On Miles Rutlin, who later became a St. Louis visual artist and gallery director before his tragically early death, see "Miles Rutlin, 26," *St. Louis Post-Dispatch*, 19 Feb. 1992, p. 4C.

[24] Vincent Terrell, "The Dash," in *Sides of the River: A Mini-Anthology of Black Writings*, ed. Eugene Redmond (East St. Louis, IL: Black River Writers, 1969), 19–22; Vincent Terrell, "The Noble Smith Affair," *Mill Creek Valley Intelligencer* 3, no. 9 (July/Aug. 1968): 29, MHS; Redmond, *Drumvoices*, 339, 342–43; Robert Elliott, "The Dream Time," in *Tambourine*, ed. Pamela White and Howard Schwartz (St. Louis: Washington University, 1968), 27, WUSC. Like much other writing that emerged from the Black Arts Movement, the latter of Terrell's stories is tinged with anti-Semitism.

[25] Troupe, author interview; Troupe, radio interview with Bobby Jackson, "JazzTracks," WCPN-FM, Cleveland, 19 July 1998; "Lindenwood to Hold Two Day Afro-American Arts Festival," *St. Louis Sentinel*, 26 Apr. 1969, p. 4; "Ex-St. Louisan One of Watts Writers in Washington U. Concert," *St. Louis Sentinel*, 1 Feb. 1969, p. 4; Troupe quoted in "Watts Poets to Stage Workshop," *Student Life* (Washington University), 4 Feb. 1969, p. 3. See also Troupe's comments on St. Louis in "Confrontation: Third World Literature and the West," speech at Washington University, 23 Mar. 1971, archive tape no. 71–13, WUSC. For Troupe's reflections on the influence of speech patterns that he heard in St. Louis's bars, churches, beauty parlors, jazz clubs, and streets while growing up, see Bill Moyers, *The Language of Life: A Festival of Poets*, ed. James Haba (New York: Doubleday, 1995), 414.

[26] Lyle, author interview; K. Curtis Lyle, radio interview with Michael Castro, "Poetry Beat: River Styx Magazine of the Air," KDHX-FM, St. Louis, 6 Feb. 2002; K. Curtis Lyle, "Primeval Mother," in *Roots and Branches*, ed. Chezia B. Thompson (St. Louis: Washington University Black Studies Program, 1973), copy at Julia Davis Branch, St. Louis Public Library.

[27] Malinké Elliott, telephone conversation with author, 2 Feb. 2004; K. Curtis Lyle, telephone conversation with author, 6 Feb. 2004. The Sweet Willie Rollbar character originated in *Tom Slick: Racer*, "Episode 10: Overstocked," Jay Ward Productions, first released 7 Nov. 1967 and broadcast as a short segment during ABC's *George of the Jungle*. The master reels of *The Orientation of Sweet Willie Rollbar* survive in Lyle's possession and are currently being remastered for video.

[28] K. Curtis Lyle, "Lemon's Brand-New-Shiny-Sky-Boat-Blues," on Lyle and Julius Hemphill, *The Collected Poem for Blind Lemon Jefferson* (Mbari Records 5002, 1971; rereleased Ikef Records, IKEF05, 2002), reprinted in *Roots and Branches*; Lyle, "Poetry Beat"; Léopold Sédar Senghor, "Speech and Image: An African Tradition of the Surreal," in *Poems for the Millennium*, vol. 1, ed. Jerome Rothenberg and Pierre Joris (Berkeley: University of California Press, 1995), 565.

[29] Quincy Troupe, "Confrontation: Third World Literature and the West," speech at Washington University, 23 Mar. 1971, archive tape no. 71–13, WUSC; Redmond, *Drumvoices*, 347. As Philip Brian Harper puts it, such work does not attempt to overcome division in the black population, but strives "repeatedly to articulate it in the name of black consciousness." Harper, "Nationalism and Social Division in Black Arts Poetry of the 1960s," *Critical Inquiry* 19, no. 2 (Winter 1993): 239. Henry Louis Gates, Jr., for example, famously dubbed the Black Arts Movement the "shortest and least successful" black cultural movement in U.S. history. Gates, "Black Creativity: On the Cutting Edge," *Time* 144, no. 15 (10 Oct. 1994): 74–75.

[30] "Blackness in Color: Visual Expressions of the Black Arts Movement," catalog essay for exhibit at the Herbert F. Johnson Museum, Cornell University, 26 Aug. to 22 Oct. 2000. BAG's educational effort in this arena became especially necessary following the 1965 demise of St. Louis's People's Art Center, originally established through the Federal Art Project of the Works Progress Administration. During its twenty-three years of existence, the center had served thousands of children and adults while providing the first racially integrated visual-arts classes in the city. Martin G. Towey, "Design for Democracy: The People's Art Center in St. Louis," in *Art in Action: American Art Centers and the New Deal*, ed. John Franklin White (Metuchen, NJ: Scarecrow Press, 1987), 89–94.

[31] Lyle, author interview.

[32] Cruz, author interview; Emilio Cruz, curriculum vitae, c. 2000, on file with author; Eric Hanks, "Emilio Cruz," in *St. James Guide to Black Artists*, ed. Thomas Riggs (Detroit: St. James Press, 1997), 126; Mary King, "Emilio Cruz Exhibit Reflects Influences of Three Worlds," *St. Louis Post Dispatch*, 11 Nov. 1969, p. 3B, and John Brod Peters, "Emilio Cruz Show at Loretto Hilton," *St. Louis Globe-Democrat*, 22 Nov. 1969, p. 6H, both in Emilio Cruz file, FASL; Norman Lloyd, on-site evaluation, 16–17 July 1969, folder 2722, ICAP-RAC; Cruz quoted in Adams, "Black Artists' Goal"; M. A. Carley, "Emilio Cruz," *New Art Examiner* 24 (June 1997): 42; Eleanor Heartney, "Emilio Cruz at Steinbaum Krauss," *Art in America* 86, no. 2 (Feb. 1998): 107–09. By the time he came to St. Louis, Cruz had been awarded a John Hay Whitney Foundation Fellowship for 1964–65 and a Cintas Foundation Fellowship for 1965–66, and had participated in group exhibitions around the country.

[33] Oliver Jackson, curriculum vitae, 2001, on file with author; Diane Roby, "Oliver Jackson: On Making," *International Review of African American Art* 13, no. 3 (Fall 1996): 51–52; Elizabeth Wright Millard, "Oliver Jackson: Former St. Louisan Featured at Art Museum," *St. Louis American*, 6 Sept. 1990, pp. 1B, 2B.

[34] Mary King, "Paintings by Oliver Jackson Interpret Capetown Massacre," *St. Louis Post-Dispatch*, 8 Oct. 1973, p. 3C, in Oliver Jackson file, FASL; Jackson, author interview; Jackson quoted in David M. Roth, "Gestural Giant: A Conversation with Artist Oliver Jackson," *San Jose Metro*, 28 Oct. 1993, p. 33. Julius Hemphill performed at the 1973 exhibit opening for Jackson's "Sharpeville Series" at the Loretto-Hilton Center in St. Louis.

[35] Hughes, author interview; St. Louis City Art Museum, *Bulletin*, July/Aug. 1971, 7; Mary King, "Hughes Art Show," *St. Louis Post-Dispatch*, 3 Oct. 1968; Mary King, "Art Show At College," *St. Louis Post-Dispatch*, 8 Oct. 1969; Saint Louis Public Library, press release, 2 Feb. 1972, in Manuel Hughes file, FASL.

[36] Mary King, "Black Artists Show Work," *St. Louis Post-Dispatch*, 24 July 1970, in Manuel Hughes file, FASL; Oliver Jackson, interview by Jan Butterfeld, in catalog for "Oliver Jackson," exhibit at the Seattle Art Museum, 17 Sept.–7 Nov. 1982.

[37] Redmond, author interview; Lake on the community college incident in Cassandra Johnson, "Esoteric Expression," *PROUD Magazine* 1, no. 6 (June/July 1970): 21, MHS. Reviews highlighting BAG "profanity" include "Old and New Afro Music BAG Blends," 2; and Ernestine Cofield, "AIR Team Party Brings Out Whole Families," *St. Louis Sentinel*, 21 June 1969, p. 10.

[38] Portia Hunt, telephone conversation with author, 9 June 2004; Rutlin, author interview; Elliott, author interview; Elliott, audiotaped comments.

[39] Elliott, audiotaped comments; Hunt, author interview; Carroll, author interview; Gary Froeschner, personal communication to author, 29 Apr. 2002. On the "anti-structural tropes" that erased separations between spectator and stage in other Black Arts Movement theater, see Harry J. Elam, Jr., *Taking It to the Streets: The Social Protest Theater of Luis Valdez & Amiri Baraka* (Ann Arbor: University of Michigan Press, 1997), 48.

[40] Shipton, 825; Shelton, author interview; Elliott, author interview; Terrell, author interview; Richard Alan Nichols, personal communication to author, 9 Mar. 2004.

[41] Carroll, author interview. For a critique of the effects of anti-poverty subsidies on black theater in the U.S., see Geneviéve Fabre, 245–46.

[42] Elliott, audiotaped comments; Michael Newton, letter to Norman Lloyd, 13 Aug. 1969, and Kenneth W. Thompson, summary of interviews with Merrimon Cuninggim and Gene Schwilk, 16–18 Sept. 1969, both in folder 2722, ICAP-RAC.

[43] Kenneth W. Thompson, summary of interviews with Merrimon Cuninggim and Gene Schwilk, 16–18 Sept. 1969, and Norman Lloyd, summary of interview with Katherine Dunham, 20 Oct. 1969, both in folder 2722, ICAP-RAC; Newton and Hatley, 194. For general comments on controversial Danforth Foundation grants to inner-city organizations, see Cuninggim, *Private Money and Public Service*, 57, 101. On funding as a way to strengthen moderate forces, see sociologist Herbert Haines's definition of "radical flank effects," in his *Black Radicals and the Civil Rights Mainstream, 1954–1970* (Knoxville: University of Tennessee Press, 1988), 181–82.

[44] Kenneth W. Thompson, summary of interviews with Arts & Education Council officials, 21 Mar. 1968, and A. Donald Bourgeois, letter to Norman Lloyd, 1 Apr. 1968, both in folder 2720, ICAP-RAC; Norman Lloyd, summary of interview with Katherine Dunham, 20 Oct. 1969, and Kenneth W. Thompson, summary of interviews with Merrimon Cuninggim and Gene Schwilk, 16–18 Sept. 1969, both in folder 2722, ICAP-RAC. Based on what they heard from the Danforth Foundation, Rockefeller Foundation officials concluded with displeasure that BAG's "lessons and teachings have been mainly for blacks, not whites." Ibid.

[45] Emilio Cruz, author interview; Elliott, audiotaped comments; Norman Lloyd, summary of interview with Katherine Dunham, 20 Oct. 1969, folder 2722, ICAP-RAC. Dunham did continue to receive smaller grants from the Danforth Foundation, but her budget was also strained by spending cutbacks at Southern Illinois University, which gave the PATC financial support.

[46] Richard C. Sheldon, memo to files, 12 Aug. 1970, GEN 70 (HA), Black Artists' Group, FFA; Rutlin, author interview; Danforth Foundation, payment schedule of grants to the Arts & Education Council of Greater St. Louis, 1968–69, released to author by the Danforth Foundation, St. Louis; Carroll, author interview; Terrell, author interview; Loewenstein, author interview; Hemphill, interview by Stitt, tape 3 of 4; BAG, "Black Artists' Group: Proposal for a New Theatre," unpublished typescript, 1970, 23–24, MHS; Christine Bertelson, "Directing Drama Workshop for Black Artists' Group," *St. Louis Post-Dispatch*, 20 Aug. 1970, p. 4F; Arts & Education Council of Greater St. Louis, "Summary of Arts Development Committee Recommendations," 15 Dec. 1969, provided to author by Patricia A. Tichacek of the Arts & Education Council.

[47] Emilio Cruz, curriculum vitae, c. 2000, on file with author; Danforth Foundation, "The Urban Program of the Danforth Foundation," n.p.; Elliott, audiotaped comments; Vincent Terrell, letter to Resist, 14 Dec. 1972, in Resist Collection, box 1, "Applications 1970–72 denied," Manuscript Holdings, Watkinson Library, Trinity College, Hartford, CT; Terrell, author interview; Shelton, author interview; "2 Charged in Arson at ROTC Building," *St. Louis Post-Dispatch*, 24 May 1970, p. 1A; C. D. Stelzer, "Howard's End," *Riverfront Times*, 16 Feb. 2000; "Theatre," *PROUD Magazine*, May/June 1972, p. 32, MHS.

[48] Cathee Allen, "BAG: Black Artist Group," *PROUD Magazine* 2, no. 6 (June/July 1971): 30–31, MHS; Dickerson, author interview; Lyle, author interview; Redmond, *Drumvoices*, 384; program to New Music Circle's "Catalytic Celebration," 1969, in New Music Circle Records, sl 483, box 1, folder 1, WHMC. While performing at Oberlin, Julius Hemphill met the cello student Abdul Wadud, who became one of his most constant recording and performance partners over the next several decades.

[49] Luisah Teish, *Jambalaya: The Natural Woman's Book of Personal Charms and Practical Rituals* (San Francisco: Harper & Row, 1985), 26–32; Patrick Chike Onwuachi, "Religious Concepts and Socio-cultural Dynamics of Afro-American Religious Cults in St. Louis, Missouri" (Ph.D. diss., Saint Louis University, 1963), 60–61, 93–94, 151. The St. Louis Fahamme temple was known at various times by other names, such as the Ethiopian Temple of Islam and Culture and the Negro Culture College.

[50] Dickerson, author interview; Luisah Teish, "Big Mommas and Golden Apples," *Ms. Magazine* (Oct./Nov. 1999); Teish, *Jambalaya*, 29; Allen, 30–31. On Dunham's use of ritual in the East St. Louis context, see Chapter 10 of Joyce Aschenbrenner, *Katherine Dunham: Dancing a Life* (Urbana: University of Illinois Press, 2002).

[51] "'Y' Black Festival August 28," *St. Louis Argus*, 21 Aug. 1970, p. 5B; Allen, 30–31; Dickerson, author interview; Mike Heffley, *The Music of Anthony Braxton* (Westport, Conn.: Greenwood Press, 1996), 64, 139n64; Teish, *Jambalaya*, 33–34. These high school students included Carolyn Zachary, Etta Jackson, and A. J. Dickerson, Sr.

[52] Eric Charry, "A Guide to the Jembe," *Percussive Notes* 34, no. 2 (Apr. 1996): 66–72; "Conversations with Mor Thiam" and Fred Onovwerosuoke, "Mor Thiam: Maverick Drummer Extraordinaire," *The Voice of African Music: A Newsletter of the St. Louis African Chorus* 5, no. 1 (Winter/Spring 1998): 2; Teish, *Jambalaya*, 33–34; Allen, 30–31; Dickerson, author interview. Thiam collaborated with BAG artists but was never a member himself. Following the summer 1971 departure of A. J. Dickerson, Sr., for California, the role of Chaka was taken over by Tillman Whitley. For biographical notes on Omawali Dance & Drum Ensemble participants Majadi Tangulifu, Johari Endesha, and Kalimu Endesha, and discussion of their political activities in St. Louis, see Lang, esp. 114–16.

[53] Muthal Naidoo, *The Search for a Cultural Identity: A Personal Odyssey*, Indic Theatre Monograph Series, no. 1 (Durban, South Africa: Asoka Theatre Publications, 1993), 3, 7; Muthal Naidoo, "A Personal View of South African 'Indian' Theatre," *Theatre Journal* no. 49 (1997): 36n18. See also T. G. Ramamurthi, *Apartheid and Indian South Africans: A Study of the Role of Ethnic Indians in the Struggle against Apartheid in South Africa* (New Delhi: Reliance Publishing House, 1995). Ronnie Govender would later win the Commonwealth Writers Prize for African Literature. While at Indiana University, Naidoo directed an adaptation of Eldridge Cleaver's *Soul on Ice* in Mar. 1969, using David Baker's jazz ensemble for the performance. Linda Alis, "Black Theatre Production Set Mar. 26–27," *Courier-Tribune* (Bloomington, IN), 25 Mar. 1969, sec. 2, p. 12.

[54] Bertelson; Naidoo quoted in Carter Stith, "Music and Dance for Benefit," *St. Louis Post-Dispatch*, 6 Aug. 1971; Naidoo, author interview; Hunt, author interview.

[55] "Black Artist Group to Perform Series," *St. Louis Argus*, 4 Sept. 1970, p. 13A; "Black Expression at BAG," publication unknown, Sept. 1970, in "Black Artists' Group" file, FASL; "Deltas to Present St. Louis Group," *East St. Louis Monitor*, 8 Oct. 1970; Sonia Sanchez, "Sister Son/ji," in *Wines in the Wilderness: Plays by African American Women from the Harlem Renaissance to the Present*, ed. Elizabeth Brown-Guillory (Westport, Conn.: Greenwood Press, 1990).

[56] Bertelson; Naidoo, author interview; Malcolm X with Alex Haley, *The Autobiography of Malcolm X* (New York: Grove Press, 1965); Wole Soyinka, *The Trials of Brother Jero and The Strong Breed: Two Plays* (New York: Dramatists Play Service, 1969); "Black Artist Group to Perform," *East St. Louis Monitor*, 3 June 1971, p. 9; program to Black Experience Theater, "The Trials of Brother Jero" and "Mission Accomplished," Forest Park Community College, 4 June 1971, on file with author; Stith, "Music and Dance for Benefit"; "St. Louis Committee on Africa," *PROUD Magazine* 3, no. 1 (Jan./Feb. 1972): 13, MHS. The play based on *The Autobiography of Malcolm X* was called *Volunteered Slavery* and traced the events in the book's "Laura" chapter.

[57] Naidoo, author interview; Hunt, author interview.

[58] Richard Krantz, "Love and Unity Rally Depicts Freedom in Talk, Skit, Dance," *St. Louis Globe-Democrat*, 6 July 1970, p. 10A; "Black Mothers Rally at Old Courthouse," *St. Louis Post-Dispatch*, 6 July 1970, p. 3B; Naidoo, author interview; Hunt, author interview.

[59] Michael S. Harper, *Dear John, Dear Coltrane* (Pittsburgh: University of Pittsburgh Press, 1970). Harper knew Oliver Jackson from their graduate school days together at the University of Iowa. When he formed the African Continuum group along with Jackson and Hemphill, he was an associate professor of English at Brown University, but held a visiting fellowship at the University of Illinois in Urbana, allowing him to travel more frequently to St. Louis.

[60] Aten, author interview; BAG, flyer for "Song for a Fallen Warrior," 23 Sept. 1971, on file with author; Ajulé Rutlin, "The Dragon," *The Outlaw*, n.d., 12–13, in "Black Artists' Group" folder, FASL.

[61] Jackson, interview by Butterfeld.

Chapter Five Notes

[1] Hemphill, interview by Stitt, tape 3 of 4; Pascal James Imperato, "Contemporary Adapted Dances of the Dogon," *African Arts* 5, no. 1 (Autumn 1971): 28–33, 68–72. On Donald Suggs's gallery, see "The Life Forces: Ritual and Ceremony," *PROUD Magazine* 3, no. 2 (Mar./Apr. 1972): 19–20, MHS.

[2] Baikida Carroll, telephone conversation with author, 11 Jan. 2004; Julius Hemphill, *Dogon A.D.* (Mbari Records 5001, 1972; rereleased Arista/Freedom, AL 1028, 1977).

[3] Robert Palmer, "Dogon A.D.," in *Setting the Tempo: Fifty Years of Great Jazz Liner Notes*, ed. Tom Piazzo (New York: Anchor Books, 1996), 244.

[4] Bill Smith, "The Oliver Lake Interview," 3. On the BAG big band, Baikida Carroll, interview by Frank Tafuri, n.d., in OmniTone Records press kit for Carroll. According to BAG's 1970 list of members, the collective's musicians were reedmen Julius Hemphill, Oliver Lake, J. D. Parran, and James Jabbo Ware; trumpeters Floyd LeFlore and Baikida Carroll; percussionists Charles "Bobo" Shaw, Carl Davis (later Rashu Aten), and Bensid Thigpen (brother of the legendary drummer Ed Thigpen); bassist Arzinia Richardson; and trombonists Victor Reef and Joseph Bowie. Baritone saxophonist Hamiet Bluiett was a member until his September 1969 departure from St. Louis. Other frequent participants not on the formal membership rolls included pianist John Hicks, drummers Philip Wilson and Jerome "Scrooge" Harris, bassist John Mixon, and trumpeters Lester Bowie and David Hines, all St. Louis natives. See membership list in BAG, "Black Artists' Group: Proposal for a New Theatre," unpublished typescript, 1970, 2, MHS.

[5] Porter, 192–93; David H. Rosenthal, "Jazz in the Ghetto: 1950–70," *Popular Music* 7, no. 1 (1987): 55; Lars Bjorn with Jim Gallert, *Before Motown: A History of Jazz in Detroit, 1920–60* (Ann Arbor: University of Michigan Press, 2001), 37–44, 108; Herman Gray, *Producing Jazz: The Experience of an Independent Record Company* (Philadelphia: Temple University Press, 1988), 26–27; Michael Cuscuna, author interview. Regarding disappointing sales for former Coltrane sidemen at Impulse Records, Michael Cuscuna notes the exception of Pharoah Sanders, whose 1969 album *Karma*, with East St. Louisan Leon Thomas, sold rather briskly.

[6] Gray, 26–27.

[7] Gray, 88–89; Michael J. Budds, *Jazz in the Sixties: The Expansion of Musical Resources and Techniques*, 2nd ed. (Iowa City: University of Iowa Press, 1990), 121; Coleman quoted in *Down Beat: Music '67* (Chicago: Maher Publications, 1967), 75.

[8] Donald Byrd, "Music without Aesthetics: How Some Non-Musical Forces and Institutions Influence Change in Black Music," *The Black Scholar* 9, no. 10 (July/Aug. 1978): 3.

[9] Kelley, "Dig They Freedom," 18; Horace Tapscott with Steven Isoardi, *Songs of the Unsung: The Musical and Social Journey of Horace Tapscott* (Durham, N.C.: Duke University Press, 2001), 82–167; Charley Gerard, *Jazz in Black and White: Race, Culture, and Identity in the Jazz Community* (Westport, Conn.: Praeger Publishers, 1998), 91–92. Tapscott later changed the name of his Underground Musicians Association (UGMA) to the Union of God's Musicians and Artists Ascension (UGMAA).

[10] Radano, 90; Jarman quoted in Shipton, 808; Gerard, 95–96; Valerie Wilmer, *As Serious as Your Life: The Story of the New Jazz* (London: Allison & Busby, 1977), 215–17.

[11] "1950s: Social Influences," *International Musician*, Oct. 1996, 40–41; Stephen Laifer, "Merged Locals Are Windows on Changing Times," *International Musician*, Feb. 2003; Charles Elwin Rose, "The American Federation of Musicians and Its Effect on Black Musicians in St. Louis in the Twentieth Century" (M.Mus. thesis, Southern Illinois University, 1978), 41–44, MHS. Local 44's charter was revoked at the AFM national convention in June 1931, on the one day (out of five convention days) when the Local 44 representative was not present to contest the charges. The white Local 2 then set up a subsidiary branch for black musicians with discriminatory rules and no voice for its members in governance, until Local 197 was chartered in 1944. Ibid. Regarding defense of union prerogatives, Delmark Records founder Bob Koester noted that during the 1950s, St. Louis's black musicians were far less willing than their white counterparts to play for less than union scale. Koester, interview by Eric Sandweiss, Chicago, 5 Apr. 1997, tape 1 of 2, unedited transcript, MHS. On general union discrimination in St. Louis, see James Neal Primm, *Lion of the Valley: St. Louis, Missouri, 1764–1980*, 3rd ed. (St. Louis: Missouri Historical Society Press, 1998), 442.

[12] Rose, "The American Federation of Musicians," 41–44, 72–74. Members of the black Local 197, leery of losing the gigs they did control, joined Local 2 in voting against a merger in 1970. The elected officers of Local 197 were given temporary executive positions with the merged union until the 1976 general election, when all blacks were eliminated from the executive board, with the exception of former Local 197 president George Smith, who had received a permanent slot as vice president of the merged union. Ibid., 73. Local trumpeter Charlie Rose explains the importance of the black union hall, claiming that through most of the 1960s, "basically the only way a young musician could learn about jazz was through the union, because that's where all of the musicians would hang out." Rose, author interview.

[13] Hemphill, interview by Stitt, tape 2 of 4; Carroll, author interview.

[14] Redmond, author interview; Hemphill, interview by Stitt, tapes 2 and 3 of 4.

[15] Ingrid T. Monson, "Doubleness and Jazz Improvisation: Irony, Parody, and Ethnomusicology," *Critical Inquiry* 20, no. 2 (Winter 1994): 286–87; Abrams quoted in Radano, 89; Hemphill, interview by Stitt, tape 2 of 4; Madden, 26; Carroll, author interview. On Sun Ra's strict conduct code for his musicians, see John F. Szwed, *Space Is the Place: The Lives and Times of Sun Ra* (New York: Pantheon Books, 1997), 117.

[16] Scott Saul, "Outrageous Freedom: Charles Mingus and the Invention of the Jazz Workshop," *American Quarterly* 53, no. 3 (2001): 400; Coleman quoted in A. B. Spellman, *Four Lives in the Bebop Business* (New York: Pantheon Books, 1966), 139; Shepp quoted in Frank Kofsky, *Black Nationalism and the Revolution in Music* (New York: Pathfinder Press, 1970), 145; Mitchell quoted in Litweiler, "The Free Jazz Movement," 27. Saul argues, however, that Mingus's angry outbursts at unruly audiences were in part "a canny collusion with a stunt-hungry public."

[17] Lincoln T. Beauchamp, Jr., "Joseph Jarman Interview," in *Great Black Music: Ancient to the Future*, ed. Beauchamp (Chicago: Art Ensemble of Chicago Publishing, 1998), 72; Holder, author interview; Ware, author interview.

[18] Jung, "A Fireside Chat with Baikida Carroll"; "Black Artists Concert Series," *St. Louis Globe-Democrat*, 27 Jan. 1970; "BAG to Give Four Sundays in February," *St. Louis Sentinel*, 31 Jan. 1970, p. 4. Historian Robert K. McMichael describes an "emerging integrationist subculture" in early 1960s free jazz, one defined by "the historically unique co-presence of black autonomy and authority" and a "white affirmation of black authority." McMichael, "'We Insist—Freedom Now!': Black Moral Authority, Jazz, and the Changeable Shape of Whiteness," *American Music* 16, no. 4 (Winter 1998): 375–416.

[19] Rosenthal, 52; Ranelin, author interview; Rob Backus, *Fire Music: A Political History of Jazz* (Chicago: Vanguard Books, 1976), 77–78; Tribe, *Message from the Tribe—An Anthology of Tribe Records: 1972–1977* (Universal Sound, USCD5, 1996); Herb Boyd, "Cookin' in the Motor City, Part 2," *Metro Times* (Detroit), 24 Sept. 1997; Litweiler, *The Freedom Principle*, 183. The Artists Workshop was founded in 1966, the Creative Musicians Association in 1968, and Tribe in 1969. Joseph Jarman comments on an appearance with the Artists Workshop in "Art Ensemble of Chicago: Great Black Music!" *Ann Arbor Sun*, 18 Aug. 1972, pp. 8–9. Artists Workshop materials are archived in the John and Leni Sinclair Papers, Bentley Historical Library, University of Michigan, Ann Arbor.

[20] "AIR-BAG Performances: July 1968–July 1969," Folder 2722, ICAP-RAC; *St. Louis Sentinel*, 10 May 1969, p. 5; "Festival of Music to Be Held," *St. Louis Globe-Democrat*, 8 May 1969; "Black Artist Group to Give Concert," *St. Louis Globe-Democrat*, 21 May 1970; Oliver Lake, curriculum vitae, c. 1975, on file with author; Karl Evanzz, personal communication to author, 25 Nov. 2003.

[21] Nessa, author interview; Carroll, author interview; Lester Bowie and Malachi Favors, radio interview with Ted Panken, WKCR-FM, New York, 22 Nov. 1994; Litweiler, "Oliver Lake/Julius Hemphill," 34–35.

[22] Ajulé Sunni Rutlin, "The Theft of Black Music," unpublished typescript, May 1976, on file with author. Break-even point from Rosenthal, 55.

[23] Rick Kennedy and Randy McNutt, *Little Labels, Big Sound: Small Record Companies and the Rise of American Music* (Bloomington: Indiana University Press, 1999), 159, 162–66, 170–71; Nessa, author interview; Robert Koester, personal communication to author, 29 July 2003; Robert Koester, interview by Eric Sandweiss, Chicago, 5 Apr. 1997, tape 1 of 2, unedited transcript, MHS.

[24] Nessa, author interview; Gray, 24–25, 88; Porter, 219, 232–33; Gary Giddins, *Riding on a Blue Note: Jazz and American Pop* (New York: Oxford University Press, 1981), 192–93; David G. Such, *Avant-Garde Jazz Musicians: Performing "Out There"* (Iowa City: University of Iowa Press, 1993), 79. After being spurned by established record companies, for example, Tribe in Detroit formed Tribe Records, pressing small batches of 500 to 1,000 LPs while offering the label's resources to other musicians. Ranelin, author interview; Backus, 77–78.

[25] Hemphill, interview by Stitt, tape 3 of 4; K. Curtis Lyle, conversation with author, 30 July 2003; Peter Occhiogrosso, "Somewhere There," *Different Drummer* 1, no. 12 (Oct. 1974); Jack Chambers, "Julius Hemphill: Dogon A.D.," *Coda* 10, no. 12 (Mar./Apr. 1973): 16.

[26] Marshall, author interview; Loewenstein, author interview; Universal Justice Records, promotional flyers, c. 1974, on file with author; Universal Justice quote from liner notes to Human Arts Ensemble, *Under the Sun* (Universal Justice Records, UJ-104, 1973).

[27] Marshall, author interview; Loewenstein, author interview; Wilmer, 237; Nessa, author interview. For reviews of the Human Arts Ensemble's *Poem of Gratitude* and *Whisper of Dharma*, both on Universal Justice Records, see Will Smith, "Human Arts Ensemble," *Down Beat* 41, no. 6 (28 Mar. 1974): 29.

[28] Parran, "The St. Louis Black Artists' Group," 4.

[29] Giddens comment in Shipton, 803–05; John Coltrane, *Ascension* (Impulse Records, AS-95, 1965); Bill Smith, "Lake Interview," 3.

[30] Lake quoted in Adams, "Black Artists' Goal."

[31] Hemphill quoted in Cassandra Johnson, "Esoteric Expression," *PROUD Magazine* 1, no. 6 (June/July 1970): 20, MHS; Michael J. Budds, "The Art Ensemble of Chicago in Context," *Lenox Avenue: A Journal of Interartistic Inquiry* 3 (1997): 66; Lewis, "Singing Omar's Song," 81. Some musicians of an earlier era also rejected the term "jazz"; see Burton W. Peretti, *The Creation of Jazz: Music, Race, and Culture in Urban America* (Urbana: University of Illinois Press, 1992), 71, 133–34. "I don't play free jazz," quipped Hamiet Bluiett; "I expect to get paid for my music." Stern, "Stars on the Rise: Hamiet Bluiett," 24.

[32] Jordan and Zabor, 62; Tejuoso, 77–79; Lester Bowie, "Fresh Air"; Aldon Lynn Nielson, *Black Chant: Languages of African-American Postmodernism* (New York: Cambridge University Press, 1997), 240; Kelley, "Dig They Freedom," 23.

[33] Bill Smith, "Lake Interview," 3–4; "BAG Concert Set for Sunday," *St. Louis Sentinel*, 25 Oct. 1969, p. 2; BAG, flyer for "Song for a Fallen Warrior," 23 Sept. 1971, on file with author; Carroll quoted in Danson, 16; Bill Smith, "Lake Interview," 6. In 1976, Lake explained his attitude toward musical labels: "I can say 'Black music' sometimes, or 'creative music,' but it's all music. Only thing is that all the music I'm involved with is coming from the Black tradition and from the Black reference point." Quoted in Valerie Wilmer, "Lakeside Developments," *Melody Maker*, 6 Mar. 1976, 42.

[34] Oliver Lake, "Separation," in liner notes to Lake, *NTU: Point from Which Creation Begins* (Arista/Freedom Records, AL 1024, 1976; rec. 1971). Lake explored these themes in a more formal setting while teaching a course on the history of black music at Webster College in St. Louis. Lake, curriculum vitae, c. 1975, on file with author. He later used his poem (under the title "No Separation") in various New York concerts, including a Mar. 1976 performance at Studio Rivbea. See Robert Palmer, "East, Midwest Meet in Jazz-Rock Beat of the Lake Quartet," *The New York Times*, 7 Mar. 1976, p. 45.

[35] Phillippe Carles, "Bartholomew 'Bazzi' Gray," *Jazz Magazine* (Paris) no. 207 (Jan. 1973): 10, trans. J. Marina Davies.

[36] Barnes, "Life of Oliver Lake"; Bill Smith and David Lee, "Julius Hemphill," *Coda* no. 161 (June 1978): 8; "BAG to Appear with Superlatives," *St. Louis Argus*, 17 July 1970, p. 7A; Carroll quoted in Danson, 12, 14. Critic John Litweiler, reviewing a 1969 BAG performance in Chicago, identified in the various BAG combos' sounds "the ghosts of territory bands, rural bluesmen, Mississippi riverboats, Missouri ragtime, and occasional Archie Shepp records." Litweiler, "Oliver Lake/Julius Hemphill," 34–35.

[37] Elliott, audiotaped comments; Parker, "Floyd LeFlore Interview," 17; Ehrlich, author interview.

[38] Jost, 163; Chuck Nessa, radio interview with Mike Johnston, "Anything Is Possible," WCMU-FM, Mt. Pleasant, MI, 10 Nov. 1993; Bowie quoted in Terry Martin, "Blowing Out in Chicago: Roscoe Mitchell," *Down Beat*, Apr. 1967, 20–21, 47–48; Lake quoted in Bill Smith, "The Oliver Lake Interview," 3. See also Roscoe Mitchell's comments on the contrast between the New York and Chicago environments in Shipton, 805.

[39] Hemphill quoted in Johnson, "Esoteric Expression," 21; Universal Justice Records, promotional flyers, c. 1974, on file with author. For an idea of the types of world music broadcast on KDNA, see KDNA/KDHX Radio Tapes, sl 536, WHMC.

[40] James Marshall, letter to author, 20 Aug. 2003; Marshall, author interview; Loewenstein, author interview; "Lover's Desire," on Human Arts Ensemble, *Under the Sun* (Universal Justice Records, UJ-104, 1973; rereleased Arista/Freedom, AL 1022, 1975); Universal Justice Records, promotional flyers, c. 1974, on file with author; various artists, *Music of Afghanistan* (Folkways, FE 4361, 1961); "Whisper of Dharma," on Human Arts Ensemble, *Whisper of Dharma* (Universal Justice Records, UJ 103, 1972; rereleased Arista/Freedom, AL 1039, 1977). Michael Castro later memorialized an evening playing the nagaswaram with Lake and members of the Human Arts Ensemble in his unpublished poem "Nagaswaram Players in All Saints Church with Oliver Lake."

[41] Weinstein, 16–17, 177; Kelley, "Dig They Freedom," 22; Budds, *Jazz in the Sixties*, 16–17; Szwed, *Space Is the Place*, 137.

[42] Aten, author interview; "Africa," on Oliver Lake, *NTU: Point from Which Creation Begins* (Arista/Freedom Records, AL 1024, 1976; rec. 1971). On Griot Galaxy, see Gerald Brennan, "Faruq Z. Bey," *Signal to Noise*, Summer 2003.

[43] Elizabeth Gentry Sayad, *A Scarlet Thread: Collected Writings on Culture and the Arts* (St. Louis: Patrice Press, 1991), 89–92; Roland Jordan, personal communications to author, 21 July 2003 and 16 Feb. 2004. J. D. Parran, for example, frequently performed twentieth-century classical clarinet works, while Oliver Lake studied with the principal clarinetist and flautist at the St. Louis Symphony Orchestra. "3 Events at Community Music School," *St. Louis Sentinel*, 15 Mar. 1969, p. 6; Elliott, author interview.

[44] Baikida Carroll later pointed to a few examples: "Anthony Braxton did a concert where he climbed up on a ladder and was dropping things into a trash can; it was totally bizarre. We were reading scores with colors and all kinds of different notation. It was really an incredible period." Quoted in Danson, 13. Robin D. G. Kelley notes that, although the AACM's members routinely dismissed critics who claimed that their music was influenced by John Cage, AACM saxophonist Joseph Jarman had collaborated with Cage for a 1965 concert. Kelley, "Dig They Freedom," 16; see also Peter Welding, "Caught in the Act: Joseph Jarman," *Down Beat* 33, no. 1 (13 Jan. 1966): 35.

[45] Neil Butterworth, *A Dictionary of American Composers* (New York: Garland Publishing, 1984), 113–14; *Who's Who in American Music: Classical*, 2nd ed., ed. Jaques Cattell Press (New York: R. R. Bowker & Co., 1985), 130; New Music Circle, "Catalytic Celebration" program, Apr. 1969, in New Music Circle Records, sl 483, box 1, folder 1, WHMC; Frank Peters, "Music Circle Festival," *St. Louis Post-Dispatch*, 12 Apr. 1969; Jean Ehmsen, "Music Synthesis," *St. Louis Post-Dispatch*, 12 Apr. 1969; John Brod Peters, "New Music Circle Completes Week-Long Culture Festival," *St. Louis Globe-Democrat*, 13 Apr. 1969; Greg Hoeltzel, personal communication to author, 10 Aug. 2003. For more on the Guise and its leader, organist and In-Men veteran Greg Hoeltzel, see Harry Young, liner notes to Bob Kuban and the In-Men, *Look Out for the Cheater* (Collectables Records, COL-5688, 1996). On Custer's time in St. Louis, see Gaye Vasilas, "Interview with a Composer and Educator," *St. Louis FM Guide*, 4 Nov. 1968, 4, 11.

[46] Porter, 201; Budds, *Jazz in the Sixties*, 80; Emmett George Price, III, "Free Jazz and the Black Arts Movement, 1958–1967" (Ph.D. diss., University of Pittsburgh, 2000); Lorenzo Thomas, "Ascension: Music and the Black Arts Movement," in *Jazz among the Discourses*, ed. Krin Gabbard (Durham, N.C.: Duke University Press, 1995), 261; Kofsky, 139–40. On the diversity of responses in the jazz world of the mid- and late 1960s, see, for example, Scott Saul, *Freedom Is, Freedom Ain't: Jazz and the Making of the Sixties* (Cambridge, MA: Harvard University Press, 2003), 302–36.

[47] Hemphill quoted in Johnson, "Esoteric Expression," 20; Oliver Lake, interview by *Le Jazz* website (no longer online), May 1998; Bluiett quoted in Chip Stern, "Stars on the Rise: Hamiet Bluiett," *Down Beat* 45, no. 15 (7 Sept. 1978): 24; Bowie quoted in "Art Ensemble of Chicago: Great Black Music!" *Ann Arbor Sun*, 18 Aug. 1972, pp. 8–9. Lake makes very similar comments in Rusch, "Speaking with Oliver Lake," 4–5. See also Famoudou Don Moye's remarks in Mike Hennessey, "Art Ensemble of Chicago," in *Great Black Music: Ancient to the Future*, ed. Lincoln T. Beauchamp, Jr. (Chicago: Art Ensemble of Chicago Publishing, 1998), 84. But Baikida Carroll explains that, at the time, he was attracted to socialist realism and was attempting "a didactic use of the arts to develop social consciousness." Carroll, author interview.

48 "Farmer and Seale to Speak at Different Gatherings Monday," *Yale Daily News*, 16 May 1969, p. 1; advertisement for "In the Spirit of Malcolm: A Festival of Revolutionary Culture," *Yale Daily News*, 16 May 1969, p. 8; "Seale Roasts 'Pigs,'" *Yale Daily News*, 21 May 1969, pp. 1, 4, Sterling Memorial Library, Yale University, New Haven, CT; Gilroy, *The Black Atlantic*, 36. According to Malinké Elliott, it was usually the collective's musicians who objected most vociferously to the participation of whites in BAG's internal affairs. Elliott, author interview.

49 Lake quoted in Johnson, "Esoteric Expression," 21; Hemphill, interview by Stitt, tape 3 of 4; Joseph Bowie, author interview; Carroll, author interview; Danson, 13; Bill Smith, "The Oliver Lake Interview," 3; Litweiler, "Oliver Lake/Julius Hemphill," 34–35; Parker, "Floyd LeFlore Interview," 16.

50 Parran, "The St. Louis Black Artists' Group," 3; Redmond, author interview; "Old and New Afro Music," 2; Parker, "Floyd LeFlore Interview," 16.

51 Parran quoted in Randall Roberts, "Donkey Business: The Unheard Music Series Reissues Funky Donkey," *Riverfront Times* (St. Louis), 18 Apr. 2001; Lake quoted in Bill Smith, "The Oliver Lake Interview," 6, emphasis in original; Lake and Hemphill quoted in Johnson, "Esoteric Expression," 20–21, emphasis in original.

CHAPTER SIX NOTES

1 Hemphill, interview by Stitt, tape 3 of 4; Wilmer, *As Serious as Your Life*, 222.

2 Jackson, author interview. On the termination of the local Model Cities Agency, see Kerstein, "The Political Consequences of Federal Intervention," 164. Due in part, perhaps, to the minor backlash generated by its Inner City Arts Project grant, the Danforth Foundation in October 1970 narrowed the scope of its urban affairs program such that future commitments would be judged solely on their educational merits. Danforth Foundation, "The Urban Program of the Danforth Foundation."

3 Shipton, 825; Rutlin, author interview; Elliott, author interview.

4 Terrell, author interview; Hunt, author interview; Shelton, author interview; Rutlin, author interview; Hemphill, interview by Stitt, tape 3 of 4. On the sale of BAG's Washington Boulevard building in Apr. 1971, see CB-930, 1968–72, Assessor's Office, City of St. Louis.

5 Teish, *Jambalaya*, 34; Dickerson, author interview; Naidoo, author interview; "Theatre," *PROUD Magazine*.

6 Luther Thomas, liner notes to Thomas, *Banana* (Atavistic, UMS/ALP 215, 2001, rec. 1973); Marshall, author interview; Rutlin, author interview; Loewenstein, author interview.

7 Floyd LeFlore, author interview; Parker, "Floyd LeFlore Interview," 14; Lake quoted in Shipton, 825.

8 Bowie quoted in Jordan and Zabor, 60–61.

[9] Henry Martin and Keith Waters, *Jazz: The First 100 Years* (Belmont, CA: Wadsworth Group, 2002), 264; Radano, 142; Shipton, 813–16; Beauchamp, "Lester Bowie Interview," 41–43; Barry Kernfield, "Moye, Don," in *The New Grove Dictionary of Jazz*, ed. Kernfield (London: Macmillan Press Ltd., 1988), 143.

[10] Martin and Waters, 264; Shipton, 813–16; Valerie Wilmer, "Caught in the Act: Art Ensemble of Chicago," *Down Beat* 37, no. 12 (25 June 1970): 26; Szwed, *Space Is the Place*, 278–91. For some of the Parisian venues used by AACM performers, see Michel Fabre and John A. Williams, *A Street Guide to African Americans in Paris* (Paris: Cercle d'Etudes Afro-Américaines, 1996), 53, 63–64, 78, 144–45, 149–50.

[11] On authorities' attitudes toward foreigners following May 1968, see Tyler Stovall, *Paris Noir: African Americans in the City of Light* (New York: Houghton Mifflin Company, 1996), 278–80. Bowie narrates the Art Ensemble's expulsion from France in Beauchamp, "Lester Bowie Interview," 41–43; "Art Ensemble of Chicago: Great Black Music!," *Ann Arbor Sun*; Jordan and Zabor, 61–62.

[12] Floyd LeFlore, author interview; Lincoln T. Beauchamp, Jr., "Famoudou Don Moye," in *Great Black Music: Ancient to the Future*, ed. Beauchamp (Chicago: Art Ensemble of Chicago Publishing, 1998), 60–61; Backus, 47; Parker, "Floyd LeFlore Interview," 14; jazz journalist Will Smith quoted in David Jackson, "Profile: Julius Hemphill, Oliver Lake," 32.

[13] Carroll, author interview; Danson, 14; Oliver Lake, *NTU: Point from Which Creation Begins* (Arista/Freedom Records, AL 1024, 1976).

[14] Baikida Carroll, telephone conversation with author, 11 Jan. 2004; Oliver Lake, letter to Valerie Wilmer, 15 Nov. 1971, on file with author. Thanks to Valerie Wilmer for providing this document.

[15] Floyd LeFlore, author interview; Parker, "Floyd LeFlore Interview," 15; Human Arts Ensemble, *Whisper of Dharma* (Universal Justice Records, UJ 103, 1972; rereleased Arista/Freedom, AL 1039, 1977); Baikida Carroll, personal communication to author, 3 July 2003.

[16] Stovall, 235; James C. Hall, *Mercy, Mercy Me: African-American Culture and the American Sixties* (New York: Oxford University Press, 2001), 12.

[17] William A. Shack, *Harlem in Montmartre: A Paris Jazz Story between the Great Wars* (Berkeley: University of California Press, 2001); Stovall, 232–33, 235–38, 243; Michel Fabre, *From Harlem to Paris: Black American Writers in France, 1840–1980* (Urbana: University of Illinois Press, 1991), 273; Stan Britt, *Long Tall Dexter: A Critical Musical Biography of Dexter Gordon* (New York: Quartet Books, 1989), 84–100.

[18] Danson, 14; Parker, "Floyd LeFlore Interview," 15; Joseph Bowie, personal communication to author, 28 May 2003; Floyd LeFlore, author interview; Francis de Marmande, "Hier est aujourd'hui," in *Festival d'Automne à Paris 1972–1982*, ed. Jean-Pierre Leonardini, Marie Collin, and Joséphine Markovits (Paris: Messidor/Temps Actuels, 1982), 277–80.

[19] Philippe Carles, "Salon d'Automne: Black Arts Group" and "Salon d'Automne: Mohammed Ali/Black Arts Group," *Jazz Magazine* (Paris) no. 206 (Dec. 1972): 48, trans. J. Marina Davies.

[20] Floyd LeFlore, author interview. For general information on the American Center, see Fabre and Williams, *Street Guide*, 143–45.

[21] Joseph Bowie, author interview; "Jazz En Direct: Noel McGhie Quintet/Black Arts Group/Joachim Kühn Trio/Robin Kenyatta Quartet," *Jazz Magazine* (Paris) no. 207 (Jan. 1973): 10–11; Fabre and Williams, *Street Guide*, 143–45, 149–50, 163; Radano, 183; Barry McRae, "Beyond the Mainstream: Oliver Lake and Joe McPhee," *Jazz Journal International* (London), Feb. 1980, 25; Parker, "Floyd LeFlore Interview," 15; BAG, *In Paris* (BAG 324 000, 1973); Barry McRae, "Black Artists Group," *Jazz Journal International* (London) 28, no. 2 (Feb. 1975): 46.

[22] Danson, 14; Bill Smith, "The Oliver Lake Interview," 2; "Shaw, Charles," in *The New Grove Dictionary of Jazz*, ed. Barry Kernfield (London: Macmillan Press Ltd., 1988), 441; Laurent Goddet, "Black Artists Group et Portal au Palace," *Jazz Hot* (Paris) no. 294 (May 1973): 23.

[23] Gaillot, author interview; Floyd LeFlore, author interview; Maurice Cullaz, "Black Artists Group of St. Louis," *Jazz Hot* (Paris) no. 296 (July/Aug. 1973): 23–24; Davis with Troupe, 329; Paul Tingen, *Miles Beyond: The Electric Explorations of Miles Davis, 1967–1991* (New York: Billboard Books, 2001), 155. Gaumont also introduced the St. Louisans to a childhood friend, the guitarist Philippe Gaillot, who then collaborated with BAG members in Paris and at New York's La MaMa theater.

[24] Philippe Carles, "Jazz En Direct: Bazzi Gray," *Jazz Magazine* (Paris) no. 211 (May 1973): 30–31; Fabre and Williams, *Street Guide*, 145; Bill Smith, "The Oliver Lake Interview," 7; Philippe Carles, "Bartholomew 'Bazzi' Grey," *Jazz Magazine* (Paris) no. 207 (Jan. 1973): 10.

[25] Parker, "Floyd LeFlore Interview," 15; Carles, "Salon d'Automne: Black Arts Group"; "Jazz En Direct: Noel McGhie."

[26] Shaw quoted in Cullaz, 23. Critical remarks quoted from Carles, "Bartholomew 'Bazzi' Grey"; "Jazz En Direct: Noel McGhie"; Carles, "Jazz En Direct: Bazzi Gray"; Carles, "Salon d'Automne: Black Arts Group."

[27] Danforth Foundation, "The Urban Program of the Danforth Foundation"; Malinké Elliott, telephone conversation with author, 2 Feb. 2004; Lexa, author interview. Several recent foreign-language books take the Institutet för Scenkonst as their topic; see, for example, Cecilia Lagerström, *Former för Liv Och Teater: Institutet för Scenkonst Och Tyst Kunnande* (Hedemora, Sweden: Gidlunds Förlag, 2003).

[28] Malinké Elliott, telephone conversation with author, 2 Feb. 2004; Lexa, author interview; "Theatre," *PROUD Magazine*, 32; Hemphill, interview by Stitt, tape 3 of 4.

[29] Hemphill, interview by Stitt, tape 3 of 4.

[30] Ibid.

[31] Stovall, 278–80; Fabre, *From Harlem to Paris*, 274; Lake quoted in Milkowski, 24. "Well, if you have thirty million blacks over here, we will see how much music you'll like then," went Lester Bowie's stock reply to Europeans when queried on the contrasting responses to the Art Ensemble on each side of the Atlantic. Quoted in Tejuoso, 78.

[32] Hemphill, interview by Stitt, tape 3 of 4; Parker, "Floyd LeFlore Interview," 15; Oliver Lake, curriculum vitae, c. 1975, on file with author; Danson, 14.

[33] Rutlin, author interview.

[34] Ajulé Rutlin, curriculum vitae, c. 1986, on file with author; Floyd LeFlore, author interview; Gregory J. Marshall, "Caught in the Act: Julius Hemphill Ensemble," *Down Beat* 43, no. 1 (15 Jan. 1976): 40, 46; Rusch, "Speaking with Oliver Lake," 3l; Luther Thomas Human Arts Ensemble, *Funky Donkey* (Creative Consciousness Records, CC-1001T, 1977; rereleased Atavistic, ALP/UMS215, 2000; rec. 1973); Roberts, "Donkey Business."

[35] Litweiler, *The Freedom Principle*, 197. On the successive "waves" of AACM members, see George E. Lewis, "Experimental Music in Black and White: The AACM in New York, 1970–1985," *Current Musicology* nos. 71–73 (2001–02): 100–157.

[36] Elliott, audiotaped comments.

Chapter Seven Notes

[1] Peter Occhiogrosso, "Rivbea: An Historic Festival," *SoHo Weekly News*, 20 May 1976, p. 35; Vladimir Simosko, "Studio Rivbea: Spring Festival," *Coda* no. 149 (July 1976): 9; Howard Mandel, liner notes to *Wildflowers: The New York Loft Jazz Sessions* (Knit Classics, KCR-3037, 2000). For the lineups and scheduling, see "Studio Rivbea: Spring Music Festival," advertisement, *The Village Voice*, 17 May 1976, p. 114.

[2] *Wildflowers: The New York Loft Jazz Sessions*, nos. 1–5 (Douglas/Casablanca, NBLP 7045-9, 1977).

[3] Chuck Berg, "Record Reviews: New York Loft Jazz," *Down Beat* 44, no. 14 (Aug. 1977): 22.

[4] Brian Case, "De-subdued Baritone," *Melody Maker*, 24 Jan. 1981, 26; Wild, "Bluiett, Hamiet," 130–31; Barry McRae, "Avant Courier: Hamiet Bluiett," *Jazz Journal International* (London) 36, no. 11 (Nov. 1983): 10; Chip Stern, "Stars on the Rise: Hamiet Bluiett," *Down Beat* 45, no. 15 (7 Sept. 1978): 24, 45–46; Gene Santoro, *Myself When I Am Real: The Life and Music of Charles Mingus* (New York: Oxford University Press, 2000), 314, 317, 325, 332.

[5] Stern, "Stars on the Rise," 24; Ware, author interview; Shipton, 819; Lewis, "Experimental Music in Black and White," 100–157.

[6] Ware, author interview; Sam Stephenson, "Nights of Incandescence," *DoubleTake* no. 18 (Fall 1999); LeRoi Jones, "New York Loft and Coffee Shop Jazz" [1963], in Jones, *Black Music* (New York: William Morrow & Co., 1968), 92–98; Stanley Crouch, "Rashied Ali and the Lofts: Up from Slavery," *SoHo Weekly News*, 24 June 1976, Newport Jazz Festival Supplement.

[7] Michael Winkleman, "The New Frontier: Housing for the Artist-Industrialist," *New York Affairs* 4, no. 4 (1978): 54; James R. Hudson, *The Unanticipated City: Loft Conversions in Lower Manhattan* (Amherst: University of Massachusetts Press, 1987), 23, 27, 31; Alanna Siegfried and Helene Zucker Seeman, *SoHo: A Guide* (New York: Neal-Schuman Publishers, 1978), 5, 17; Lawrence Alloway, "SoHo as Bohemia," in *New York: Downtown Manhattan, SoHo*, ed. Ursula Block and Kurt Thöricht (Berlin: Akademie der Künste, 1976), 143–45, 149.

8 Alloway, 143; Winkleman, 54–55; Hudson, 79–80; Stephen Koch, "Reflections on SoHo," in New York, ed. Block and Thöricht, 107; Sharon Zukin, Loft Living: Culture and Capital in Urban Change (Baltimore: Johns Hopkins University Press, 1982), 10–11. The uncertain legal status of residential lofts until 1975 prevented landlords from obtaining institutional financing to upgrade properties to residential code standards.

9 Ali quoted in Stanley Crouch, "Jazz Lofts: A Walk through the Wild Sounds," The New York Times Magazine, 17 Apr. 1977, p. 40; Hudson, 27; Emanuel Tobier, "Setting the Record Straight on Loft Conversions," New York Affairs 6, no. 4 (1981): 35–36. Average annual rents for Central Business District lofts remained steady from the 1950s through the mid-1970s. The stable price of floor space paired with high vacancy rates suggests that, in the early years, the conversion of industrial space to arts and residential uses did not drive up prices and create prohibitive conditions for industry—though this would change markedly beginning in the mid-1970s. Ibid.

10 John Litweiler, Ornette Coleman: The Harmolodic Life (London: Quartet Books, 1992), 120–22; Joan La Barbara, "SoHo: A Community of Cooperating Artists," in New York, ed. Block and Thöricht, 253.

11 W. A. Brower, "Sam Rivers: Warlord of the Lofts," Down Beat 45, no. 19 (16 Nov. 1978): 21–22, 39; Simosko, 9; New York City Directory, 1970, NYPL; Wilson, author interview. Studio Rivbea was located at 24 Bond Street, and the Ladies' Fort at 2 Bond Street. During the mid-1970s, Rivers's building was owned by photographer Robert Mapplethorpe and painters Joseph Kosuth and Virginia Admiral, among others.

12 Siegfried and Seeman, 116–17; Crouch, "Jazz Lofts," 42; Crouch, "Rashied Ali and the Lofts"; Fischer quoted in Robert Palmer, "Loft Jazz Goes on a Three-Day Toot," The New York Times, 4 June 1976, p. C1; Susan Mannheimer, "Jazz Lofts," SoHo Weekly News, 18 Apr. 1974, pp. 16–17. Thomas Markus remarks that in buildings open to the public, "inhabitants" function as the controllers, while "visitors" occupy space as subjects of a system, whether as audience members, inmates, shoppers, or churchgoers. If, as Markus asserts, spatial "depth indicates power," then in the typical jazz performance setting, the "shallow visitor zone" indicates control by the proprietor or institution. Here, the spectator does not have access to the physical and metaphorical "backstage areas" described by Erving Goffman in his discussion of "impression management." The loft performance venues overturned these standard spatial layouts, modifying extant power relations between spectator and performer, proprietor and visitor. See Thomas A. Markus, Buildings and Power: Freedom and Control in the Origin of Modern Building Types (London: Routledge, 1993), 13–17.

13 Ornette Coleman, Friends and Neighbors (Flying Dutchman, FDS-123, 1970); David G. Such, Avant-garde Jazz Musicians: Performing "Out There" (Iowa City: University of Iowa Press, 1993), 81–82; John Szwed, "Free on Third: New York City Artists' Collective," The Village Voice, 8 May 1990, p. 81; Peter Occhiogrosso, "Thriving from a Loft," SoHo Weekly News, 30 Sept. 1976, pp. 34–35; Bluiett quoted in Clifford Jay Safane, "The World Saxophone Quartet," Down Beat 46, no. 16 (Oct. 1979): 29. For a description of the loft scene alongside New York's concurrent disco and punk scenes, see Jonathan Mahler, New York: 1977 (New York: Farrar, Straus & Giroux, forthcoming 2005).

14 Saul Steinberg, "View of the World from Ninth Avenue," cover illustration for The New Yorker, 29 Mar. 1976; David Jackson, "Profile: Julius Hemphill, Oliver Lake," 32–33; Hemphill, interview by Stitt, tape 3 of 4; Sayad, author interview; Bill Smith, "The Oliver Lake Interview," 2; Danson, 14.

[15] Jackson, "Profile," 32–33; Danson, 14–15; Robert Palmer, "Music: Environ 'Workshop' Offers Exciting Jazz," *The New York Times*, 20 Aug. 1976, p. C15; Peter Occhiogrosso, "Listen to This: The Music of Bluiett," *SoHo Weekly News*, 10 Mar. 1977, p. 34.

[16] Mannheimer, 16–17; "Listen to Loft Jazz," *SoHo Weekly News*, 23 Sept. 1976, p. 39; Robert Palmer, "Bluiett Performs Blends of Jazz with Saxophone," *The New York Times*, 7 Feb. 1978, p. 11; "Openings: Lester's Licks," *The Village Voice*, 8 Jan. 1976, p. 57; Barbara Lee Horn, *Ellen Stewart and La Mama: A Bio-bibliography* (Westport, Conn.: Greenwood Press, 1993), 100; Lindberg, author interview; Gaillot, author interview.

[17] Emery, author interview; Ehrlich, author interview; Lindberg, author interview; Terrell, author interview; Hewitt, 18. Two members of this revamped version of the Human Arts Ensemble, James Emery and John Lindberg, went on to form the String Trio of New York, which played its first concert at the La MaMa Children's Workshop Theatre in February 1978. On the Human Arts Ensemble's 1977–78 European tours, see Jan Rensen and Rinus van der Heijden, "Bobo Shaw: The Human Arts Ensemble/Association," *Jazz/Press* (Holland) no. 52 (June 1978), 10–11; Fabre and Williams, *Street Guide*, 127; and Denis Constant, "Jazz en Direct: Human Arts Ensemble," *Jazz Magazine* (Paris) no. 269 (Oct. 1978): 12.

[18] Rusch, "Speaking with Oliver Lake," 3; Hemphill, interview by Stitt, tapes 3 and 4 of 4.

[19] David Jackson, "Profile: Julius Hemphill, Oliver Lake," 33; Rusch, "Speaking with Oliver Lake," 5; Such, 80. On lack of media attention, see also Sam Rivers's retrospective comments in David Mittleman, "Improvise or Shut Up: Jazz Titan Sam Rivers Keeps on Blowing," *Miami New Times*, 9 Dec. 1999.

[20] Crouch, "Jazz Lofts," 40; Zukin, 118–19; McCandlish Phillips, "Musicians' Group Plans Jazz Fete," *The New York Times*, 19 Mar. 1973, p. 47. Lineups for these and many other loft festivals of the late 1970s can be found in *NYC/Jazz*, held at the Performing Arts Research Library, NYPL.

[21] Rivers quoted in Hubert Saal, "Jazz Comes Back!" *Newsweek*, 8 Aug. 1977, p. 56; Radano, 156–57; Porter, 215–39, 369–70n51; Carroll, author interview; Ware, author interview; Clifford Thornton, "Black Solidarity Festival," *Down Beat* 37, no. 14 (23 July 1970): 30.

[22] Robert Palmer, "Jazz Lives in New York," *Rolling Stone* no. 248 (22 Sept. 1977): 20–25; Pines, author interview; Morgenstern, author interview; Occhiogrosso, "Rivbea: An Historic Festival"; Robert Palmer, "New Jazz from the Midwest Moves East," *The New York Times*, 9 May 1976, p. 18. On the 1976 and 1977 New York Loft Jazz Celebrations, see *The New York Times* reviews on 4, 5, 7, and 8 June 1976, and 3 and 6 June 1977. In the festival's second year, the Brook replaced Sunrise Studio among the four venues used.

[23] Danson, 14–15; McRae, "Beyond the Mainstream: Oliver Lake and Joe McPhee," 25; Oliver Lake, curriculum vitae, c. 1975, on file with author; Emilio Cruz, curriculum vitae, c. 2000, on file with author; Cruz, author interview; Troupe, author interview.

[24] Litweiler, *Ornette Coleman*, 120–21; Peter Occhiogrosso, "Listen to This: Julius Hemphill and Bloods," *SoHo Weekly News*, 31 Mar. 1977, p. 38; Peter Watrous, "Julius Hemphill, Saxophonist and Composer, Is Dead at 57," *The New York Times*, 4 Apr. 1995. See also Hannah Charlton, "Breaking out of Uniform," *Melody Maker*, 6 Dec. 1980, 23.

[25] Hemphill quoted in Peter Watrous, "Using a Saxophone Opera to Recount Black Culture," *The New York Times*, 6 Dec. 1990, p. C17; Hollie West, "Mixed-Media Work," *The Washington Post*, 4 Nov. 1978, p. B4; Malinké Elliott, telephone conversation with author, 15 June 2004. Ralph Ellison himself once appeared in the audience for a performance at Brown University. Acquaintances remember the older writer chastising Hemphill afterward for using *Invisible Man* materials without permission, though Hemphill quickly disarmed the older writer with conversation about their roots in neighboring Texas and Oklahoma. Lyle, "Poetry Beat."

[26] Robert Palmer, "Ralph Ellison in Mixed-Media Setting," *The New York Times*, 2 Jan. 1981, p. C14; Richard Harrington, "Evocations in Jazz; Julius Hemphill & the City Saga of 'Long Tongues,'" *The Washington Post*, 12 Feb. 1987, p. C1; Geoffrey Himes, "Sax: Peaking In 'Tongues,'" *The Washington Post*, 29 Sept. 1989, p. N22; Bill Shoemaker, "Julius Hemphill and the Theater of Sound," *Down Beat* 53, no. 2 (Feb. 1986): 22; Watrous, "Using a Saxophone Opera"; Jon Pareles, "Tour with Saxophones through Black History," *The New York Times*, 8 Dec. 1990, p. 19; Malinké Elliott, telephone conversation with author, 15 June 2004. During the 1960s, the Crystal Caverns had changed its name to the Bohemian Caverns.

[27] Bill Smith, "The Oliver Lake Interview," 2. Record sales estimates are from author interview with Michael Cuscuna, who headed the Freedom subsidiary of Arista Records during the mid-1970s.

[28] On India Navigation, see Ben Ratliff, "Bob Cummins, 68, a Producer in Manhattan's Loft-Jazz Scene," *The New York Times*, 10 Sept. 2000, p. 48. On Arista's 1970s foray into jazz, see Radano, 249.

[29] Lake quoted in Clifford Jay Safane, "The World Saxophone Quartet," *Down Beat* 46, no. 16 (Oct. 1979): 28; Lake quoted in Daniel King, "Fire Music: Lincoln Center Thaws Its Cold War on Jazz Activism," *The Village Voice*, 12 Mar. 2003.

[30] Anthony Braxton, *New York Fall '74* (Arista Records, 4032, 1974); Francis Davis, *In the Moment: Jazz in the 1980s* (New York: Oxford University Press, 1986), 42, 44–46; Fred Jung, "A Fireside Chat with Hamiet Bluiett," *Jazz Weekly*, www.jazzweekly.com, Aug. 2001; Safane, 26; Hemphill, interview by Stitt, tape 4 of 4. Murray was married for several months to poet and playwright Ntozake Shange, who spent part of her childhood in St. Louis, and the couple performed poetry/jazz amalgams in several of the New York lofts.

[31] Paul Pines, *Tin Angel* (New York: William Morrow and Company, Inc., 1983), 16; Pines, author interview; Peter Occhiogrosso, "Listen to This: New York Saxophone Quartet," *SoHo Weekly News*, 3 Feb. 1977, p. 33; Peter Occhiogrosso, "Playing the Field," *SoHo Weekly News*, 24 Feb. 1977, p. 38; Stanley Crouch, unpublished interview by Jonathan Mahler, 21 Oct. 2003; Hemphill, interview by Stitt, tape 4 of 4.

[32] Barnes, "Visit to St. Louis Stirs Memories of '60s for Julius Hemphill"; Hemphill, interview by Stitt, tape 4 of 4; Woodward, "Four Saxmen, One Great Voice," 46.

[33] Murray quoted in Woodward, "Four Saxmen," 47.

[34] Jung, "A Fireside Chat with Hamiet Bluiett"; Francis Davis, *In the Moment*, 49.

[35] Chip Stern, "Faces: World Saxophone Quartet," *Musician, Player and Listener* no. 18 (May–July 1979), 29; review quoted from Stern, "The Hard Blues of Julius Hemphill," 44; Hemphill quoted in Safane, 28; Jung, "A Fireside Chat with Hamiet Bluiett." Similarly, Stanley Crouch described the manner in which the World Sax Quartet took the stage at Avery Fisher Hall during the 1982 Kool Jazz Festival: "Entering with a mar.ing dance step that rhymed with the chant they were playing . . . , [the group] proceeded to play a set that was breathtaking in its comprehension and compelling in its passion." Crouch, liner notes to World Saxophone Quartet, *Revue* (Black Saint, BSR0056, 1982).

[36] Woodward, "Four Saxmen" 46; Hemphill quoted in Gene Santoro, *Stir It Up: Musical Mixes from Roots to Jazz* (New York: Oxford University Press, 1997), 137.

[37] Litweiler, *Ornette Coleman*, 137–38. On conflicts between loft artists and discos, see Jim Stratton, "Keeping Aloft," *SoHo Weekly News*, 6 May 1976, p. 8; and Roz Kramer, "Vibrations from the Loft," *SoHo Weekly News*, 10 Mar. 1977, p. 5. Photographer Stan Ries, a mid-1970s tenant of 24 Bond Street along with Studio Rivbea, remembers that late-night music in the lofts often generated complaints from other tenants, but that formal complaints were rarely filed with the city because all of the tenants were technically occupying their lofts illegally. Complaints became more common, however, when changes in the zoning laws gave tenants legal status. Ries, personal communication to author, 9 Mar. 2004.

[38] Robert Palmer, "New Jazz Thrives at the Public," *The New York Times*, 2 June 1978, p. C11; Robert Palmer, "Jazz at the Public Has a New Name and Variations on Its Theme," *The New York Times*, 12 Sept. 1980, p. C12; Emery, author interview; Mark Kernis, "Avant-Garde Jazz Climbs out of the Loft," *The Washington Post*, 4 May 1979, Weekend Section, p. 16. On referenced BAG concerts, see Robert Palmer, "Loft Jazzmen Move Uptown to Recital Hall," *The New York Times*, 2 Oct. 1976, p. 14; Robert Palmer, "New Jazz: Oliver Lake," *The New York Times*, 23 May 1978, p. C6; *NYC/Jazz* 2, no. 3 (24 Jan. to 28 Feb. 1979); Robert Palmer, "Baikida Carroll's Septet," *The New York Times*, 22 Oct. 1979; Gary Giddens, "Oliver Lake Seeks the Right Time," *The Village Voice*, 25 Sept. 1978, pp. 94–96; Robert Palmer, "Julius Hemphill Brings 12-Man Ensemble to the Public," *The New York Times*, 3 Nov. 1980, p. C14; Carroll, interview by Tafuri.

[39] Emery, author interview; Such, 82. Already by February 1978, critic Robert Palmer was describing a packed house at La MaMa as "somewhat rare now that the lofts are no longer centers of downtown jazz activity." Palmer, "Bluiett Performs Blends of Jazz with Saxophone."

[40] Tobier, 37–38; Hudson, 71, 102–03, 123; urban planner quote from Winkleman, 37, 54–55; Zukin, 4, 13, 96, 121. Sociologist Sharon Zukin, in her study of the transformation of New York's loft districts, claims, "For a while, various sorts of 'nonproductive' use can coexist in this infrastructure. The creative disharmony is interesting and sometimes even elegant. But sooner or later, a contradiction develops between the production of art and other, higher-rent uses." Ibid.

[41] Carter Ratcliff, "SoHo: Disneyland of the Aesthete?" *New York Affairs* 4, no. 4 (1978): 68; Hemphill, interview by Stitt, tape 4 of 4.

[42] Bluiett quoted in Palmer, "The Pop Life," *New York Times*, 22 July 1977, p. C17; Morgenstern, author interview. On musicians feeling typecast by the label "loft jazz," see, for example, pianist John Fischer's comments in Robert Palmer, "A Jazz Festival in the Lofts," *The New York Times*, 3 June 1977, p. C18. Indeed, one of the loft scene's most prolific musicians was the saxophonist Monty Waters, a mainstream veteran who had migrated to New York from San Francisco during the late 1960s. Robert Palmer, "Monty Waters in Loft Jazz Series," *The New York Times*, 5 Apr. 1977, p. 38.

[43] Wilson, author interview; Robert Palmer, "The Pop Life," *The New York Times*, 15 July 1977, p. C18; Palmer, "The Pop Life," 22 July 1977, p. C17; Eugene Chadbourne, "Loft Jazz," *All Music Guide*, www.allmusic.com.

[44] Hudson, 111; Winkleman, 50.

Epilogue Notes

[1] Hemphill, interview by Stitt, tape 1 of 4; Ken Gewertz, "Requiem for Sax and Canvas: Carpenter Center Project Commemorates a Friend," *Harvard Gazette*, 18 May 2000. Hemphill passed away on Apr. 2, 1995, in Manhattan of complications from diabetes.

[2] Lake quoted in David Jackson, "Profile: Julius Hemphill, Oliver Lake," 32. BAG's definition of "community," however, was never the wider metropolitan community. Oliver Jackson observes that more recent discussions of BAG present the group as if it had been "spun out of St. Louis with the blessings of the larger cultural community," when actually, he claims, garnering civic support "was like pulling teeth. It was an appeasement at best." Jackson, author interview.

[3] Shirley LeFlore, author interview; Hemphill, interview by Stitt, tape 1 of 4.

[4] Such, 84; Ajulé Sunni Rutlin, *Travels with Douglas and Hamid* (Tucson: Eneke-the-Bird, 1983), 6, on file with author; Lawson; Shirley LeFlore, author interview; Mason, author interview; Bluiett quoted in Minderman, 60; Thomas Crone, "No Place Like Home," *St. Louis Post-Dispatch*, 8 June 2004. One poetry collection that emerged from the Creative Arts & Expression Laboratory is *Wordwalkers*, ed. Shirley LeFlore and Jabari Asim (St. Louis: CAEL, 1988), SCSL.

[5] Carroll quoted in Danson, 14.

Selected Bibliography

Adams, Robert. "Black Artists' Goal Is Art That Tells It Like It Is." *St. Louis Post-Dispatch*, 13 Apr. 1969.

Allen, Cathee. "BAG: Black Artist Group." *PROUD Magazine* 2, no. 6 (June/July 1971): 30–31. At MHS.

Andrus, Gorden F. "Washington University: Students Trigger Reform." *FOCUS/Midwest* 7, no. 45 (1969): 32–36.

Aschenbrenner, Joyce. *Katherine Dunham: Reflections on the Social and Political Contexts of Afro-American Dance*, edited by Pat A. Rowe. Congress on Dance Research Annual XII. New York: Congress on Dance Research, 1981.

Barnes, Harper. "Jazz Threads through Life of Oliver Lake." *St. Louis Post-Dispatch Everyday Magazine*, 14 Feb. 1993.

___. "Out of Diversity, LaClede Town." *St. Louis Post-Dispatch Sunday Pictures Magazine*, 2 Nov. 1969, pp. 2–7.

___. "Visit to St. Louis Stirs Memories of '60s for Julius Hemphill." *St. Louis Post-Dispatch*, 9 Apr. 1989, p. 3E.

Beauchamp, Lincoln T., Jr., ed. *Great Black Music: Ancient to the Future*. Chicago: Art Ensemble of Chicago Publishing, 1998.

Berkeley, Ellen Perry. "LaClede Town: The Most Vital Town in Town." *Architectural Forum* 129, no. 4 (Nov. 1968): 57–61.

Bertelson, Christine. "Directing Drama Workshop for Black Artists' Group." *St. Louis Post-Dispatch*, 20 Aug. 1970, p. 4F.

Bleck, Timothy. "Black Liberators Represent Type of Militancy Unknown in St. Louis before This Summer." *St. Louis Post-Dispatch*, 17 Sept. 1968.

Brower, W. A. "Sam Rivers: Warlord of the Lofts." *Down Beat* 45, no. 19 (16 Nov. 1978): 21–22, 39.

Bushnell, Don D., and Kathi Corbera Bushnell. *The Arts, Education, and the Urban Sub-culture: The National Survey of the Performing Arts for Minority Youths*. Santa Barbara, CA: The Communications Foundation, 1969.

Carles, Philippe. "Salon d'Automne: Black Arts Group." *Jazz Magazine* (Paris) no. 206 (Dec. 1972): 48.

Castro, Michael. "The Origins of River Styx." In *Seeking St. Louis: Voices from a River City, 1670–2000*, edited by Lee Ann Sandweiss, 851–57. St. Louis: Missouri Historical Society Press, 2000.

Cofield, Ernestine. "AIR Team Party Brings out Whole Families." *St. Louis Sentinel*, 21 June 1969, p. 10.

Crouch, Stanley. "Jazz Lofts: A Walk through the Wild Sounds." *The New York Times Magazine*. 17 Apr. 1977, pp. 40–42, 46.

Cullaz, Maurice. "Black Artists Group of St. Louis." *Jazz Hot* (Paris) no. 296 (July/Aug. 1973): 23–24.

"Culture through AIR for Inner City." *St. Louis Sentinel*, 19 July 1969, p. 10.

Cummings, Charles Kimball. "Rent Strike in St. Louis: The Making of Conflict in Modern Society." Ph.D. diss., Washington University, 1976.

Danson, Peter. "Baikida Carroll." *Coda* no. 192 (Oct. 1983): 12–16.

Ehmsen, Jean. "Music Synthesis." *St. Louis Post-Dispatch*, 12 Apr. 1969.

Fabre, Michel, and John A. Williams. *A Street Guide to African Americans in Paris*. Paris: Cercle d'Etudes Afro-Américaines, 1996.

Gray, Herman. *Producing Jazz: The Experience of an Independent Record Company*. Philadelphia: Temple University Press, 1988.

Haskins, James. *Katherine Dunham*. New York: Coward, McCann, & Geoghegan, 1982.

Heath, G. Louis. "Corrupt East St. Louis: Laboratory for Black Revolution." *The Progressive* 34, no. 10 (Oct. 1970): 24–27.

Helmreich, William B. *The Black Crusaders: A Case Study of a Black Militant Organization.* New York: Harper & Row, 1973.

Hewitt, Paulo. "Debunking the Funk." *Melody Maker*, 13 June 1981, 18.

Hudson, James R. *The Unanticipated City: Loft Conversions in Lower Manhattan.* Amherst: University of Massachusetts Press, 1987.

Jackson, David. "Profile: Julius Hemphill, Oliver Lake." *Down Beat* 42, no. 12 (19 June 1975): 32–33.

Johnson, Cassandra. "Esoteric Expression." *PROUD Magazine* 1, no. 6 (June/July 1970): 19–22. At MHS.

Jordan, Philippa, and Rafi Zabor. "Lester Bowie: Roots, Research, and the Carnival Chef." In *The Jazz Musician*, edited by Mark Rowland and Tony Sherman, 49–69. New York: St. Martin's Press, 1994.

Jost, Ekkehard. *Free Jazz*. 1974. Reprint. New York: Da Capo Press, 1994.

Judd, Dennis R., and Robert E. Mendelson. *The Politics of Urban Planning: The East St. Louis Experience.* Urbana: University of Illinois Press, 1973.

Kathriner, Danny. "The Rise and Fall of Gaslight Square." *Gateway Heritage* 22, no. 2 (Fall 2001): 32–43.

Kelley, Robin D. G. "Dig They Freedom: Meditations on History and the Black Avant-Garde." *Lenox Avenue* no. 3 (1997): 13–27.

Kennedy, Rick, and Randy McNutt. *Little Labels, Big Sound: Small Record Companies and the Rise of American Music.* Bloomington: Indiana University Press, 1999.

Kenney, William Howland. "Just before Miles: Jazz in St. Louis, 1926–1944." In *Miles Davis and American Culture*, edited by Gerald Early, 25–39. St. Louis: Missouri Historical Society Press, 2001.

Kenyatta, Malinké (a.k.a. Robert Elliott). *Black Theatre Notebook.* St. Louis: privately published, 1971. At MHS.

Kernis, Mark. "Avant-Garde Jazz Climbs out of the Loft." *The Washington Post*, 4 May 1979, Weekend Section, p. 16.

King, Mary. "Emilio Cruz Exhibit Reflects Influences of Three Worlds." *St. Louis Post-Dispatch*, 11 Nov. 1969, p. 3B.

———. "Paintings by Oliver Jackson Interpret Capetown Massacre." *St. Louis Post-Dispatch*, 8 Oct. 1973, p. 3C.

Kofsky, Frank. *Black Nationalism and the Revolution in Music.* New York: Pathfinder Press, 1970.

Kornblet, Donald. "In Search of the Model City: Fighting for the 'Goodies.'" *FOCUS/Midwest* 5, no. 38 (1967): 28–33.

Krantz, Richard. "Love and Unity Rally Depicts Freedom in Talk, Skit, Dance." *St. Louis Globe-Democrat*, 6 July 1970, p. 10A.

Lewis, George E. "Singing Omar's Song: A (Re)construction of Great Black Music." *Lenox Avenue* no. 4 (1998): 69–92.

Lipsitz, George. *A Life in the Struggle: Ivory Perry and the Culture of Opposition.* Philadelphia: Temple University Press, 1988.

———. "Like a Weed in a Vacant Lot: The Black Artists Group in St. Louis." In *Decomposition: Post-Disciplinary Performance*, edited by Sue-Ellen Case, Philip Brett, and Susan Leigh Foster, 50–61. Bloomington: Indiana University Press, 2000.

Litweiler, John. "The Free Jazz Movement: New Music in Chicago." *FOCUS/Midwest* 6, no. 41 (1968): 26–29.

———. *The Freedom Principle: Jazz after 1958.* New York: William Morrow and Co., 1984.

———. "Oliver Lake/Julius Hemphill." *Down Beat* 36, no. 12 (12 June 1969): 34–35.

Mannheimer, Susan. "Jazz Lofts." *SoHo Weekly News*, 18 Apr. 1974, pp. 16–17.

Marshall, Gregory J. "Caught in the Act: Julius Hemphill Ensemble." *Down Beat* 43, no. 1 (15 Jan. 1976): 40, 46.

McRae, Barry. "Avant Courier: Hamiet Bluiett." *Jazz Journal International* (London) 36, no. 11 (Nov. 1983): 10–11.

___. "Beyond the Mainstream: Oliver Lake and Joe McPhee." *Jazz Journal International* (London), Feb. 1980, 25–26.

Meyer, Gerald J. "Percy Green's Tactic: Stir Public Outrage." *St. Louis Post-Dispatch*, 12 July 1970.

Milkowski, Bill. "Oliver Lake: Sax in the Hip Pocket." *Down Beat* 50, no. 5 (May 1983): 22–24.

Naidoo, Muthal. *The Search for a Cultural Identity: A Personal Odyssey.* Indic Theatre Monograph Series, No. 1. Durban, South Africa: Asoka Theatre Publications, 1993.

Newton, Michael, and Scott Hatley. *Persuade and Provide: The Story of the Arts and Education Council in St. Louis.* New York: Associated Councils of the Arts, 1970.

"Old and New Afro Music BAG Blends." *St. Louis Sentinel*, 31 Aug. 1968, p. 2.

Ottenheimer, Harriet. "The Blues Tradition in St. Louis." *Black Music Research Journal* 9, no. 2 (Fall 1989): 135–51.

Palmer, Robert. "Dogon A.D." In *Setting the Tempo: Fifty Years of Great Jazz Liner Notes*, edited by Tom Piazzo, 243–47. New York: Anchor Books, 1996.

___. "Loft Jazz Goes on a Three-Day Toot." *The New York Times*, 4 June 1976, pp. C1, C17.

___. "New Jazz from the Midwest Moves East." *The New York Times*, 9 May 1976, p. 18.

Parker, David. "Floyd LeFlore Interview," *Cadence* 18, no. 6 (June 1992): 11–17.

Patterson, Ernest. *Black City Politics.* New York: Dodd, Mead & Company, 1975.

Peters, John Brod. "All-Negro Cast in 'The Blacks.'" *St. Louis Globe-Democrat*, 2 Aug. 1968, p. 2N.

___. "Negro Artists Open New Training Center." *St. Louis Globe-Democrat*, 15 Mar. 1969.

Piety, Harold R. "Revolution Comes to East St. Louis." *FOCUS/Midwest* 6, no. 42 (1968): 14–17.

Porter, Eric. *What Is This Thing Called Jazz?: African American Musicians as Artists, Critics, and Activists.* Berkeley: University of California Press, 2002.

Radano, Ronald M. *New Musical Figurations: Anthony Braxton's Cultural Critique.* Chicago: University of Chicago Press, 1993.

Redmond, Eugene. *Drumvoices: The Mission of Afro-American Poetry—A Critical History.* Garden City, N.Y.: Anchor Books, 1976.

___. "Indigenous Struggle Pays Off." *FOCUS/Midwest* 6, no. 41 (1968).

Roach, Jeannette E. "KDNA—for the Entire Community." *Greater St. Louis Magazine*, Aug. 1969, 16–19.

Roby, Diane. "Oliver Jackson: On Making." *International Review of African American Art* 13, no. 3 (Fall 1996): 50–57.

Rusch, Bob. "Speaking with Oliver Lake." *Cadence* 2, no. 5 (Feb. 1977): 3–6, 12.

Safane, Clifford Jay. "The World Saxophone Quartet." *Down Beat* 46, no. 16 (Oct. 1979): 26–29, 66.

Santoro, Gene. "Marty Ehrlich." *The Nation* 262, no. 10 (11 Mar. 1996): 34.

Saul, Scott. *Freedom Is, Freedom Ain't: Jazz and the Making of the Sixties.* Cambridge, MA: Harvard University Press, 2003.

Schoenberg, Sandra, and Charles Bailey. "The Symbolic Meaning of an Elite Black Community: The Ville in St. Louis." *Missouri Historical Society Bulletin* 33, no. 2 (Jan. 1977): 94–102.

Shipton, Alvyn. *A New History of Jazz.* New York: Continuum, 2001.

Simosko, Vladimir. "Studio Rivbea: Spring Festival." *Coda* no. 149 (July 1976): 8–10.

Skinner, Olivia. "Jazz Is His Bag," *St. Louis Post-Dispatch*, 18 Feb. 1970.

Skovgârd, I. B. "Luther Thomas in Denmark." *Jazz Special* (Denmark), First International Edition, 2002, 93–96.

Smith, Bill. "Human Arts Ensemble." *Down Beat* 41, no. 6 (28 Mar. 1974): 29.

___. "The Oliver Lake Interview." *Coda* no. 147 (May 1976): 2–7.

Smith, Bill, and David Lee. "Julius Hemphill." *Coda* no. 161 (June 1978): 4–10.

Stern, Chip. "Stars on the Rise: Hamiet Bluiett." *Down Beat* 45, no. 15 (7 Sept. 1978): 24, 45–46.

Stith, Carter. "Music and Dance for Benefit." *St. Louis Post-Dispatch*, 6 Aug. 1971.

Stovall, Tyler. *Paris Noir: African Americans in the City of Light.* New York: Houghton Mifflin Company, 1996.

Such, David G. *Avant-garde Jazz Musicians: Performing "Out There."* Iowa City: University of Iowa Press, 1993.

Teish, Luisah. *Jambalaya: The Natural Woman's Book of Personal Charms and Practical Rituals.* San Francisco: Harper & Row, 1985.

Tejuoso, Olakunle. "The Jazz Connections: Interview with Lester Bowie." *Glendora Review: African Quarterly on the Arts* (Nigeria) 2, no. 2 (1997): 74–83.

Van Deburg, William L. *New Day in Babylon: The Black Power Movement and American Culture, 1965–1975.* Chicago: University of Chicago Press, 1992.

Watrous, Peter. "Julius Hemphill, Saxophonist and Composer, Is Dead at 57." *The New York Times*, 4 Apr. 1995.

Wilmer, Valerie. *As Serious as Your Life: The Story of the New Jazz.* London: Allison & Busby, 1977.

Wood, Sue Ann. "Reviving Their African Heritage." *St. Louis Globe-Democrat,* 5 July 1969.

Woodward, Richard B. "Four Saxmen, One Great Voice." *The New York Times Magazine,* 12 Apr. 1987, 46–47, 72.

Wright, John A. *Discovering African-American St. Louis: A Guide to Historic Sites.* St. Louis: Missouri Historical Society Press, 1994.

Zukin, Sharon. *Loft Living: Culture and Capital in Urban Change.* Baltimore: Johns Hopkins University Press, 1982.

INDEX

Coleman, Montez, x

Coleman, Ornette, 150, 157, 166, 218–219, 238–39

Collected Poem for Blind Lemon Jefferson, The, 118–19

Collective Black Artists (CBA), 226–27

Collins, Georgia, vii, 29, 57, *59*, 61, 69, 101, 132

CORE, 45–47, 81

Cruz, Emilio, vii, 58, *76*, 81, 83, *123*, 132, 228; BAG arts supervisor, 120–22; joins BAG, 69–71

Cruz, Pat, 58, 79, 81, 83; joins BAG, 69–71

Cuninggim, Merrimon, 130

Cuscuna, Michael, 231

Custer, Arthur, 176–77; "Songs of Freedom, Love and War," 177

Davis, Miles, iv, 3, 4

Dickerson, A. J., Sr., 137

Dogon A.D., viii, xv, 145–48, 231

Dudley, Carl, 25–26

Dunham, Katherine, xvi, xxi, 56, 61, 68, 130; opens PATC, 48–52

Durgin, Russ, 19–20

East St. Louis, Illinois, 40–42, 113; opening of PATC, 49

Ehrlich, Marty, 78, 89, 92, 173, 223, 247

Elliott, Malinké (Robert), vii, 38, 57, *91*; antiwar protests, 86, 95; as BAG stage director, 105–06; "Dream Time, The," 116; early life, 19–20; in New York, 228–30; in Sweden, 205–06; leaves BAG, 132; *Orientation of Sweet Willie Rollbar, The*, 118, 229; *Poem for a Revolutionary Night*, 101–05

Emery, James, 223

Evanzz, Karl, 78, 160

Faulk, Thurman, 92

Fowler, Sherman L., x

Funky Donkey, 208–09

Garnett, Ruth Miriam, x

Gaslight Square, 67–68

Gateway Theatre, 67–69

Gaumont, Dominique, 202

Gray, Bartholomew "Bazzi," 202–03

Green, Percy, 46, 81, 83

Gunn, Russell, x

Harold, Keyon, x

Harper, Michael, xiii, 141

Harris, Darryl, 206

Harris, Jerome "Scrooge," 7, 17, 47, 72

Hayden, Chris, x

Hemphill, Julius, vii–xv, *11*, 14–15, 22, 69, 141, *146*, *169*, *181*; AACM, 17; army life, 12; audience reaction, 183; *Collected Poem for Blind Lemon Jefferson, The*, 118–19, 163; college life, 12; director of AIR Program, 57, 130; *Dogon A.D.*, 145–48, 163, 231; early life, 9–10; expelled from BAG, 189; expelled from World Sax Quartet, 233; in New York, 221, 228–30; in Paris, 206–07; in Sweden, 206, 207–08; *Orientation of Sweet Willie Rollbar, The*,

Naidoo, Muthal, vii, *139*, 143; BAG theater director, 137–41; leaves BAG, 190
Nashville, Vernon, 8, 77
Neal, Larry, 38; *Poem for a Revolutionary Night*, 99, 101–05
New York loft scene, 216–44
NTU: Point from Which Creation Begins, xxiii, 194–95

Omawali Dance & Drum Ensemble, 134–37
Orientation of Sweet Willie Rollbar, The, 117–18, 229
Osby, Greg, 78

Paris arts scene, 197–98
Parran, J. D., xviii, 8, 86, 208
PATC, v, ix, 48–52, 130
Performing Arts Training Center. *See* PATC
Pines, Paul, 233–34
Poem for a Revolutionary Night, 99–105, *104*

racism, viii
Ralph Ellison's Long Tongue, 228
Ranelin, Phil, 159
Redmond, Delano, x
Redmond, Eugene B., iv–xi, xvi, 27, 112, 119, 133, 182, 249; early life, 41–43; *Ode to Taylor Jones*, 50
Richardson, Arzinia (Carl), 17, 199
Rivers, Bea, 213–14, 219
Rivers, Sam, 213–14, 219, 242
Rutlin, Ajulé (Bruce), vii, 32, 47, 57, 69, 75, 88, *91*, 161, 208; after BAG, 249; becomes BAG chairman, 131–32; early life, 18; poetry and music, 114–16; *Song for a Fallen Warrior*, 142

segregation, viii, xx, 2, 6
Shaw, Charles "Bobo," 20, 87, 114, *201*; "Lover's Desire," 174; in New York, 222–24; in Paris, 195; starts Universal Justice Records, 163
Shelton, LeRoi, 20–22, *21*, 47, 132
Song for a Fallen Warrior concert, 141–42
"Songs of Freedom, Love and War", 177
St. Louis, xv–xvi, 2–15, 17–27, 32–62, 65, 85, 153; and BAG, 35, 127; music scene, 2–4, 172–74; race relations, 37; rent strike, 82–84; union discrimination, 153–54; Ville, the, 6–7
Studio Rivbea, 213, 219, 242
Sumner High School, 6–7

Teish, Luisah, *135*; BAG dance director, 133–34; leaves BAG, 190
Terrell, Vincent, 47, 87, 116, 132; BAG theater director, 106; early life, 20
theater program (BAG), 105–11
Thiam, Mor, vi, ix, *60*, 136
Thomas, Luther, 78, 208–09, 223
Thomas, Reginald, x
Touré, Askia, 38, 39
Troupe, Quincy, vii, 117, 119, 133, 228
TSOCC Players, 20, 29, 100